# BECK! ON A BACKWARDS RIVER

# BECK! ON A BACKWARDS RIVER

## The Story of Beck

*Rob Jovanovic*

*Virgin*

# For all my family –
## thanks for your help and support

First published in Great Britain in 2000 by

Virgin Publishing Ltd
Thames Wharf Studios
Rainville Road
London W6 9HA

A catalogue record for this book is available
from the British Library.

ISBN 0 7535 0451 0

Typeset by TW Typesetting, Plymouth, Devon
Printed and bound by CPD, Wales

# Contents

# Preface

Oh, hindsight, what a wonderful quality.

I spent my first stateside visit, in the autumn of 1990, flitting around Southern California. I can remember one particularly hot October afternoon spent up at the Griffith Observatory, looking out over the amazing urban landscape – Los Angeles stretches out for almost 40 miles in front of you – not realising that just a couple of miles in front of me, in Loz Feliz, I might have been able to track down a young avant-garde folk singer by the name of Beck Hansen. I may even have been able to catch one of his legendary early shows and saved myself a lot of backtracking to write this biography. Instead I went to see the LA Dodgers at nearby Dodger Stadium.

Oh, hindsight, you could have saved me, and all the following people, a lot of work.

## Acknowledgements

I will start this Tom Hanks-like list of thanks and debt-paying by pointing out a few names that have paved the way for this book to actually happen, so my thanks go to Mark Paytress (then at *Record Collector*) for commissioning my first Beck article; Marcus Gray for giving me the inspiration to start writing in the first place; and of course Ian Gittins and all at Virgin for saying, 'Yeah – go for it . . .'

My wife, Carolyn, deserves many thanks for her encouragement, proof reading, patience and understanding (the amount of CDs, tapes, videos, magazines and books that I have stored in every nook and cranny around the house would drive anyone crazy). Paul Hellier's devotion to translating many French articles for me is commendable, even if the first quote that he translated came out as 'I'm just a little pedal who plays folk' – things got better from there! I must also give a mention to Mark T, Gino, Chris P, Kev, Dave, Simon, Neil, Paul S, Colin, Roy, Tim and Denise – all who gave much encouragement and brought me back down to earth when required.

Beck once related his music to architecture and said that 'It would be a walled community with a lot of different houses. You would be able to walk into any one of them and you'd feel welcome.' The same could also be said for his fans. During the writing of this book I was lucky enough to meet some great people and make some new friends. Special mentions are in order for the following:Brian Bauer (co-organiser of the Beck tribute CD *Fresh Takes On Old Slabs* – see http://members.aol.com/mrchonk for ordering information); Marie Cox (co-road trip member, May '99, photographer supreme and title chooser – thanks for everything); Deborah Gilmore (webmistress of 'Slo-jam Central' (http://earth.vol.com/~debber//beck/mainpg2.html) – thanks for the research and parcels!); Cathy 'Ethylester' Illman (a whole chapter could have been missing if it wasn't for your time and effort); and last but not least – Joseph Andrew 'Aloha' Milbury – thanks for the pictures, you came through in a clutch situation when my camera didn't work. Keep it reel!

The following posse all gave valuable advice and help on all manner of Beck-related subjects (as well as taking the time to send me lots of goodies) and generally helped to make a tough job a little bit easier. So, as they say, the 'props' go out to:

John C. Book, Tim Borneman, Cathy Brillon, Erika Y. Brinda, Lee Cannon, Mr Chonk, Mary D. Decicco, Wendy Diplock, Luke (eggy!) Eygenraam, Dustin Patrick Fitzgerald, Adam Flaherty, Ben Goldberg, Carlos D. Giffoni, Dustin Harjo, Levi Klau, Tony Linkin, Doreen Lobelle, Ehren Meditz, Sitar Mody, Deirdre Mullins, Hunter Neisler, Shauna O'Brien, Graham Palmer, Chris Quigley at *Level* magazine, Tom Reed, Lily Simonson, Paul Smernicki at Polydor, Geoff Snack, Wietze Spjikerman, Toni Strickroth (the nitemare hippie girl), Pete Tognetti, Abby Travis, Truck, Todd M.R. Tue, Keith Zehr and Flo – thanks for the tour on your day off!

I must also mention Chris Barlow and all who submitted book title and cover ideas.

The staff of the following stores helped make the collecting of Beck material all the more enjoyable and in some cases even cheaper than expected: Moby Disc (LA), Selectadisc (Nottingham), Arcade Records (Nottingham), Minus Zero Records (London), Espirit, Energy, Opal and all the independent stores on Melrose (LA).

Overall, this has been a very interesting and educational year, even if the ability to drag myself to the keyboard was sometimes difficult. I think P.J. O'Rourke came close to summing it up when he observed, 'The average commute time is now about 38 minutes. But I work at home and it takes me an hour to get to my desk.'

I'm always keen to hear from Beck fans so if you feel inclined, drop me a line at robj@innotts.co.uk.

As he usually has something interesting to say, I'll give the last word of the introduction to Beck: 'All you've seen so far is "This is a test", not the actual broadcast. Prime time has not come on yet. I've got a million ideas.'

*Rob Jovanovic*
*Paris, October 1999*

# 1 Lord Only Knows

*California, July 1970*

BY 1970 THE ACID REVOLUTION, hippie idealism and spirit of sixties San Francisco summers were as shot and faded as flower power. The Beatles had split a few months previously, the spectre of Vietnam was casting a shadow across the country. The explosion of pop and rock music that had left its imprint so memorably on the previous decade was about to receive a trio of casualties. Amidst this tide of change, in a boarding-house in downtown Los Angeles just before midnight on 8 July, David Campbell and Bibbe Hansen had their first baby and named him Bek David Campbell. Three months later Jimi Hendrix would be gone; a month later, in nearby Hollywood, Janis Joplin would follow; and within a year Jim Morrison would be dead in Paris.

At the time rock stardom probably didn't seem a popular choice for your first-born's career, but twenty-five years later this view would seem a little different. By the end of the millennium, little Bek David Campbell would be known as Beck Hansen and even better known simply as Beck. But in the hundreds of interviews he has given, you could never really be sure what was fact or fiction, and when you just about had it figured out he would pull the rug from under you.

It was not just the poor unsuspecting journalist who was getting the run-around either. When Beck's buddy Thurston Moore of Sonic Youth interviewed him for MTV in 1994, he received a masterclass in question avoidance that would have made any politician proud:

Thurston Moore:    I wanted to ask about who you are. I've asked a few people but I don't seem to be able to get any straight answers. So Beck, is Beck your real name? Were you christened Beck?

Beck:    (Just stares at Moore, then takes off his boot and throws it across the studio.)

Further questions were greeted by Beck holding a walkman to his mic and playing back a stream of incoherent noise.

The basics of Beck's background were established by *Rolling Stone* magazine who managed to scratch the surface as Beck gave away some of his story: 'I was born in Los Angeles. My parents lived in a rooming house near downtown. My mom had just come from New York, and my Dad was from up north. They were very young. My mom was 18 or 19 when they had me. Then, later on, we moved to Hollywood and lived just off of Hollywood Boulevard.'

This is the starting point for any Beck biographer: Beck has a unique family tree – one which juxtaposed artistry with relative poverty and which involved Beck from an early age in a series of cultural shifts which have had an inevitable influence on the eclectic nature of his work. Despite the tendency of some writers to portray Beck as emerging from the privileged position of having an artistic family, his early life was spent bouncing around between his mother and grandparents. Neither of their households were particularly prosperous and he quickly had to learn how to fend for himself as well as helping to support his family.

The independence instilled into him from an early age has no doubt helped Beck, if only subconsciously, to make up his own musical mind and not follow trends or movements. His Los Angeles upbringing has certainly ensured that he does not fit into the clichéd idea of a Californian and he is always keen to stress that he is from East LA, among the immigrants from Mexico and Central America.

'I was originally raised by a family of people who were from New York, and my father was from northern Canada, so I grew up in the shadow of the eastern culture.' When his mother remarried it was to a Mexican and Beck's upbringing took another turn.

As for Los Angeles itself, and Silverlake where he now resides, it's somewhere Beck has come to embrace later in life: 'I grew up hating it. Sometimes it has this feeling of a deserted place; there's millions and millions of people, but they are all in their cars and houses. That's why I live in this neighbourhood; it's one of the few places in Los Angeles where you can walk.'

Although LA is now his home, Beck was travelling from an early age as he divided his time between LA and Kansas. Indeed, Beck's upbringing could be described as just about as different from the average white American upbringing as you could reasonably get. Of course, the young Beck didn't know that it was different, he just accepted it as normal. This early travelling gave his grandfathers a chance to influence his future development to a slight degree and it's here the story begins.

Beck's maternal grandfather was the performance artist, Al Hansen. Spending time with his grandson, Al undoubtedly had an influence on Beck, both personally and artistically:

> I think my grandfather influenced me like anybody in your life influences you. People's character and ideas tend to rub off on you, whoever you're around. It's not like he ever sat down and said, 'Here's how to make art.' He had a bottomless stream of plans and hustles and dreams, and he always had a lot of young people around him. He was always giving young artists advice, but I was a musician.

Al Hansen was born in Queens, New York in 1927 and later spent long periods in Germany, beginning with his military service there in 1945. It was in Germany during World War II, so the story goes, that he daily passed a bombed building which had a piano half hanging out of a room several floors up. He grew steadily more fascinated by this piano, walking by day after day, until one night he crept back after dark and pushed it out of the building. This would become a centrepiece of his performance art pieces or 'Happenings' and he later titled it 'Yoko Ono Piano Drop' after his friend and contemporary in the 1960s.

3

On returning to the States he set up home in New York, where he studied and married an actress-model-poet by the name of Audrey Ostlin. The two had a daughter, Bibbe, who turned out to be the spitting image of Audrey. While studying in the 1950s he became more interested in performance art and got involved with the Fluxus movement, a collection of artists specialising in different fields, the most famous member of which was probably Yoko Ono. They embraced experimentation and their attitude was summed up in the saying, 'If you know what the end product is going to be then it isn't experimenta-tion.' This was applied to painting, sculpture, dance, music and the Happenings which were wild, unrehearsed theatre pieces. Al performed at several early international Fluxus Festivals and Beck would resurrect this style of performance in the late 1990s.

In 1965 Al Hansen published *A Primer of Happenings and Time Space Art*, about his art beliefs. Around this time he was also involved with Pop Art and Andy Warhol's Factory scene. He began churning out thousands of collages, mainly based around the image of the Venus de Milo. Al became good friends with John Cage in New York and, as Beck described, was on the scene when Andy Warhol was shot.

'He actually ran into Valerie Solanas as she was on her way out of the Factory from shooting Warhol. He made a book about it called "Why Shoot Andy Warhol?" It's really beautiful.'

Al became the catalyst for many Fluxus and Pop Art events and his enthusiasm encouraged those around him to create and go on to greater things. According to Beck, 'He was the life and soul of the Fluxus party. He would hook up everybody together. At his funeral all the Fluxus people were there, and all the Pop Art people, and they all talked about how mischievous he was. He didn't really play the game, though. He would get drunk and insult the gallery owner's wife and get banned. He was the Bukowski of the scene.'

When Bibbe was in her early teens, tragedy struck: Audrey suddenly died at the age of only 37. Her obituary appeared in an August 1968 edition of the *Village Voice*. At about this time Al had started teaching at Rutgers University in New Jersey. As Bibbe began accompanying her father on his visits to The Factory, she became the youngest Warhol Superstar, appearing in a film called *Prison* with Edie Sedgewick. She also had numerous roles in Al's Happenings.

It wasn't until he was well into his teens that Beck really understood that his mum had been around with Andy Warhol and his scene.

'I'd gotten into the Velvet Underground's first record, and I pulled it out and started looking at it,' he says. 'My mom saw that I was into it and said, "I know them." I said, "Tell me about that stuff." I already sort of knew about it, but it hadn't really connected until then.'

He quickly downplays the effect of having his mother seen as some sort of 1960s guru.

> She was involved with Warhol, very briefly, as a dancer and was in one or two short movies. They would just set somebody up and film them for five minutes and call it a movie. By the time she was 15 or 16 she had moved back west and she met my father. I think, to her, The Factory was just a bunch of grown ups. It wasn't really where she was at. From everything she's told me, it was just a bunch of speed-freaks hanging around and sometimes someone would bring out a camera. I don't think it was as crazy as it seems now, looking back. You know, that time period, anything in the 60s, but especially something like that scene, is always blown up into this larger-than-life thing. The whole Factory thing, it was really just Andy's scene. It wasn't really a life-impacting situation.

At the end of the 1960s Bibbe moved to Los Angeles where she met the son of a Canadian Presbyterian minister by the name of David Campbell. He was a tall, soft-spoken man and later Beck would develop a very close facial resemblance to him: the two would be referred to as 'two peas in a pod'. Campbell had been born in Canada but at an early age his family moved to Seattle and later to New York. He started playing the violin at the age of nine and later studied at the Manhattan School of Music. He moved to Los Angeles in the late 1960s and studied The Beatles, Rolling Stones and Leonard Cohen and would play their tunes on his violin to the cinema queues in Westwood Village.

After he and Bibbe married they had a pair of sons; first Beck, in 1970, and soon after came Channing, who was to go on to study art in San Francisco. In the early 1970s Campbell would take the young Beck along on his various musical outings, 'My father was a bluegrass musician, he played violin. When he left to play in the street, he took me in a sort of rucksack,' recalls Beck.

This early start in music didn't inspire Beck to take it up himself however.

'I heard him play here and there, but it wasn't like I went into the living room and people were jamming or anything,' he explains. 'I just remember that he was always working. I liked what he played, but it wasn't like I went out and picked up an instrument and started playing myself. It wasn't until a lot later that I picked up an instrument.'

Indeed Campbell did work a lot and, as Bibbe was also working, Beck was often packed off to stay with Campbell's parents who were then living in Kansas. His paternal grandfather had his parish in Kansas and the environment was the opposite of Beck's LA home.

Looking back, Beck can remember that his Kansas grandparents weren't sure what was going on: 'I had a kind of weird home, I think they were kind of concerned.' It was here that Beck was really left open to a lot of music for the first time by the unlikely influence of listening to Presbyterian hymns. 'That music influenced me a lot, but not consciously, there's something biblical and awkward and great about all those lyrics,' he says.

Later, after he had discovered the blues and its links to the rhythms of rap, he connected it all back to the religious songs of his past: 'The religious energy of a minister in front of his congregation is pretty similar to rock and roll energy. The grunt and the groan and the punctuation of a sermon is similar to the grunt and the groan of a soul singer or rapper. It's all connected to the blues.' Despite David Campbell's upbringing, he now studies 'Asian religious philosophies via Scientology'.

Campbell's hard work paid off as he garnered a reputation as an expert string arranger who was much in demand. He played viola on 'Song for Adam', a track on Jackson Browne's debut album, and soon after was part of Carole King's touring band at the height of the popularity of her breakthrough album *Tapestry*, which directly led to his role as string arranger on her *Rhymes and Reasons* album.

'It was sort of straight into the fire,' he told the *LA Times*. 'I had studied orchestration, but here was the biggest-selling artist of that era and I'm doing real work on her next album.' This also led to later work with Linda Ronstadt, the Rolling Stones, Neil Diamond, Willie Nelson and Bob Dylan. He also played viola on a couple of classics, Marvin Gaye's 'Let's Get It On' and Bill Withers's 'Lean on Me'. Despite this professional success, Campbell's personal life was not so rosy and he and Bibbe split in the mid-seventies. After this split Beck chose to take his mother's maiden name, Hansen, as his own and he didn't see a whole lot of his father for the next few years.

By the autumn of 1974 Beck started school in Los Angeles and was immediately an enigma to the authorities there as he remembers:

> When I first started school, I was four or five, the administrators and the teachers, and the certifiers, the paper registering people of the world gave the 'c' to me. I don't think they could deal with b-e-k. It would always become b-e-c-k and I guess I got tired of saying 'no, b-e-k.' So I just went with it. Somehow I think it gave me a little more weight. I thought maybe as a kid, I was a small kid, with a name like that I was going to float away.

Soon after starting school Beck had his first on-stage performance – as a donkey. It almost scarred him for life: 'All I remember is that one kid was the goat, one was the horse and one was the giraffe. I had to get up to the front and say, "The donkey goes eeyore." Everybody started laughing and I thought I'd done something really wrong. I was horrified. It turned me off performing for a long time.'

Around this time Beck began seeing more of his grandfather, as Al Hansen occasionally stayed with Bibbe on his West Coast trips. Al surely deserves some credit for some of Beck's unique lyrical styles.

'When I was about five, I was trying to get my Grandfather to explain what rhyming was,' he recalls. 'He explained it to me and "pull down your pants and do the hot dog dance" was my first lyric. My grandfather got a kick out of that.'

As well as his performance pieces, Hansen was now working on bizarre sculptures, often prepared by recycling garbage. A later chapter in this book will detail these links between Beck and his grandfather but this story that Beck told to *Rolling Stone* is a good example of their artistic closeness:

> He was this strange phenomenon, you know, who'd come from out of nowhere. I remember he came to stay with us when I was about five, and he brought with him bags full of junk and magazines, cigarette butts, all sorts of refuse and materials that he would use for his art pieces. I had some old toys that had broken and didn't work stored in the back room somewhere. He found an old rocking horse, the kind you buy at K-Mart, made out of plastic with springs on it. And he offered me five bucks for it, which, for me, was an unheard-of quantity of money. I immediately said yeah, he could have it. But I couldn't understand what he would do with it, what use he could have for it.
>
> So I came back from school one day and saw this thing sitting at the side of the house, vaguely familiar but somehow completely unrecognisable. He had taken the thing and glued cigarette butts all over it, severed the head off and spray painted the whole thing silver. It was this metallic headless monstrosity. I think I was interested, but something within me recoiled as well. It was, it was so raw: something so plain and forgotten suddenly transformed into this strange entity.
>
> At the time, it was more of a curiosity to me. But in retrospect, I think things of that nature gave me the idea, maybe subconsciously, that there were possibilities within the limitations of everyday life, with the things that we look at that are disposable. Our lives can seem so limited and uneventful, but these things can be transformed. We can appoint ourselves to be, to be alchemists, turning shit into gold. So I always carried that with me.

While getting a certain amount of artistic inspiration from his grandfather Beck seemed to be totally uninterested in music at an early age. The playing and arranging of his father didn't immediately inspire Beck and he was exposed to a number of other influences that also had little or no effect on him at the time. He claims that the first music he can remember at home must have been a musical comedy, one of those Broadway pieces of rubbish that my mother listened to at the house. There were very few records at our house and there were some absolute horrors with melodies that made me want to vomit. The first record I really adored was 'Ruby Tuesday' by the Stones. I knew nothing about them, not even that they were English. It was that song that I loved, that simple melody.

Other early musical memories include 'Listening to *Rubber Soul* when I was five, though I'm not sure how that's filtered into what I do now. And I remember hearing "Hot Child in the City" while driving to school.'

In the light of Beck's upbringing it is easier to understand his claims not to have been aware of a lot of 1970s music. Listening to a Beck record, one is tempted to jump to the conclusion that he has listened to a lot of popular music from that time. The truth is very different. 'It's sort of strange for me because I totally missed the 70s,' he said recently.

Sometimes there's this notion that I'm this encyclopaedia of 70s culture which isn't really true – I know much less than anyone else in the band. I wasn't even aware of most of the music in the 70s . . . maybe Blondie and Devo. You know sometimes people will say 'Hey, that sounds exactly like so and so, you must have listened to a lot of their stuff' and often I haven't even heard of them. I don't think I even heard Black Sabbath until I was 19 or 20. I just wasn't exposed to it – it just wasn't in our house. My mum would just play show tunes and stuff like that all the time.

After a few short stays, Al Hansen moved in with his daughter for a longer spell towards the end of the 1970s. Beck recalls: 'When I was very young he lived in the garage for a couple of years. This was probably about 1977, '78. I didn't have a lot of contact with my grandfather, but seeing how he worked gave me a lot of confidence. Seeing the way he worked, I never felt that I had to have schooling in order to create. He was this presence; he got people excited about the scene.'

Al would take Beck and Channing on scavenging missions along Sunset Boulevard for materials to use. 'He used specific materials – cigarette butts, matches, Hershey Bar wrappers,' Beck told *VH-1* in 1998. 'My art is a little less focused. I tend to use ephemera from computers, diskettes, there's imagery from muscle building. Instead of all those things at the end of the week that you'd throw in the dustbin, I keep them and my grandfather would keep them as well – try to turn something disposable into something beautiful.'

While Al would take trash and turn it into art (what Beck referred to as 'Turning shit into gold'), Beck has been tagged with doing something similar in his music by taking many different styles and combining them into one song. When discussing this 'recycling', Beck agrees with the principle to some extent. 'On a certain level that's right on,' he admits, 'but when you say "recycling", it cheapens the aesthetic a bit and makes the music sound second-class. I think the process has a gracefulness and a dignity to it, so I like to say my music is orchestrated, an organisation of disparate elements.'

Times were now becoming hard for the Hansen household and Beck remembers that some things taken for granted by other kids were not the case for him and Channing: 'We stopped having Christmas when I was very young, because we couldn't afford it. I remember one year my brother and I made a Christmas tree out of cardboard. We cut it out and stuck it on the wall. It was a traditional sort of thing, but it was depressing. It always is if you haven't got any money.'

When Q magazine asked him directly if the family was poor he avoided the question, merely saying, 'You could say that. I don't want to talk about it. Where I come from financially doesn't inform my music.'

Throughout this impoverished time, Beck and Channing were close. When not hanging out with Al, they would be left to their own devices as Bibbe would be working.

She believed in a 'hands-off' approach to bringing up the boys. 'She's just a chain-smoking, make-your-own-dinner kind of mom,' says Beck.

To her credit, Bibbe has never tried to claim any of Beck's musical abilities to be part of his upbringing. She simply says, 'He's an original. He did it all completely on his own. I wouldn't have a clue as to how Bek became Beck.'

With little or no money the two brothers had to make up their own entertainment. 'When I was little we used to have these missions,' he reveals. 'We'd strip down to our underwear and have a destination – like the supermarket eight blocks away. We had to make it there and back without getting arrested or beaten up or pregnant.'

With Bibbe usually out at work it was a time of adventure and discovery for Beck:

> As kids, me and my brother always had to fend for ourselves. We had to learn how to cook and to feed ourselves all the time, I started cooking pretty young. It was kind of a necessity really. My parents would be working, my dad would be off for a week somewhere, and you'd get hungry. You'd think, 'I want a hamburger,' but then you'd think, 'how do you make a hamburger?' So you sort of figure it out. I remember when I was a teenager going to shows and me and my brother were the youngest ones there. We were the only kids around.

The latter half of the 1970s saw a new musical entity on the West Coast – a strange new beast called punk. Al Hansen saw something in this new music that appealed to his artistic nature and he became involved in the scene. The Masque club had opened in July 1977 and hosted bands like X, The Germs and The Go-Go's before having to be closed in early 1979 because of fire regulations.

'My Grandfather was into that whole Masque scene,' says Beck. 'He hipped my mom to bands like The Screamers and The Bags and The Plugz.'

Soon Bibbe was well into the scene and playing mother to a whole host of punks who needed a place to sleep for the night. Beck wasn't overly keen on this situation.

> I wish she'd done all that stuff when she was a teenager, 'cause she was definitely not that open then. There seems to be a point, and this is true for a lot of my friends too, where their mothers reach their mid-forties and turn into freaks. They become teenagers again. She's definitely become more open-minded. My brother and I were sort of left to our own devices. Again, it was the same with a lot of people my age. They weren't very parented. In fact, almost everybody I know was like that. It wasn't an LA thing, more a sixties-seventies thing. That generation was definitely . . . I don't want to say self-centred, but maybe self-focused.

Beck found it difficult to get used to walking into the kitchen in the morning to be faced with a punk or two at the breakfast table.

> I just remember all these people sprawled about looking like thrashed parrots. Very colourful and debauched but very sweet too. They were normal people, they just smelled a little funny. She would let punks stay at our house who didn't have a place to stay. She claims that Darby Crash [lead singer of The Germs] crashed out a few times on our living room sofa. She was older but felt kind of sorry for them.

For Bibbe, it was a breath of fresh air. 'Punk was like the best thing I'd heard in years, so there was always a peanut butter and jam sandwich and a couch,' she says. Her involvement with the punk scene eventually led to her playing guitar in the Los Angeles ensemble, Black Fag with Vaginal Creme Davis, a 6ft 7in African-American drag queen and performance artist.

After spending the end of the 1970s in LA, Al moved to Cologne in Germany and Bibbe met Sean Carrillo, a Mexican artist, whom she married. Carrillo's parents had moved from the northern Mexican town of El Paso to LA where he was born in 1960, one of nine children. He became an artist, later owned Troy Cafe with Bibbe for five years, and has recently spent some considerable amount of his personal time documenting the career of Al Hansen.

As a result of this remarriage Beck suddenly had a half Mexican family: 'Even now I feel more comfortable being around Mexican people than anyone else. Half my family was Mexican. It's just the way of life that was around me growing up. It's very natural with them. I can feel out of place with other people, but not with them.'

For a while they lived in Hollywood, which was still affordable before the 1980s property boom. The area had been in decline for a while, as Beck recalled at length to *Rolling Stone*:

> I spent my childhood watching the decline of Hollywood Boulevard, watching the dying embers, the final light of the Hollywood era, fade into decay. I remember certain relics of the 40s and 50s Hollywood eras still around when I was growing up.

They had the lunch counters, shoeshines and family owned businesses, which have now turned into rock-poster shops and bad souvenir shops. We lived near Tiny Naylor's, which was a monument from the age of the 50s drive-in coffee shops. It was just a megalopolis of hamburgers and milkshakes, that whole – you drive up, and the waitress puts the tray on your car. They still had that up into the 70s. And right next to that was Ali Baba's, a Middle Eastern restaurant with belly dancers, and on top of it was a two- to three-story statue of Ali Baba. Then in the early 80s, all that was suddenly gone. The developers came in and tore it all down and turned it into giant condominiums and block apartments. I remember seeing LA just transformed within a couple years. All of a sudden there were mini-malls everywhere. The 80s came and conquered. And it erased a lot of the heritage of that city. It's not the same city at all.

Beck would spend his weekends riding his bike around Hollywood Boulevard where he'd see the break dancers and hear Grandmaster Flash. 'My funk came from being eleven years old on a Saturday night hanging out on Hollywood Boulevard with all the break dancers,' he says. His new family then moved to South Vermont Avenue in Los Angeles.

The apartments that the family inhabited were fairly small and Beck never had a room to himself: 'When I was growing up, I used to share the living room with my little brother – he slept on the couch, I slept on the floor. He liked to listen to Leonard Cohen's *Songs From A Room* while he fell asleep, but it was so dark and creepy, it gave me nightmares. Especially the song where he takes his son, Isaac, up to the mountain and kills him.'

Later on he claims to have had to sleep in a sleeping bag under the kitchen table. The next move was downtown to Hoover & Ninth Street, a neighbourhood which had a lot of Koreans and Salvadoran refugees, and once again Beck had to change schools.

By this time, around 1983, Beck was buying music for himself during the family's trips to LA thrift stores. He now had the chance to pick up some cheesy second-hand albums:

I was really into easy-listening records. I had all the Mancini records and Jobim. It was the early 80s, so it wasn't really campy or retro, I just had a genuine affection for the music. The second hand store would have a bin of records, Mancini and stuff like that. It was five records for a dollar. You went to the Salvation Army and there'd be some elderly person who'd just passed away, and you'd end up buying all their junk. There wasn't any Top 20 stuff.

The financial circumstances of the family would improve, but at this time things were still pretty tight where money was concerned. As Beck admits:

It was a little rough. By the time I was a teenager, we were living on the edge of things. I would say we were economically depressed, we were basically living in a ghetto. But I wouldn't want to sell myself as some kind of rags to riches story because that reduces it to something soulless. It was an impoverished childhood, but it was rich in other ways. Where I grew up wasn't your typical, homogenised, one-track frame of mind, there were a lot of other things going on. Everyone was outside all the time, there were mariachi bands, animals running down the middle of the street. We lived in a one bedroomed apartment, five of us in a tiny space. If you're 13 or 14, all you want is to be alone. So I would go to the library and spend days there. I just stumbled onto a lot of stuff, got into some different books, but then there are a lot of other ones that I've just totally missed.

While Beck's somewhat unconventional parental upbringing would stand him in good stead to look after himself in the future, his schooling left a lot to be desired. By the age of about 14 he just gave up going; it was a combination of not being mentally stimulated, not really relating to a lot of the kids at school and living in fear of his life for being the only white kid around. Beck explains:

I wanted to go to school more than anything. I would never want to give the idea that I left because I didn't think school was important. It was just the circumstances that I was in. We lived in a one-bedroom apartment, and it was pretty crowded in there. There were sometimes five or six people at a time when I was a teenager. I have a brother. He's younger than me. And when you're a teenager, you want space, you want time alone. Also, the part of Los Angeles where I was going to school, it wasn't exactly the safest. It was a hard-core school, there were lots of hard-core gangs. I was the only white guy in my neighbourhood, which was fine by me, but not for some.

I didn't really have any friends, it felt kind of like a waste of time to me. It wasn't education at all, more like mass day care, a sort of unorganised way of killing time.

He wasn't against the idea of education, he really wanted to learn, it was just that what he wanted to learn was different from what he was being taught.

I was a kid who was in love with the idea of books before I could even read them. The education system in America depends on where you grow up. In my part of LA it was completely backward. I remember being in an English class, aware of being taught the same thing year after year. It never went anywhere and there was nothing interesting. But I knew there were interesting things out there and I knew there were possibilities.

During his years of fame and fortune, Beck has often been asked if he harbours any regrets about dropping out so early and his answers always confirm that he does. As he told *Rolling Stone*: 'Oh, yeah, definitely. More than anything I envy my friends that got to go to college. I thought maybe I would work for a few years and save money to go to college, but that never worked out. I went to New York instead and was playing music. I thought I would eventually go back to school, but I never have.'

He is also memorably quoted as saying, in his best Groucho Marx voice, 'I'm sure there's something good about high school, but not any of the ones I went to.'

It wasn't just at school where he felt like the odd man out: he was the only white kid in his East LA neighbourhood which led to his being in some hairy situations on an almost daily basis. While he doesn't really like to expand on this, he has said that there was some 'pretty bad-ass shit going on. Getting chased by kids with lead pipes everyday.' The frequent escapes he was required to make also turned him into something of an athlete: 'I guess it made me tougher, but I'm not tough for tough's sake. I don't really have the mass. I've been in fights. I've been in chases more. I'm a pretty fast runner, I think I was the fastest runner in my neighbourhood.'

The area where he lived was very Latino in atmosphere. 'I grew up around Central Americans and Mexicans,' Beck recalls. 'It was, I dunno, really urban, there were still chickens running around in the street and people passed out on the sidewalk.' But he quickly found himself caught in something of a cultural Catch-22 – living in a half-Mexican family excluded him from white culture, but at the same time his colour excluded him from the local gangs: 'I felt completely alienated from suburban white culture, even intimidated by it. I couldn't relate to kids my own age and color because I didn't live the way they did. But at the same time I couldn't hang with the Salvadoran gangs on my street, 'cos to them I was the "Whetto", the weird white kid.'

The positive side to living here was that it exposed him to a real mix of diverse ethnic influences: 'Visually, where I grew up was such a collage of culture,' he recalls. 'The business on the corner, it wouldn't just be a video store, it would be a video store-slash-furniture-slash-accounting-slash-income tax.'

In the hours of free time, before he discovered blues and folk, he immersed himself in *Star Wars* – he claims to have watched the original trilogy about fifty times – and James Bond. Both of these would have indirect effects on his music. He could often be seen in his Star Wars Stormtroopers mask, which in later years he could be seen wearing in the 'Loser' video and onstage.

And it was the James Bond link that was eventually to lead to his love of noise and punk after he bought a Pussy Galore record.*

'Pussy Galore was a James Bond character so I bought it. I was a total Bond freak. It was so distilled and pure, it had all the elements, just turned up.'

But it wasn't 'noise' that started Beck on his current path, it was folk and blues. The story of how he first connected to these genres has been told many times, and each time the facts are

---

*Pussy Galore were the band that opened the door to one of Beck's later musical passions – noise rock. From their beginnings in Washington DC, they set about offending as many people as possible with their brand of hardcore punk/noise. They put out five albums and five EPs in a seven-year span which included titles like 'Dial M For Motherfucker' – obviously an influence on some of Beck's early song titles. In 1992 they split and guitarist Jon Spencer formed the Jon Spencer Blues Explosion with whom Beck would later work.

slightly different. So here is an all-encompassing version which you can cut and paste to suit your own preference.

At the age of {15, 16, 17} Beck {stumbled upon, found, was given} an old record by Mississippi John Hurt.* This happened at {the library, a friend's house, his aunt's, his parent's}.

> It was shrink-wrapped, [he remembers] it hadn't even been opened, and it was this insane close-up of his face, sweating, this old wrinkled face, and I took it. I was going to return it, but I didn't. I loved the droning sound, the open tunings, the spare, beat down-tone. And his voice was so full. He just went through so much shit, and it comes across really, really amazing. This wasn't some hippie guy finger picking in the 70s, singing about rainbows. This was the real stuff. I stopped everything for six months and was in my room finger picking until I got it right.

The only things he'd really listened to before hearing this album were 'trucks going by outside and helicopters with spotlights looking for criminals'. He didn't relate to the plastic synthetic sounds of many eighties bands:

> By being a kid in the 80s and seeing how fake and artificial all the music was, and feeling disconnected from it – all this Huey Lewis and the News stuff didn't make an impression on me – and stumbling across Blind Willie Johnson, Woody Guthrie. This kind of stuff is really potent and pure. It kind of shook me up. It all seemed so possible. None of the pop music in the 80s seemed like you could be part of it. You just had it inflicted on you. Now I hear music on the radio, and it's guitars. It sounds a little more possible. Hearing Woody Guthrie, it's like 'Oh, that's guitar.' He's just sort of talking. He's just a person.

Inspired by his find he immersed himself in listening to as much of the stuff as he could afford; he also got himself a guitar and taught himself to play: 'I got a nylon stringed guitar and that's what I learned to play on. I remember saving up for a while and I finally got an old Gibson – the same model that

---

*Mississippi John Hurt taught himself to play in the 1920s and recorded some material for Columbia. However it didn't sell very well and he returned to farming. Amazingly, years later in 1963, he was tracked down at the age of 71 and persuaded to record again. He could still sing and play well and he continued to play live until his death in 1966, having found a new generation of fans.

Woody Guthrie used. It didn't sound good when I tried to play a pop song but it sounded good when I tried to play a folk song.'

The folk and blues sounded so pure to Beck, especially when compared with the phoney, fake-sounding music on the radio. He hadn't even liked the blues before because of what he'd heard: 'I'd never liked the blues before,' he said, ''cos I thought it was all just hoochie-coochie Chicago stuff. Oh God, really boring. Then I heard Son House* and it was the most lonesome, strange, really sparse, heavy wooden-sounding music ever.'

Beck was really taken by the tradition and honesty of the songs that he was learning and hearing: 'I was very uninspired to make music until I stumbled upon Mississippi John Hurt, Woody Guthrie, those kinds of musicians. It was just a guitar, and I liked the sound of it. It was really simple, the antithesis of the 80s. Once I discovered this traditional folk music, country music, Delta blues, I had a whole world to get lost in.'

He wanted to get to the essence of the music, not later exponents of the pure sound as he saw it:

> I dig Leadbelly. He's like the most powerful 12-string player. You can't copy his music, you can't even play it, because it's coming from hands that are three times bigger than normal hands, you know. I never really got into Pete Seeger. There's a sort of grandfather quality to him that's sweet but it seems a little corny. I never really got into Arlo Guthrie, either. I was more interested in Woody Guthrie because he was more stripped-down, more connected with traditional music. Early Arlo Guthrie music had a 60s kind of reality about it. The 30s kind of reality of Woody Guthrie is more what I felt connected to.

Another finger-picking inspiration was the Carter Family. He also found they had a connection to the religious music that he'd been exposed to ten years earlier at his grandparents in Kansas: 'There's this whole tradition of beautiful religious music that I love,' he acknowledges. 'Like the Carter family, who came down

---

*Eddie James 'Son' House was possibly the most important of the Delta Blues innovators. His passionate playing was best represented on his 1930s recordings for Paramount and he was a great influence on both Robert Johnson and Muddy Waters, both blues greats in their own right.

from the hills of Bristol, Tennessee to be recorded by Victor Records; they had these really strange, really beautiful harmonies.'

It wasn't until years later that he found contemporaries that had similar musical loves. In 1993 on their *Unplugged* recording, Nirvana covered Leadbelly. This came as real shock to Beck. He recalls:

> It was a strange moment to hear Cobain sing Leadbelly, because that was a song I'd been playing as a teenager. Leadbelly, Mississippi John Hurt, Woody Guthrie – anywhere I could, I was banging out those songs. And people wouldn't respond until maybe I'd accidentally play something Led Zeppelin had covered, and then people would recognise it as 'the Led Zep song.' I'd kind of finally given up on that music and started experimenting with drum machines when I heard Cobain do that. It was like, 'What? Oh my God. Where was that audience before?' But it was good to have that music recognised.

Beck soon had a collection of all the blues, country and folk greats, Jimmie Rodgers, Woody Guthrie, the Carter Family, Mississippi John Hurt, Mississippi Fred MacDowell, Blind Willie Johnson, Son House, Blind Blake and Skip James . . . the list just goes on. But one name is conspicuous by its absence – Robert Johnson: 'I was never drawn to Robert Johnson much,' he admits. 'A lot of that stuff had a hyped-up, clichéd aspect. I was attracted to guys like Skip James. When he sings about the devil you get a feeling of true evil.'

It wasn't too long before Beck started to see, or rather hear, the possibilities in the blues, even though it was a while before he actually experimented with them. Mance Lipscomb, a relatively unknown Texas farmer-turned-guitarist, became one of Beck's favourites:

> When I first got into Delta Blues I could hear the hip hop beats in the music. It would just be Son House playing a slide guitar by himself, but there was this implied hip hop beat in everything he was playing. Mance Lipscomb, too, had a lot of funk in him. I remember thinking it would be great some day to experiment with that. It's all related, it all goes back to the rhythm and the African influence. It's been filtered through so many different

times and genres, but it's still just as strong as ever. I fantasised about combining slide guitar and hip-hop music. The first time I met somebody [Carl Stephenson] who had some equipment and knew how to loop up a beat, that's the first thing I did. It had been on my mind for years, and it was great to finally hear it.

It seems like 'Loser' was just an accident waiting to happen.

If Beck had been born ten years later this love of the blues might never have happened. He liked the fact that it was difficult to get the records, that they weren't just something that you could walk into the local corporate record store and buy: 'I can't imagine dealing with the blues now. I remember when I was younger you really had to search and dig the stuff up. It was all kind of obscure, you even had to find 78s. They didn't have the 3-CD Son House reissue box set.'

With some basic songs under his belt, Beck began to experiment with some live performances. These consisted of blues and folk covers and goofy spoof songs that he just made up on the spur of the moment. The venues were street corners, parks and on buses. Remembering this, he laughs: 'I just carried my guitar everywhere. I was just kind of ready for any sudden jamboree that might befall me. I used to play down at Lafayette park, near where I used to live as a kid, and all these Salvadoran guys would be playing soccer and I'd be practising a Leadbelly song. They would just be shaking their heads. Once in a while a ball would sail over my head.'

He also played at MacArthur Park, not exactly the safest of places, where David Bowie had filmed some scenes for *The Man Who Fell To Earth*. On the buses he gave the public-transport-loving minority of Los Angeles some unusual sounds to help them on their journey: 'I'd get on the bus and start playing Mississippi John Hurt with totally improvised lyrics. Some drunk would start yelling at me, calling me Axl Rose. So I'd start singing about Axl Rose and the levee and bus passes and strychnine, mixing the whole thing up.'

He tended to choose the longer bus routes so he didn't have to break up his 'set'. A favourite route was the Vermont line down through south central LA and back around up to Hollywood. Occasionally he'd be joined by some other musician but usually he was just left by himself to the stares and occasional abuse from the other passengers. He didn't make much money from this pursuit but he reckons that if he'd changed his songs he might have. 'It all comes down to "Hey Jude",' he says. 'I think the most successful street musicians I've seen in my time were the ones who just played "Hey Jude" all day and all night.'

At the same time as these early forays into the live arena he was trying out some crude home taping too. By the age of 16 he had begun making tapes by recording on to one cassette player, then playing along with that cassette and recording on to another. This was repeated until the sound was completely distorted; the screwed-up tape speed gave his voice a helium-like vocal effect which Beck still occasionally uses. Despite all this musical activity, the plain fact was that Beck was now in low-paid employment and probably would be for a long time. He would hire himself out as a removal man or sometimes get a stint working in a local video store. It was all pretty demoralising.

One bright point occurred, however, when his mother packaged him off in the summer of 1987 to Germany to spend some time with his grandfather. He had $150 spending money and the chance to explore a little of Europe. Al had spent the early 1980s establishing the Ultimate Akademie, an art school that he set up there with Lisa Gieslik. It was here that Beck began keeping notebooks of collages that he put together. These would eventually form part of the Playing With Matches exhibition.

'I lived there for a while,' said Beck of the Akademie. 'It was very free. Somebody would get the idea to start a band, and that night we'd be performing on the radio, and there'd be a local news crew interviewing us.'

'I went to visit my grandfather who lives in a spa town in Germany,' Beck told a French magazine. 'I made the most of it, drinking some water and taking baths. My Grandfather was fairly well known, he inspired me enormously when I was young.' To see what is perhaps the most obvious part of Al coming out from Beck you should look at Al Hansen's *Intermedia Poems*. The series of cut-out newspaper headlines arranged on a page in the form of a poem could be lyrics from a Beck song:

'Pitfalls in the promised land/Robbers plunder the night train/English cloud received with silver lining/Cash bottlenecks pinch profits.'

In the end, Beck saw Al not as a mentor but one of many people who have shaped the way that he has evolved himself: 'I don't really think of Al as a teacher, any more than anybody else in my life. We all have relationships, friendships, that will eventually become pieces of who we are. It's hard for me to dissect what part of me is Al and what part of me is my friends from junior high. My other grandfather was a Presbyterian minister, so where that fits in, I don't know.'

On his return to Los Angeles Beck found himself back in the same old depression that he'd left behind. His next move was to decide that he'd take a chance and get some action before it was too late. He set his sights on the Big Apple and went cross-country to see if his luck might change and set him on to a brighter course.

But it was not all to go quite as smoothly as he had hoped. Beck was about to hit some trouble.

# 2 Trouble All My Days

I N ORDER TO BREAK OUT from the rut into which he was sinking in California, Beck decided to make a drastic move before it was too late. Although he may have been planning his escape route for a while, when he actually got around to making his move it was because he saw an advertisement for cheap bus tickets and just went for it. He decided to take a chance and, with guitar in hand, transported himself to New York with a view to expanding his musical sphere and experiencing the big city atmosphere.

Beck had slowly been realising that he'd probably spend the rest of his life in low-paid employment, moving from job to job and never leaving Los Angeles. 'I didn't have rich parents to support me,' he explains, 'so I knew I was in for years of menial work. I decided to spend a few years seeing what was out there, before I was locked into a dead-end job.'

His chosen destination was New York as he wanted to sample the city that had been home for his mother and grandfather. It helped that the Greyhound buses were offering a special promotion, allowing travel anywhere in the country for $30. So on the spur of the moment he bought two tickets, one for himself and one for a girlfriend. New York was about as far from LA as possible, so Beck would be getting good value for his money.

Despite his blues education, he didn't really see going cross-country as either a romantic 'beat' thing to do, nor as the traditional hobo occupation of 'riding the rails'.

There was no romanticism left in it by that time. As a teenager I'd read all the Beat literature; I'd read all about the folk revival of the 60s. I knew that was all gone. It wasn't about that. I was intensely into the blues, country blues, but I knew it wasn't a romantic thing. The blues came out of hardship, misery. I think in the 60s it was romanticised, the wise-old-bluesman thing, but I didn't really have any illusions about it. You spend about two minutes in the downtown LA Greyhound bus station and your romanticism about taking a bus trip across America will be eradicated and exterminated immediately.

As Beck says, he was accustomed to low-budget, long-distance travel, having previously visited grandfather Al in Germany. 'I was used to going somewhere with no means, not really knowing anybody, sort of making my way through it. I dunno, I was naive. I tend to trust people.' If there were going to be any sticky situations along the way he felt that he'd had a good grounding in looking after himself in some of LA's more notorious areas: 'At that point I'd seen some fucked-up shit: people machine-gunned on my front lawn; coming out in the morning and playing with the bandages when I was a little kid.' Compared to growing up in this warzone-like environment, a 3,000-mile bus trip with little or no money was a tea party.

So, in mid-1988, he booked his ticket with a girlfriend and set off with his guitar, a little cash and nothing much else. 'It must have taken at least a week to get there,' he moans. 'I stopped off here and there. Went through the South.'

It was in the South that he had one of his scarier moments:

At some point in the middle of west Texas, the sun was going down, and I realised that all the straight people, all the working people, had gotten off the bus and everyone left was a drug fiend or an ex-con. I remember one of them whispering in my ear as soon as I fell asleep: He was going to slit my throat. I knew I was descending into the heart of America. I was discovering the heartland at that moment.

He would later write a song entitled 'Heartland Feeling' which, although not about that exact encounter, was probably inspired by seeing the many miles of nothingness across the country and the feelings of vast open expanses as depicted in the atmosphere of songs by Springsteen and Mellencamp. His general plan was to eat food from vending machines, sleep on overnight bus hops from city to city and spend the day wandering around each town before the following night's jaunt.

A decade later he told Barney Hoskyns in *Mojo* about his recollections of the journey:

> I was immersed in stuff like 'The Anthology Of American Folk Music' when I was growing up. Of course a certain amount of it was romantic and macabre and intriguing and fascinating. That faraway strange quality is definitely something I gravitated towards when I was younger. I guess travelling through America, I realised that a lot of strangeness is still out there, only maybe it's a little more frightening because it's alive here and now.

If any of that 'strangeness' came too close to him he was sure to ward it away with a nifty little manoeuvre he learned along the way. 'Whenever anyone looking a little sketchy came my way,' he laughs, 'I'd start swinging my guitar around or start doing handstands or something. The best way to drive these people off is to pretend you're insane.'

Somewhere along the way, the bus drivers went on strike and almost scuppered his plan of reaching the East Coast. This turn of events did, however, allow a few free rides as some kids taught him how to sneak on to a bus without paying. 'The guys who loaded the baggage were all driving the buses,' he says. 'And it was fairly chaotic and the buses were all overcrowded so it was pretty easy to sneak on.'

He also hitch-hiked for part of the journey when the buses were too overcrowded even to sneak on. Even this wasn't up to the romantic idea of hitching from coast to coast though, as Beck ended up getting a ride from an optometrist: 'It's never like a movie, he just picked me up, we talked about laser-corrective eye surgery for an hour and a half, then he dropped me off.'

Eventually after the long and winding journey, the bus at last pulled into the Port Authority Bus Terminal in Manhattan. This isn't the nicest of places at the best of times (although it has been immensely cleaned up in the last few years) but Beck arrived like a pauper in the promised land: 'It was the whole cliché, I had like $8 in my pocket like a total idiot with a guitar and nothing else.'

At least he had his girlfriend. Well, he thought he did: 'I think

I got on the wrong subway train somewhere along the way . . .' he explained, but whatever did happen, no sooner had they arrived than she dumped him.

Without a place to stay Beck had to live rough, at least for a little while. He spent the summer looking for somewhere to work and live and did manage to hold on to a few short-term jobs like checking in people's coats at a bookstore. Without any money or prospects he just went with the flow: 'I just trusted that I'd find somebody who'd let me crash here or someone who knew about a job, and I'd get a job for a while. I never pushed to get anywhere. I just always trusted that I would end up where I was supposed to go. That was always my belief. And that would happen to greater or lesser degrees. If I ended up in a weird place, I'd just make the best out of it.'

One of the 'weird places' that he ended up in was working for the YMCA:

> For a while I was working on the Upper East Side at the YMCA, taking ID photos. Me and this Russian guy who didn't speak any English. We would just sit there every day, and they didn't need two people for the job. I'd press the button and he would pull the film out. It was really weird. We'd sit there for six hours just looking at each other like there was nothing to say. I'd be like, 'So where in Russia are you from?' He didn't know what I was talking about. Like one person would come in every hour and ten minutes. There would be like this really hard-core 45-year-old Jewish lady, 'I wanna see the picture.' And they freak out when they see the picture. They'll be like, 'No I have to get this done over again.' But we were told specifically: 'No matter how much they want their picture taken again, you don't take their picture again.' So we would have to deal with some chick like, 'I cannot have a card where I look like this!' And I'd be trying to convince her, 'Lady you look great.' And the Russian guy, he'd be looking wistfully off into the corner, thinking about Siberia or something.

He actually managed to save up a little cash and was hoping to rent a small place of his own. It wouldn't be the Hilton, but it would be his: 'I found it hard to live in New York, it was tragic. I had saved up this money from working at the YMCA, and I gave it to this woman, who I was going to rent an apartment from, she was a junkie and she split town with all my money. I was screwed, and it was all downhill from there.'

While the financial and accommodation situations went downhill from there, the artistic and musical scenes were just about to flourish. He'd already done a little street-corner busking and began to trek further afield, jamming along with the freestyle rappers in Tompkins Park Square. 'That's where I first started rapping,' he recalls. 'There would be these homeless hip-hop freestyle things happening. We would get up there and do some folk-rap. The seeds of a lot of what I do now came out of that time.'

Eventually his stay in New York took a positive turn. It happened one day when he was just hanging out around Avenue A as usual with his beat-up guitar. 'I remember literally standing on the street and running into some people, and when they saw I had a guitar, they said, "here's an open-mic night – why don't you come?" And I was scared to death to play.'

Despite his initial fear, that was all the invite he needed and soon he was in the 'Lower East Side freak-out folk noise Delta blues Pussy Galore scene' as he put it. From then on he'd busk during the day, and play at night, but not much else: 'I didn't work. I just spent a couple of years sleeping on couches and being penniless. Just playing music. There's just all these people there making music and there's always a place to crash, and there's always something going on every night. I played on the streets for money. It's really hard to find work there.'

What he'd accidentally stumbled upon became known as the 'Anti-Folk scene'. It had begun with John S Hall, a Brooklyn native who grew up in Greenwich Village, and his friend Lach, owner of the Chameleon Club. Hall was originally a spoken word artist who later found more widespread recognition with the band King Missile.*

---

*As a stream-of-consciousness poet at The Fort on the Lower East Side, Hall gained a reputation as an interesting live spectacle. He soon added music to his excellent vocal abilities, both spoken-word and singing. He needed extra help to play the music as his musical expertise began and ended with his playing of the triangle, but as he managed to blend in his flow of spoken-word prose with a few actual songs, he formed King Missile Dog Fly Religion (later shortened to King Missile) in 1986. With this band, Hall released six albums in seven years (the last three on Atlantic Records) before they split up in 1994.

Hall's spoken word gigs had been well before the anti-folk scene appeared around him as he remembered: 'I started out in poetry readings and open mic nights as a spoken word artist, then I went and got musicians to put music behind my work.' When asked to recall the scene he's not too sure what it was himself: 'I couldn't really tell you much about anti-folk. It was something my friend Lach started in response to all the boring folk clubs that were thriving in New York, but shutting out new artists.'

The overall feel was exactly what its title suggested. A punkish rowdy selection of folk songs delivered by performers that stomped and screamed around the stage – the total opposite of the 1960s Joan Baez, James Taylor types that had, in the eyes of the performers, taken folk away from its raw roots. Beck explains: 'There was a real anti-Bob Dylan feeling in that scene. There was this need to move on, and not linger in his shadow. Which is a hard thing to do. I mean anyone who picks up an acoustic guitar and a harmonica, immediately you're doing a Dylan. But we wanted to break through that. And that's where I started writing songs.'

He had originally been performing his old blues and folk standards with all the energy that he could muster, but soon began slipping in his own words to the original melodies and then later writing his own material from scratch: 'That scene was the whole punk rock thing, which was right on for me. Punk was always sort of my favourite. But all I had was an acoustic guitar, and no one wanted to play with me. Here was this whole scene with people with just acoustic guitars punking out really hard.'

So he just 'punked' out every night and became friends with everyone in the scene. Michelle Shocked, Cindy Lee Berryhill, radio-host Kristin Johnson, Paleface, King Missile, Roger Manning and Kirk Kelly all came through this movement to achieve differing degrees of recognition on their own.

One of the most well-known performers to come out of this bunch was Cindy Lee Berryhill. Also from the West Coast, having been born in San Diego, she started out in a punk band before going solo. She was – and is – a singer-songwriter in the classical vein, but she presents her songs in a very modern context. Although she was around the anti-folk movement she hasn't really carried any of its legacy with her in the music that she's produced since. Popular opinion is such that her 1987 debut album is still her best. Like Beck, she too returned to California in the early 1990s.

Another female singer-songwriter on the scene was Michelle Shocked. Her father had introduced her to country bluesmen like Big Bill Broonzy and Leadbelly as well as contemporary songwriters like Guy Clark and Randy Newman. From 1983 onwards she spent years travelling around between Texas, New York and Holland honing her style of tradition-rooted folksiness with a strong post-modern feminist perspective and punk attitude. The latter of these dovetailed nicely with the scene that was blossoming at the decade's turn.

Beat Poet Allen Ginsberg was also around the 'anti-folk' scene and years later he had a conversation about it with Beck:

Ginsberg: Yeah, I knew some of them, I used to sing with them sometimes.

Beck: Well, I was playing the traditional stuff and first I was really down with 'Anti-folk.' That's basically what the term was. It was separating themselves from all the new-age sounding stuff. The safe, watered down stuff. That charged me up, and I came onto the idea of taking the traditional music and coming up with different words.

Ginsberg: That was my idea. Except I was too old to do it, and I didn't know how to play guitar.

Beck: To me it was incredible. Of course I was only 18 at the time and it was all really new and being in New York was really intense. I had a blast during that time. I was pretty much struggling, trying to play as much as possible. Lach and all these people took me right in y'know. They were so friendly.

As well as acoustic guitar, Beck would play banjo, harmonica and anything else that could get him on-stage. He fell in with poet performer Mike Tyler, the publisher of *AIR* – the American Idealism Rag. Tyler recalls that time with Beck: 'He could get up on stage with somebody else and play the harmonica or the guitar or sing or hum or bang something and it just always seemed perfect. All the false alternative hypocrisy just seemed to fade away when I saw him.'

Beck wanted to continue the tradition of the original folk music but put his slant on it: 'I wasn't trying to do anything like what Dylan did with the original music. That was part of the anti-folk idea, to keep the basic style but not to write typically, you know . . . singer-songwriter songs. I was trying to keep my songs cut down, tight, not like Dylan's half-poetic style.'

He soon overcame any initial stage fright and became a regular at clubs like ABC No Rio, the Chameleon and the Pyramid. 'It gave me a chance to play the music, and everybody in the scene would come to the shows. It was a little bit of support.' Indeed everyone would support everyone else. Beck remembers going to see anarchists the Missing Foundation then 'trying to get some of that energy off an acoustic guitar'. On stage he could be a dervish and didn't need a band or technology to help him:

> Before I had a drum machine I had my foot, I would just stomp the thing. It was an insular scene, but there was a lot of space within there to do almost anything you wanted. I remember going in and getting as drunk as possible and getting up and playing a few tunes. We could take our cue from KRS-One, rewrite an old Woody Guthrie song, make it something totally different. It felt powerful because we didn't need guitars, amps, a practice space or anything; everyone was a one-person band.

In New York, he wrote early versions of songs that he'd re-work later like 'Pay No Mind', 'Cut 1/2 Blues', 'Totally Confused' and 'The Fucked Up Blues'. He also put together his first tape of original material played on only a banjo and harmonica. The tape was – surprise, surprise – titled *Banjo Story* and copies are still circulating among fans today. 'Let's Go Moon Some Cars', 'Goin' Nowhere Fast' and 'Sucker Without A Brain' would also end up on the *Fresh Meat And Old Slabs* tape for his mother's birthday five years later but would never be officially released. The songs on this tape are really the lowest of the lo-fi, mixing traditional country and blues arrangements with the bizarre lyrical twists that would become Beck's trademark.

Cover of *Banjo Story* cassette, New York, 1988

The scene really gathered some momentum and everyone was getting into the spirit of 'claiming back folk music'. If Leadbelly had been there, he would have been stomping and yelling with the best of them. Beck claims:

We were going back to the roots of country blues and the original Woody Guthrie, Jack Elliott-type folk of the 50s. It was our reaction to the whole 60s and 70s folk thing, which ended up as James Taylor and Cat Stevens and all those women with quivering voices who sang about white birds and unicorns. We were taking back the folk music that had got such a bad name, living out our fantasies of putrid homelessness and distilled malt liquor.

It might seem like a cliché now, but Beck and co. of the anti-folk scene were a group of people who were reviving the real essence of alternative long after everyone else had forgotten what 'alternative' had originally meant. As Beck says:

I guess you could say that was a time of realisation or de-realisation, forgetting what you know and starting over. It still felt that something was possible, that there was no way it was going to get turned into something commercial, that it would always remain true, that you wouldn't be able to work a formula out for it. There was a feeling that 'We will not be fooled.' It was innocent in the sense that it wasn't a post-post-post-post-thing, you know?

The songs' subjects could be absolutely anything; one memorable (or forgettable, depending on your taste) song was about a packet of potato chips. Beck himself had an early, unrecorded song about a train that went around the country destroying everything in its path. As he explains:

We were writing about really mundane things and trying to get to the essence of them. We were singing songs and getting over what it's like to be 'here right now'. I remember thinking it was great, because there were all these people playing folk music really aggressively. I'd always thought folk music had a bad rap, being cracked up to be this overwrought, really sensitive muck. It was great to hear people shouting and yelling. It was like the music was supposed to be.

After his rejection of synthetic mid-eighties pop in favour of the raw, ragged feel of the blues, this folk-attack was right up his street. He also began writing songs because it was the only way to get a whole night at the Chameleon club: 'Lach wouldn't book me for a whole night unless I wrote my own songs. So I said, "OK", and I went and got a pen and wrote five songs about things like pizza or waking up after having been sawn in half by a maniac – stuff like that. He finally gave me a Friday night.'

Beck especially liked the fact that it all had some history. 'The whole scene inspired me to add something to the tradition,' he is quoted as saying. When asked about the 'everyman' tone of his views he really warms up:

It should just become your own song. That's what I like about folk music. It's just everybody's songs and everybody can take a song and reinterpret it their own way and change the words. Music's become unhealthy. It used to be a communal thing. Now you go and watch a couple of people do it. I think that's why all these kids start moshing, 'cause that's the only thing that they can give back.

Sadly, the anti-folk scene has not been well-documented. Most of the contributors to this scene that went on to any kind of fame did so without taking much of the 'anti-folk' sound with them. There are no live tapes in general circulation, no videos or even much in the way of official releases at the time. The lack of documentation wasn't helped by the fact that the music press of the day paid virtually no notice to what was going on, so live reviews or interviews are non-existent.

The best way to hear what the songs might have sounded like is to listen to early Beck tapes like *Golden Feelings* or *Fresh Meat And Old Slabs*, but even these were recorded after he had returned to Los Angeles. Word of mouth is the only route back into the 'anti-folk' scene. By this route, it is known that Beck could sometimes be seen on stage in his Star Wars Stormtrooper mask, or writhing around on the floor while still playing a harmonica, or just jumping about playing percussion on whatever was in range for him to hit.

He really embraced the punk aesthetic mixed into a roots style. Beck also realised that there were no restrictions when it comes to subject matter or songs. It was this discovery that set him on his current course. Whereas he'd spent a few years learning to copy the old blues songs with which he'd fallen in love, he was now confident enough to add noise, bizarre percussion and wacky vocals to his songs. The structure of the songs he was writing didn't have to follow any traditional patterns and his lyrical subjects could be absolutely anything that he dreamt up. All the limits usually put on popular music had been removed and Beck was free to follow his heart to whatever strange musical places it would take him. The breaking of these boundaries was the trigger for Beck to start writing songs at an ever-increasing rate and he would follow these anti-rules throughout his career, through crude home-made tapes and on to major label albums sold the world over.

The fact that a lot of the artists had little money made the punk ethic of doing your own thing with whatever you did have ring more true than ever: 'A lot of us were playing folk music because we couldn't afford all the instruments. And, Jesus, it was New York, where were you going to rehearse with a band? All we had was an acoustic guitar and energy. It was cool, it was abstract, it was stand-up comedy and free-form lyrics. It was the time. It was a current of creative electricity.'

One of the people Beck really clicked with at the time was Paleface.* This New York native was one of the earliest exponents of what became the 'anti-folk' movement as he brewed up a mix of booming acoustic guitar and clever lyrical plays on subjects like disillusionment with the 'American Dream'. After Beck started playing at a few shows, it was just a matter of time before the two got together. For a time they were great friends and Paleface let Beck sleep at his place for quite some time.

Nowadays, though the friendship seems to have been broken, Beck still has fond memories of him:

> We hung together for a long time, I usually mention him. But I guess people don't know him, they usually know Roger Manning or Cindy Lee Berryhill so they include those names, because interviewers tend to leave out names. He was a good friend for a while. And then there was some kind of falling out. I think I was staying at his house and he got sick of me, so he kicked me out. I couldn't find a place to live and couldn't hook up a job to save my life. So, he was a sport. He was a really good guy. He let me crash on his sofa a lot. But I think after a few months it got a little tiring for him.

Paleface also mixed hip-hop and folk and obviously had some influence on Beck's music. However, the two didn't keep in touch, as Beck admits:

---

*Paleface was spotted at Lach's Chameleon Club by Danny Fields (ex-manager of the Stooges and the Ramones) and signed to Polygram. In 1991 he released an eponymous debut and had a minor hit-single with 'Burn And Rob'. After a less than successful tour in support of the Crash Test Dummies he was dropped by Polygram. Four years later he had a second album out on Shimmy Disc, backed by a punk band, and his last release 'Get Off' appeared on Elektra in 1996.

I called him once and he just hung up on me. That was maybe 1991 or 1992. So I just kind of gave up. But I thought he was really talented, he was one of the best. The thing I remember was 'Ex Ox Ho Folk', that was a tape he made on a four track. In that scene, he was one of the fixtures definitely. But he was kind of a moody guy, I couldn't tell if he wanted me to hang out, or get out of his face.

Another friend of Beck's from this era was acoustic punk fiend, Roger Manning – not to be confused with Roger Manning Jr from Beck's current band. Manning has been described as 'the de facto spiritual leader' of the anti-folk movement and was just about to release his debut LP on the legendary SST label when Beck arrived in New York. The two frequently crossed paths at the Chameleon on open-mic night and at casual all-night jams in Tompkins Square Park. When asked about Beck's early New York shows that featured a lot of Mississippi John Hurt and Leadbelly covers, Manning recalls that 'It was like seeing the ghost of Woody Guthrie.'

Manning's views on what can and can't go into a song's lyrics are very similar to Beck's: 'People think lyrics have to be poeticised and formal but my lyrics are the way I talk; if I wouldn't use a word in a conversation, I won't use it in a song.' Beck agrees in typical 'Beckian' speak:

> I just let whatever comes out, come out. Some of it I keep, some I toss out, some I turn into giant cigarettes and smoke 'em. Everybody's got their own songs, too. Everybody should turn off their TV machines and make up their own songs about whatever comes to mind: their couch, their friends, their loaves of bread. There should be so many songs out there that it all turns into one big sound, and we can put the whole thing into a pickup truck and let it roll off the edge of the Grand Canyon.

Manning describes his own songs as movies: 'The words are the movie, and the music is the soundtrack,' he told the *San Diego Union-Tribune*. 'They're true movies about things that really happened, because life is the best story there is.'

Beck had a different outlook on his early lyrics: 'Set your guitars and banjos on fire,' he advises, 'and before you write a song, smoke a pack of whiskey and it'll all take care of itself'.

Both artists were fond of lo-fi technology, although from a

financial perspective they didn't have much choice about it. Both recorded their debut albums on four- and eight-track equipment. Another similarity is their love of low-budget acoustic guitars. 'I'd swear by any good-quality plywood guitar,' says Manning, who adorned his with a collection of stickers similar to Beck's legendary 'Jazzercise' guitar. 'It's taking your guitar as a tool,' explains Beck. 'It's not some priceless object. It's something you're supposed to make noise on.'

One of the downsides of the bohemian, 'sleep-anywhere' lifestyle was the frequency of muggings and robberies. Beck was on the receiving end of more than his fair share of these during his time in New York. 'These gangs, they just assume you must be some rich student because they see the guitar,' he bemoans. 'Usually I'd only have about two bucks, which would just make them madder.' One time he was on the end of a beating so bad that it put him in hospital. 'I remember coming out of the hospital and the sky had this apocalyptic rust hue. The winters were very bitter there. Both my eyes were black, but you know . . . I didn't have many options at the time.'

Beck has this to say about his time in the Big Apple: 'I didn't have a plan when I hit New York. LA at that point was just a cultural void. It's amazing to me that this whole hipster culture has emerged since the early 90s. In New York there was a lot of really stimulating stuff happening and I got right into it. After a while it was like I'd always been there.'

But, despite his settling in to New York and his involvement in its anti-folk scene, it wasn't to be his permanent home. As the nineties dawned, Beck decided enough was enough. Tired of being beaten up, having no money or no home, he went back out west: 'I was tired of being cold, tired of getting beat up. It was hard to be in New York with no money, no honey, no thermostats, no spoons, no Cheerios. I kinda used up all the friends I had. Everyone on the scene just got sick of me. I got jumped by this Puerto Rican gang and I was all wrecked up. It was January, and incredibly bleak, so I pulled myself together and went back to California.'

So the great adventure had come to an end. Whether Beck had always meant to return home after two years isn't clear, but that's what he did. Without too many ties to the Big Apple he knew that his time there was up. The 'anti-folk' scene was breaking up, having run its natural course; the artists that had contributed to it were slowly moving away from the scene – both figuratively and literally.

When Beck left the East Coast he took with him an important education in both life and music. He had always been fairly independent but his financial situation in New York had made him even more so. He had also become even more independent in his music. By the time he was back home he was starting to make music that was original and came like a slap in the face to those who heard it.

His folk and blues roots were now mixed in with noise and indie-rock influences and his experiences in Tompkins Park Square paved the way for him to bring rap into his special mix too. These ingredients would later prove very fruitful and change his life, but before he had all the accolades thrust upon him, he had a few more years of hardship ahead. He started on the next phase of his story by heading back to LA and moving in with his brother, Channing.

# 3 Loser

EARLY 1990 AND BECK WAS BACK in East Los Angeles where he'd started, but with a lot of experience under his belt. He soon reverted to his old routine of small-time jobs by day and trying to get a gig by night. He was also beginning to write his own material at an ever-increasing rate, refining his lyrical skills and his humour. He had come to the conclusion that LA was his home and he had to accept that.

'As an adult, I came to realise it was a part of me, if you hate it, you end up hating a part of yourself,' he said. 'So eventually I was reconciled with the fact that this is me whether I like it or not.' This was the place where he really felt comfortable despite his sometimes lowly circumstances. 'It's like the family you grew up in; you don't agree with how it is, but it's your family.'

He managed to get some money saved and decided to buy a car, but his luck seemed to be continually running out:

> I found a car in the newspaper for $100. I had it for one day, then the engine blew up on the freeway, and that was kinda shot, because if you don't have a car in LA you spend more time waiting for a bus than you do at your job. Then someone gave me a bicycle and it got stolen. Finally someone gave me a skateboard, but that went too. Then I was just reduced to my feet. I was expecting my shoes to get stolen.

Despite the seemingly constant stream of setbacks he continued writing new material and playing unannounced. Usually this was done by jumping on stage while a band was setting up. Some nights his whole set would be new songs. Many of these would be based around in-jokes with the small groups of friends who'd come along to see him. This led to many humorous little tunes, some of which would later be recorded and released. In these, Beck placed most emphasis on the lyrics. 'The words are the most important part to me,' he claims. 'Because if the words suck, then I can't listen to something . . . that's all I've had. I never had money to buy equipment and have a band with a big sound. All I had was an acoustic guitar, you can only go so far, so I had to make up everything else with having words that would interest people . . . I'm not that well-read. I didn't go to High School. I'm not really educated.'

Beck's home in East LA was often changing during this time, from the shadow of the Griffith Observatory in Los Feliz up to Echo Park and also Silverlake, constantly moving from Bibbe's to Channing's to various boarding houses and rented accommodation and then round again. At one point he claims to have lived in a Downtown alley with just rats for company. This was likely made to sound a little more dramatic than it actually was; probably not by Beck himself but by 'Chinese Whispers' as the story was repeated.

He did admit that he lived rough for a short time in Los Angeles and he may have had rats in one or two of the apartments that he rented for a little while, but the image of his spending a lot of time in an alley with just rodents for company is a bit too much of a Beck-myth. He did, however, live just off Sunset Boulevard, behind 'Tang's Donut Shop'. Here he could hang out at 4 am getting his fill of donuts while watching the homeless guys playing high-speed chess. He and his friends had a random way of deciding how to spend an evening: it was based on a revolving Podiatry sign. On one side was a cartoon of a foot and some crutches; the reverse side depicted a happy smiling foot. At around dusk the gang would convene to see which way the sign pointed when it was switched off for the night. If the happy side faced the house they'd head out for the night; if it was the crutches side they'd call it a night and stay in.

The jobs that Beck endured were haphazard and soul sapping. 'I used to shift trash and unload trucks. I also did a bit of breakdancing in the street,' he says. He also seems to have painted a large portion of LA single-handedly: 'I painted the whole inside of that place electric pink. We worked all night. For days all I saw was electric pink,' he recalls of his experiences painting the interior of a lingerie shop near the Victor Borge 'Star' on the Hollywood Walk Of Fame. He'll also point out numerous shop signs that he's painted around East LA if you ask nicely.

Through much of this job changing he again felt alienated just as he had at school. Before going to New York it had been because of his only-white-kid-on-the-block situation and the feeling of being removed from white suburban culture. Now it was more down to the fact that he hated watching TV and therefore, he didn't. 'I'd rather stare at a blank wall,' he claimed. The feeling of not quite fitting in with workmates continued until one night at a friend's house he caught a glimpse of a TV sitcom.

'I suddenly realised,' he exclaims. 'Oh my God, everyone I'm working with is imitating a sit-com. That's why I couldn't relate to them.'

One of the more painful employments he undertook was to wear a little hat and work as a hot dog waiter at a rich kids' birthday party. He recollects: 'The party was at a rich spread on Brentwood on a big tennis court turned into a roller skating rink. It was a lot of work carrying the hot dogs and the cart with the umbrella up the endless stairs. The girls were seven or eight years old and real snooty. Too snooty to even eat hot dogs. We got stiffed on the $15 pay and stuck with 200 hot dogs.'

More manual jobs included working as a refrigerator and furniture remover and, famously, as a 'leaf blower'. This very Californian profession involves wearing a kind of rocket pack on your back, with a vacuum cleaner attached and you go to the rich folks' homes and literally blow the leaves from their otherwise pristine lawns. Beck later mentioned this job in his 1994 single 'Beercan' ('I quit my job blowing leaves/Telephone bills up my sleeves', he sang). The leaf blower itself would later make a memorable on-stage appearance, and Beck acknowledged the debt of noise-music to this garden machinery: 'It's a very large population here, there's a leaf blower contingent. There's no union that I know of so far, but there's certainly a spiritual brotherhood. They are the originators of noise music. It's like a cross between a Kramer guitar and a jet pack.'

Finally, Beck ended up back in the video store: 'I was on the lowest rung of video store employees. We weren't allowed to sit down and we were only allowed to listen to this oldies radio station that was piped in. They would play "Doo Wah Diddy" at six o'clock every night. It was a little demoralising.'

In the autumn of 1992 it became just a little too demoralising and Beck began collecting unemployment checks. The $4 per hour video store job would be the last one he ever had.

During the construction of this eclectic employment CV Beck could, on many evenings, be found in and around the coffee-house and punk club circuit of Los Angeles and its environs, with bashed-up guitar in his hand, rope-strap dangling, and harmonica in pocket.

'I'd realised, when I heard that first Pussy Galore record, that fuck what you think music's supposed to be – just go do it!' That is exactly what he'd set about doing.

'People always say I came from the coffee-houses,' states Beck, 'and I played there, but mostly I played in the punk-rock clubs and the all-ages . . . in punk-rock clubs, there's a lot more energy.'

The venues that Beck did find himself in were as colourful as they were diverse. Al's Bar on South Hewitt, by the edge of Little Tokyo in downtown Los Angeles, has been described as LA's answer to Liverpool's 'The Cavern', meaning it was dark and damp. Raji's started life as a curry house before becoming a hard rock club and playing host to the likes of Guns N' Roses and The Replacements. It, like the rest of its block on Hollywood Boulevard, has now been demolished.

Highland Grounds, also located in Hollywood, opened right at the dawn of the decade and has since played host to all manner of acoustic performers. It is actually a restaurant–wine-bar–coffee house and Beck appeared here more than once. Club Spaceland was Beck's local venue on Silverlake Boulevard and was also a hangout for the Dust Brothers.

Other venues were visited along the way like The Onyx, Fuzzyland, and the Pik-Me-Up, not forgetting Cafe Troy and of course Jabberjaw where Beck would later get his big break. He was now writing at such a prodigious rate that he was constantly changing his repertoire at these venues. As he puts it: 'I'm someone who likes to do creative things every day, writing songs, something more new and interesting, instead of playing the same stuff every day. When I was playing around in LA, once I had played a song live, I wouldn't play it anymore. I was playing at Al's Bar on Friday, then on Tuesday at the Pik-Me-Up. I'd have all new songs.'

His ever-growing live reputation gave rise to a slot supporting the then not-so-famous San Francisco punks Green Day. But more often than not he was playing to small crowds. Scott Cymbala, of Fingerpaint Records, remembers seeing Beck play at Cafe Troy: 'There were like ten or twelve people there. It was great because there were no expectations. It was pure and honest. He didn't have to live up to the crowd's expectations.' Two years later Beck would release an album on Cymbala's label.

At this time Bibbe Hansen was now co-owner of the Troy Cafe in Downtown Los Angeles and also ran a second-hand clothes store where a young girl by the name of Leigh Limon worked. Through her work at the shop Leigh met Beck, the two began seeing each other. They and are still together now, seven years later, and Leigh helps Beck with his choice of clothes for concerts, TV appearances and photo shoots.

Beck also made some new friends in the music scene with whom he had similar tastes and styles. With Martha Atwell he formed a short-term band called Ten Ton Lid, specialising in playing Carter Family and Louvin Brothers* covers. Both of these groups had featured amazing harmonies so it would have been interesting to hear any recordings of the Beck–Atwell shows. Beck had already been covering the religious inspired country of the Carter Family from his earliest days with an acoustic guitar. At one Ten Ton Lid show in the Saugus mountains, so the story goes, they encountered Mike Tyson who was in training for a fight with Buster Douglas. The fighter was so 'impressed' with what he heard that he climbed on stage in a little Santa Claus hat and relieved himself on the drum-kit.

---

*The Louvin Brothers, Ira and Charlie, had been one of the leading traditional country music duos of the 1950s, as well as writing for other artists. Emmylou Harris's 'If I Could Only Win Your Love' was one of their compositions.

For Beck, finding people who shared his musical vision and tastes was paramount and Carla Bozulich was one such person: 'Carla Bozulich of the Geraldine Fibbers, Ethyl Meatplow and Possum Dixon were really receptive, which is really a hard thing to find in LA. Most of the time there isn't a musical community, there isn't any kind of connection between bands, so when I met those people it was more of a family.'*

Bozulich collaborated with Beck just as he had made his Geffen debut in 1994: 'Carla called me up before *Mellow Gold* came out, she had written some songs with a country flavour, and we got together and did some stuff on a four-track at my house. Some of those songs turned out to be Geraldine Fibbers songs.'

The Geraldine Fibbers made their recording debut in 1994 with the *Get Thee Gone* mini-album on which Beck guested before a full length album, *Lost Somewhere Between The Earth And My Home*, was released on Virgin in 1995.

Beck also hung out, and later recorded, with the girls from That Dog. Anna Waronker was the sister of Joey Waronker, soon to be Beck's drummer, and was the chief songwriter and guitar player. Sisters Petra and Rachel Haden were daughters of jazz legend Charlie Haden (who would himself appear on *Odelay*). The third member of the Haden triplets, Tanya, sometimes played cello with them. In 1992, Anna Waronker, then even younger than Beck (she was 18), recruited a drummer, Tony Maxwell, to complete the line-up. That Dog signed to Geffen in 1993 and, after some college airplay and gigs in and around Los Angeles, they joined Beck on his first real tour in support of *Mellow Gold*. In the years following this tour Beck worked with the band on a handful of projects and they have supported him on several tours.

Although there was no actual 'movement' in Los Angeles, like the anti-folkies in New York, there was a bonding of these like-minded bands and poets. Beck could often be spotted at

---

*Bozulich had been in Neon Vein and then Ethyl Meatplow, which could best be described as a 'pseudo-industrial-alternative-dance-rock' trio. They released three singles before their only album, *Happy Days Sweetheart* in 1993. The Geraldine Fibbers had originally formed as a side project between the members of Ethyl Meatplow and Glue.

poetry readings by Exene Cervenka, of X, or Wanda Coleman, and he appeared in a documentary by French film-maker Sophie Rachnal about the LA poetry scene. Scott Cymbala was part of the scene.

'It was definitely good just to hang out. Everybody knew each other. There was always something going on, you could go to see a show or a reading or a party.' Beck remembers that he began to embrace the LA way of doing things: 'The clubs and parties may be many miles apart, but they were there if you could scratch the surface to see what was going on.'

The West Coast also had a great diversity of musical styles thrown into the mixing pot – Latino, Mariachi and hip-hop. As Beck acknowledges: 'That was my world. Still is. I found myself rejecting so much new music, everything that is part of our culture. Then a couple of years ago, I just spun all around and decided to embrace it all. Y'know, the machines, the rap, the loud guitars, every sort of emotional level. And just go with it all.'

Just 'go with it all' he did – 'all' being the operative word. His unique brand of traditional folk-blues-country was mixed with the Latino-Mariachi-hip-hop of LA and his own love of indie guitar rock. It was all topped off with his wit and sense of observational humour, not to mention his family background of performance art. This heady brew made a Beck show in the early 1990s a wondrous sight to behold.

But he often had a hard job to get on a stage in the first place. He'd jump up before a support band or while the main band was setting up their equipment. Mostly the audience wouldn't have a clue who he was or maybe he'd have a few friends in the audience. In the main nobody cared who he was or what he was singing: 'I'd only have two minutes and everyone was drunk so I'd sing my goofy stuff, that was my whole shot. I was like a side act in bars. I would come on and play to please the inebriated. That's why I have a lot of songs with the devil in them; it was the only way to get the attention of people who were drunk. That's how to get people's attention anytime, in fact – just bring the devil in.'

Sometimes even the goofy stuff didn't get the reaction he was looking for so he decided to start adding a little more to get the crowd involved: 'Originally I was just playing with a guitar, but no one really cares here unless you are putting on some kind of show. So I started to get people from the audience and other bands to back me up, and the shows turned into these free-for-alls; I wouldn't have any idea what the show was going to be.'

Sadly these shows weren't really documented because every one was different. 'Sometimes I'd only play one or two songs,' Beck remembers. 'It would be all stories or trying to orchestrate these audience participation events. It was fun.' The audience participation included one night where he got the whole place to empty and follow him across the street to a petrol station where he put on an 'al fresco' performance. 'Every show I would try to pull some kind of stunt like that,' he explains. 'I was just trying to break down the whole structure of a stage and an audience and stretch it out a bit.'

Another time he played a whole show where his lyrics were prompted by a friend at the back of the club using a walkie-talkie headset to give Beck words to work into his songs. Sometimes he'd arrive on stage in a Star Wars Stormtroopers mask to the sound of a disco version of the Star Wars theme.

An early gig of this type didn't go down well with Johnny Depp when Beck played at his Viper Room club. 'They obviously didn't like us,' hoots Beck, 'because in the middle of the set they cut the electricity and dropped the curtain on us.' Beck's trusty acoustic guitar, 'Jazzercise', was set on fire so many times it had to be retired. Clips of these on-stage antics can be glimpsed in the 'Loser' video.

The chain of events that led to Beck musically breaking through weren't catalysed by any of his on-stage antics or bizarre comedy tunes but by his traditional folk songs. In August 1991, Rob Schnapf, co-owner of the tiny Bong Load Custom Records label, was wandering around the Sunset Junction Street Fair in LA. Beck was playing his stuff on the Hully Gully stage and, allegedly, Schnapf was stopped in his tracks and heard to mutter 'What the hell is this?'

About a week later, Tom Rothrock (also a co-owner of Bong Load) was talked into checking out a gig at the Jabberjaw coffee club by his friend Jon Neuman. Members of The Actors Gang were sharing the bill with the quaintly monikered Dicktit. In between the two bands, Beck jumped on to the stage. He was in his then-trademark outfit consisting of his battered acoustic guitar, held on by a piece of rope, his harmonica and two microphones.

After hearing 'Cut 1/2 Blues', Rothrock was convinced that he should get Beck to record for his label. He immediately asked Beck about working together and reported back to his partner who remembered Beck from the street fair.

'What hit me about Beck,' enthused Rothrock, 'was that here was this self-contained folk artist who'd be great to make records with.'

When Beck thinks back about it he sees the whole process beginning from a chance in a million: 'It was a total fluke, I was playing at this place called Jabberjaw, this all ages place in LA. This guy came up to me and said he liked the songs I'd played, and we got talking and it turned out he was a record engineer, so he offered to record some stuff. We got together and we did some songs.'

At this time Beck had been adding some rap to his repertoire and had even covered Ice Cube in a few shows. 'That was around 1991,' he recalls. 'I started thinking that somehow the hip-hop and folk thing could work together.'

For a while Beck didn't see Rothrock, but his second meeting led to the turning point in his life: 'I ran into him again and we got talking about rap music. I was telling him about how I'd do a lot of rap sorta things where I'd just stomp my foot and shout out all these lyrics. And he said "Oh, I've worked with a guy who does rap music" – and after work one day he called me and said "Do you want to come down tonight and I'll introduce you."'

The producer in question was Carl Stephenson. Born in Washington, DC, by an early age Stephenson had moved with his family to Olympia, WA, which would become the spiritual home of the US underground music scene. He later moved to Houston where he worked with the Geto Boys. This gangsta-rap group were one of the most extreme of the early 1990s, having trouble getting stores to stock their x-rated albums and at times even struggling to find a label willing to distribute their material.

Eventually Stephenson became disillusioned with their attitudes and he moved to LA in 1990 to begin putting together his 'Forest For The Trees' project. Along the way he met the guys from Bong Load.

On a hunch that something good might be in the offing, Tom Rothrock took Beck to Stephenson's house and waited to see what might transpire. 'I went down there and he had a drum machine and a sampler,' says Beck. 'I brought my acoustic guitar and started playing some folk songs.'

Stephenson, however, wasn't overly impressed with what he was hearing and his irritation wasn't disguised. 'He was really bored, like he couldn't care less,' recalls Beck. 'I think I remember him walking out of the room. It was a pretty awkward situation.'

Rothrock, though, encouraged Beck to keep playing and he hit upon a slide guitar riff that would go down in musical history. 'I went back to the guitar and started playing this slide riff, and he [Stephenson] said, "Oh, that's cool",' recalls Beck. 'He recorded it and stuck it over a drum beat.'

Stephenson sampled Dr John's 'I Walk On Gilded Splinters' and an anthem was born. To finish off the instrumentation Beck added bass and played around with some instruments that Stephenson just had lying around. In this way a little sitar was added to the mix. With the backing track complete, Rothrock and Stephenson went out for pizza, but they left the tape rolling on a loop. Beck had been fooling around doing a little rap but he thought that it was the worst rap he'd ever heard so he sang 'I'm a loser baby, so why don't you kill me' as a chorus and added a similar line in Spanish, 'Soy un perdidor' ('I'm a loser').

By the time Rothrock and Stephenson returned Beck had written the entire lyric. They recorded the vocal and that was it.

'When we recorded "Loser", that was the first time I ever rapped,' says Beck. 'The chorus should have been, "I can't rap worth shit." ' They also did 'Steal My Body Home'. 'The whole thing was said and done in a couple of hours,' he adds. 'I went home, and we didn't see the guy for a year, and I totally forgot about it.'

It would be a long time before 'Loser' was actually released. In the meantime Beck released a debut single, 'MTV Makes Me

Want To Smoke Crack', on Flipside Records in 1992. This track was another of Beck's humorous little ditties about the poor state of the once influential TV channel. The single also featured Beck's 'To See That Woman Of Mine' with two tracks by Bean on the other side. He'd been approached by the independent Flipside label some time after the initial Carl Stephenson session and he agreed to let them release this live favourite. Despite the catchy melody and funny lyrics this song failed to catch many people's imaginations and slipped through the cracks. It was the first pressing of 'Loser' that made everyone sit up and take notice.

By March 1993, Bong Load had enough money to get 500 copies of 'Loser' pressed. KXLU in Los Angeles picked up on it and soon after KCRW did too while the END radio station in Seattle started it off in heavy rotation. Soon afterwards stations were calling Bong Load from all over the country wanting a copy.

'Before the record even got pressed there was all this excitement, there were bootlegs right away,' remembers Tom Rothrock. 'By the fall all these heavy-duty commercial stations started playing it. They didn't even have copies,' laughs Beck. 'They were making cassette copies off of someone who had a copy of the vinyl.' And by September the influential station KROQ in Los Angeles was on the bandwagon too.

This over-exposure soon had people flocking to his shows. He wanted to beef up his gigs a little and the first requirement on his list was to add a drummer. He met one in the shape of Don Burnette, aka 'Dallas Don', at a Popdefect show at Toe's Tavern in Pasadena. Burnette also fronted the band Lutefisk and was a member of 3D Picnic, Plain Wrap and Theloneous Monster. He would accompany Beck on his first radio sessions as well. Beck also admired Don giving a live performance of the Rush concept album *2112* in its entirety at a Silverlake club.

Releasing a song called 'Loser' with a chorus that says 'I'm a loser baby, so why don't you kill me' at the time he did thrust Beck unwittingly into the spotlight as a generational spokesperson figure. Richard Linklater had a film out called *Slacker*; Beavis and Butthead were everywhere showing the American youth of the day how to live their entire lives sat on a couch; Seattle's

Sub-pop records had a T-shirt with 'loser' written across the chest, while Sebadoh had a tune called 'Losercore'.

Beck, with his hit-song, was cast as the centre of this 'movement', although it is probable that the movement didn't exist outside the media's imagination. Beck himself has always disassociated himself from the generational slant that has been attached to the song:

> When we recorded 'Loser', I wasn't aware of the slacker thing, I never saw the movie, it was before they invented 'Generation X'. I was lost in my own little world. I wasn't talking about apathy or how cool it is not to care. I was just making fun of my rapping abilities. It was definitely a case of 'wrong place, right time'.
> People needed a designated candidate and I was it. I mean, I didn't even know what a slacker was! But I was too naive to fight it – you do photo shoots and they say 'Put this shirt on', 'Sit on this sofa', 'Look tired or something', and it's all perpetuated.

If people did know about the struggle Beck had had to reach this point then they ignored it: 'Even in the 80s no one I knew was succeeding or slacking off, just living normal lives and getting by. No one had time for that stuff. And I didn't grow up in a suburban environment, so I could never relate to that kind of suburban boredom. I've always been stimulated and interested in things.'

It was certainly a sign of Beck's relative naiveté that he allowed himself to be portrayed in this way and he didn't have the experience to nip it in the bud before the image had swollen to the point where he himself was being cast as a cartoon character.

The way some corners of the music media portrayed him caused Beck a lot of frustration:

> I was up in Olympia, Washington, and someone called me up and said they were going to premiere the video. The guy on the air was talking about all this slacker stuff, saying that 'Loser' was like some slacker anthem or something. I was like 'What?', I said 'Turn that TV off'. I was like 'Slacker my ass'. I mean I never had any slack, I was working a $4-an-hour job trying to stay alive. I mean that slacker stuff is for people who have the time to be depressed about everything.

His record speaks for itself, Beck is not someone who sits

around waiting for something to happen – in fact it is the opposite: 'I guess it all depends on how you define "slacker", because for me it has a negative connotation; it seems to be "young people are apathetic, they sit around making it their profession to be bored and uninspired". That's insulting because even when I didn't have the means to do much I always tried to create some activity. So in that respect I'm an anti-slacker.'

When this kind of media overload happens there will inevitably be someone standing to one side with a calculator thinking up possibilities of how to make money from the success of someone else.

Brewing giant Budweiser was first on the scene. Beck shakes his head as he remembers:

> Budweiser said 'We'll give you $250,000 for the rights to the song.' I had a lot of opportunities to become a part of the whole business machine, or whatever you want to call it. I just stayed away and did everything I could to play that song down. Not that I'm ashamed of it or anything. I'm proud of the song, but I didn't want to let it be turned into what it wasn't meant to be. Basically, it was hijacked from its original place.

It wasn't only the corporations that Beck wanted to stay away from. Many of the people who championed the song were exactly the ones who Beck had spent many of his formative years feeling alienated from:

> The people who took that song to heart were the jock people, the popular people, the attractive, stronger ones. But it was really coming from someone – myself – feeling displaced from the 80s, a time of materialism where everybody was cashing in and making money. If you went to school and you were wearing the same shoes you had a year ago, and you'd grown out of them, and your toe was coming out of a hole, it was not your time. You were not accepted. The people who embraced it represented the reason the song was written.

To downplay the song a little Beck went through a period of changing the chorus of 'Loser' whenever he played it live. On one night it could be 'I'm a schmoozer baby', or 'I'm a softie baby' or 'I'm a squeegee baby'; the next he might sing 'So why don't you hug me' or 'So why don't you squeeze me.' He didn't really enjoy having a hit and all the baggage that comes with it, as he discussed with Thurston Moore in the infamous MTV 120 minutes interview in 1994:

| Thurston Moore: | How do you feel about 'Loser' being such a massive hit? |
| Beck: | It feels like surfing through an oil spillage. |
| Thurston Moore: | I know exactly what you mean, man. |

He also wanted to make it clear that he had been fortunate to end up in the position he now found himself in and that he hadn't forgotten where he'd been just a few months previously:

A year ago I was living in a shed behind a house with a bunch of rats, next to an alley downtown, I had zero money and zero possibilities. I was working in a video shop alphabetising the pornography section for minimum wage. Believe me this has fallen in my lap, I was never any good at getting jobs or girls or anything. I never even made flyers for my shows. And until, like, six months ago, I didn't know that you could get paid for playing.

Another downside, one which Beck feels strongly about, is the simplification of a – or more specifically his – story to fit a newspaper column or magazine page. 'The thing that frustrates me is just how simplified things can be made, cut down to the lowest common denominator. How can you sum up my life, or any life, in a paragraph in *USA Today*? It takes all the dignity and all the expansiveness out of it.'

While all the hoo-ha was boiling up over 'Loser', Beck had begun to cement his reputation of being a prolific worker by also releasing his first full-length album. *Golden Feelings* was a cassette-only release on the Sonic Enemy label and first saw the light of day in January 1993. It contained 19 tracks which had built up over the previous four years or so and was sold by Beck before and after his shows. The Sonic Enemy catalogue that was given away with all of its releases had the following to say about the tape:

Beck, 'Golden Feelings' –
'Like Neil Young on cough syrup' says his lawyer and who am I to differ? Genuine and genuinely fucked-up, straight from the

heart of spooky folky noisy unaffected tales of poverty &
lucklessness, fast food & bad trips.
Thirty-five or more minutes . . . $3.00

The sleeve showed a kind of teddy bear's tea-party and
original copies are virtually unobtainable now, but second-
generation tapes and CD copies are fairly easy to get hold of if
you know where to look. Around 750 copies of the original tape
were produced and distributed up until 1995 when Sonic Enemy
was 'put on hold'. They were rumoured to be restarting in 1999
with a CD release of *Golden Feelings*. The tape showcases early
four-track versions of songs that would later get an official
release: 'No Money, No Honey', 'Totally Confused' and
'Motherfucker'. 'Trouble All My Days', 'Special People' and
'Supergolden Black Sunchild' were later included in their
original form on the 'Pay No Mind' single. The latter had its
titled changed to 'Supergolden (Sunchild)'. All three were listed
as being 'Evacuated to four track in 1998' which was interesting
as they had been recorded in 1992 and the 'Pay No Mind' single
was released in 1995.

This first 'official' release really captures the early Beck
sound. A little rough around the edges it may be but that is part
of the appeal. Beck adds little bits of crude samples between
songs, at the end of songs and before songs showing that his 'cut
and paste' leanings were already in place by the age of 22.
They're aren't many straight ahead country, folk or blues songs
in this collection and the 'anti-folk' lessons are obvious in their
effect on songs like 'Trouble All My Days' – which is a really
distorted, bent out of shape, blues tune.

Before the year was out he had also produced another tape
titled *Fresh Meat And Old Slabs*; this time it contained 21 songs
but was not officially released. In fact it had been recorded as a
birthday present for his mother, Bibbe. It included updated
versions of several of the *Golden Feelings* songs ('Totally
Confused', 'Trouble All My Days' and 'Heartland Feeling') and a
lot of the songs that Beck was playing live around LA at the
time. It was by far the strongest collection of Beck tracks so far
compiled and that fact is borne out as over half of the songs
would be released officially over the next few years.

'Go Where U Want' would later be re-worked as 'Hollow Log' and other tunes showed Beck's wicked sense of humour. 'Grease' and 'Satan Gave Me A Taco' were typical of the spoof songs that Beck would perform to keep his friends amused and grab the attention of apathetic crowd members who would be waiting for the main band to come on-stage.

'Fume' was based on a true story about two kids who drove out in a pick-up truck with a can of laughing gas. They parked up, closed the windows and proceeded to get high. Tragically though, they overdid it and were later found dead by asphyxiation.

Other songs were written about the plight of being in low-paid employment and some of the bad-luck scenarios that would feature later on *Mellow Gold*. Beck loved working in this high-speed, lo-fi way: 'That's why four-tracks are so great, 'cause you're writing it as you're recording and it's all unknown territory.' The breadth of styles showcased on this tape is impressive for someone so young and inexperienced.

Beck's first live radio appearance happened a few days after his 23rd birthday on 23 July 1993. DJ Chris Douridas had heard some of Beck's early tapes after Geffen A&R man Tony Berg had sent him a copy of 'Loser'. He invited the singer to drop in on his famous *Morning Becomes Eclectic* show on KCRW in Santa Monica. The segment began by Beck playing a Woody Guthrie spoken-word tape as an intro, then breaking into 'Loser'. A backing tape was played while Beck rapped live over the top of it. As tapes of this show circulated some people began thinking that an alternate version of the song was available due to the ad-libbing that was done. Beck changed a few words and sang about 'Oakies running around in spandex' and 'A swimming pool full of Kool Aid'.

The interview segments revealed some interesting information about Beck's early 1990s life. He said that he had lived rough: 'I lived out of my car, but not more than a couple of days, I was homeless in New York.' Also mentioned was his lack of recent employment: 'I got laid off work last fall, I'm on unemployment.'

The other songs played live were 'Mexico' (this take would later be released on the KCRW compilation *Rare On Air*), 'Death Is Coming To Get You', 'Pay No Mind' ('I used to live in like this shed, this next song, it's about being bored and sitting in the shed'), 'Whimsical Actress' and 'MTV Makes Me Want To Smoke Crack'. Part way through this last song he stopped it and declared 'Hold the show, I'm gonna bum-rush this. Start the tape, we've got to do this another way.' The tape that was played was a 'wine bar piano' take of the song and he performed the 'lounge act version' of the song with full cabaret crooner aping for good measure. Throughout the show he was accompanied by Don Burnette on drums who, during the show, would only be referred to as 'Dallas Don', the owner of the deepest voice this side of Calvin Johnson.

That night Beck and Don played at the Troy Cafe in the 10 pm show, prefaced by a rap band, Kill Whitey. By all accounts they were hanging from the rafters to get in after hearing him that morning on the radio. More sporadic gigs continued through the summer. In the following September Beck was back on the airwaves, this time on KXLU performing a session with Thurston Moore. The track 'Whiskey-Faced, Radioactive, Blowdryin' Lady' from this session appeared on a compilation album put out by the station.

During the early 1990s, Calvin Johnson's reputation grew to a point where everything he was associated with reeked of indie-credibility. He'd started out as a KAOS DJ at Evergreen university, in Olympia, Washington – one of the few students there to actually come from Olympia. In 1984 he started his own record label, K Records, and also played in the influential underground band Beat Happening. He also set up a basement studio going by the name of Dub Narcotic.

Beck had met Johnson in Los Angeles and had occasionally sent him tapes of songs that he was working on. The two shared a common love of the DIY punk attitude; even if the music they produced didn't have a recognised 'punk sound', the lo-fi, four-track approach meant they were almost bound to work together at some point. Another north-west native, Kurt Cobain, though sonically miles away from Beat Happening's off-kilter approach, shared Beck's admiration for the way that K Records was run and went as far as having its logo tattooed on his arm. While sending Johnson his tapes, Beck had threatened to travel up the West Coast and work with him. He finally made it in October 1993 for the first of two periods of furious recording.

This first session mainly showcased just Beck and his guitar on tunes like 'Whisky Can Can' and 'Hollow Log'; he also covered Mississippi John Hurt's 'He's A Mighty Good Leader'. The following January he returned to finish off some songs and record new ones with a local crew of musicians, James Bertram, Mario Prietto, Calvin Johnson, Sam Jayne and Scott Plouf, who would later be a member of Built To Spill. Chris Ballew (of Presidents Of The USA fame) also played and became a regular Beck guitarist for a while in 1994.

These sessions showed a different side of Beck to the one seen on the two tapes from earlier in 1993. This was a Beck who was acknowledging his own musical roots (as he covered Mississippi John Hurt) and delivering material in an intimate setting devoid of the goofing around that characterised much of his early material. For the first time he really seemed to be taking his music seriously and the results are impressive. It also showed that he could work with other musicians in a band setting although he would shy away from repeating this style of work until *Mutations* five years later.

The product of these two Olympia sessions would subsequently see the light of day as the *One Foot In The Grave* album, but Johnson revealed that much more had been recorded and not issued: 'He's already recorded another album for us, but it's not quite finished being mixed yet, and he's so fucking busy that it's hard to get it done. I guess I'm not aggressive enough about bugging him. I really need to, but since everyone else is pulling him every which way, I feel bad about going to him and saying "Let's finish this fucking thing." ' The material most likely came from the first session (in October 1993). Johnson added:

> It's more acoustic stuff. Half of *One Foot In The Grave* was done with a rock band, which people seem to overlook. But this time it's mainly him, and it's great. The songs are just so incredible, and he's so fun to work with. I feel like I've got a pretty good job: I get to work with all these talented people that I really admire, like Beck and Doug Nartsch and just stand back and watch them go. I'm really lucky.

As well as the album, tracks from the sessions have also appeared on Beck's three-track K Records 7″ single 'It's All In

Your Mind', which came out in 1994, and on the 1998 compilation CD *Selector Dub Narcotic* which included the track 'Close To God'.

Rumours of a second K album of this material have, not surprisingly, been circulating for a while. This rumoured album even has a rumoured title, 'A Tombstone Every Mile'. Beck, however, isn't so sure that it will see the light of day. 'I haven't had the chance to get back up there and work on it. I have a lot of stuff sitting around. I don't know if any of it's worthy to inflict on the world.' So what's left might not be in Beck's Top Ten but *One Foot In The Grave* has been quoted as his favourite album to date: 'I made *One Foot In The Grave* for me. That's the one, when I'm sitting by myself, that I really get into.'

As 1993 progressed the record company interest in Beck intensified. After 'Loser's' release in March and his KCRW appearance in July the labels began circling ever closer. Exactly how many labels were after his signature will never be known. Estimates have varied between six and sixteen, but at least three major players were in the race for sure: Capitol, Warners and Geffen. 'The whole thing got a little crazy after a while, I mean David Geffen called me at home just to express his interest and stuff. I kept thinking the record companies would go away after a few months.' Beck for one certainly wasn't going to get carried away or rush into anything. 'I'm happy that they like what I do, but picking a record company is kinda like choosing the best ATM machine,' he said.

He also thought he should put the record company reps through a little humorous test, as he explained:

> When all these record company honchos started coming to my shows in a local dive bar or hole-in-the-wall. The kind of place where there was a big pole in front of the stage. And all these limos would be pulling up with these industry people. People would be saying, 'they love your song, they're coming down, they want you to blow them away!' So I thought I would get a leaf-blower on-stage and really blow them out of the room. The ones that survived the exhaust fumes from the landscaping machine, when the smoke settled down, that's how I found

people I could work with, I guess. Put 'em to the test. Things like bringing a leaf-blower on stage, these things grew out of more of a performance type thing. I wasn't trying to be a clown. It was a comment on keeping these red stucco fake-house communities clean, the breeze from the inner cities. It had something to do with that. I had a firm agenda, and just silliness.

Almost as soon as Bong Load put out the first 12″ singles of 'Loser' in March, the labels took notice and chased Beck for most of the year. He recalls: 'The whole label thing took about eight months. I didn't want to do it first of all . . . it took a long time; sifting through the possibilities, deciding whether to do it myself or let someone else do all the work for me, all the day to day business.'

Eventually around November, after previously turning them down, he put pen to paper and Geffen were the winners of the race. A&R man Mark Kates was instrumental in signing Beck. Kates was sure they weren't going to be stung by signing a one-hit-wonder. 'When we did sign him he made it clear that he wanted to be around for 20 or 30 years,' he says, while Beck wanted to be sure his artistic integrity would remain intact: 'I went for Geffen 'cos they offered me the most control – though the least money. I think the best thing to do is to have your own label. I never realised how easy it was to put out your own records.'

Beck's legal representative, Bill Berrol, negotiated a clause in the Geffen contract that would allow Beck to release 'uncommercial' recordings on any independent label of his choosing so long as he finished the required amount of records for the major label. This was probably a wise move in Beck's case, not only because of his prolific writing but because David Geffen had previously sued Neil Young for making 'uncommercial music'.

Beck also signed up with John Silva's Gold Mountain management team which handled the affairs of Nirvana. When asked exactly what advance he got from Geffen, Beck was straight to the point as usual: 'It wasn't a million. I got some strawberries, some blueberries, a hackysack, a silver spacesuit . . .' When pressed he gets closer to the truth on this subject and concedes: 'I didn't get that much money. I got enough to pay my rent for a year and buy some equipment and stuff. But it wasn't a money deal. If I'd wanted to get a lot of money, I could've gotten three times as much.'

Beck, to his credit, was as down-to-earth about the whole situation as normal. He didn't expect, or really want, to be an instant rock star on a major label. To this day he seems genuinely shocked that people pay so much attention to him and want a piece of his action. Despite this wonderment on his part he is appreciative of the way the recording industry works. 'I was pretty aware of the music industry treadmill, the revolving door,' he said at the time of his signing to Geffen. 'I've been playing music for a lot of years, so I was always very reticent about having some business people dictate to me what I should be doing. It seemed way too foreign to me. I always did music for my own amusement, which is how anybody starts playing music.'

He was also aware that his new-found standing would put him into the media glare, a glare that would include the target of his first single. 'I know it means I'll be on MTV, which is annoying. No one wants to be saturated and over-exposed. That's like everything I'm against. Most people you meet in America are plugged into the whole entertainment thing, they have nothing to say.'

So, Beck was about to enter a new phase of his musical development, one which would see his major label debut album and an almost year-long tour with a band. It would all take some getting used to, as he talked about in early 1994: 'All the shit that's happening now is just totally insane, because if you ask anybody that knows me, they'd tell you that I've had just the worst fucking luck. This is all an avalanche of confetti and balloons and kazoos. Before, the party was just an empty room with a bare light bulb on the ceiling. It was pretty bleak.'

It wouldn't be for very much longer.

# 4 Sweet Sunshine

I N A *ROLLING STONE* INTERVIEW, April 1994, Beck was asked to describe his debut Geffen album. His reply was typical Beck and took some beating in the 'Quote of the Year' stakes:

The whole concept of *Mellow Gold* is that it's like a satanic K-Tel record that's been found in a trash dumpster. A few people have molested it and slept with it and half-swallowed it before spitting it out. Someone played poker with it, someone tried to smoke it. Then the record was taken to Morocco and covered with humus and tabouli. Then it was flown back to a convention of water-skiers, who skied on it and played Frisbee with it. Then the record was put on a turntable, and the original K-Tel album had reached a whole new level. I was just talking about that whole 'freedom rock' feeling, you understand.

Understand or not, the facts are that it was recorded between 1992 and mid-1993. Sessions took place with the Bong Load gang and later with Carl Stephenson again at his house where he and Beck had originally recorded 'Loser' two years previously. Mixed in with these sessions were a couple of trips to work with Tom Grimley at his Poop Alley Studio.

The sessions at Stephenson's were very ad hoc; frequently they'd take place in the kitchen. 'I'd be hurrying to finish a vocal before Carl's girlfriend came home from work,' laughs Beck. This, of course, gave the recording a very lo-fi quality, one which Beck wasn't aiming for: 'If I'd had access to 24 tracks when I recorded "Loser", I would have used them! I was always trying to make it sound as good as I could. I was embarrassed by a lot of my songs because of the way they sounded. This was before lo-fi became hip. I was ashamed of my music because it was so badly recorded.'

So this was not a high-tech process of putting together an album. Of course he hadn't signed to a label when he started working on this collection of songs that he'd later describe as 'Afternoon demo songs, very slow and not very energetic, not very conducive to playing a rock show in front of an audience that was excited and anticipating something'.

In some respects the fact that the album fell together in a haphazard way makes it all the more enduring but Beck would have liked a little more finesse to be added. 'The whole album had been recorded in about two weeks overall,' he remembered. 'Really it was like demos. I didn't get to take the songs as far as I wanted to.'

Sessions at Carl Stephenson's house had been fitted in when the house was empty, but this gave a hurried feel to some of the songs. 'The earlier stuff is a little more spastic because everything was done on a shortage of time,' says Beck. 'When we were recording *Mellow Gold* in 1992, we were recording in the living room-kitchen area, and we'd usually have about three or four hours to work before his girlfriend came home to make herself some food. So a lot of those songs, the impetus behind them, is this mad dash to finish and get all the parts down before his girlfriend was coming back.'

Beck's breakthrough track was re-recorded for *Mellow Gold* but when asked about it later, Carl Stephenson was unhappy about the outcome of 'Loser'. 'I feel bad about it,' he explained. 'It's not Beck the person, it's the words. I just wish I could have been more of a positive influence.'

In the years after 'Loser', Stephenson struggled against an undisclosed form of mental illness. He had trouble staying focused on anything and had bouts of destructive obsessiveness over minute details. After finishing his work with Beck he was hospitalised, but having received treatment he managed to complete and release his own project, *Forest For The Trees*, an album which Beck guests on. After its release in 1997, Stephenson had a Top 30 hit single with 'Dreams', taken from the album.

Other sessions took place at Bong Load partner Rob Schnapf's house and on Beck's own mini four-track equipment. Guests during these sessions included Beck's old keyboard-maestro pal Mike Bioto and Petra Haden from That Dog, while David Harte played drums on three tracks.

He cut down the list of songs to 12 and was ready to go ahead and release it on Bong Load in August 1993, but this was delayed when the big labels started circling. Beck laughs: 'Geffen started talking to Bong Load in about April 1993 about signing me and I just thought, "Yeah, right." So I waited . . . I wanted to finish up all the artwork and . . . mastered it, and we were about to put it out in August [1993], but . . .' then Geffen got serious and the release date was put back to the following March.

The finished album was a self-contained, minor-league sonic work of art. The opening 'Loser' riff immediately reminded most people why they bought the album in the first place and also put it out of the way so Beck could introduce 11 other new songs that the listener probably hadn't heard yet.

After getting the 'big-hit' out of the way, the listener is presented with the gently acoustic (and by now ancient) 'Pay No Mind' which conjured mental comparisons with early Bob Dylan (listen to lines like 'Give the finger to the rock and roll singer/as he's dancing upon your paycheque' and 'and the drugs won't kill your day job'). This likening to Dylan could also be stretched to 'Loser'. Where Beck sang 'Don't believe everything that you breathe/You'll get a parking violation and a maggot on your sleeve', Dylan had sung 'Don't follow leaders/Watch your parking meters' in his own 'Subterranean Homesick Blues'.

Track 3, 'Fuckin' With My Head', took Beck in a different direction again with heavy twanging guitars and a Sonny Terry-like harmonica. The funky bassline of 'Soul Suckin Jerk' highlighted that Beck was already a multi-dimensional artist and that was only five songs into his major label debut.

While *Odelay* would later show off Beck's eclectic mix of updated country, blues, rap and rock, *Mellow Gold* mixed lots of styles but many of them were different from its later, more famous follow-up. On *Mellow Gold*, 'Beercan' displays a swirling psychedelia-meets-hip-hop that assaults your senses in ways you hadn't known were possible while a few songs later 'Mother-fucker' hits you again, but this time with some death-throe guitar feedback and screaming vocals.

Courtney Love would later say that Beck and her late husband, Kurt Cobain, would have been great friends if they had ever met. This track shows that she may have been right to link them in a musical sense too, although Beck couldn't be said to share Cobain's misanthropic world view. Like Beck, Cobain had also been homeless for a while and spent some time sleeping under the north Aberdeen bridge in the winter of 1985. In between these songs had been the comedic acoustic number 'Nitemare Hippy Girl'. The way in which Beck seemed effortlessly to combine folk, rap, punk and hard-core, sometimes even in his humorous tracks, hinted at the shape of things to come.

Another comparison could be made to Dylan as many songs on this album contain a weird mix of characters and situations. Most of these came from a blue-collar world, a world that Beck knew very well, and their low-paid jobs and cheap boarding houses were taken from his direct experiences. Just check out the nitemare hippy girl (with her 'Tofu the size of Texas'), the truck drivin' neighbours fighting downstairs, the poor character washing dishes in the hotel (in 'Whiskeyclone, Hotel City 1997') or the fast-food worker who finally snaps and goes on the rampage (in 'Soul Suckin Jerk').

The album's mix of 'stream of consciousness' lyrics versus narrative stories gives a genuinely fascinating collection that is sometimes hard to peg down and the deliberate false starts and obscenities remind the listener of Beck's early home-made cassettes. With this album, Beck leapt into the mainstream but didn't really get his feet wet. Though yet to demonstrate his full genius he was starting to show glimpses of it.

After Geffen got hold of the tapes and agreed to release the album, Beck was keen to point out that this wasn't a very good overall impression of him or his music: 'Mellow Gold is probably not the best impression to give people of my music as a whole. The silly songs came from playing live at other people's shows where you only had about five minutes. In that situation, you often play something that'll make a few people laugh.'

Another mitigating factor was the way it had been recorded, the lack of an overall plan: 'It was such an anomaly in the way it fell together. It was just this concatenation of accidents that nobody could control, and it was beautiful that way.' On another occasion he explained that his recording process had been anything but conventional: 'I nailed my earlobe to the speaker, and the sound was booming through my hollow skull. And my pen was on fire so I had to write fast and not actually think about it.'

Although Beck claimed that he had a fair amount of artistic freedom, and this was pretty much true to a large extent, he did have to go along with some major label demands. The first of these was that they re-release 'Loser' in the US and release it for the first time in Europe too. One of the effects of this was to re-ignite controversy over the 'Slacker' tag and this time on a much larger scale. Again he had to field the questions of his background and outlook on life and again he shied away from any connections to the so-called 'Generation X', he denied that the 'Slacker Nation' existed at all:

> That nation doesn't really exist, does it? I don't really know that nation. I don't believe it's there. It's just a created thing because I don't really know anybody like that. Maybe when you're a kid, and you're in high school and you don't have much to do and you're just sort of hanging out, but everyone I know is working hard, myself included. That song wasn't really a response to any sort of Generation X or slacker thing. It was more a reaction to the 80s, which seemed to involve this whole winning,
> materialistic thing. This whole 'Top Gun' attitude, which for the 'have not's' was just kind of a drag. If anything it was a reaction to that. But it was meant humorously.

Time and again in interview after interview, this time around Europe too, he had to explain that the chorus of his most famous song was addressing his lack of rapping ability not a serious generational statement.

When the album finally hit the shops in early March 1994, the sleeve depicted the Armageddon figure of 'Last Man After Nuclear War' and the song titles were missing a few letters to make it acceptable for shops to stock. An in-store promo CD to be played to shoppers was edited to remove 'Fuckin' With My Head', 'Truckdrivin' Neighbors Downstairs' and 'Motherfucker', while 'Corvette Bummer' was added to beef up the playing time.

Bong Load were in charge of the vinyl version of the album which for some unknown reason carried an alternate version of 'Pay No Mind'.

When the reviewers got hold of *Mellow Gold*, all most of them had to go on was 'Loser' and maybe a few stories about his wacky on-stage antics. In the UK at least, no one had seen him live, or heard him live for that matter, so it was a blind introduction. Despite the lack of knowledge the album stood up very well to what could have turned into calls of 'one-hit wonder.' The *NME* gave it a respectable 6 out of 10, commenting: 'At his best he refuses to be what you assume he must be – an acid-fried LA novelty.' Ireland's *Hot Press* was more generous, awarding a top mark of 10 while gushing that 'Beck is well on his way to rescuing rock and roll from the mundane.'

*Q* magazine gave a glowing endorsement with 4 out of 5 and a sparkling look at his résumé: 'He's got everything going for him. He looks like a young Evan Dando; he shares management with Nirvana; Geffen are spending enough money on him to rescue Eurodisney and, most important of all, he's very, very good.' *Vox* on the other hand liked what they heard, giving a score of 8 out of 10, but got his background a little out of context: ' . . . at last grunge has a solo star to worship'. Grunge? *Rolling Stone* missed the boat somewhat but tried to cover its own tracks in its end-of-1994 issue by saying, 'Like all genius moves, only in retrospect does it seem obvious.'

As for direct feedback, Beck had received some from people in the street. Some was favourable, some less so. 'Every once in a while, somebody says, "Oh, I like your album." Mostly, people come up to me and say, "Hey, you faggot, you think you're really cool, huh?" I get most of that.'

It wasn't all abuse though. Beastie Boy Mike D was singing his praises: 'He fits into the nomadic folk tradition of Ramblin' Jack Elliott, the whole traditional coffee-house balladeer tip, but his hip-hop side legitimises Public Enemy as the real folk music of the 80s and 90s, because he draws on that aspect just as much as on anything else that he's picked up along the way.'

To coincide with the release of *Mellow Gold*, Geffen had lined up a series of promotional appearances for Beck. The first of these was a transatlantic jaunt for Beck's first TV appearance on the BBC's long-running show *Top Of The Pops*. He would be required to sing a live vocal of 'Loser' over a pre-recorded backing tape. As he had no band with him on the trip he decided to spice things up a bit. He enlisted the services of a group of elderly gentlemen to act the parts of being his band. Beck smirks on recalling the spectacle:

> It was a group of 80-year-old men playing; some were dapper, sprightly elderly gentlemen who still had hair. There was a portly guy with a Friar Tuck hairdo playing guitar. Then we had a hunched, slightly demonic old man, and he was playing drums. There's a genius part where the camera cuts to him like there's a break on drums, and he does the slowest drumstick spin ever executed in the history of rock drumming, it was really beautiful.

It went down as one of the highlights in the show's long history. 'I knew they'd totally appreciate old men. We just asked around and a bunch showed up and we picked the best. We hung out with them for two days, just playing guitars and telling stories. One of them sold sunglasses and he tried to sell me an old police-issue pair. I wouldn't buy them though.'

Back in the States, Beck was thrust into a few radio appearances closer to home. On 1 March 1994 he returned to KCRW and *Morning Becomes Eclectic* with Chris Douridas. This time he was accompanied by Chris Ballew, opening with a live version of 'Bogusflow'. After discussing how the two musicians met (Ballew went by the name Caspar, which made it difficult for Beck to find him as he was asking for the wrong guy), it was announced that Beck would be playing the following day at Aron's Records to coincide with *Mellow Gold*'s release. The interview continued about how Beck signed to Geffen. 'I counted 14 labels chasing you,' claimed Douridas, before another live track, 'Dead Man With No Heart' with Beck on banjo. Chris Ballew joined in with his trademark two string Bassitar for 'Hard To Compete'.

The interview then switched topics to ask Beck if he'd ever been in love, to which he replied, 'Once or twice, couple of hundred times.' He was also asked the inevitable question about the Slacker tag: 'Slackers are for rich people or something, I don't know what's up with slackers.' He was also asked if he felt the need to make up the 'Beck mythology'. 'Oh, no, I'm not that smart,' he gasped, genuinely surprised that anyone might think that.

This is most likely the truth. Not that he wasn't smart, but that most of the stories about him were true, even if they had been tarted up a little by over-enthusiastic journalists. 'Howling Wolves' was introduced as 'a demo for our side band' and was described as 'Sort of Bon Jovi in a vacuum cleaner'. Surprisingly, that description was amazing close to reality. *Top Of The Pops* was also mentioned. 'It was surreal, they made me sing it 11 times. Practice it 8 times, then film it, but the cameras weren't working. I was kinda tricked into it, because I said yes before I knew what it was.' The show closed with renditions of 'It's All In Your Mind' and 'It's All Gonna Come To Be'.

A week later Beck teamed up with Thurston Moore for a session at KXLU. This madcap noisefest was later sent out as an official Geffen promo cassette to college radio stations, to ensure that Beck retained his wacky image.

The early incarnation of Beck's band consisted of drummer Joey Waronker, guitarist Chris Ballew and bassist Dave Gomez. This line-up was assembled in early 1994 and prepared to begin their inaugural tour in March of that year. Big, burly Dave Gomez was a veteran of several Los Angeles hard-core bands. Chris Ballew had played with Beck on KCRW and also participated in the second *One Foot In The Grave* sessions. After touring with Beck he would go on to form The Presidents Of The USA and record two albums for Columbia.

Joey Waronker is perhaps an unlikely rock-star in his own right. He's quiet, self-consciously polite, and has been described as 'a wee bit spacey'. Not unlike Beck in some ways. He comes from a strong musical background. His sister Anna was a member of That Dog and his father Lenny was a producer and later worked as an executive with Warners. It was hanging out in the studios where his father was working that started the young Waronker on his way to being a drummer. His father worked with the likes of James Taylor and Randy Newman, giving Joey the chance to study drummers like Jeff Porcaro and Steve Gadd.

Most of Waronker's encounters with drummers of the day were positive and they'd give little hints along the way. As he recalls:

They were just friendly, and they'd hang out and play with me. I'd sit in the drum booth and watch them. I remember, the main thing that I picked up on was the drum tuning. That was the big thing. I would obsess on listening to how the snare drum sounded in the room as opposed to how it sounded in the headphones or in the play back. I'd try to imitate that at home. So I'd sit there and watch how Steve Gadd, after doing six takes, would just tweak one lug over here and one over here. It would be totally uneven, but he'd whack it and it would have his sound. I'd listen to how his cymbals were really sort of dry and dead, yet he had a way of somehow bringing a lot of sound and character out of them.

As he reached his teens his interest in drumming waned as he concentrated on his education. 'About the time I stopped playing, I had a weird realisation that I should use my mind and focus myself,' he explains. 'I just got really into school for a while.' This lasted for a while but by the age of 14 he was not only back playing again, but he was in his first band. The Radio Ranch Straight Shooters were a western swing band with a guitarist by the name of Smokey Hormel (who would later join Waronker in Beck's band).

Although his favourite music was rock, bordering on punk, Joey put his all into the band and set about learning everything he could about jazz, blues and country. He was aided by the Blasters' Bill Bateman, another drummer with a love of all musical styles. 'He was a real historian and a real serious collector. He'd see me playing and he'd be like, "You can't use a Yamaha hi-hat pedal to play this music! You're not going to be able to get the right feel." It was a little over the top, but for a 14 year old, it was actually really cool. And I became obsessed with learning about the history of music.'

On graduation from High School Waronker relocated to Minnesota and signed up at the McAllister College where he studied classical percussion. It was here that he joined Walt Mink, a band signed to an independent label. After completing his four years at McAllister, he thought things might lead somewhere with Walt Mink. 'I definitely wasn't going to join a symphony. And there was a buzz going around about the band. We had gotten a write-up in *Rolling Stone*, and it seemed like things were happening. I just sort of bit the bullet and said, "If I really need the degree, I'll come back and get it, but right now there's no time." And there hasn't been time since.'

By 1993 Waronker was trying to add a little bit of experimentation to the band, but without much success. He explains:

> I was fascinated by the way the Beatles and Brian Wilson recorded, so I was trying to integrate those kind of sounds: bells and tambourines and snare drums and timpanis and concert bass drums and vibraphones. We'd make demos and I'd break all this stuff out and then it would all get erased. Everyone in the band would kind of look at me funny, like, 'Why are you wasting our time here?' But in the back of my mind I knew that the time would come when I'd figure it out.

So he quit the band and headed back to Los Angeles. Before he'd had a chance to settle in he got a call from a friend for a session job with a singer named Beck. Waronker remembers:

> I showed up and it was so funny. Beck was like, 'I'm going to play bass. Let me show you this song. It's really simple. It has two parts. The first part is going to go like this.' And it was like, a I–V progression. 'So we do that four times and then the next section goes like this.' And he plays the same I–V progression. So we played it and I just sort of followed him and he was like, 'That's great, but make the second sections a little heavier.' So I did that and that was it. Afterwards we hung out and were talking and then we ended up just freaking out and recording sort of a noise jam. And then I split, and my friend dropped off a tape later that day. Beck put on some guitars and a tambourine and a bunch of crazy noisy things and some vocals and then tacked the noise jam that we did onto the end of it. I was blown away by how he visualised the song.

After a couple more sessions Beck asked Waronker if he wanted to go on tour in 1993. Waronker has been Beck's drummer ever since.

As they prepared to go on tour Beck commented that 'We need about two more weeks of practice, but we leave in two days. We'll work it out on the road.' The band gave themselves the moniker 'After School Special' and played only their second-ever gig together at Cafe Troy two days before they were to depart on tour. For the occasion they pulled out unrecorded tracks like 'New Wave Cocksucker Blues' and 'Teenage Wastebasket'. In response to some of his fans that night wearing the infamous Sub-Pop T-shirts bearing the name of his most famous song, he asked 'What's with all these "Loser" T-shirts. Don't you people have any self-respect?'

The next night they played their final warm-up at Fuzzyland, a roving club that changed venue from night to night. For this particular night it was stationed at a disused bowling alley with the stage set up at the end of the bowling lanes. The show was also to have doubled as the release party for Beck's compilation CD on Flipside Records, *Stereopathetic Soul Manure*, but the CDs weren't ready and that plan was shelved. The album itself was a real hotch-potch collection. Many of the tracks had been recorded with Tom Grimley who owns and operates the Poop Alley Studios which had been called 'The best recording studio in Los Angeles' by the *LA Weekly*. Grimley had filled it with 1950s era equipment and synthesisers that he'd picked up at second-hand fairs. Grimley is a multi-instrumentalist and had fronted the Bennett Orchestra. He'd also hosted the Rentals and That Dog at his studios; the latter appeared on *Stereopathetic Soul Manure* with Beck.

Those few reviews the album managed to garner found the reviewers struggling to get to grips with Beck's eclectic collection of songs. Q magazine awarded it just 1 star out of 5 and summed it up as 'For those who find Pavement a touch easy'. While it is true that some of the noisier tracks ('Pink Noise (Rock Me Amadeus)', 'Thunderpeel' and 'Rollins Power Sauce') take a few listens to get into, there are also some lush country numbers ('Rowboat', 'The Spirit Moves Me' and 'Modesto'), some great acoustic songs ('Crystal Clear (Beer)', 'Puttin' It Down' and 'Satan Gave Me A Taco') and some plain old silliness ('8.6.82', 'Total Soul Future (Eat It)' and 'Aphid Manure Heist'). If you give this collection some time you'll probably find it does reward. This vein of recording had continued with some more Bong Load sessions. Tom Rothrock claimed that 'We have about 40 songs in the can, recorded during the year following the release of *Mellow Gold*. It's more an extension of the stuff on *Stereopathetic Soul Manure.*'

The tour continued to take in major cities across the country before reaching LA again in late April. Beck took a trip to the Beale Street Music Festival in Memphis during May and the tour restarted in June. For many of the shows the crowd were surprised and even shocked to see the Beck live experience. As Beck pointed out, his audience hadn't really known where he was coming from musically having probably only heard 'Loser':

> After 'Loser' came out I think our shows became sort of confrontational. I think that song drew a certain type of audience, but at that point, I was still basically playing folk gigs. The 'Loser' thing was really a side project from my folk stuff. So there was a time where I was trying to figure out exactly what I wanted to do. Did I want to do something that was confrontational and explosive, or do something that was more country and folk-based, or did I want to create a whole different thing that I'd never really imagined before? I think I opted for the last one.

As the tour picked up the thread and took in the West Coast and Mid-Western states, some major media coverage began to ensue, with bootlegs circulating from some shows. The show at Minneapolis's First Avenue Club was reviewed in *Rolling Stone* and gave rise to the first bootleg CD, *Total Paranoia*. The set opened with the non-album 'Corvette Bummer' and included unreleased tracks like 'Scavenger' and 'Color Coordinated' plus a healthy mix of acoustic numbers and B-sides to go with the better known *Mellow Gold* songs. *Rolling Stone* noted that 'Beck seemed intent not only on shaking his erratic live reputation but on delivering a message: There's more to music than alternative rock, there's more to history than yesterday and there's more to Beck than "Loser".'

'Erratic' was perhaps an understatement. Some nights it all clicked and he was brilliant but on others the performance was patchy to say the least. It should be remembered that Beck had mostly played solo for the previous six years and he sometimes struggled to put across a good show as part of a band. The overall performances might have been up and down but Beck did manage some consistency with the solo acoustic mini-sets that he would play mid-way through the show each night.

The tour then shifted to a whole new ball-game for Beck as he went down to Australia for ten, small-venue dates and then on to New Zealand and Japan. While in Australia he and the band stopped by JJJ Radio in Sydney to record an eight-song session. After being introduced as 'The people's poet', Beck was certainly not just going through the motions of promoting his album as only one of the eight songs, 'Beercan', was from *Mellow Gold*.

*Strawberry Communion*, the bootleg of his 6 September 1994 show in Tokyo, also made the rounds. It contained an early romp through 'Minus' that would show up on *Odelay* two years later. Beck's reaction to Japan was one of love at first sight and this feeling was reciprocated. It was such a strong bond that four years later, when Beck decided to do a mini-tour with his *Mutations* album, he did so only in Japan and claims: 'Japan is my very favourite place in the whole world. I enjoy not knowing how anything around me is working. I just enjoy that constant derangement, and I'm really into that whole cleanliness thing, how you can go to the fruit store and the fruit comes out like it's from an antiseptic forest, it's so pristine and well.'

By November, *Melody Maker* was sending reporters stateside to review shows in anticipation of the forthcoming British dates. Everett True reported from Boston that 'Before tonight, I'd never seen Slayer turn into Sebadoh. After tonight, I'm not sure I ever want to again.' Despite this Beck was still eagerly anticipated. Before reaching the UK he undertook a whirlwind tour of 14 dates in 20 nights across mainland Europe, finally debuting in the UK in Manchester on 26 November 1994. Two nights later he put on a triumphant show at the Astoria Theatre in London. The set-list spun from half a dozen *Mellow Gold* songs to some unreleased tracks ('Color Coordinated', 'Casio', and 'Protein Summer') and a healthy dose of acoustic numbers ('Ziplock Bag', 'Puttin' It Down' and 'It's All In Your Mind').

While in London he stopped by at Radio 1 for an interview. When asked about his plans for the next year he replied: 'This is going to be the feedback year. The year of headphone solos. We got this helicopter thing happening. We're gonna drop musicians into depopulated areas and then get this big satellite and sorta hook 'em all up. It's kind of an unambitious year.'

He was also joined on-stage in London by session pedal steel expert BJ Cole. Cole would later fill in on a Verve tour (replacing Nick McCabe) and later still he played with Joey Waronker again, this time with R.E.M. Cole remembers that his initial meeting with Beck was arranged by the record company: 'At first I thought he was just a space cadet off of Planet Zod. But I soon realised the guy had something very interesting going on. He's got a strong vision of what he's doing and doesn't compromise for other people, but he has a thorough knowledge of all the base styles of popular music: Jimmie Rodgers, Sonny Terry, Brownie McGhee and people like that. He's a dustbin of American popular music styles.'

Beck was obviously happy with Cole's contribution because he contacted him again: 'He called me up to do a Radio 1 session with him just before *Odelay* came out. I was the only other musician on it – he played all the other instruments, including drums, which he couldn't play! My favourite bit was when he completely detuned his guitar to overdub a solo. I realised he had this atonal effect in his head, and he knew exactly how to get it. That session just sold me.'

After a few more European dates it was back to LA for another show just before Christmas, a well-earned rest and a chance to reflect on a hectic first year of major label commitments. Beck recalled the turbulence of 1994:

> At first I wasn't prepared for any kind of success at all. I was just getting used to the idea of something as basic as putting an album out, so I don't think I went into this year ready for what happened. It's been a year of intense learning and kinda struggling to figure out how it all works. The strangest thing is the way that people have come in and had an idea of what they think I am, and no matter what I've said or done, they've turned me into it. That kind of power is really disturbing.

1994 had actually seen the release of four Beck albums. As well as *Mellow Gold, One Foot In The Grave* and *Stereopathetic Soul*

*Manure* there was a 10" vinyl only release – *A Western Harvest Field By Moonlight*. Issued on Fingerpaint Records, the initial 2,000 copies each came with an original and unique finger-painting. These mini works of art had been created during finger-painting parties held by Beck and some of his friends. A second pressing didn't include the paintings and the record has now had at least four pressings due to the demand of fans. This collection includes such typical Beck titles as 'Feel Like A Piece Of Shit (Crossover Potential)' and 'She Is All (Gimme Something To Eat)', while a version of 'Totally Confused' was also included. The final track, 'Styrofoam Chicken', is cut into the vinyl such that it continues revolving and so the song never ends.

As the year drew to a close Beck wrote for French magazine *Les Inrockuptibles*. In a piece entitled 'My Year Of All Dangers' he wrote that '1994 hasn't been very kind to me. People very quickly came to a false image of me.' When asked about the speed of his new-found fame he replied: 'I've no comparison, I don't know what speed it happens for others. For me anyway, everything happens too quickly. The news goes round too quickly; records come out too quickly, trains go too quickly.' *Spin* magazine announced that *Mellow Gold* was its number 2 album of 1994 and that both 'Loser' and 'Beercan' were its number 1 singles of the year.

The overall feeling was that 1994 had been a year of intense learning for Beck. For his part, he must have felt that he'd been dropped in at the deep end, but he'd just about managed to swim – even if he was occasionally slapped in the face with a big wave. The most important thing about making mistakes in public is that you learn from them and endeavour not to repeat them. Beck obviously took this on board as he would change his band for the following year to attempt to tighten up his concerts and also to get a little more accustomed to dealing with all the media attention.

1995 started with Beck agreeing to release a new four-track single on the British Domino Records label in January. The title track was to have been the original version of 'Static'. The label was all set to go but the master tapes never showed and the project was scrapped.

With European festivals and Lollapalooza looming, not to mention his own headlining dates throughout the year, Beck juggled his band line-up again in the early spring of 1995. Joey Waronker was kept on as drummer and long-time pal Mike Bioto was brought in on keyboards. Beck recalls: 'I played piano and keyboards quite a bit as a kid. My best friend while I was growing up was this keyboard whiz, Mike Bioto. He was the archetypal 13-year-old jazz piano prodigy. I used to play with him all the time but I veered off into more of a Professor Longhair thing. I can hang a little Booker T if necessary, but I prefer to keep with the blues.'

The places for bassist and guitarist were up for grabs and auditions were held. Smokey Hormel was among the invitees but Beck couldn't immediately decide on a guitarist and Smokey took up a more concrete offer. So the job of tour guitarist went to Sunny Reinhart. Another member of the band to be added via this route was bassist Abby Travis. She kindly took time out from working with her band, The Abby Travis Foundation, to talk about her year with Beck: 'An A&R man from Geffen recommended me for the audition. We spent about a month rehearsing before the tour and he got through a lot of songs. Beck just has so many! He'd still want us to play songs we didn't really know anyways once we got out on the road.'

At the end of the tour she left to join Elastica temporarily. After five late-June warm-up dates in California it was time to join up with the big boys on the Lollapalooza juggernaut, starting on the Fourth of July in Washington state.

The Lollapalooza phenomenon was the brainchild of ex-Jane's Addiction visionary Perry Farrell who tried to take a whole festival on tour and succeeded. Farrell's self-imposed brief was to take a diverse selection of alternative acts on the road not only to a selection of major North American cities, but also to places that wouldn't normally see headline shows from major acts. The whole package included travelling side-show circus acts and all the associated stalls and curiosities that you'd find at any stationary festival. He also ensured that at least $1 from every ticket went to AIDS and environmental charities. The first Lollapalooza did the circuit in 1991 but by 1995 there was a feeling creeping in that Farrell was finding it difficult to keep the crowds happy and that they always wanted something bigger and better than the previous year.

Lollapalooza 1995 was, to some people, a great disappointment after the extravaganzas of previous years. None of the big four names of the past was available this time around – Pearl Jam, the Red Hot Chili Peppers, Smashing Pumpkins and Nine Inch Nails. Ticket sales sank; whether it was because of the absence of these bands or just because the public had grown used to this kind of tour rolling in every summer was unclear but the opening day at The Gorge only sold out on the day of the event.

Vancouver was next up and that didn't sell out at all. In Denver, where each of the previous years had been an 18,000 sell-out, only 12,000 tickets were sold. Farrell tried to keep up the profile of the event by coming out to state 'This year's line-up is a unifying thing, and what happens when you unify is that you dissolve slightly into anonymity. But it doesn't make it any less potent.' Was this a weak cover-up of a poor line-up or did he really believe in the acts that he was showcasing?

The audience apathy hit Beck pretty hard. It was his first massive venue tour and almost no one was paying him any attention. His place on the bill was after the Mighty Mighty Bosstones and the Jesus Lizard, and right before Sinead O'Connor (before she pulled out) and Pavement. Hole and Sonic Youth topped the bill. Mostly he was on early in the afternoon and was faced with seemingly miles of empty seats and a few fans that seemed to be a long way away. When asked what he remembers about the experience, it's the seats that haunt him: 'What comes to mind? Blue plastic seats. Empty. Very empty. And it's 105 degrees, and there's a small cluster of youngsters who are displaying their energetic support, but they're about a mile and a half away, and there's 10 security guys closing in on them. I think at that point there was a lot more happening at the falafel booth than where I was standing.'

Bassist Abby Travis agrees with this summation: 'I had fun. I liked that there were so many different people and bands around. Beck should have had a way better time slot though, there were indeed a lot of empty seats.' Beck also enjoyed the company of all the other bands, playing a lot of table tennis along the way. He met up with Cypress Hill on the tour and discovered that they were almost neighbours. 'I found out that we grew up not far from each other. I said I was from Pico Hill and they were like "Shit, that's right next door, we thought you were from Europe or something." '

Beck would generally perform with the band on the main stage early in the day and then return on the second stage in the evening for some acoustic songs. For the main set they had to do some rejigging to fit them into the massive venues: 'When it came to songs from *Mellow Gold*, it was hard to re-create them live. They were kind of slow – even "Motherfucker", which seems rocking, but is really pretty slow. I had made most of them up on my own, so they didn't have a bigger audience in mind. We had to change the songs to play them live to a big audience, so they'd fit the atmosphere of that kind of show.'

A typical set would be based around 'Thunderpeel', 'Pay No Mind', 'Loser' and 'Fume', with new songs introduced as the tour unwound. He played 'Novacane' and 'Diskobox' in Chicago on 15 July, and debuted 'Minus' and 'Where It's At' in Hartford.

A song he wrote along the way was inspired by the hot, faceless summer and the empty seats. It was originally called 'Electric Music And The Summer People' but was re-written as 'Devils Haircut'. However he kept the original title for a later B-side:

> The title's from a poem, from a terrible record – I can't remember what it's called, some easy listening thing from the 60s. I spent that whole summer out in these incredibly, hideously, devil-adjective, tremendously hot, intolerably humid, outdoors facilities playing at two in the afternoon, watching the half-baked youth of the summer of '95, desperately trying to connect with them. It was futile. The original idea behind the song is a last gasp call to arms for everybody to come together – it was a somewhat cynical title. But it sounds good. 'Let's don't be like everyone else', that seemed to be the current of that summer of '95. It was inverted homogeny, everyone's trying so hard to be different, but they're all the same.

Later he would appear with acoustic guitar in hand for a low-key set on the second stage. 'I remember the stages being, like, a mile apart. I remember racing on a golf-cart thing – just flying through the mud. It's about as off-road as Lollapalooza got.'

When he arrived he would put on a magical set of tunes from his back catalogue: 'Rowboat', 'Hollow Log', 'Asshole' and a cover of 'John Hardy' were favourites. Sometimes he'd finish up with an amazing medley that could include any number of songs like 'Mexico', 'Satan Gave Me A Taco' and even 'Ozzy'. While these performances lacked some of the spark from his early 1992 shows, where he also played with basically just an acoustic guitar, he managed to strike up a better rapport than he had managed on the main stage with his band.

It was another example of his ability to put forward an on-stage persona that could connect with all types of people when he could actually talk to them, as he had during his early LA shows, but at the moment he struggled to do this when they were half a football field away. This on-stage attitude was something that he would refine over the next couple of years until he could achieve the same intimate feeling at the much larger venues and festivals.

Major magazines gave column space for artists on the tour to submit tour diaries. In hers, Courtney Love was quoted as saying 'Wish Kurt could've been here to meet Beck, he would've liked him a lot.' It was an observation that obviously could never now be tested but nevertheless it's likely to have been true. Beck himself submitted a tour journal that subsequently underwent some heavy analysis by readers on his stream-of-consciousness, Kerouac styled observations.

The tour ended on 18 August at the Shoreline Amphitheatre in San Francisco. Beck put on an energetic show including 'Fuckin' With My Head', 'Thunderpeel', 'Novacane', 'Where It's At', 'Beercan' and two versions of 'Loser'.

The touring didn't end with Lollapalooza. It was off to Europe for more dates starting at the prestigious Reading Festival. 'As I recall Reading was one of the best shows we did,' according to Abby Travis. This show was filmed and some parts have since been broadcast on MTV Europe. Further festival appearances followed in Belgium, France, Holland, Switzerland, Austria and Spain. By mid-October he was back in California to play at Neil Young's annual Bridge School Benefit concert.

*   *   *

It was only after the tour ended that it was revealed that Beck had had to deal with the deaths of several people close to him during the previous months. Not only had he had to get through the second consecutive year of long arduous touring and the soul sapping of Lollapalooza, but he had also kept his grief to himself, as he later explained: 'In the past year I've had several people close to me die. The shock mechanism that is stimulated when you hear about it was being pressed down all last year and at one point it didn't even pop back up.'

As well as the death in Germany of his grandfather he'd had to cope with the passing of Jac Zinder, the LA club promoter and music critic who'd been the first to write about him in *Spin* in 1993. He also had two friends die of AIDS and a friend of his mother's had died after being hit by car. Most of these losses had been private, but the last one was also professional as he lost an occasional member of his band, his pedal steel player, Leo LeBlanc: 'We opened for Johnny Cash and it was Leo's last show. He died about two weeks later. I hadn't realised that he was battling cancer. I called him up to do the show and he said "I can't play pedal steel, I'm getting this operation and I can't really play it, but I can play lap steel." So he played that.'

So many personal losses in such a brief time must have taken their toll on Beck and as 1995 ended for him he had a choice: he could either take a complete break to gather his thoughts or he could decide to work his way through it. He opted for the latter and in the aftermath of all this tragedy he had to pull his thoughts together as he began thinking about his follow-up to *Mellow Gold*.

Throwing himself into his work was no doubt, at least in part, a reaction to all that he'd been through. 'At the time I was thinking "Am I gonna write a bunch of songs about death?" ' he recalls. 'But I wanted to get more into the celebratory aspect of these people being alive.'

That is exactly what he did, managing to put the sadness behind him to produce one of the most stunning albums of the 1990s. He had already been working on it in part during 1995 and soon the fruits of this labour would be thrust upon an unsuspecting world to great acclaim.

# 5 Where It's At

B Y 1995, BECK AND LEIGH were living together in Silverlake while Channing had moved north and was studying Art in San Francisco.

Beck had begun work on the follow-up to *Mellow Gold* almost as soon as his debut album was released. He started by composing songs on guitar and piano but despite racking up almost twenty tunes he decided against using most of them. These singer-songwriter tracks included 'Feather In Your Cap', 'Brother', 'Cold Brains' and 'Ramshackle'. The latter actually made it on to his next album while some of the songs attempted at this time later found their way on to the more acoustic environment of *Mutations*, as Beck explained: 'I tried to record "Dead Melodies" and "Canceled Check" for *Odelay*, but they just didn't fit. I approached *Odelay* as a sound project and not as a performative thing.'

Random sessions continued when they could be fitted in between touring commitments, and Beck worked with Beastie Boys collaborator Mario Caldato Jnr on some songs described as '8 minute multi-layered country and western classics'. During the early part of 1995 Beck wanted to put down some more songs before setting out on an extensive summer of touring. He wasn't really getting into the stuff that he'd worked on the previous year. 'That stuff wasn't really turning me on,' he said. A change was required. It came in the shape of two DJs with a home studio just minutes from Beck's house.

The Dust Brothers, Mike Simpson and John King, had met in 1985 and teamed up to DJ a college radio show in Claremont, CA. They soon found themselves producing tracks for Tone-Loc,

Def Jef Young MC and other rappers on the Delicious Vinyl label. They set up their own studio, PCP Labs, in Silverlake, a district of East LA, and started work on an album of their own.

After putting down a collection of instrumental tunes they talked about working with the Beastie Boys on the follow-up to the new rude rappers, *Licensed To Ill* debut album. The Boys heard the tracks that King and Simpson had been working up for their own album and asked if they could rap over the top of them – thus *Paul's Boutique* was born and soon became one of the most influential rap albums ever.*

One of the amazing things about *Paul's Boutique* is the amazing amount of samples used. This isn't too surprising given the Dust Brothers' eclectic record collection. Mike Simpson once bought 15,000 records from a collector in one go. This would later help towards broadening the horizons of Beck's next album.

John King (aka 'King Gizmo') is a classically trained musician into blues, rock and punk while Mike Simpson (aka 'E-Z Mike') is more into funk – a combination that dovetailed nicely with Beck's embrace-all-styles methodology. The PCP Labs studio is basically their house with 'stacks of weird old gear', according to Mike Simpson: 'The living room is a live room, so when artists come here it's just a loose, laid back environment.' This is exactly the atmosphere that Beck wanted to record in, one which went right back to his *Mellow Gold* sessions with Carl Stephenson.

'I prefer to record in houses,' he claims. 'I can't go into those big studios. It's too much like a laboratory or something. Too scientific.'

In January 1995 the Dust Brothers and Beck met and the trio decided to have a go at recording something to see how they worked together. Beck recalls: 'I didn't have a place or anywhere to set up a studio. I knew the Dust Brothers had one in their house, so essentially we just hooked up. There was no agreement, we were just going to record a song for fun and see how it came out.'

---

*An aside to this story is that while working at the PCP Labs, a carpenter by the name of Mark Ramos Nishita came by to fix a broken gate. He ended up playing keyboards for the Beastie Boys and became Money Mark, later releasing two solo albums in the late 1990s.

He started dropping by more and more, but it was still informal and no one ever said that it would go on to form an album. They just experimented and waited to see what came out. 'At times it was a descent into madness, as all good endeavours should be. I was so exhausted after touring with *Mellow Gold* and the whole overload of the "Loser" thing that I probably should have taken six months off. But I had all this stuff I needed to get out and I wanted to push myself. I was afraid that otherwise I might just settle like a stone at the bottom of the ocean and just stay submerged forever.'

While Beck might have had definite ideas about what he wanted to accomplish, Mike Simpson did too, as he explains:

Modern records are very predictable. Usually if you listen to a song for 30 seconds, you get it – you know where it's going, you know what's gonna happen, you know what to expect. We wanted to try to keep the music exciting so that you have to listen to the whole song, or else you're going to miss the best part. When I listen to old records, they have a certain sound you can feel – when you turn it up, you can feel it in your body. When I listen to stuff from the 80s and 90s, it's all very clean and precise, but I don't feel it. We use all this technology to get some amazing technical performances, yet we still want to create that sound that has some emotional impact.

This seemed to sit well with Beck and the three hit it off immediately. As Simpson says: 'We could tell from the first day in the studio that we were going to have a lot of fun making this record. He was just amazingly talented and the ideas were just flowing from day 1. We were basically just like kids in a sandbox, having fun with our toys.'

The dynamics between the three allowed input from any of them into any part of the recording process. There were no defined roles for any of them, except that Beck had to sing! He remembers that it was very informal:

We'd just go in the studio and we were all kind of doing stuff together production-wise. It wasn't one of those scenarios where the producer comes up with the track, and then the singer comes in and does their thing. That's kind of an old-school way of doing it. I started playing the music by working 4-track, doing the music myself, and recording it myself, so I still had particular ideas about how I wanted it to sound.

I played the instruments, Mike Simpson did a lot of the turntable scratching stuff. Mike, John and I picked out the samples together from whatever was lying around in the studio. I would write and record a song and one of us would grab a record and find a little something that fitted.

Mike Simpson recalls that it was good for them all to start as equals on a clean page in order to get the ideas flowing:

We just started from scratch with Beck, just the three of us collaborating with a blank slate. It was like a free-for-all; he's a classic songwriter but also a big fan of weird sounds; we had a pop sensibility but at the same time we're into disparate off-sounding shit. Between us we had an insanely eclectic record collection, so we got the vibe going by listening to everything from the obvious old funk and psychedelic rock records to crazy country and really cheesy religious records, not so much for a melodic line but more of an overall sound.

The sessions were basically split into two distinct sections which each gave rise to a distinctly different set of songs. Before he embarked on the Lollapalooza dates he'd been working on a series of songs that were dense, abrasive sound collages. 'Hotwax' was the first one they worked on and other early tracks included 'Novacane', 'High Five' and 'Where It's At'. 'Minus' was also recorded, one of the few songs that Beck had written before he started work with Simpson and King. 'Most of the songs hadn't been written, I went into the studio and built those songs piece by piece,' recounts Beck. Work was initially slow and some of the songs took two weeks each to piece together.

Beck then went out on tour and tried some of these songs live. While doing so, he realised that to balance the album, he'd have to change the writing style for the rest of the sessions on his return. 'After doing those songs live, I decided I wanted to have more melodies. I wanted to have some kind of balance in there.'

He was also disappointed at the response the new tunes received. 'I remember playing these songs at Lollapalooza and nobody cared what I was playing and all the reviews were always awful, so I expected it to be a curiosity, expectations were low.' The break for touring was possibly the major factor that turned the album around: 'We had a long break and it was a good division,' says Beck. On his return the songwriting style and recording process were changed drastically. Instead of working for weeks on one song they sometimes did two in a day and Beck went for songs with a lot more melody.

This second period of recording produced some of the most memorable songs on the album: 'Jack-ass', 'Sissyneck', 'Lord Only Knows' and 'Devils Haircut' were all quickly finished. 'The New Pollution' was written and recorded in one afternoon. 'He had a definite vision,' says John King of Beck's return. 'But he seemed really comfortable masterminding his own songs and at the same time letting go of them to let us do our thing.' Beck was in the midst of a creative high and tried his hand at everything. As King recalls: 'You toss an idea his way. And instead of immediately rejecting it, he'll turn it into something fantastic. He looked in the *Recycler* [a free "buy and sell" newspaper] one day, saw a guy in Santa Monica was selling Indian instruments. Two hours later he came back with a sitar and tamboura. He said, "The guy tuned it up for me and taught me how. Let's record something." '

After months of working on the new songs they were almost there, just the final mix needed some work. 'Mixing it was where the real work was,' recalls Beck. 'Recording it was mayhem, but mixing it we'd just sit there for hours and hours 'til we turned green.'

Although some of the new songs hadn't had overwhelming reviews, one that stood out was 'Where It's At'. Beck, however, had not thought ahead to how the songs would be performed: 'I was never concerned as to how it would sound live. I was embracing the album as a totally different art-form.'

Another tune that would become a live favourite was 'High Five (Rock The Catskills)' which even included Beck's first foray into classical music with a sample of Schubert's 'Unfinished Symphony'. Beck recalls: 'We'd started talking about classical music. We grabbed that off the shelf. Nobody was sure if they liked it, but it ended up staying on there. A lot of things we'd just throw into the soup. A lot of times we'd get rid of it later. I must have had twelve keyboard parts for "Where It's At", but only two of them are in the song. Each song was like that.'

The album was all but complete by the end of 1995. The Dust Brothers kept themselves busy by starting their own label, Nickel Bag, and Mike Simpson took an A&R position with DreamWorks SKG (he helped sign the Eels). They also worked with some more Hanson's (on 'Mmmbop') and tried again to get that elusive Dust Brothers album back on track – after all they had been trying to record it since 1985. 'Something always gets in the way,' laughs Simpson. 'We're really fortunate to have all this work, but I can't wait to set aside some time for ourselves. That's when we'll get really busy.'

With the music side of things finished, Beck had to give his creation a name and decide on a cover. The song 'Lord Only Knows' had originally been called 'Orale', but then fate stepped in. Beck explains: 'Odelay comes from a Mexican slang word, just part of the LA language. I had a song called "Orale" and the engineer mis-spelled it so I thought I'd use the phonetic spelling to describe where I come from culturally. "Odelay" doesn't have an exact meaning but can be used in terms of "Way to go!", "Alright!" or "Right on!" '

'Lord Only Knows' was not the only song to get a name change late on; 'Novacane' was originally called 'Novacane Express', 'Minus' was known as 'Minus (Karaoke Bloodperm)' and on early promo tapes, 'Devils Haircut' was still referred to as 'Electric Music And The Summer People'. Beck had also teased a few journalists with the title of the album, referring to it as both 'Mellow Tinfoil' and 'The Sensuous Casio'.

The Hungarian Sheepdog on the cover also came to be used almost by accident. 'I was flipping through a book of dogs,' Beck remembers. 'I was looking for a dog at the time. I just laughed so much at this ridiculous canine monstrosity being made to jump over this hurdle.' That was the final piece in the puzzle. 'The whole time making it I thought it would be a disaster. I thought it was going to be a beautiful way to go out, a beautiful disaster.' Well, he would soon be proved wrong, but the album release was still six months away.

With his new album complete, Beck took up an invitation to tour as an acoustic opening act for Sonic Youth in Europe. The

Advert for first solo UK gig, March 1996

tour took in several countries and received some major media coverage in the UK with Beck getting some good and bad press. Mostly Beck played a set of 10–12 songs that many of the crowd had never heard before. A couple of songs were usually from *Mellow Gold* but most of the audience had only heard 'Loser' so they spent their time chatting away or shouting for his hit song.

Mark Luffman reported for *Melody Maker* at La Riviera in Madrid that 'Beck doesn't deserve to get away with this. Mediocre songs sung poorly, played worse. What makes Beck think we give a shit?' On the other hand, Kitty Empire, writing about the show at Le Zenith in Paris, could hardly wait for the new album: 'It's impossible to gauge whether the finished product will pack the same punch.' But she loved the show, saying 'The frenzied beatbox leaves the rest of us breathless, phew!' The song 'Mexico' was commonly broken into three parts and scattered throughout the set because 'It's too long to sing in one go' and old favourites like 'Heartland Feeling' and 'No Money, No Honey' were resurrected for the tour. After these dates were over it all went quiet for a couple of months in anticipation of the new album.

The completed masterpiece that was 1996's *Odelay* was astounding. It would, like any new release, immediately get people searching for ways to define and pigeon-hole it and to file it nicely away under a genre of their choosing. But unlike the majority of new releases *Odelay* would defy their attempts at characterisation and maybe even make them think up new categories that only it could fit into. Some of the influences were obvious and plentiful but the way in which the songs had been assembled (sometimes including many styles in one track) was something new and exciting.

Beck was paying his musical dues, but in his own unique way. His early love of the Casio showed up at the end of 'Novacane'; his Mexican heritage again surfaced with a Spanish chorus on 'Hotwax'; early 1980s rap parties were acknowledged on 'Where It's At'; 'Devils Haircut' contained a blues lyric but in a rock setting; country music was updated on 'Sissyneck' and 'Jack-ass', but it still sounded legitimate; and for the first time Beck included a real pop song, 'The New Pollution', which in turn tipped its hat to the Beatles and other sixties bands.

While at first listen the album may have sounded like a bit of a mess, it only went to show that first listens could be deceptive. The danger when adding layer upon layer of sounds is that the producers might overdo it and not know when to say enough is enough. Repeated listens to this album, though, prove that Beck and the Dust Brothers got it right on just about every occasion – and 'High Five' may be the only occasion they overdid it. The jubilation that Beck had talked about including in response to the deaths that he'd had to contend with is evident in the overall feel of the record, even if specific songs might not seem to contain it – 'Ramshackle' and 'Derelict' spring to mind.

Beck's lyrical style had moved on enormously in between *Mellow Gold*'s songs and these new ones. Gone were the seemingly straight-ahead narratives and blue-collar situations – Beck's last job had been over three years ago. His observations were more oblique and even downright confusing. If any lyrical comparisons could be made it would again be to Bob Dylan whose It's All Over Now, Baby Blue' was also sampled on 'Jack-ass'.

The mix of styles and the sometimes odd lyrics combined to give songs that were fresh and inspiring while at the same time containing something that made the listener think that they might just have heard a particular song somewhere before. Somewhere that they couldn't quite put their finger on.

This was 1990s music at its best. It was something that no one else was doing, or had ever done. Of course it soon spawned the wannabes (Bran Van 3000, Cake and 1000 Clowns to name but three) but the fact is that they are just following a formula, Beck's formula. The copycats will always be trailing behind because they don't have Beck's history and musical education to put into play. In the space of one album Beck managed to turn around the people that didn't care much for him after *Mellow Gold* and the Lollapalooza tour of '95. Beck had seen the future but it was taken from the past.

'Ramshackle' provided an odd, acoustic end to the album after all the shenanigans that had gone before it. Was Beck giving a hint about the direction of his next album? He was later to admit openly that 'Diamond Bollocks' was put at the end of 1998's *Mutations* to lead the way on to 1999's *Midnite Vultures*, so was he doing the same here?

Beck's next step was one of his finest moments to date, with the release of a new single, 'Where It's At', in mid-June 1996. This song had been tried out during some of the Lollapalooza dates but the recorded version was amazing. Beck says of the track: 'There's a lot of experimenting going on, but there's also grooves. Without them, this would be a pretty abrasive record. If you took out the keyboard, guitar and bass, there's all this noise and shit – me breathing through these distortion boxes. I sound like some imploding cyber-donkey. That's kinda subversive.'

The refrain of 'Two turntables and a microphone' became a Beck trademark and is mentioned in just about every article written about him ever since. 'It's a tribute to the old house parties,' says Beck. 'I'm not talking about house music – I'm talking about the old-school rap house parties. We're talking two turntables and a microphone.'

The weekend before the single was released, and the album in the US too (the UK had to wait an extra week), Beck was invited by the Beastie Boys' Adam Yauch to play at the Tibetan Freedom Concert in San Francisco's Golden Gate Park. The Saturday saw sets by Pavement, the Foo Fighters, Smashing Pumpkins and the Beastie Boys. Beck appeared on the Sunday, in front of 60,000 along with Bjork, De La Soul, Sonic Youth and the Red Hot Chili Peppers. The concert was filmed and a triple-CD set was later released containing performances from both the 1996 and 1997 shows. After his acoustic set, Beck popped into LIVE 105 for a special edition of *Modern Rock Live* with Adam Yauch. He played three live songs and participated in some lively discussion about the festival and Tibet related issues.

To top off a busy weekend, Beck then relocated to Los Angeles for the *Odelay* release show/party on Monday, 17 June 1996. It took place at Tower Records on Sunset Strip and consisted of Beck playing a short set to a few hundred fans at midnight. CD shelves had been pushed back to allow a regular stage and PA to be set up. He was joined by Justin Meldal-Johnsen on bass and Sonic Youth's Steve Shelley on drums.

Beck was in fine form, taking the stage initially with just a drum machine and guitar. He messed around with the drum machine (as he had at the Tibet show), speeding it up to give the crowd some jungle beats, before slowing it right down, saying that this new style should be called 'Tundra'. He improvised a song called 'John Tesh Blues' and he played 'Asshole' before introducing his two bandmates for 'Fume' and 'Lord Only Knows'. He ended the show with some free-style rapping over a human beatbox volunteer from the crowd and then a version of 'High Five'.

Finally, the waiting was over and the album was in the hands of fans and reviewers alike. The album started modestly (it entered the UK chart at number 18 and slightly higher in the US at number 16) but has now gone on to sell in excess of 3 million copies world-wide.

The reviewers were pretty much unanimous in their praise for the album, a fact that took Beck by surprise. 'I saw a few reviews and was completely floored,' he said. Two of the major US monthly magazines gave the album top marks. *Spin* gave it 10 out of 10 and *Rolling Stone* 5 out of 5, saying '*Odelay* takes Beck's kitchen-sink approach to new extremes while also managing to remain a seamless whole; the songs flow together with intelligence and grace' before ending with the question, 'Could the future of rock 'n' roll be a snot nosed slacker with a bad haircut, an absurdly eclectic record collection, two turntables and a microphone?' *Details* claimed the album was 'Everything you could want from a subterranean blues-sick homey' before giving it 9 out of 10.

In the UK, Beck received one of the few negative reviews from David Stubbs in *Melody Maker*. Stubbs, who may now be looking back and realising that this was one of the most ill-advised reviews of any album ever, said: 'This album, for all its mess and energy, seems debilitated and shot through with all the wasted, lifeless mirthlessness that's afflicted American music for years.' After three-quarters of a page of such comment he ends his monologue of badly chosen negative anti-hype by saying that *Odelay* is 'goofing off its responsibilities to offer us something urgent and inspirational in our lives. I'm bored.' On the other hand, *Q* magazine awarded 4 out of 5, concluding that Beck is 'Possibly the hippest person in the world.'

One theme running through the reviews stuck in Beck's side though: 'In every review that I'd pick up it would say "Manchild Beck". What do I have to do? I've got hair on my chest. I'm 26. I mean, granted I look young. I always take it as a little disrespectful. It's like I'm not to be taken seriously.'

He also had to defend against some comments about the lack of any understandable lyrics. This could be the one valid criticism of the album as a whole. But for Beck, that kind of argument was irrelevant. 'They're meaningful to me, I'll get 3 or 4 subject ideas for a song and just mix them into this tapestry, it becomes a little more dense.' In any case, did everything have to be spelt out for the listener? 'I'm trying to invoke an atmosphere, as opposed to the specific events or specific story.'

Pavement frontman Stephen Malkmus had become a good friend of Beck's and the two had similar approaches to lyric writing. Did the fact that Malkmus sang 'Focus on the quasar in the mist, the Kaiser has a cyst and I'm a blank want-list' make Pavement's 'Stereo' any less of a great song? Probably not, and the same should be said for Beck singing 'Tyin' a noose in the back of my mind' or 'She's alone in the new pollution' on this album.

Bong Load again dealt with the vinyl version of the album, which came with a fold-out poster of the CD sleeve. This was released two months after the CD and tape versions. In the UK the regular 13 tracks were augmented by an extra one – 'Diskobox' and a limited edition run of CDs added another in 'Clock' which was not listed on the packaging.

The advance tapes of the album had been sent out with one sample that had to be removed at the last moment. On 'Sissyneck' there was a sample from a 'Cell Phone Barbie' saying 'Oh cool, let's get together. Oh, right, great. You could get a pizza, with my sister, on Friday,' but Mattel, the toy giant, made some last-minute protests. Beck explains: 'Mattel made us take it off the record. They said if we tried to approximate it in any form, we would be ruined. We thought we may be able to get away with it, but we played it for an 8-year-old, and she immediately shrieked with recognition, screaming, "Cell Phone Barbie! Cell Phone Barbie!" '

Despite the legal pressure the sample can still be heard when the song is played live.

Many people were fooled into thinking that there were hundreds of samples on the album, à la *Paul's Boutique*. Beck admits that if he didn't know, he'd have been fooled too: '*Odelay* sounds like samples, even to me, but there really isn't a whole lot of sampling on the record. The Them sample and a few others were obvious, but mostly it was me playing stuff on instruments. The sampling that's there is along the lines of frosting on a cake that I baked myself.'

One of the unsung guests on the album is the relative unknown Paulo Diaz who plays tablas and saranghi on 'Derelict'. 'Those are all instruments with a craft that takes years to master,' says Beck. 'But they're very interesting just as raw sounds. I'm not trying to cop a Beatles thing; it just comes from a genuine love of the music.'

Other memorable moments on the album include, on 'Ramshackle', jazz legend Charlie Haden playing upright bass below Beck's acoustic strumming and on 'Hotwax' Beck breaks out the Spanish chorus again. 'Yo soy un disco cabrado, yo tengo chicle en mi cerebro' which roughly translates as 'I am a broken record, I have bubblegum in my brain'. 'It's in my contract,' laughs Beck. 'Every album has to have a Spanish chorus. 'Cos that's the formula – that bilingual shit drives 'em crazy. Spanish people don't even know I'm singing in Spanish – that's the sad thing.'

In the many interviews that accompanied the album's release Beck spoke of some of the processes that went into making the whole thing work. Some of the now better-known songs were almost cut:

> There are a few good songs on the album that weren't going to be included because I thought I didn't like them. For instance we completely wrote and recorded 'The New Pollution' in four hours. When we finished, I hated it. There was no way it was going to be on the album. Later, it grew on me as a kind of lightweight tune.
>
> I wanted this album to be the kind of album they made in the 60s, when people experimented with whatever they felt like – folk, country, chamber music, Eastern sounds.

But sometimes Beck had just too many ideas. However, occasionally he found that he could jam them into one song: 'It had been a couple of years so I had a lot of ideas fermenting. That's what "High Five (Rock The Catskills)" is all about – having too many ideas and throwing them together and watching them just kind of explode.'

One oft mentioned instrument that was used in recording the album was the Moog synthesiser. Beck explains: 'I tried to keep the Moog sound to a minimum on the album. It's such a trendy instrument now and can easily be overused. I used the Moog mostly for textures and kept it low in the mix rather than push it up front like "Hey everyone, look at me, I'm playing a Moog!" '

'Devils Haircut' received a lot of attention, with people speculating as to just what Beck was talking about. In interviews, Beck was not very forthcoming about the song's contents; instead he wanted people to make their own mind up:

> I would like to say that everyone should have their own idea of what that song means, from the most obvious – 'Oh, gee, I got a bad haircut', to something incredibly involved and academic.
> For me, I had this idea to write a song based on the Stagger Lee myth.* The chorus is like a blues lyric. You can imagine it being

---

*The 'Stagger Lee' myth is one of the oldest pieces of folklore in American music. Coming from an African-American heritage, the song 'Stack O'Lee Blues' has been alternatively called 'Stackolee' or 'Stagolee' among others. It was famously recorded by Mississippi John Hurt in 1928, but had already been around for about seventy years even then. The song tells of the violent events around a young black man 'Stagolee', culminating in his execution of someone who beats him at craps.

sung to a country-blues guitar riff, 'Got a devil's haircut – in my mind.' And all the images in the song, 'Something's wrong/My mind's fadin'/Everywhere I look there's a devil waitin'', it's a blues song. So that's where I wrote it from. And that's why I get frustrated when people say, 'Oh, that's a bunch of gibberish.' It's the way you perceive it. Maybe people just aren't patient enough to get into it.

'Devils Haircut' was just one of the songs to get a vigorous treatment in the remix room. Noel Gallagher, Mike Simpson, Mickey P and the Dust Brothers combined all had a go at this track. Beck was unsure about some of the remixes attempted but most were eventually released on some format. He says:

There was a bunch of songs that got remixed but none of them were very good. Some of the Mo'wax guys did a track and the Beastie Boys' producer, Mario Caldato Jnr did something too. It was mostly just people I knew, except Tricky, who remixed a track without my knowledge. It sounded like he just turned on this drum machine that was falling apart and left the room while my vocal track was playing somewhere in the background. I think it was meant to be a dis. We're still trying to find Lloyd Price* to get clearance for the samples the Dust Brothers used on the 'Where It's At' remix. It sounds much better than the original version.

At the time of *Odelay*'s release Beck revealed his lack of confidence in its quality, probably down to some of the less than overwhelming reviews for the new material he'd played at Lollapalooza the previous summer. 'Early on with *Odelay* we thought the record was going to bomb, but we just kept at it. I think these days, being successful takes a lot more hard work than it used to.'

Beck also took time out to talk about the many styles employed on *Odelay*:

It's more trying to have a musical language, sort of like a tool box or something. A whole lot of different stuff. I don't know

---

*Lloyd Price had had his finest moments in the 1950s when his brand of New Orleans R&B gave him a slew of Top Ten hits in the US and the occasional one in the UK. He even reworked 'Stagger Lee' and took it to number 1 in the US in 1958.

where it comes from. Music's there, it's everywhere.
Whatever comes out, comes out. I don't really filter it. I don't
pick up a guitar and say 'okay, now I'm going to do riff #27.'
There's something sort of defeating about surrendering to
one style. There's not much room to move around. It's very
narrow. I just feel like I don't want to have any restrictions. If
it's more open-ended like that, then anything can happen.

He could go from describing the Schubert sample as a 'palette
cleanser' to discussing the reaction he received from other
artists about his rapping:

The more hip-hop artists I meet, the more I find they're down
with me. I've never made any effort to put on anything that I'm
not. You know, I don't come from suburbia, so I'm not some
suburban kid puttin' it on. On some levels I relate to it, but I
definitely make it my own and I don't try to imitate it. But I'm
always surprised. I've had people from South Central come up to
me and say 'Oh, man, we're all down with your shit, all the
brothers are rocking your album.' They're pretty open-minded,
most of the hip-hop community, and they're much more aware
than people give them credit for. They're tuned in.

After the *Modern Rock Live* performance Beck appeared on three
other shows in mid-June 1996. On KOME in San Jose he showed
up to play 'Jack-ass' and 'Curses'. On KROQ he did a commentary
on a number of tracks from the album with what can only be
described as an American version of Stuart Hall who found
everything about the interview and album immensely hilarious.

Finally he returned to his spiritual radio home – KCRW's
*Morning Becomes Eclectic* with Chris Douridas. The two talked
about the cover art for *Odelay* and a bit about the family history.
Beck played a few solo tunes as the band wasn't quite assembled
yet and Joey Waronker was in the Caribbean on his honeymoon.
The highlight was an acoustic guitar and harmonica run through
'Jack-ass'.

The official *Odelay* tour kicked off on 27 June 1996 at the
Galaxy in Santa Ana, California. Beck really wanted the whole
deal to be more high-profile than the *Mellow Gold* dates.
He arranged for some elaborate costume changes and

choreographed dance moves. 'I get all my moves from Hong Kong movies, Mexican TV and Arabic TV,' he claimed. 'They have really good moves on Arabic TV, especially on the pop music variety shows.'

As for the costumes, he would appear for the encore in a rhinestone nudie-suit: 'I actually rented those Nudie suits. They cost anywhere from $6,000 to $20,000. I couldn't afford them at the time, so I found a place that rented them. They had two suits that fit me perfectly; they looked like they were made for me. The reference was really more of a country thing.' He also explained the thoughts behind the wearing of them: 'The suit makes me feel kinda feminine, kinda weird. It's shining and silly and I enjoy it. I always fantasised about having one when I was younger. I was very much enamoured of 1950s Country & Western – Hank Snow, Hank Williams – they had amazing suits.' But more often than not the whole 'country' point was missed and all people talked about was the Elvis connection. 'People started to take it as an Elvis thing, so I retired them,' he complained.

He also reshuffled the pack of touring musicians. He added Justin Meldal-Johnsen on bass, Greg 'Smokey' Hormel on guitar and Theo Mondle on keyboards, while retaining Joey Waronker on drums. And he gave them all stage names – Meldal-Johnsen was christened as 'Shotgun', Hormel as 'Smokestack', Waronker became 'Showboat' and Mondle was known as 'Hounddog'.

When asked about the personnel changes he said:

> I've played with four different bands, because I started this whole thing on my own and a band was an afterthought. I finally hipped myself to what I needed from a band, and I hooked up with a great ensemble. And these cats are all riding the same wave. Before, it was like one person was on the beach, another was getting pulled out by a riptide, one was body-surfing and another one was being eaten by eels. I was the lifeguard trying to rescue myself at that point.

Abby Travis had moved on to play for a while with the UK's Britpop icons, Elastica, and Beck seemed to be tired of the revolving-door policy of his band members: 'My last bass player joined Elastica, my last guitar player joined Porno For Pyros, the axeman before him is in the Presidents Of The United States Of America. My band's like a quarantine farm team, we spay and neuter people to go on to other bands.'

Very little was ever known about Theo Mondle except that he played keyboards, was in his forties, was from Bangladesh and smoked a pipe. A little more is known about Justin Meldal-Johnsen. He's not from Bangladesh, and as far as we know he doesn't smoke a pipe. He does sometimes wear tight pink trousers though. He had previously played with the LA band Medicine, appearing on the album *Her Highness* and co-writing one song, 'A Fractured Smile'. After leaving school he worked as a studio production co-ordinator, a position he has filled on several Beck recordings. He also played with Electric Company, Tori Amos, Amnesia and Pet before joining Beck's band.

One of the new members, Greg Hormel had almost become Beck's guitarist in the early spring of 1995 before the Lollapalooza tour. Like Beck, he comes from a musical background. Hormel explains: 'My mother was a ballerina and her grandfather was a classical pianist. My dad played piano, as did his brother – who is the guy who invented spam. My uncle was a jazz pianist/recording pioneer – one of the early multi-track experimenters. He owned a studio called Village Recorders. Steely Dan, The Band and Fleetwood Mac worked there in the 70s. I fell into playing guitar and drums.'

Hormel moved from the West Coast to New York to study as an actor and work as a waiter in the early 1980s but after that didn't work out he returned to Los Angeles in 1984. 'In LA, in 1985, I met Paul Greenstein, who had a western swing band called the Radio Ranch Straight Shooters,' he recounts. It was to change the course of his performing career. 'He asked me to join. We opened for X and the Knitters. We had a 15 year old drummer named Joey Waronker, it was his first band and he was just incredible. He was a neighbour of my parents and I became his friend. He was so young that we couldn't play clubs with him.'

The Radio Ranch Straight Shooters didn't have an explosive recording career. In fact it amounted to just one song, 'The Next Big Thing', on a country compilation called *The Hollywood Round-Up*. They also had a brief appearance on MTV's *The Cutting Edge*.

The following year, with the death of Hollywood Fats, guitarist with local band the Blasters, Bill Bateman asked Hormel to be in the band. Smokey agreed to be the fourth guitarist in the Blasters history and Bateman set about teaching him to play the blues. He played with the band from 1988 until 1992. This tenure was a relatively successful one as Hormel remembers: 'We toured Europe in 1991 and had especially big followings in Italy and Scandinavia.'

After he left the Blasters, he and Joey Waronker formed the Lotus Eaters, an industrious undertaking:

> We were going to do this ambitious thing of playing as an improvising ensemble. We would accompany spoken word artists. We did a few performances and then Joey left with Beck. I auditioned for Beck in 1995, but I was booked for a Bruce Willis tour of Planet Hollywood's. Beck just couldn't make up his mind in time so I just left with Bruce Willis. Beck's song 'Loser' was already a million seller but the Bruce Willis gig was in Jakarta which was a really exciting exotic place that I wanted to see. I think Beck wasn't able to take his music seriously yet. I think he was intimidated by good musicians. He felt like I was a really good musician. At the time I thought he just didn't think I was good enough. It worked out because that tour was a disaster for Beck.

While disaster might be a tad too strong a description of the 1995 tour, Beck was unhappy enough about it to change his touring band for the third time in three years for the *Odelay* dates. Only Joey Waronker survived.

Talking to Hormel, it soon emerges that he and Beck have very similar ideals in the sound and presentation of songs: 'I always loved the feedback thing because I grew up on Hendrix. Beck is surprisingly traditional in his musical mind. He comes from a country blues background. When he was a kid he taught himself to play like Mississippi John Hurt. He listened to a lot of Jimmie Rogers so we have that in common.'

When the two got together for the second time, Beck put Hormel through his paces: 'I wasn't very familiar with the experimental guitar players like Sonic Youth, which Beck was into, but I learned what to play by copying it off the record. Beck likes things a little off and sloppy. On some songs I'll even detune the guitar to get that vibe, approaching it like a non-player.'

The roles were reversed though when it came to some of the choreographed routines on-stage between Hormel, Meldal-Johnsen and Beck: 'It's pretty collaborative. I've been bringing in videos of old soul programs. I had Jackie Wilson and James Brown on Shindig. We would work on that. Beck's a good dancer and he seems to be getting ready to push that further.' The results of these video lessons can be seen in the promo clip to 'The New Pollution' and on-stage during songs like 'Devils Haircut'.

The longest serving member of the ensemble was Joey Waronker, but for such an enterprising drummer he could well have felt snubbed that most of the drum work on *Odelay* had passed him by. This would sometimes spread to the live shows too, as the new album contained many drum samples and effects which would require some taped material to be played in the show. Waronker explains: 'We had all of the things that we thought may need to be looped on separate tracks. We'd start with stuff that I could imitate, and erase it. Then we'd erase stuff that anyone else could imitate, and sometimes we were left with just a click track and a few weird things, so it's as organic as possible. Sometimes we would strip everything away, so we wouldn't have to use a click track at all.'

The overall show became so diverse that, as Waronker says, any musicians playing this material would have to be able to change styles with little or no effort: 'Beck's whole thing is so diverse, so he needs musicians who can go from the hip-hop thing to more poppy stuff, to punk, to folk, to country. All of which he does pretty beautifully. There just aren't that many musicians who can do that. The challenge has just been to do it all and make it sound cool. That's taken a long time.'

Waronker is forgiving when it comes to being left out of the recording process:

The records are really well conceived and made in a certain way, for a reason. And right now, I'm intrigued by watching Beck work because I feel like there's something important going on. I'm not thinking, 'I'm a drummer and I need to express myself.' Which I question from time to time, like, 'Wait a minute. I AM a drummer! I should be in a rock band, playing everything.' I would like to be better represented on an album, but it's sort of a weird time.

Beck's next album would be produced in a more traditional way. *Mutations* was recorded live in the studio with the whole band and little or no studio trickery. Waronker was not totally excluded on *Odelay*, though, as he added drums to two tracks and percussion to three more. To fill in his free time he worked as a session drummer for a number of bands.

If you were to examine the difference closely between the recorded *Odelay* songs and their live counterparts you'd see, or rather hear, that Waronker adds the kind of new things to each song that a machine couldn't do night after night: 'I feel that Beck and I have a really good rapport. As a musician, what I want to achieve with this band is to be able to read minds. I think that's the best way to be. So I put all my energy into trying to figure out what Beck's going for and just trust that I will interpret that and make it better.'

The initial part of the *Odelay* tour saw Beck playing European festivals, sometimes early in the evening with a time slot that only allowed a shortened set. One of these was the Phoenix Festival at Stratford in England and filmed for UK TV. 'It's a very medieval scene here,' Beck laughed. 'Y'know, bodies passed out and refuse and debris all about. Human specimens of all sizes and forms. I can't imagine after four days of this what the derangement of consciousness will be.'

One of the first headlining shows was at Amsterdam's Paradiso Club on 21 July 1996. Here it was witnessed what the rest of the tour would shape up like. The show started out with a triple whammy of 'Fuckin' With My Head', 'Devils Haircut' and 'Novacane'. The set then settled into the rhythm of slow-quiet songs followed by loud-fast songs, before the acoustic interlude that included 'Truckdrivin' Neighbors Downstairs', 'No Money, No Honey', 'Puttin' It Down' and 'Rowboat'.

This skeleton would continue throughout the tour with some refinements. Beck was taking this opportunity in the tour to use

Flyer for gig at start of *Odelay* tour, June 1996

a lot of sea-faring imagery and quotations: 'The beats came forth, surged like a wave and on that crest a rhythm was born,' he said of the album. He was often seen on stage in an old-fashioned sailor's jacket and peaked cap, sometimes smoking a pipe too. He would give monologues along the lines of 'The seafaring aspect is the theme of the tour we're embarking on now. With storm clouds on the rise we will sail headlong, and headstrong, and headless, if need be, towards that destination.'

In August 1996 the tour set sail across the US and Canada. On 20 August, *Mojo* magazine in the UK sent a reporter to write a two-page review of the show in Buffalo: 'He displays the confidence in the power of *Odelay* to kill the curse of "Loser" by trotting out his signature song barely a third of the way into the set. It's an act of dismissal, and it catches the crowd off guard.' However the power of the live show compared to the album was questioned: 'The quartet assembled for this tour do a reasonable job of approximating the patchwork, but they aren't yet capable of providing the dimension that's always missing when studio wizardry hits the road.' It was a criticism that held some water, particularly early in the tour, but one which fell away as the months passed (especially with the addition of DJ Swamp after Christmas).

A permanent record of this part of the tour was captured on 22 August in Toronto when the *OdeBeck* MuchMusic TV special was filmed. Ten songs were recorded, eight of which were from the new album.

1 September 1996 saw a night away from the regular tour as Beck played what started out as an acoustic show at the tiny Maxwell's in Hoboken, New Jersey. In a show for the ages he worked his way through his acoustic back catalogue, taking numerous requests from the audience. Included in the set were an early version of 'Cold Brains', 'Girl Dreams' and 'Painted Eyelids'. Beck took frequent requests on the premise of 'It's got to be something I can play on acoustic guitar. I've never heard of half of those songs!'

After 'One Foot In The Grave' he invited the 'Three 'S's' – Showboat, Stagecoach and Smokestack – on to the stage from the audience, for a band rendition of 'Painted Eyelids'. Money Mark was then added to the fray on keyboards. 'We've been on the road for about two months, three months, six months,' declared Beck. 'We've been on the road for about three decades, but now we're going back in time.' The band gave sterling performances of 'Ramshackle' and 'Rowboat' before a beautiful version of 'Totally Confused' which Beck aptly introduced by saying, 'We've been on the road for about three minutes'.

The evening was rounded off with an amazing medley which included 'Pay No Mind', 'I Get Lonesome', 'Truckdrivin' Neighbors Downstairs', 'Alcohol', 'Cyanide Breath Mint', 'Painted Eyelids' and 'Fuckin' With My Head'. Beck played it solo with just his acoustic guitar and managed to jump between songs and lyrics with consummate ease. Seven minutes later Beck ended it to rapturous applause by declaring 'Man! That wasn't a medley, that was an orgy!'

After the New Jersey show he then hung out in the Big Apple for a week before making his network TV debut on David Letterman's CBS show to perform 'Where It's At'. Two weeks later he was back on the road through the South, reaching home in mid-October.

One new song now becoming a regular in these shows was the then unreleased 'I Wanna Get With You (And Your Sister Debra)', later to be released as simply 'Debra'. This classic 'slo-jam' proved to some that Beck was more of a 'White Prince' than just his size and work-rate indicated: the falsetto tale of his obsession with 'Jenny from JC Penny' and her sister Debra could easily have been written by the Artist Formerly Known As Talented. It had apparently been recorded for *Odelay* but left out at the last minute. It also didn't fit the mood for *Mutations*, but later showed up on *Midnite Vultures*.

These comparisons continued to evolve after *Odelay*, and for good reason. Both artists are (or in Prince's case were) prolific and extremely talented; both are gifted multi-instrumentalists and can work in a variety of different musical environments. But while Prince is too often hemmed into the admittedly brilliant trademark sound of his keyboard-driven rock-pop-funk hybrid, Beck has been able to change his 'sound' easily from album to album – never staying in one musical place long enough for it to become stale. A second difference is Beck's ability to mix sometimes eclectic influences into the body of a single song – possibly one of his most special talents and certainly one which is unique. Prince has also managed this on occasion but Beck has a far wider range of genres at his disposal: on top of the funk, rap, pop and rock that Prince has employed, Beck's list includes blues, country, Mariachi, Latino and folk too. I don't recall hearing too many Prince harmonica solos that can match Beck's 'One Foot In The Grave'!

A reviewer once said that 'nobody has come closer to equalling the imp of the perverse at his 80s peak', but I believe that in another ten years Beck will have proved superior in both variety and quality. When *Midnite Vultures* was released in 1999 though, Beck took a step closer to such comparisons.

Back on the tour, a two-week trip to Japan was followed by another visit to Europe. To hype up the UK dates, *Melody Maker* sent a reporter to Tokyo, where Beck was having a four-night stand, to interview him and review the live show before it hit the UK in December. The hype was also swollen by the

November release of 'Devils Haircut' as a single with a UK-only release of a remix by Oasis songwriter Noel Gallagher who gushed that 'Beck's a hero of mine, hopefully there'll be more collaborations in the future.' Beck however was more reserved in his appreciation of Oasis:

> I haven't really been paying too much attention, but I thought they were good at the MTV awards. The remix came about because my A&R guy had been hanging around with Oasis and he asked Noel if he was down with it, and he was. That was as much as I had to do with it. I felt very honoured by Noel's interest, I would never think that he would have the time to do something like that. I mean I wouldn't have the time to remix one of my own songs, no matter how much I liked it.

As Beck's UK dates approached, the bootleggers of the world united to blaze a trail of live CDs from his European shows. The show at The Cirkus in Stockholm gave rise to the bootleg *Cirkus* – which came with four CD-ROM video tracks from the show too – and Le Bataclan in Paris produced the CD *Loser*, which included a rare live outing for 'Derelict'.

On 9 December 1996 the *Odelay* tour made its UK indoor debut at the Academy in Manchester. In one of the more energetic shows of the tour so far, Beck dedicated 'Thunderpeel' to 'All the Spice Girls and Spice Boys'. Q magazine gave a two-page spread for coverage of the show, concluding that it was 'Stunning'.

'Crowds in Germany or France, say, take a little more time to loosen up,' Beck told Q. 'Here the audience go the full distance. It's very rewarding to have that connection when you're on stage.'

This near hysteria continued the following night at London's Brixton Academy in a show broadcast on BBC Radio 1. The show was supposedly attended by members of Oasis, Pulp, Damon from Blur, Elastica and other members of the Britpop community. All were blown away, but unfortunately not (as some might say) by a leaf-blower, only by the music. This show would end up as a bootleg CD, *Swinging London*.

A hectic six months came to an end with a couple of Christmas radio show concerts for KROQ's *Almost Acoustic*

*Christmas* in Los Angeles and LIVE 105's show at the Cow Palace just outside San Francisco with the Beastie Boys. *Rolling Stone* decided in their year-end issue that 'Beck is rock & roll's man of the year – even if he only looks 12.' This was only one of the many awards bestowed upon Beck at the end of 1996; others included: *Alternative Press* (2nd Best Album), *Melody Maker* (8th in Album Of The Year and 1st in Best Male Artist), *Spin* (Artist Of The Year and Album Of The Year), *Rolling Stone* (Artist Of The Year and Album Of The Year), *Village Voice*'s Pazz & Jop Poll (Album Of The Year) and *NME* (Album Of The Year).

1997 would turn out to be even busier for Beck than the second half of 1996. He opened the year in New York where he made his *Saturday Night Live* debut, playing 'Where It's At' and 'Devils Haircut', and took part in a mini comedy sketch with Kevin Spacey and Michael Palin. He stayed on in New York to play a show at the Roseland club before going home to play two songs on the Radio Free LA benefit on 20 January. He chose Woody Guthrie's 'I Ain't Got No Home In This World Anymore' and the rare 'Don't You Mind People Grinnin' In Your Face'.

The early part of 1997 saw a new addition to the touring line-up: a DJ – something that Beck had never had before. DJ Swamp (he never gives away his name or age in interviews) was born and bred in Cleveland, Ohio. It was here that as a 15 year old he bought a drum machine from Trent Reznor, then a salesman at a Cleveland music store. Swamp reminisces: 'Watching Nine Inch Nails get bigger and bigger, seeing Trent come up, that inspired me. It was like, "Wow, this guy who sold me a drum machine when I was 15 is becoming the biggest rock star in America." I drove that inspiration into DJ-ing, which was something, I would say, nobody was really doing at that time, using that kind of energy towards turntables.'

Swamp brings a rock attitude to his DJ skills and this helped him become the 1996 US DMC Champion: 'The way I DJ, I would say, is more from a rock attitude than a hip-hop attitude. I've always been really conscious of not trying to exploit DJ culture. I give the props where the props are due and follow a motto of "just be yourself".' After his US success he qualified for the DMC/Technics World DJ Mixing Championships in Italy where he came second. Unhappy with his placing he smashed a record in two, removed his T-shirt and scratched 'swamp' into his chest. When asked about this he says calmly but resolutely, 'I don't really want to talk about the contest' and that is the end of that.

He had an album of his own released called *Swamp Breaks* before making a home video of himself mixing and scratching some tracks from *Odelay*. He sent a copy of this to Beck's then tour manager, Ben Cooley, who passed it on to Beck. 'He goes against the grain, tries new stuff,' says Swamp about Beck. 'He's not afraid to experiment. Same kind of thing that I'm into. I'm into all music, whatever. If it's on vinyl I'll scratch it.' A week later Swamp received a call from Beck and was invited to join the tour. He's been there ever since: 'Basically I'm supposed to help recreate live what's done on the recordings. A lot of times we get the samples pressed up on vinyl and rather than triggering it from a sampler, I'll scratch it in from a record. I also add a lot of things that weren't on the original recordings, so that separates it as a live thing.'

Joey Waronker says he loves having Swamp in the band to bounce sounds off: 'It's a little like playing with a drum machine, because of the sounds and because he's coming from such a hip-hop background. He's used to turntables and drum machines. It's a whole different feel, so I find myself adjusting and playing more drum machine-type beats. But he also plays a lot of weird sounds, atmospheric stuff, a lot like a percussionist.'

The difference was certainly felt in songs like 'Sissyneck', 'Jack-ass' and 'Where It's At' which all had new life breathed into them after Swamp came on board. Waronker concurs: 'I think at first, Swamp really didn't consider himself a musician, and now he's realising that he has this rhythmic gift and a sense of dynamics. It's a bizarre thing because it's such a new instrument and I think he's used to the concept of just being a DJ or playing loops. But in this band he's being forced to be more of a percussionist.'

The tour got back into full flow in early February 1997 and Beck mixed things up, not only with the addition of DJ Swamp, but by adding some old favourites and new songs to the set on a nightly basis. For instance he added 'Alcohol' and 'Canceled

Check' in Vancouver, a new version of 'Ozzy' and 'Don't You Mind People Grinnin' In Your Face' in Oregon; 'Sleeping Bag' and 'Fume' were also plucked from obscurity. The tour took a temporary break after the show in Las Vegas on 21 February as Beck had the task of flying to New York for the Grammy Awards.

Beck had previously been nominated for a Grammy for Best Male Rock Vocal Performance for 'Loser'. This time around he actually walked away with two, 'Best Alternative Music Performance' for *Odelay* and 'Best Male Rock Vocal Performance' for 'Where It's At'. He didn't even know that he'd been nominated: 'Nobody called, because everyone assumed I knew. For about a day, I remember walking around not knowing. Someone in line at the supermarket congratulated me. I said "Thanks. That's nice." It was a little surreal but it feels good to be validated, to be acknowledged. For a while, I was one of the scapegoats for the whole slacker-Generation X thing. Somehow the perception changed, and I'm grateful.'

Of course an event like the Grammies brings out millions of photographers from all manner of magazines, not just ones dedicated to music. In the aftermath of the awards, photos of Beck were splashed across a myriad of publications. One shot that was used many times over showed him backstage with David Campbell. Beck had rarely spoken of his father over the previous few years and the fact that he had changed his name to Hansen hinted at some kind of falling out between the two. If this was the case then the two must have had a reconciliation as the photos suggested and the fact that Campbell was working on some of Beck's B-sides adding some string arrangements backed this up. Campbell also spoke about his son publicly for the first time: 'It's not surprising at all that he got to create all this brilliant work. The thing that is amazing to me is that he's managed to bring so much of the world into what he does. It's not your average stuff.'

Beck commented on his dad: 'He always had an ear for the weirder harmonies. That's probably what he passed to me.' It also became apparent that Campbell was working as hard as ever, as he joked: 'I'm a monk. You have these spurts where you go to do a session, you're active and social. But the rest of the time you're there with a blank computer screen. Eight-

and 12-hour days just sitting there writing, just on my own with no interplay, feedback . . . anything.'

This hard work was paying off though. At one point during 1997 Campbell had arrangements on 11 of the USA's 200 best-selling albums, including the soundtracks to *Armageddon* and *City of Angels*, and collaborations with Hole and the Goo Goo Dolls.

As well as being photographed at the awards with his father, Beck was accompanied to the event by his long-time girlfriend, Leigh Limon, of whom he commented: 'I've been living with my girlfriend for about 5 years now. She comes along with me for the good tours, because you need a little stability to deal with all the chaos. There's a lot of patience required. Obviously, occasionally she pulls out her AK and puts a few caps in my ass, but mainly it's good, we're a team. It's not some kind of tug-of-war.'

Leigh is almost a female equivalent of Beck, slightly shorter, slight of frame and stylish in dress-sense. Normally reticent about their relationship, Beck was prepared to say this: 'She knew me when I was a penniless nothing. She liked me long before anybody else did. And that's important. I mean, like any relationship, you have your work, and you talk about work, and if something's fucked up, your partner will comfort you.'

As usual Beck was surprised even to be considered, let alone win: 'I never had any expectations of winning a Grammy,' he said. 'It wasn't something I was set on, that I was hoping and praying and starving for. But it is incredible!' He felt that the loosening of the Grammies towards accepting more innovative artists certainly worked in his favour: 'I do think they're opening the umbrella a little bit to include stuff that isn't standard Grammy fare. On the other hand, I think in my case, I'm somewhat of a traditionalist to them; I'm working from a place that maybe someone who came up on folk rock or singer/songwriter stuff can relate to. Maybe that's it.'

On the back of these honours he jetted over to London for an appearance on the *TFI Friday* TV show, where he played his new single 'The New Pollution' and was filmed dropping a rubber chicken into a giant cooking pot (don't ask why). While in the UK he took advantage of his schedule to play a couple of shows, at London's Kilburn National and Cardiff's University before flying back to Florida to continue the tour.

He continued on the road through March and April 1997 (picking up a BRIT Award as 'Best International Male' along the way – beating Bryan Adams, Prince, Babyface and Robert Miles) before ending this North American leg of the tour on 25 April at the Universal Amphitheatre in LA.

It had been a busy, but exciting few months and he took time out to talk about how things were progressing:

> So much air-travel can be like an endurance test. Your fingernails disappear pretty quickly and so do the fingernails of your soul. Tom Waits reckons that if you fly somewhere it takes a couple of days for your soul to catch up, and I know what he means. If there had been an evolutionary build-up to aeroplanes, it would be different. We could have done with at least another thousand years of hang-gliding. But I'm into refining the show as much as possible, so I guess it's cool.

He also commented on the people that were coming to see his shows. 'An incredible cross-section of people come to our shows, like total dreadlocked, spacerocker guys, White Zombie-lookin' dudes, Korean businessmen, little teenybopper kids and old blues fans – it's pretty sick.'

If sickness was to be judged on this criterion, it would only get sicker as Beck flew into the UK for his longest-ever tour there in early May. Before he got down to business he stopped by Jools Holland's *Later* show to record three live songs – 'Devils Haircut', 'Jack-ass' and 'Sissyneck'. The last of these was released as a single to tie in with these dates. The following week was spent playing in Manchester, Birmingham, London, Nottingham, Glasgow and Newcastle.

After a few more US dates he then played a surprise acoustic set in Los Angeles on 12 June 1997. The occasion was the premiere of his friend Steve Hanft's film, *Kill The Moonlight*. Beck played 'Leave Me On The Moon', one of his contributions to the soundtrack, 'Rowboat' and covers of 'Waitin' For A Train' and The Doors' 'Light My Fire'. After a short break, his next show was a big one, the Glastonbury Festival in England.

As is typical for the Glastonbury Festival, the fields at the site

intro
thunderpeel
novakane
new pollution
hotwakks
derelikt
minus
sissynekk
feather in yr. kap
rowboat/lonesome
jakkass
where it's @
devil's hairkut
swampsolo
high-five

Set list from Nottingham gig, May 1997

were deep in mud when Beck arrived for his set on the opening Friday of the festival. On a main stage bill headlined by the Prodigy, he had to follow Phish, Echo and The Bunnymen, Terrorvision and The Levellers. The last of these bands had received a severe pelting of mud bombs during their set and Beck was fearing the worst before going on stage. As it turned out he needn't have worried because after a few early shots the crowd got into his set to such an extent that by *One Foot In The Grave* the whole site was clapping along.

The show was broadcast in part by the BBC and reviewed by Andrew Male the next day in the *Glastonbury Daily* which was distributed every day at the festival:

### THE LOSER TAKES IT ALL / BECK, PYRAMID STAGE, Friday 27th
The mud clods lie peppered around the main stage, testament to both a standard performance by the Levellers and the fact that a poor show at Glastonbury '97 will no longer be tolerated.

Backstage, Beck is understandably wary, changing out of plastic burgundy safari jacket into a more sensible lilac windcheater. Initially this seems like a wise move, for as the diminutive heart-throb American and his geek wrecking crew take the stage, a considerable volley of dirt hits the flooring. However, halfway into the robotic breakbeat suave of third song 'Novocane', the sod lobbing suddenly stops and, miraculously, everyone in the Glastonbury Festival appears to be jumping up and down.

It isn't surprising – the guy is a human dynamo, throwing bizarre body-popping shapes and yelping guttural squawks like a more manic version of Steve Martin in 'the Jerk'.

Seeing this sudden shamanic power, the young lad swifts into call and response hip-hop mode, yelling 'all the freaks over there! Give it another 15 per cent!' With the 60s breakbeat loungecore of the 'New Pollution' and the dreamy grunge singalong of 'Loser' it seems like Beck can do no wrong, even when he tries.

Despite Beck swifting into the decidedly non festival slow-jam that is 'Debra' everyone is still going insane, causing him to break down in tears in mock emulation of a young, white James Brown. Soon the whole band are mock weeping and Beck is slamming into the lunatic voguing of 'Sissyneck'. This is, without a doubt, proper entertainment. After a spookily slowed down version of 'Devils Haircut' the band exit, only to return with Mr Hansen bedecked in a ridiculously impractical rhinestone cowboy attire jumping and hollering through the dirty party funk of 'High Five'.

Wild, filthy and downright stupid, Beck's was the perfect Glastonbury performance. And the rhinestone suit remained perfectly clean. Rare praise indeed.

Rumour has it that Beck chose to unwind after his Glastonbury gig by stripping down to his vest and underwear and having a bounce on a space hopper. Beats the hell out of a martini . . .

More festival appearances followed before he hooked up with the HORDE ('Horizons of Rock Developing Everywhere') Tour for the middle third of its schedule alongside Neil Young, Kula Shaker, Blues Traveller, Ben Folds Five, Morphine and several other B and C list Indie bands. After several years through the 1990s as a poor man's Lollapalooza this touring festival finally bit the dust in 1999.

Another high-profile appearance ensued at the Bizarre Festival in Cologne, Germany. The show was broadcast on German TV's *Rockpalast* show and turned up on the *Pulling Up Roots* bootleg CD. He then flew back to the UK (for about the hundredth time in twelve months or so it seemed) to play at the V97 festivals in Leeds and Chelmsford.

The first week in September 1997 saw the release of the final single from *Odelay* – 'Jack-ass'. The CD featured several versions of the title song plus 'Burro', a Mariachi version of it sung in Spanish. This week also saw a trio of TV appearances. The first was a return to David Letterman's *Late Show* to perform 'Jack-ass', then he stopped by the MTV Music Video Awards to perform 'The New Pollution' and pick up several awards for 'Devils Haircut' and 'The New Pollution'. The final stop was at the 'Sessions at West 54th' studios for a live taping of 15 songs. 'This'll be our last show until next year,' declared Beck. He was almost right. The band performed at the Farm Aid benefit in Illinois, including a duet between Beck and Willie Nelson on 'Peach Pickin' Time In Georgia'.

As 1997 drew to a close, 'Deadweight' was released as a single from the soundtrack to *A Life Less Ordinary*, the Ewen McGregor/Cameron Diaz film. Beck took the opportunity to display another style that he had mastered – the Brazilian bossa nova sound of early 1970s South American counter-culture exponents like Os Mutantes. 'It's one of those things where you hear it and it instantly attacks your immune system 'til you're completely at its mercy,' says Beck for this style. 'It has all the elements – the groove, the beats and an insane melodic flair.' Beck would continue this genre experiment with 'Tropicalia' on *Mutations*.

Beck's fashion sense was honoured by VH-1 in the autumn of 1997 as he picked up the 'VH-1 1997 Fashion Awards: Most Fashionable Artist' award and gave one of the most entertaining acceptance speeches of all time:

Thank you VH-1 people for embracing my appearance
and bestowing this award,

certifying the apparel and accoutrements
which have clothed me this past season as measuring up
to the stringent standards upheld in this arena of style.
With gratitude I claim this award and dedicate it to those who
have aided me in breaking the fashion barrier:
namely Leigh Limon for her impeccable guidance
whether I am attired in uniform or civilian clothes,
buckskins or bloomers,
kimonos or cat socks,
lingerie or long johns;
cerements or tube socks,
espadrilles or chapeau,
loin cloth or poncho,
skivvies or layette;
gabardine or crash helmet,
dashiki or camisole,
sombrero or tutu;
jackboots or skullcap,
codpiece or ascot,
Members Only jacket or Yashmac
– whether naked or arrayed in the finest livery
I will strive to be worthy of this shimmering ideal
and scrape brute yet fondly on this zig-zag rampart.
Thank you.

The last two live performances of the year were totally out of character with the shows that he'd been putting out for the past 18 months. Both took place at LA's El Rey Theater. The first was a country show featuring country classics like the 'Redball' and 'Peach Pickin' Time In Georgia' mixed in with Beck's own country compositions like 'Rowboat' and 'Sissyneck'. He also took the opportunity to play a selection of as-yet-unrecorded songs, some old, some new. These comprised 'Cold Brains', 'Static' and 'Dead Melodies', all of which would be released within twelve months.

The final show was a surprise as Beck played as the opening act for Bob Dylan. A somewhat ironic combination considering the comparisons that had been made between the two over the years. Again a few future *Mutations* songs were included: 'Cold Brains',

'Sing It Again', 'Dead Melodies' and 'Nobody's Fault But My Own'.

It is perhaps not an exaggeration to say that for Beck and his fellow musicians, producing and touring *Odelay* had grown into a mission in itself, to open people's ears to a kind of music that didn't follow laid-down rules and formulas. As Beck put it: '*Odelay* was not an easy record to put over to people. It took two and a half years touring, and most of that time we were trying to convince people every night that they actually like this music. Not following a formula or jumping on a current sound is definitely a bit more work.'

Others again sought to make a few bucks from Beck's music. It was reported that the Miller Brewing Company would pay $10,000 for 15 seconds of 'Where It's At'. The offer was allegedly later upped to $100,000 but Beck still said no.

To see in the New Year he headed to Sydney, Australia, for some well-earned rest and relaxation.

At least that's what everyone thought.

# 6 Mutations

A LTHOUGH BECK FANS could be forgiven for not realising at the time, the impact made by a small press conference in the southern US on Halloween 1997 would be a lasting one on Beck's band.

A hand-picked gathering of journalists were invited to the R.E.M. office in Athens, Georgia for some startling news. R.E.M. drummer Bill Berry would be leaving the band with immediate effect. The stressful *Monster* tour during 1995 had seen health problems affect Mike Mills, Michael Stipe and, most seriously, Bill Berry himself. Berry had been rushed to hospital while on tour in Switzerland and was operated on for a double aneurysm. Several months of concerts were cancelled but eventually the tour was completed and all of the band returned to full health.

After releasing *New Adventures In Hi-Fi* in 1996 (an album that had been mostly recorded on the road) the band reconvened to start work on their next studio album (which was eventually released as *Up* in 1998) and Berry dropped the bombshell that he was to retire from music completely. The band decided to carry on as a three-piece with the plan that additional musicians would come in to help with recording and touring duties as and when required.

Eventually it emerged that the drummer of their choice would be Joey Waronker and this would later cause conflicts as touring schedules clashed, leading to rumours of Waronker quitting Beck's band to join the Athenians full-time. By the end of 1999 these rumours would become true, but these troubles were away on the far horizon as Christmas 1997 saw Beck's star rise even higher. In the UK, *Melody Maker* named him as the

Best Solo Artist of the year, an award that was duplicated by the *NME* in their Brat Awards. In the US, *Spin* readers voted Beck as both Best Artist and Best Male Singer.

The most outlandish award, however, came from *Select* magazine: they put Beck at the number one position of the '100 Most Important People In the World' (the Dust Brothers made it in to number 29 on the list). The December 1997 issue carrying this feature also came with a free, three-track Beck CD which contained 'Clock', 'The Little Drum Machine Boy' and 'Totally Confused'. Beck spoke about the repetitive tag of being labelled the 'Coolest Man In The World':

> I'm not really conscious of people saying that. If anything, I'd be the first to refute it. I'm willing to make a fool of myself, if that defines coolness. I really don't give much of a shit about how I'm perceived or about trying to fit into the matrix of a market place or tastes. I just go on a more instinctual level. Cool is something that's foreign to me. Maybe I should move to London, then I can soak up the glory. In LA, like in any hometown, you're rejected. I'll go to a club here and it's 'oh yeah, that guy.' I've been around forever. These are people who saw me playing coffee houses, smashing my phone machine on-stage, doing some random act in a local club – they take me for granted.

He also fought off connections with the Hansons of 'MmmBop' fame. This was getting more difficult as it became more widely known that they too had worked with the Dust Brothers. In typical Beck fashion he quashed the connections by saying 'I ain't riding around in the seat of that Hansonmobile. I'm not even in the side-car. I'm in the tow truck.'

The long rest that Beck promised he'd take after the end of the *Odelay* tour just didn't happen. Despite being on the road for the best part of two years, Beck didn't show any signs of slowing up. To start the new year Beck made some more changes to his touring personnel. The major adjustment was the keyboard swap of Theo Mondle with Roger Manning Jnr, not to be confused with the Roger Manning (not junior) from the anti-folk scene ten years earlier. Manning Jnr had been a member of various bands before landing a job with Beck.

He'd started out with the pretty much unheard of Beatnik

Beatch, who put out one album (*At The Zula Pool*) in 1987, before forming the critically acclaimed Jellyfish. Jellyfish may have dressed like psychedelic Sixties throwbacks but their music was not in keeping with their image. Sounding more like Badfinger crossed with Squeeze they put out two great albums in the early 1990s, *Bellybutton* and *Spilt Milk*. As Jellyfish dissolved, Manning joined forces with co-writer Eric Dover to form Imperial Drag. After a self-titled debut album they set off on tour with an opening slot for Alanis Morissette and then their own headlining tour of the US and Canada.

When Imperial Drag ended, Manning again bounced back, this time with the formation of the Moog Cookbook with Brian Kehew. This duo put out two hilarious albums of instrumental cover versions, not surprisingly heavy on the old synthesiser. A highlight of the Cookbook's short-lived career was when they played an in-store show in Los Angeles which Michael Jackson inadvertently walked into, whereupon Jacko was given a copy of the duo's CD. Manning Jnr also toured with Justin Meldal-Johnsen as guests of French band Air.

After a few weeks of rehearsing with Beck and band, Manning Jnr was given the stagename of Shotgun and bundled down under with the rest of the crew which included two more additions. The horn players, known as the Brass Menagerie, were invited to join the band full time after some one-off guest appearances. David Brown was a long-time friend of Beck and had played with the likes of The Creatures (Siouxsie Sioux's side-project turned full-time band) and Ben Lee (the 20-year-old Australian wonder-kid signed to the Beastie Boys' Grand Royal label); while David Ralickie met Beck through mutual friend Mike Bioto and had played with Natalie Merchant (ex-lead singer with indie-folksters 10,000 Maniacs) as well as with David Brown's band Brazzaville.

Beck and band played a New Year's Eve show on the beach at the Bondi Pavilion in Sydney before a hectic few days began. Two days at the amusingly titled Mudslinger Festival in Perth on 3 and 4 January 1998 were followed by a 1,400 mile hop to Adelaide for a show on the 6th then another 400 miles for shows in Melbourne on the 8th and 9th. The next four days were spent travelling up the eastern Australian coast with dates in Sydney and Brisbane before flying down to New Zealand for a further two dates. After playing at the Wellington Town Hall on 18 January, the *Odelay* tour was effectively over after twenty long months. Beck and the band were due a well earned rest and of course they were going to make the best of it . . . weren't they?

But Beck for one was in no mood for resting: 'It had been three years since I recorded *Odelay*. I was restless and anxious to get back in the studio and do something creative. I had just gotten off my tour, and I knew I wanted to work with Nigel [Godrich], who happened to be in L.A. on somebody else's album.'

In fact Nigel Godrich ran into Beck's management at an Oasis gig in Los Angeles. He takes up the story:

> The next day I got a phone call. Basically Beck wanted to do a record with his band because he'd never really recorded with them, and he was trying to figure out who to get as a producer. And they'd sort of mentioned my name, but they thought that it was a bit of a long shot to fly me out just to see if it would work. But then because I was in town, it was like it was all meant to happen. So basically I had a meeting with Beck, went round to his house and had a cup of tea and we sat and talked about stuff.

'We got together,' confirms Beck. 'But he had to fly back to England after a week. So it had to be very spontaneous and quick.'

It was planned that Godrich would spend a weekend in the studio with Beck to see how the pair got along, then if it seemed OK he would return a month later and they'd have two weeks to do the album. Beck had a good-sized collection of songs to choose for this project; many of which, like 'Dead Melodies' and 'Cold Brains', pre-dated *Odelay*.

He decided to let Leigh have a say in which tracks would be recorded for the album: 'In the weeks before the recording sessions, I played a number of older songs out of my notebook for my girlfriend and let her decide which I should record. And she sort of said, "I like that one . . . and that one . . ." Other than that, I had no big plan.'

Godrich used his time before going into the studio to get up to speed with Beck's previous work. He admits that previously he had a few misconceptions about Beck: 'He's very quiet and studied and obviously very intelligent. For some reason, I actually thought he'd be a bit more aggressive and loud. All the kind of rap stuff on *Odelay* is pretty aggressive, but he's quite cerebral. I guess as well my exposure to him previous to that had only been the singles off *Odelay*. So I went away and listened to the whole of *Odelay* and thought, "Bloody hell, what does he want me to do?" '

For the trial studio sessions they booked the weekend of 21/22 February at the semi-legendary Oceanway Studio (formerly the United Studio) on Sunset Boulevard. It had been the scene of the recording of 1970s hits like *Bridge Over Troubled Water* and numerous songs by the Beach Boys and Mamas & Papas. Nigel Godrich was ecstatic about the choice of studio, as he enthused to *Melody Maker*: 'Oceanway is the best studio I've ever worked in. The desk was the forerunner to this American desk called an API – it was called a Delcon and it was all gold. Basically it's a great studio because the gear – as is the fashion – is fairly vintage, but everything works, it's maintained really well. It had quite a small control room and a very, very big live area with a separation booth which we put the drums in.'

The two songs to be attempted over the weekend were 'Cold Brains' which was pencilled in to be the album's opener and 'Electric Music And The Summer People', the old B-side which was due to be overhauled as a surf-style song. Godrich saw both tracks as complicated in their own way and thought that they would be a good indication of how things could work out.

' "Cold Brains" was the first thing we recorded and we sort of finished that in a day,' says Godrich. At the end if you listen carefully, you can hear Beck say to Godrich, 'Yeah, I like that a lot.'

'Then we did a version of "Electric Music And The Summer People",' Godrich enthuses, 'this surfing version. It was amazing, just completely over the top. It had this sitar solo and four keyboard solos and huge timpanis and stuff. It didn't make it onto the album, but it would be the kind of song that would be good for a film soundtrack. After that we kind of looked at each other and he said, "Hey, we could do an album in two weeks." '

The song did in fact make it on to the Japanese version of the album and on to some CD EPs that came out the following year. So the scene was set. Godrich had to return to England briefly but flew back out again in March 1998 where sessions were due to start on the 19th. 'I like the challenge, I like working with limitations,' said Beck about the time constraints, but in this case he didn't have much choice in the matter.

The band had only a short time to prepare too. A few nights of rehearsals at Beck's house and the songs they'd previously played live were all they had to go on. Right up until the last day the song choices were still being refined. Beck was working on the lyrics into the early hours of 19 March in order to have them ready for when they all met at the studio. In the time between the initial weekend and the start of recording proper he had decided to go for more of the traditional singer-songwriter acoustic-type songs in the vein of 'Cold Brains'.

Godrich remembers the instructions that Beck gave on returning to the studio: 'He had come back, saying "Listen, we're gonna do a lot more songs like 'Cold Brains'. Not so freaky like 'Electric Music'." '

'Static' was the first song to be completed. While Godrich was mixing it, Beck went back out into the studio and began rehearsing the next song, 'O Maria', with the band. As only about an hour per mix was taken, they got into a rhythm of record, mix/rehearse and then repeat. According to Godrich, to get the vaudeville feel for 'O Maria' they had to 'fuck up the piano sound' as they only had a grand piano. It was recorded live with the horns and Roger Manning Jnr's Hammond organ dubbed afterwards. 'Originally the trombone solo – which is a particular favourite of mine,' recalls Godrich, 'was at the end and we did a bit of a hash edit that you can hear quite clearly to stick it in the middle.'

By the first Saturday the band was playing so well that more and more of the material was just recorded live. As Godrich recollects:

'Sing It Again' was completely live apart from one guitar overdub. The vocal is live as well. We got a really good set-up going and he sang it really well. We did about four takes and I edited between three of them, I think. The drums were separated but the rest of them were literally in the same room, just all looking at each other. You get bits of sound bleeding between tracks, but it adds something . . . you get a sense that the people are in the same room. And he was singing so well, I could just sort of edit the track around his vocal. Even the guitar solo is live.

One of the oldest songs attempted was 'Canceled Check' which Beck had written in Japan in 1994. Again they wanted to affect the piano's sound, Godrich says, this time to get a honky-tonk feel: 'We detuned the grand piano and stuck paper clips on the hammers to get that honky-tonk sound. Because most of the notes have three strings, if you detune one of them slightly flat, you get that kind of chorusy sound. So that was a pretty straightforward backing track and then everything was overdubbed on top.'

Beck remembers this song well. The car crash of an ending to the song was memorable indeed:

We'd been recording very, very late into the night and I couldn't figure out how to end the song – it needed some finality to it. We had this room full of percussion, piles and boxes of percussion, which we'd rented for the record and there was all kinds of crazy Brazilian stuff, stuff that looked like medical tools and handmade African stuff and timpani drums and all this stuff we hadn't got around to using and it was costing a lot of money so I felt it was going to waste. So in a moment of inspiration or idiocy, I don't know which, we all just descended into the room, we had the engineer turn on all the mics and myself and the other musicians went crashing through the room. It was just a melee of 3am madness and it was a nice release, it was therapeutic, there were people flying through the air, and I think there were people bleeding actually.

The only single to come from the album, 'Tropicalia', recalled the Latin feel of 'Deadweight'. Beck said it was the middle part of a Latin trilogy that he was working on. It managed to cause some problems for the band but they eventually pulled it off memorably. It was the first time that Justin Meldal-Johnsen had played an upright bass and Smokey Hormel struggled with, but overcame, the quica. Godrich laughs: 'We got all the percussion going by getting everybody to do four sets of percussion with all the shakers and stuff lying around the studio. The vocal was difficult because it was so fast and the breakdown was something that they figured out while rehearsing. So many things were happening so quickly.'

The chaos that was building up in the studio, and the fast turnaround time for songs, was starting to cause some problems. While still working on 'Tropicalia', David Campbell arrived to arrange the strings for 'We Live Again' and with just an hour before the string players arrived they had still not recorded the backing track for them to play with. Nigel Godrich got them to bash one out in double time and save the day from even more confusion: 'In half an hour we knocked out the backing track to that – harpsichord, upright bass and acoustic and stuff. I had this Scott Walker album that I was listening to and I was just sort of thinking about the reverb they had on it, how amazingly over the top it is . . . so that's why "We Live Again" has got so much reverb on it.'

With the first week almost over, they still managed to complete another song. 'Dead Melodies' took just three hours from start to finish, with Joey Waronker playing on an improvised drumkit including an ash tray and a petrol can. 'It was definitely that children-let-loose-in-an-expensive-recording-studio vibe,' says Godrich. 'It was slightly different for each song, but I ended up thinking "Wow, this must be the way they used to make records." '

It became apparent that a theme was starting to appear: decay, death, failing relationships, misery. As Back said later:

> It's sort of a poetical crutch. It's easier to write about things that are falling apart than things that are beautiful and perfect. That's the nature of creation; as soon as something is perfected and realised, it's immediately decaying and falling apart. That's part of the process, the first rule of the universe. But sure, a lot of these songs are blues songs, so I tend to look into that landscape. Maybe some of the lyrics are bleak, some of them are a comment on vacuousness – y'know, Disneyland is as much a wasteland as Death Valley is.

But in his own way he did put some humour in there:

> Some of them are funny, too. There's a humour to 'Cold Brains'. I'm talking about a leg in the gravel and abandoned hearses and stuff like that. They're kind of silly, pseudo-romantic imagery. I guess they're more serious songs and I'd saved up enough of them to have an album's worth. Over time I think certain songs start grouping together, they pair off. It's like a party: you can invite a lot of different people, but certain people are just gonna stick to themselves.

The last weekend of recording saw some of the more pivotal songs put to tape – as it was tape they were using, a contrast to both Beck's and Nigel Godrich's works prior to this album. In this case Godrich saw the use of tape as good in the overall scheme of getting the album done: 'I use computers and stuff as well, but with bands I prefer to cut the tape. With computers, you leave yourself with too many options because you can undo everything. When you cut your tape, you're cutting it and you have to make a decision and you can move forwards. Being able to go back five steps is not necessarily a good thing for the creative process, y'know.'

'Nobody's Fault But My Own' is one of the album's most complex-sounding songs but the way Nigel Godrich tells it, it was a piece of cake:

> Beck had an idea for an Indian song and he got in touch with these two guys who were Indian music freaks from some university. We cut that whole backing track pretty much live which is why it's got that vibe. It's a big bass drum and Beck playing guitar and the Indian stuff . . . it all kind of went down together and then we overdubbed more Indian stuff. I think that's probably the best song because it's kind of got two choruses.

The sitar on the song comes and goes throughout the track, something that Beck discussed the following November:

> I've used a sitar on almost every record I've done. To me it's just a wonderful sound, it's evocative. A lot of times I try to get the guitar to get that sound of a sitar, that undulating drone. I tend to record a song with instruments playing all the way through,

on every track, and then at the end of the day it's a matter of subtracting, taking things away, and opening up the space. That's why you only hear things in bits and pieces, it's tastier that way.

The next song was even tastier and, even by Nigel Godrich's standards, a really accomplished piece of work. 'Diamond Bollocks' was totally out of keeping with the rest of the album. Its inclusion was in doubt right until the end, then added as a bonus track in the US although it was listed as a regular track elsewhere in the world. At one point it was going to be the second song. 'It would have been like, get the listener all settled down and comfortable, then this would come along and get them in a headlock!' laughs Beck. The song was the only one actually written in the studio, as Nigel Godrich explains:

Beck had an idea that we wanted to do a bit of a rock opus. It was almost like, y'know, throw an idea into the machinery and see what comes out. We did four different sections of music with the intention of splicing them together. One of them turned out really cool, so we ended up making it longer and turning it into the verse. I spliced it and copied it and copied it again, so it's almost like a loop, but not quite. The beginning section is like a pastiche French thing with a harpsichord and then the second section was like a spy thing and then there was the acid rock section. Then he just wrote a melody over the top of it, but that one took nearly three days.

'Bottle Of Blues' was a straight-ahead bumping bluesy track, completed in half a day. It summed up the approach to this album in its straightforwardness, as Beck says:

There wasn't a lot of technology involved. Just a simple tape machine. With these songs I just didn't need to get bogged down in any technology, I'd written them on piano and guitar, they were more reflective. One of the reasons that I wanted to go back to this more traditional approach was that there are limitations with technology; there are so many possibilities, you get caught up in the possibilities, you can lose track of the moment.

Godrich recalls the genesis of 'Lazy Flies': '[It] was one that we started on the night before I had to leave. We worked until five in the morning and that was just a double-tracked acoustic played to a percussion shaker thing that Joey was doing and then he put the drums on afterwards. We carried on working on it the next day, but we were so tired by the time he did the vocal.'

The very last track was 'Runners Dial Zero', a strange title that Godrich explained to the *NME*: 'It's what came over the PA when the girl at the reception wanted one of the runners to do something. You'd just hear "Runners dial zero . . ." all the time and he didn't have a title for this last song, so that became it. It's a beautiful track, and basically we just got a fucked-up vocal sound and a fucked-up piano sound. I actually left before that was mixed, my cab turned up to take me to the airport.'

Beck also remembers the hurried goodbyes: 'I was doing vocals at the end and we had to run out in the rain and put him in a towncar and send him on his way.' The wonder-producer had run his body into the ground with the marathon two weeks but enjoyed the different approach to the album:

> We were trying to keep the momentum going because that was the thing that everyone was getting off on. I remember him saying that it was like having a party and not having to do the washing up, because you mix as you go and everything's finished. Usually you have your freak-out recording bit and then you have to tidy up at the end. We were digging the fact that it was all going very quickly and we were having to make the decisions as we went along.

Beck later told KROQ: 'They had to slow the record down, because I made it so fast that it was at a frequency nobody could hear. This is a fruitful time in my younger life,' he continued. 'I feel like I've got a lot of work to do.'

Godrich, meanwhile, could leave the studio knowing that by the end of the millennium he had worked on some of the 1990s' best albums: Radiohead's *OK Computer*, R.E.M.'s *Up*, Pavement's *Terror Twilight* and Beck's *Mutations*.

To get ready for some upcoming European dates Beck played a one-night stand at the Galaxy Theater in Santa Ana. The show included 'Tropicalia', 'Cold Brains', 'Diamond Bollocks', 'Nobody's Fault But My Own' and 'Electric Music And The Summer

People' – all from the album, which was surprising considering that Beck had said he wouldn't be touring with *Mutations*.

One of the first European shows should have been the Universe 98 festival in the UK. Beck's name stood out from a mainly dance orientated roster of acts and it was to have been his only UK appearance of the year. Then, merely weeks before the event, it was cancelled due to poor ticket sales and Beck was left without a UK date.

After the Universe 98 debacle, Beck might have been forgiven for thinking that someone was trying to tell him that a UK performance during 1998 was not a good idea. As it happened, the UK phenomenon of the past year had been The Verve and they were due to play a homecoming gig on 24 May, the same day that Universe 98 had been pencilled in. The show, hyped in the UK weeklies as *the* musical event of the year, was to be at Haigh Hall, a stately home on a hillside overlooking Wigan – The Verve's hometown. Adding to the hype would be a live BBC radio broadcast and delayed TV transmission later that night. The only problem was that as of April, no other acts had been finalised. In the wake of the Universe 98 disappointment, Beck was therefore soon lined up to support The Verve along with John Martyn and DJ Shadow.

After playing in Denmark the previous day, Beck arrived in Lancashire to a grey overcast sky and the prospect of having to win over 35,000 mainly male fans who had probably heard little or none of his music apart from 'Loser' or maybe 'Where It's At'. As it happened he went down a storm, while debuting 'Diamond Bollocks' and 'Nobody's Fault But My Own' to the audience. He then flew to Portugal for one show in Lisbon. This was filmed and shown in part on MTV Europe.

Back in the US, ten large outdoor venue dates were played. All contained mainly *Odelay* material, 'Deadweight', 'Loser' and a sprinkling of *Mutations* songs. All of the songs debuted at Santa Ana in May were played along the way, but no new ones and never all of them on the same night. Fans would have to wait until the next year for some full *Mutations* shows.

As the summer progressed, reports began to emerge that the original plan of Bong Load handling the release of the album was changing and the release date was pushed back from June to November. Beck explains:

Bong Load were gonna put it out in June and it was all going ahead. We had it mastered, all the artwork was done, and then I was about to go over to Europe to do these shows in May, when Geffen called and said, 'Y'know, we'd really like to put this out, we really like this record.' I thought it would be too mellow for them: it wasn't even an album that I planned on performing live, that contributed much to where I'm going in a bigger musical sense. It's nothing like the next record I was working on. So I was a little bit surprised. I thought people would gravitate towards it and discover on their own. Anyway, they really wanted it and they ended up buying it.

Although it wasn't clear at the time, this change would later cause numerous problems between Geffen, Bong Load and Beck, and it would also, perhaps inevitably, lead to a much higher profile for the album when it was finally released. Beck, however, is dismissive of the whole business:

Bong Load could've put it out if they wanted to. They got a shitload of money, so it worked out for everybody. It doesn't matter to me, I record my albums and mix them, and I send them to the record company. To me the whole debate is absurd, I mean, is the music good or is it bad? I don't get hung up on the personality who made the song. I don't care the way somebody's dressed or who they slept with.

The final deal was the same as it had been for his previous Geffen albums. Geffen would release the CD and cassette while Bong Load would handle the vinyl.

August saw an appearance in Japan at the Mt. Fuji Festival and the taping and filming of a couple of interviews that would later be circulated as the Electronic Press Kit for the forthcoming album. The album was eventually released three months after originally planned. Bong Load put out the vinyl with a free 7" single containing 'Diamond Bollocks' and 'Runners Dial Zero' as they didn't fit on the 12" record. German and Japanese versions of the CD also carried extra tracks, but all would later be available on various CD singles.

The thing that may strike you initially when you listen to *Mutations* and compare it to Beck's previous output is his vocals. Clearly much more effort was put into the recording of his vocals than before and the product is impressive. A criticism of *Odelay* could have been that the vocals were a little flat and unfeeling. The *Mutations* songs needed an authentic delivery to match the songs' hauntingly understated production, and that's what Beck managed to give them.

This delightfull collection of songs is low-key as opposed to lo-fi as on his previous acoustic effort, *One Foot In The Grave*, and that is down to the twin factors of Nigel Godrich and the quality of the studio used. Godrich gives a much rounder production than on *One Foot . . .* but also the songs are much stronger, with a greater emotional depth. While casual observers were surprised that there weren't samples and beats all over the place, pre-Geffen fans wouldn't have been so shocked by the content, only maybe by the polish and the delivery of the songs. Full of mournful yearning, Beck conjures up atmospheres reminiscent of *White Album*-era Beatles in places.

Beck's lyrical scene-setting is also more accomplished than any of his previous work and the fact that the lyrics were printed and presented with the album backs up the theory that he was more confident with the words on this album than ever before. Of course no Beck album would be complete without some silliness and Beck manages to leave some song-intro speech and comments as tracks fade out, while the 'Canceled Check' ending is a glorious, masterful piece of noise.

This record sounds like the band are playing live in one room, quite an achievement for his first attempt at really recording with them. An even bigger achievement is actually pulling off such an album at this stage in his career. What other major artist would try to do an album like this, especially after the success of *Odelay?*

'I was gonna put it out as this low-key affair,' stated Beck, 'but it just grew into what it is now.' What it had grown into was an eagerly awaited album that was reviewed all over the place. Almost every UK newspaper carried a review of it. At the time of *Odelay* most of them wouldn't have given him the time of day. In the US, *Spin* gave *Mutations* 8 out of 10 while *Raygun* said it was 'A delicious reminder that we can count on Beck to give us something worth listening to more than once.'

The UK press was almost unanimous in its praise for the

change in direction. *Uncut* awarded 5 out of 5, saying 'This could be Beck's masterpiece.' The *NME* gave 8 out of 10 and reckoned 'Yet as Beck's ancient voice becomes all the more intimate, the mischievous angel takes a turn for the worse, tapping into a timeless mythology of melancholy', while in *Mojo* Jim Irvin declared that 'If he can keep these parallel strands going he'll soon be pop's most important practitioner.' *Melody Maker* simply said that it was 'A quiet album of considerable scope and a pleasure from start to finish.'

In *Select*, however, John Harris gave 3 out of 5 but raised a whole host of questions; Who is Beck? What does he do? Where does he go? What is he like? Even on this more 'personal' album these were not questions that could be answered directly by listening to the music. Similar questions were raised in the *NME* where Beck answered some of them at least. 'Knowing about where I went, what time I went to bed and who I did this with and that with,' he responded. 'That style of confessional songwriting – you don't really know the person. You know the mannerisms and their habits. Who the person is, I think, is what inhabits their dreams. So the imagery in the songs is probably more me, or the essence of who I am.'

The *NME* tried to delve further but while he didn't ignore questions Beck didn't give too much away. 'I'm probably locked up in my thoughts a lot of the time,' he said. 'Although my friends and girlfriend are pretty good at occupying me with chores and barbecues and errands – lots of day-to-day things. But left to my own devices I can get pretty lost.' Did he try to guard his privacy? 'No, I wouldn't say so. I don't live in a bank, I'm not locked away in a safe.'

As was becoming tradition, Beck played a session for KCRW shortly after the release of the album. This time it was his longest stay at the station, lasting for almost an hour, and the full band was also in attendance. Starting with 'Cold Brains' they ran through seven *Mutations* tracks and added 'Debra' and a teasing preview of 'Hollywood. Freaks' at the end.

Describing the new album as 'My take on the evolution of songcraft', Beck took part in many interviews around this time, despite the original plan just to let the album slip out without any fuss or fanfare. 'This album is more of a parenthetical addition to the equation, it's not the big bottom line' was a quote Beck used time after time. 'Basically, I went into the studio with no preconceived ideas, and we recorded and mixed the whole album in 14 days. My goal was to make a timeless record, not a record for the Nineties, not country music with a Nineties electronic sauce all over it either, because that has already become something of a cliché.'

The album, with all its lyrics of social decay, death and withered relationships, entered the *Billboard* chart at number 13. It was Beck's highest chart entry. As the New Year of 1999 came around many magazines had Beck on the cover and some detailed interviews inside. Beck spoke of the overall mood on *Mutations*:

> I've always wanted to make a homogenous, coherent album. So this time, I really wanted to make a subdued record with one beautiful mood. Also, that way, I've finally made a record that my girlfriend likes to listen to, because she didn't like my other records. And I like my girlfriend, so it's about time I made some music for her. She chose me when I was penniless and unknown, and that makes her about the most important person in my life. I just felt I should scale that down and let the music take centre stage again. Not that I'm going to be straight and super-serious; I'm perfectly willing to be the clown. I would get bored otherwise. And I do think it's important to weave a sense of humour through the music, while retaining some modicum of dignity.

Around the time of *Mutations* Beck mentioned Leigh in a few more interviews than normal. The two had been living in Pasadena but moved back to Silverlake in late 1998 claiming that the Pasadena house was too big for the two of them.

Beck's songwriting style and methods were also put under the microscope:

> I think my lyrics are sometimes concocted in a backwards manner. I wrote a song recently about all these catalogues that come in the mail, I wrote this ridiculous song. Then a few days later I came back and wrote, with the same melody and all, I wrote about some born again town that I was reading about. Then I wrote another one about a bunch of weight-lifters and

then I just merged the three together and they become all these elements just distilled into this tune.

He also took part in some conversations that were 'deep and meaningful, man'. He was constantly asked about his place in musical history and how he has taken elements of musical traditions, updated them and turned them into something new. These were often linked into some millennial connection about how things will musically progress in the next century, as if in some way it'll all suddenly be different:

> I don't like to think in terms of decades of micro-era. I think this whole century is one continuous contemporary musical moment. It's all relevant. Son House is still relevant. Edith Piaf is still relevant. And the Damned are still relevant. It's all from the same banquet table. That said, there is a style of production from the 60s and 70s that really excites me. They were bringing in all kinds of instruments, a little fuzz guitar mixed in with some baroque music. I don't find that kitschy, I find it cool and contemporary. Maybe it's idealistic to think you can use all of music to get an idea across, but actually I think it's just compositional. All the sounds that have gone before out there are your orchestra, and you have to figure out the parts for them.

And he told the *NME*:

> I don't know if there's a word in English for what the nature of the universe is. There's a whole lot of words, I think there is an absurdity. The whole thing is a dance y'know, it's silly and then it's dumb; it's the same circle. It's the same snake eating its tail to find out what its ass tastes like. Just when I think I've broken through to the next place in my life, I realise I'm doing the same things I was doing when I was 12, or when I was 19. You think you're gonna evolve into something else, and in a way do, but on another level you never learn anything.

1999 was to see what he had learnt. He spent a large part of it working on his next album with some new guests and managed to play a few shows too. The new album would be shrouded in secrecy as famous names came and went from his Silverlake home – Johnny Marr, Beth Orton and Kool Keith among them. As anticipation for his 'official' *Odelay* follow-up mounted, he became the centre of numerous lawsuits between Bong Load, Geffen and himself.

The last year of the century would prove to be an interesting one for Beck, to say the least.

# 7 Mixed Bizness

A T THE CENTURY'S END Beck found himself in turbulent waters. Not only was he working on a new album, planning a mini-tour and making TV appearances, but he would, later in the year, be involved with a trio of lawsuits, lose two of his band and have his debut tape *Golden Feelings* reissued as a CD without his consent. And he would also release a blockbuster of an album and set off on a world tour.

In January 1999, Beck opened what would be a busy, and controversial, six months in New York City. First he popped back to his old haunt, *Saturday Night Live*, for a quick nationwide showcase of 'Nobody's Fault But My Own' and 'Tropicalia'. The following night, 10 January, he played a long-awaited show at the Town Hall, an off-Broadway gem of a theatre. The show was seen as such an event that British magazines *Mojo* and *Q* had reviewers in the audience as did the *Hollywood Reporter* and *New York Times* among others.

In contrast to the shows that he'd played in December, this one was much more *Mutations*-based. After a shaky start of 'Cold Brains', 'Bottle of Blues' and 'Sing It Again', the full band shifted into gear for a memorable acoustic evening. 'We only had a day to rehearse,' Beck offered as an explanation for the slow start, and it had been almost a year since the band had recorded the album so some slack was given. The show really took off after Beck played a solo slot, mid-set, including the rarely played cover of Mississippi John Hurt's 'He's A Mighty Good Leader' and the old blues standard 'Stagolee'. The set then swerved through a phalanx of genres including western, blues and Latino before ending the show with 'Jack-ass'.

This week also saw the release of the soundtrack to *The Hi Lo Country*, a film starring Woody Harrelson and Patricia Arquette, which featured the Beck–Willie Nelson duet of Floyd Tillman's 'Drivin' Nails In My Coffin'. The Thursday after the New York show should have seen Beck play again, this time in Las Vegas. However, Joey Waronker had suddenly fallen ill with pneumonia and Beck cancelled the show rather than bring in another drummer and re-scheduled the gig for May, just after the planned Japanese tour in April. The band split their separate ways and Beck headed home to Los Angeles for a well-earned break.

But the man wouldn't lie down and the next month was equally busy. After a one-off show with English electro-folkster Beth Orton* and Jon Brion,† he did manage some studio time and supposedly put down some tracks with Orton and rapper Kool Keith.‡ He also recorded two new songs, 'Diamond In The Sleaze' and 'One Of These Days' – both would be released in the coming months.

The end of the month saw Beck in an awards frenzy. He showed up at the Grammies to present the Record Of The Year award and also at the Rock The Vote ceremony to present an award to Neil Young. If that wasn't enough he then picked up an award of his own with another BRIT for 'Best International Male Solo Artist'. Although he wasn't in London to collect the prize, a short film was played of Beck jogging through a finishing line tape and celebrating with the award.

Beck's next public outing was on 21 March 1999 when he played an after-show party following the Oscars at the House Of Blues in Los Angeles. The show included a cover of Eddy Grant's 'Electric Avenue' and a new song, 'Jockin' My Mercedes'. The show was broadcast live over the Internet for those who weren't lucky enough to be among the audience of 1,200.

---

*Beth Orton is England's foremost 'electro-folkster' and released her second critically acclaimed album in March 1999. She plays simple folk tunes and sometimes throws some trippy beats into the mix too – obviously something that Beck could relate to. She is also friends with Beck's video collaborator Steven Hanft and he directed her 'Best Bit' video.

†Jon Brion is the former 'Til Tuesday guitarist – the band that previously featured Aimee Mann and released three albums between 1985 and 1988 on Epic.

‡Kool Keith, aka Dr Octagon, is a rapper with a difference. He's the world's most famous Black Elvis, going as far as gluing a black plastic 'Elvis-wig' to his head.

*Mutations* had sold very well in Japan and Beck decided to play a small series of shows there for his Japanese faithful. Starting off with two nights in Tokyo, most dates consisted of a heavily *Mutations*-based set with a few 'hits' thrown in for good measure. Disposable cameras were given out to members of the crowd and the results were later displayed at the official Beck website. After a few provincial dates the band returned for two more shows in Tokyo. The whole thing was over in ten days. To coincide with the tour a new Japanese-only single was released, 'Nobody's Fault But My Own', and came with the two new songs from earlier in the year, 'Diamond In The Sleaze' and 'One Of These Days' – which had also been played at a couple of the shows.

To break up the long journey home the entourage stopped off for a show in Hawaii. It was played to a predominantly military crowd and included more upbeat and *Odelay* material than the Japanese shows. Mid-set Beck left the stage while the rest of the band introduced themselves as 'Rainbow Warrior' and did a version of 'Pass The Dutchie'.

Following on from the Japanese dates Beck found himself in an unusual situation – the middle of a series of law suits and counter-suits. The legal wranglings reached back over a year to the recording of *Mutations*. Beck had originally intended it to be for Bong Load, but after hearing it Geffen executives paid a fee to the independent label for the rights. Matters were further complicated as, during 1998, Geffen's parent company, Polygram, was purchased by Universal. Beck had been in the midst of negotiating a new royalty rate on his contract when the Geffen representatives lost their jobs as part of the Universal take-over. Beck was allegedly not happy with the new representatives. The combination of these two events eventually led to Beck's decision to want out of the whole mess.

On 23 April it was reported that Beck informed both Geffen and Bong Load that he was no longer required to fulfil the obligations of his contract. He cited the 'California Seven Year Rule' (California Labor Code Section 2855), a statute that states that personal service contracts can only run for seven years. Therefore, under that ruling, his contract would cease at the end of 1999. This law has been invoked before by Metallica and others, but never challenged in a court of law by the record company.

The following Monday, 26 April, both labels filed individual lawsuits against him in the California Superior Court, asking the court to enforce the contracts and to determine damages against Beck. Geffen's suit alleged that Beck approached them in order to renegotiate his contract in May 1998 even though it still had over 18 months to run. They claimed that he owed them a further four albums.

A few weeks later, on 10 May, Beck filed counter-suits. The lawsuit against Geffen alleged copyright infringement by the label for releasing *Mutations* and also alleged that Beck was owed his advance and royalties for *Mutations* which at the time of the suit had sold well over 400,000 copies. The suit further stated that Beck found himself working with a different set of record company employees 'who apparently decided to place improper exploitation of Beck's work above contractual and copyright obligations'. The lawsuit against Bong Load sought $500,000 in damages as well as release from his contract.

In the midst of all this courtroom drama, Beck managed to get out and play four more dates. To begin with, 6 May saw the rescheduled show from January hit Las Vegas. The tiny Tiffany Theater, inside the Tropicana Hotel & Casino, played host to Beck and band in a dinner theatre setting. The assembled 'Beck freaks' were arranged in cabaret style booths which the band clearly found amusing.

'Well, we feel real safe,' smirked Justin Meldal-Johnsen.

'We normally get Visigoths gnawing on each other's thighs,' cracked Beck. 'This cafeteria thing is . . . nice.'

A mainly *Odelay* set was interspersed with 'Tropicalia', 'Girl Dreams' and Musical Youth's 'Pass The Dutchie'. DJ Swamp was in full effect and after his solo the band returned in wild costumes (Beck wore a cape, Justin Meldal-Johnsen a pink vest and tight pink trousers while Joey Waronker had a heavy metal wig perched on his nonce) for an even wilder charge through 'Electric Avenue' and 'Devils Haircut'. It was quite a sight to behold.

Two days later the whole caboodle had relocated across the Mojave desert for a weekend homestand in Los Angeles. It had been two years since Beck had last played in his hometown and the anticipation was at fever pitch. The venue was the Wiltern Theater, an art deco beauty, the interior of which could pass for an inside-out version of the Chrysler Building. The first night was filmed for future broadcast on the TV network HBO and was heavy on *Mutations* material.

After being greeted on-stage by shrieking reminiscent of the Beatles in about 1964, the band put on about as good an acoustic-rock show as you could hope to see anywhere. Nine *Mutations* songs got an airing and were impeccably played by all. The normal band was present along with two extra string players, a sitar player and Jay Dee Maness on lap-steel. The new song 'One Of These Days' sounded better than the recorded version and Beck dipped into his back catalogue to come up with an unexpected rendition of 'Lampshade'.

He prefaced this with a hilarious ten-minute story about how he broke his collarbone at a New Year's Eve party and then later rebroke it falling out of a bunkbed when he was awoken by a screaming cat at his bedside. He finally brought the house down with a funked-up 'Debra' and a chaotic 'Devils Haircut'. The latter saw widespread instrument destruction, Roger Manning standing on the piano with a keyboard between his legs while flapping his trademark cape in a vain attempt to fly, and Beck being piggy-backed off stage by Justin Meldal-Johnsen.

After the show, Beck looked back at the gig in a kind of haze. 'I took some caffeine tablets just before the show because I was so tired,' he explained, 'but now I don't remember too much about it, the first half anyway. It seemed like everything was going at 80 miles an hour but in slow motion.'

The following night it was more of the same although 'Canceled Check', 'Sleeping Bag' and 'Diamond Bollocks' found their way into the set. That, as Beck said himself, was 'the beginning and the end of the *Mutations* tour'. A week later he played at a Sony Playstation launch party, putting on a show similar to the Vegas extravaganza of earlier in the month, but mainly consisting of *Odelay* material.

One major point that the Vegas and LA shows highlighted

was Beck's distinct two-pronged attack on modern music. While in Vegas he was the flamboyant showman with all the beats, good-time tomfoolery and manic sound assaults, two days later in LA he was the serious, traditionally based musician playing a laid-back set and chatting with the audience. The fact that he is simultaneously carrying these two halves of his personality forward is pretty amazing. If he carries it on, it will be even more of an accomplishment as most artists would be happy to master just one or other of the facets of this almost schizophrenic performer.

As the last summer of the millennium reached its mid-point, the official Beck website gave fans the chance to see the recording of the next album via weekly video updates. The five minute clips were directed by Bart Lipton and invariably concentrated on the comings and goings at the Dust Brothers' Silverlake studio. The release date for the album was now tentatively pencilled in as November 1999, lawsuits permitting. That would be the earliest that Beck fans could expect anything new from Beck either recorded or live as Joey Waronker was on tour with R.E.M. until October.

In the meantime Beck had given plenty of hints as to the direction of his 'official' follow-up to *Odelay* and no doubt some red herrings too. 'It will be positively artificial,' he claimed. 'It's going to be like one of those "Best of the 90s" party discs. The 90s ain't over yet. Give me another year, because I'm getting ready to drop some party jams. The first part of the decade you weren't allowed to party; it was the introspective half of the 90s. Now we've got to make up for lost time.'

He also waxed lyrical about the future of his work and the copycats that he was 'inspiring' (though he didn't mention Bran Van 3000 and 1000 Clowns by name):

I was a little disappointed no one followed Marilyn Manson's lead. I guess they will soon. There's always this two-year gap before the copycats come out. But the point is not to look like Marilyn Manson after there is a Marilyn Manson. And the point is not to sound like Nirvana or imitate the Beastie Boys or try to be the Beatles again. It's more about raising the stakes. It seems like the great bands were always upping the ante a little bit and doing their own thing. Every time a band raises the ceiling a little bit, there's a little more air for all of us. More room to go up.

The first week of July saw Beck make a couple of live guest appearances. First he joined Brazilian legend Caetano Veloso in Los Angeles for a few songs where Veloso also played an instrumental version of 'Tropicalia'. Four nights later he was on stage again as he borrowed Beth Orton's guitar at the El Rey Theater to play a last-minute guest support role under the name 'Silverlake Menza'. He strummed his way through four *Mutations* tracks – 'Cold Brains', 'Lazy Flies', 'Tropicalia' and 'Nobody's Fault But My Own'.

Behind the scenes, July marked the end of the recording of *Midnite Vultures* and the beginning of its mixing. It had all been kept pretty quiet, but now it was revealed that Beck had been planning the album for a long time. He'd actually started work on the official *Odelay* follow-up way back in January 1998, before the sessions for *Mutations*, but had shelved the project after a computer intervened.

'I tried to start the record before *Mutations* but the computer destroyed one of the songs, so I took that as a sign,' sighed Beck. This hard-drive crash left him looking at 'the huge mountain I had to climb', so he had meandered off to record *Mutations* instead. He'd spent the first seven months of 1999 recording a large number of songs from which he would select twelve for inclusion.

Most of the album had been recorded at Beck's Silverlake home and co-produced by Mickey Petralia, a long-time LA DJ, engineer and club promoter, with help from occasional Beck guitarist, Tony Hoffer. Some sessions had taken place at the Dust Brothers' PCP Labs studio although only two of the finished tracks actually made it on to the album. After over a year in the studio the mixing gradually gathered pace until by late August Beck had completed over 30 tracks, with the final six weeks taken up with 18-hour working days:

This record is a two year project that we crammed into one year. It easily could have taken another year if we'd done it in a civilised manner, if we hadn't completely surrendered our lives.

It was an awful lot to bite off. I knew how much work it took to make *Odelay* and I knew that the level of production and programming I wanted on the new album would be immensely time-consuming. It turned out to be that and then some.

Indeed; if you thought the production and layering on *Odelay* had been intensive then you hadn't heard nothin' yet. 'Sometimes we'd spend 16 hours on 4 seconds of music. I figured this was a chance to get that deep,' says Beck. The co-producing duo of Petralia and Hoffer spent time creating and editing the beats for programming by using a computer and a 'techno map' which allowed them to give Beck multi-layered grooves to work with. It wasn't all computer created however. All of the touring band appeared at some point or other and Beck got them to play with a free spirit as they had on *Mutations* tracks like 'Diamond Bollocks'.

'It was really exuberant, and we all got wild,' says Justin Meldal-Johnsen. 'Everything was rendered in a really passionate way, and often the tracks were built from the mistakes we made.'

While the finishing touches were being applied to the packaging and other technicalities, a whole set of spanners was thrown into the works. First an unauthorised reissue of Beck's debut tape, *Golden Feelings*, came out as a CD and then the longest surviving member of Beck's band, Joey Waronker, announced that he'd be leaving the fold. To cap things off it then emerged that Smokey Hormel would also be saying adios.

Sonic Enemy, the original *Golden Feelings* label, had supposedly gone under in 1995, but by the autumn of 1999 rumours were emerging of their resurrection. By September it was possible to buy one of 1,000 first-pressing CDs of the original album. The problem was that Beck had not been consulted about the re-release as Beck's management team member Shuana O'Brien explained: 'It came out without our knowing.' The problem was further complicated as the album was not considered to be bootleg nor was it thought to be a legitimate release. In the end it seems as though nothing will happen and Sonic Enemy will continue to press and sell copies.

The second dilemma, though more serious, was perhaps more predictable. Joey Waronker spent much of 1999 playing with R.E.M. and although he did return to add his playing skills to five songs on *Midnite Vultures*, it became apparent that his heart now lay elsewhere. He decided that he wanted to do some production work of his own and the conflicts of playing on two bands, that would both require his services in 2000, were too much to take on. As Waronker puts it:

It's not about leaving one band to join another. I've been asked to participate with R.E.M. for events scheduled for next year. Plans for their next album are already on the blackboard. I have this sense I'll still be involved with Beck, even if it's just to help break in the next musician, I'm really lucky to have worked with him for six years. I know that in fifteen years, Beck will be right where R.E.M. is now. He has that in his heart.

R.E.M.'s manager Bertis Downs pointed out that Waronker isn't 'joining' R.E.M., but that, for now, he is 'the right drummer' for the band. R.E.M. themselves had always maintained that Bill Berry would never be replaced in their line-up. It's possible that Hormel's and Waronker's appearances at the Coachella Festival will be their last gig with Beck.

As October progressed, things stepped up a gear as news about the new album began to leak out. First it was that the title would indeed be *Midnite Vultures*, then the track-listing was released and then advance copies of the new single, 'Sexx Laws', began to circulate. Beck himself was busy shooting a video for the single and warming up for his appearance at the Coachella Festival in Indio, California. After an appearance at the food court of the UCSB Student Center in Santa Barbara, 6 October, he rushed up to Fresno for another show at the Satellite Student Union on the 7th. The following weekend saw his Coachella set which included the new songs 'Debra', 'Mixed Bizness', 'Sexx Laws' and 'Pressure Zone'.

By mid-October the anticipation was at fever pitch and Beck played host to the world's media in New York to speak about the album:

I've had the luxury of being underestimated. In a way, I think this is the first time that people will be expecting more than I'll probably be able to give. *Odelay* surprised a lot of people who had written me off. And *Mutations* surprised some other people because they assumed it was all cut-and-paste, a very artificial smoke-and-mirrors type of sound. I don't know what this album will mean to people.

It's true that a lot was expected, and probably to a degree he was always going to be fighting a losing battle, but the album was pretty close to meeting the expectations of its quality. The content, however, possibly threw people off a little as it was something of a re-invention of Beck's public image. He'd never been quite so rude.

Prince comparisons were inevitable once the album was out but Beck had given an indirect hint earlier in the year when he said, half seriously but also with neat irony:

I'm sure the next record I do will annoy a lot of people. It's not finished yet, but I'm sure it's not for everybody. It's like *The White Album* and *The Black Album* arm wrestling. I think it'll eventually become 'The Beige Album', but I hope it doesn't become too beige, because I think of beige as the colour of complete resignation and conformity. Maybe it'll be 'The Fuchsia Album'.

When asked to sum up the record at the time of its release he simply said, 'This album is sexcapades in the biosphere. A lot of music was inspired by the R&B world. People like Silk.' The question was: what the heck was this going to sound like? The answer is quite simple. It sounded stunning.

The album opens with something that Beck hasn't used to open an album before – horns (the Brass Menagerie have parts on four of the album's tracks). 'Sexx Laws' sets the lyrical mood for the album, if not the musical tone. 'Can't you hear those cavalry drums/Hi-jacking your equilibrium,' Beck sings, as if to tell the listener what is going on. 'Brief encounters in Mercedes Benz/Wearing Hepatitis contact lens/Bed and breakfast and away weekends.' This is Beck at his most lustful. He'd used the chorus from this song in concerts for the past couple of years, often falling to one knee, preacher-like, to scream 'I wanna defy the logic of all sex laws.'

The album then proceeds to explain just how he'd like to achieve that goal. 'Nicotine & Gravy' continues the theme, and raises the stakes too, as he promises that 'I'll feed you fruit that don't exist/I'll leave graffiti where you've never been kissed.' To some, this may be a Prince-by-numbers track but listen to it again and you get all manner of mood changes within one song. Admittedly the opening (and lyric) isn't a thousand miles away from Prince, circa 'Controversy' or 'Purple Rain', but the many twists and turns take in an operatic bridge section, some aggressive strings (including David Campbell on viola) and for the first time on a Beck album, some scratching from DJ Swamp. As the song comes to an end, a distinctly Eastern rhythm comes into play and carries the song to its conclusion. You can easily understand why these songs took hours and hours to come up with just a few seconds of music as the depth of sound and attention to detail are amazing.

'Mixed Bizness' is one of the album's highlights and sounds as though it came straight from a mid-70s funky Blaxploitation soundtrack. The call and response chorus again recalls Prince and while the whole band appears on the track, Tony Hoffer adds the wah-wah guitar. For 'Get Real Paid' Beck mixes in some weird synthesiser trickery with what could be an unreleased Kraftwerk demo and what sounds like a robotic, arcade machine vocal observing that 'We like the boys in the bullet-proof vests/We like the girls with the cellophane chests' – at least with lyrics like these, fans could rest assured that some things never change.

Beck had been saying for the best part of a year that he was being influenced by R.Kelly and all the R&B radio stations in LA. 'Hollywood Freaks' is the most obvious product of this:

> I love listening to the beat stations, Power 106 and all that. It's always been over the top, the super R&B shit which is so slick, but I'm addicted to it. It's so evil, but so unbelievable, the production, the slickness and the commerciality. You can plug right into that culture by hearing those songs, the sexuality. Last year, when Montell Jordan came out, it was like, 'What the hell is this?' He's singing gangbanger lyrics, but it's sort of lightweight R&B singing. It's kind of twisted that way.

Beck's take on this was originally known as 'Jockin' My Mercedes' when he played it at a show in February.

'Peaches & Cream' continued the recurring themes of sex and

food. 'We're on the good ship ménage à trois,' crows Beck. 'You make a garbage man scream.' This sly melodic seduction bumps and grinds its way to another mid-song reinvention as the Arroyo Tabernacle Men's Chorale requests that the object of Beck's desire 'Keep your lamplight trimmed and burning'.

'Milk & Honey' is the hardest rocking song on the album and recalls Lynyrd Skynyrd via The Black Crowes, with Johnny Marr* on guitar. Of course, being Beck, he couldn't just let this be a straightforward arena-rock song. The mid-section becomes a kind of disco strut (which Cameo could have been in on) with horrible 80s disco-drums and laser-beam sound effects before Beck goes all husky and whispers, 'I can smell the VD in the club tonight' and a woman bizarrely asks, 'Excuse me please, can you tell me how to get to the Soviet Embassy?'

The most out-of-place track on the album is also one of the best ones. 'Beautiful Way' is the track on which Beth Orton adds her talents to back up Beck's vocals. The song is a beautifully tender, country-tinged ballad that would have fitted well on *Mutations*. The lust of the earlier tracks is nowhere to be heard as some gorgeous pedal steel swirls about the chorus. To end the album is the fairly well-known, to Beck concertgoers at least, 'Debra'. A staple of the live set since the middle of 1996, this is the track that Beck just had to include. The recorded version is a little more refined than the live one but it brings the album to a nice close, the gentle horns evoking a late-night atmosphere as the album is put to bed. But of course sleep is the last thing on Beck's mind. 'You got a thing that I just got to get with/And you know what we're gonna do,' calls out Beck in his best falsetto.

So the Great White Hope for the twenty-first century didn't let anyone down despite the high expectations that were set for him. He managed to add new styles of songwriting to his repertoire and reached back to some early 1980s electro-funk inspirations to add to his new-found love of R&B. In the tour that would follow Beck would surely be spreading his 'lurve' all over the world.

*   *   *

---

*Johnny Marr is the ex-guitarist with the legendary Smiths and a Beck fan. After the 1987 breakup of The Smiths he formed Electronic with New Order's Bernard Sumner and Pet Shop Boys' Neil Tennant; and also teamed up with Matt Johnson's The The.

Of course, none of this might have been possible if the legal situation hadn't been resolved between Geffen, Beck and Bong Load. It was all kept pretty hush-hush but Beck did reveal that 'Any musician on a record label believes they're not getting what they deserve. In my case, it was brought to my attention that it was grossly unfair. It was below what any musician off the street would be getting as far as a deal goes.'

As far as the lawsuits are concerned, Beck dismissed them by saying: 'It was all perfunctory legal manoeuvring, and in the end it worked itself out.' As far as the new deal goes, it seems that, although it's unconfirmed, Beck now has a better royalty rate but it is now more difficult for him to release other projects on independent labels – one of the things that drew him to Geffen in the first place. Despite whatever did go on behind closed doors, the main thing that concerned the fans is that he had a new album out in November 1999 with minimal delays.

So with a loud new album and world tour looming, Beck was about to enter the twenty-first century in fine form. In just a decade he'd gone from LA unknown to New York unknown and back to LA unknown again. He'd been thrust into the spotlight with 'Loser' and managed to avoid being a one-hit wonder, while using the independence allowed him at an early age to keep his musical visions unspoilt by trends or fads. He let his music evolve naturally from blues-folk to punk-hard-core to rap-indie-pop and eventually to R&B-funk – there wasn't a deliberate re-invention in sight, just a master musical brain gently ticking over. Undoubtedly, the stability in his personal life with Leigh has allowed him to develop musically and he's almost bound to explore even more new musical avenues as his career progresses.

So Beck is now all set to take another step up the ladder of greatness. But after all the razzamatazz that is bound to accompany his 2000/1 tour, what then? Will it be back to an acoustic environment? Will it be another sound and sample fest? Or will it be something totally unexpected and new? With Beck, you never can tell. In the end it might, again, all come down to a random matter of chance.

In 1996 Beck was asked where he thought he might ultimately end up. Although he wasn't sure where it might be, he sure was going to enjoy the journey:

It's all a chance thing. It's a chance that I got home early from work one day, and that a friend called and told me to go to this other guy's house, and that I came down and he had this drum machine and an eight-track, and we did 'Loser' in three hours. I could have just as easily gone out and got a beer with a friend and that would have never happened. All of these things are just kind of chance. Hopefully I'll be making banda music down in Mexico City, something like that.

# BONUS NOISE –
# APPENDICES

# I MTV Makes Me Want To Smoke Crack – Videos

Beck's videos have been almost as inventive and groundbreaking as his songs. With a visual arts grounding given by his grandfather and a good friend in independent film-maker Steven Hanft, he has a good basis from which to take the almost dead art of the 'pop video' on to greater things. This appendix aims to collect together the stories behind Beck's videos, to look into some of his more memorable TV appearances and document his links to film soundtrack work.

After starting out with the hastily constructed 'Loser' video, Beck soon came to master the art of videos and by 1997 he had won five MTV Video Music awards. His main collaborator has been Steven Hanft; the two met before *Mellow Gold* came out at a Melvins show and soon hit it off as a creative partnership. In return for some songs for a film he was working on, Hanft agreed to make a film for 'Loser' and the partnership has been going strong ever since.

Thurston Moore wrote of meeting the pair in *The Face* magazine: 'Beck introduces me to his friend who he's having do a video to "Loser" and has never even viewed more than a minute of MTV. His friend can't even look at me and his handshake is like a dead washcloth. He seems completely alien and lost to any social interchange.' Despite this slightly odd introduction to Hanft he proved that he could make damn good films, but with no thanks to the channel that shows most of them.

'MTV is so boring, I hardly ever watch it. I don't even have cable. I'm just into making weird little movies with music,' Hanft told *Rolling Stone*. 'I try to make them as fucked up as I can, I'm really into making something like a dream, and in videos you can get away with that.' For someone who was influenced by Captain Beefheart he's pretty much achieved that goal.

Hanft grew up, and still lives, in Ventura, California. After getting his Masters Degree in film from Los Angeles Cal Arts College he went to New York but later returned home broke after six months and took a job with Greenpeace. He continued making short films and for a short time even fronted his own band called Loser.

> I like getting weird images but shooting them really normally. Instead of using a wide-angle lens or flashy editing, you just shoot it straight. But it's a weird image to start with, so it becomes surreal. Like the line-dancing scene in 'Where It's At' looks like something straight off the Nashville Network, but in the context of the Beck song, it becomes really weird. I love that. Films, videos, rock & roll – it's all part of the same thing to me. Anything that's weird or funny or bizarre, you can just look at it and go, 'Man, that's art.'

Beck also got into directing his own videos. After part-directing some of the earlier ones, he took total control with 'The New Pollution' and was enthusiastic about the project:

> I enjoy making videos. I have a lot of ideas. I spent about five weeks of my life doing the video for 'The New Pollution', and, damn, it's a lot of work, but it's satisfying in the end. It was a bit shocking to have this picture, something visual in my head, translated into existence. I'm used to being able to do that with sound, to have an idea and approximate it in a song, but not with an actual picture. It's frightening to take something that you dream or daydream or imagine, something you've conjured up in your thoughts from out of nowhere, and put it into existence on a screen. There's something wrong about that, something very disturbing when you can do that. It's a power that we shouldn't have. But it's exhilarating.

Despite the exhilaration it isn't something Beck has got into the routine of doing regularly. He has enlisted the help of other respected directors such as Mark Romanek and Michel Gondry too.

How serious should videos be? 'It's very silly; most of it's not serious at all. And I think that's what videos should be,' says Beck. 'I think videos should be more about just ruining everything you've built up in the music. I think you should just go and blow it all up by making a bunch of dumb, funny imagery.'

## **Promotional videos** *(in alphabetical order)*

### **Beercan** (1994)
A Steven Hanft video, this one plays on the line 'Winos throwing frisbees at the sun' as a gang of winos go on the rampage. They break into houses and raid cupboards, smashing anything that gets in their way. Beck is seen briefly wearing a fluffy jacket and playing guitar

while having foam blown at him. Black Fag member Vaginal Creme Davis can be seen strolling around a field in a dress and other guests in the film are Buzz Osborne of the Melvins and the band Sukia.

## Computer Chips And Salsa (no release date)

By early 1998 stories were starting to emerge that there would be a Beck longform video by the end of the year. Indeed the Steve Hanft page of the Bong Load website listed a 'Beck Tour 97' film as being 'in progress' under the title 'Computer Chips And Salsa'. Hanft had shot some footage of the *Odelay* tour and plans were to also include performance art, comic sketches and unreleased Beck videos in the final cut. By late 1999 there was still no word of a release date or even of an actual release.

## Deadweight (1997)

This is the only one of Beck's soundtrack contributions to be released as a single and thus the only one to have its own video. Innovative French director Michel Gondry was called in to perform the honours on this tie-in with the Ewan McGregor–Cameron Diaz movie *A Life Less Ordinary*. Previously he'd directed well-received clips for Bjork (including 'Bachelorette', 'Joga' and 'Human Behaviour'), Foo Fighters and Sheryl Crow. Right from the off he wanted to get away from the traditional film tie-in videos that alternately involve clips of a band playing 'live' with scenes from the film in question. 'Soundtrack videos always seem to go with the film rather than the film going with the video,' he explains. 'I wanted to do something different. We reversed all the situations so it looked like the film was shot after the video.'

The song begins with Beck in a business suit sat at a desk on a beach working away amidst sunbathers and children playing in the sand. As the song progresses his day starts to mirror clips from the film – a toy car is tossed into the sea from the beach and is followed by a clip from the film of a car crashing down a hillside, Beck punches the air and a villain in the film is knocked down. Beck's character then goes on vacation from working on the beach to sitting on a deckchair in an office. Before setting off he packs a suitcase with framed pieces of wallpaper – the walls of his house are papered with giant photographs! After a series of such reversed situations (Beck's 'shadow' walks down the street while the 'real' Beck is dragged behind along the sidewalk on his back and a man walks down the road carrying a car on his shoulders) Beck goes to the cinema to see *A Life Less Ordinary* but instead he sees footage of himself on the screen, much to his pleasure. Beck himself was not previously a great fan of soundtrack videos: 'A lot of times it's pretty gratuitous,' he says. 'You are sort of a slave to whatever footage they give to you; it's basically a commercial – so you try and make it a little more artistic.'

From Michel Gondry's perspective he felt it all worked out pretty well, even if he and Beck didn't work too closely together. 'He was very nice and simple when we filmed it, but we didn't collaborate beforehand. I don't think he's the sort of guy who goes to ten meetings in a row.'

### Devils Haircut (1996)

Directed by Mark Romanek, this is not only one of Beck's best videos, but one of the best of the 1990s. Beck explained that the two had similar influences to apply to this film. 'We'd both seen *Midnight Cowboy* and liked the way the movie looked,' he told MTV. 'I was talking about a lot of French cinema, the 1960s and New Wave cinema and how it had some really cool effects. The freeze-frame into the zoom, these optical zooms, so we just incorporated things like that. The idea was just to make something simple, to set a mood.' The zooms used in the video gave it a striking feel, but originally it was going to be even more stark. 'We followed sort of a French new wave thing, where the image holds for a couple of seconds. Originally we were going to have only 8 shots and slowly zoom in on each one, but we changed it later,' Beck explained.

Filming took place in New York City early in the morning to avoid disruption but it still meant that the crew had to close a few streets. The general theme of the video is Beck walking along, wearing a brown leather jacket and cowboy hat and carrying a ghetto blaster. At the end of each scene the camera freezes and the frame zooms into Beck's face. After seven different scenes, as the song comes to an end, the frozen zooms are re-shown – but this time they zoom into the background behind Beck to show a couple of fellows dressed in black who are spying on our singer as he walks the streets.

A live version of 'Devils Haircut' was recorded in Lisbon during May 1998 and has been shown on MTV in the UK.

### Flavor (1996)

Beck not only sang on this Jon Spencer Blues Explosion track but he agreed to appear in the video too along with another guest, Beastie Boy Mike D. Directed by Evan Bernard, the video shows the Blues Explosion visiting a restaurant where Beck is the chef and also a DJ. He manages to chop vegetables while falling asleep and spin some discs too. Eventually the band get their meal with some bits of broken

*Above* Beck's grandfather Al Hansen (centre, white-gloved), the Fluxus artist, poses with Andy Warhol (front, 2nd right) and other friends of the Factory, March 1968 (*Fred W McDarrah*)

*Right* Beck's mother, Bibbe Hansen, reading at the Al Hansen-inspired Playing With Matches exhibition, New York City, September 1998 (*Lily Simonson*)

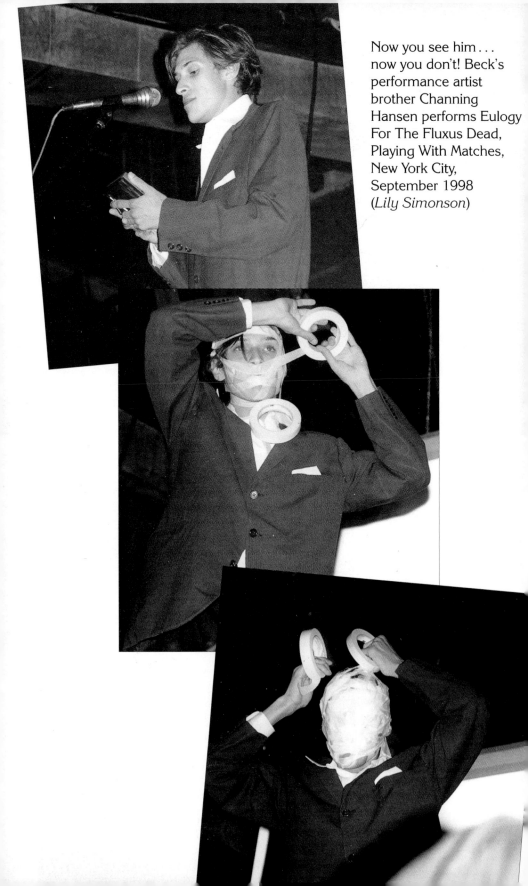

Now you see him . . .
now you don't! Beck's
performance artist
brother Channing
Hansen performs Eulogy
For The Fluxus Dead,
Playing With Matches,
New York City,
September 1998
(*Lily Simonson*)

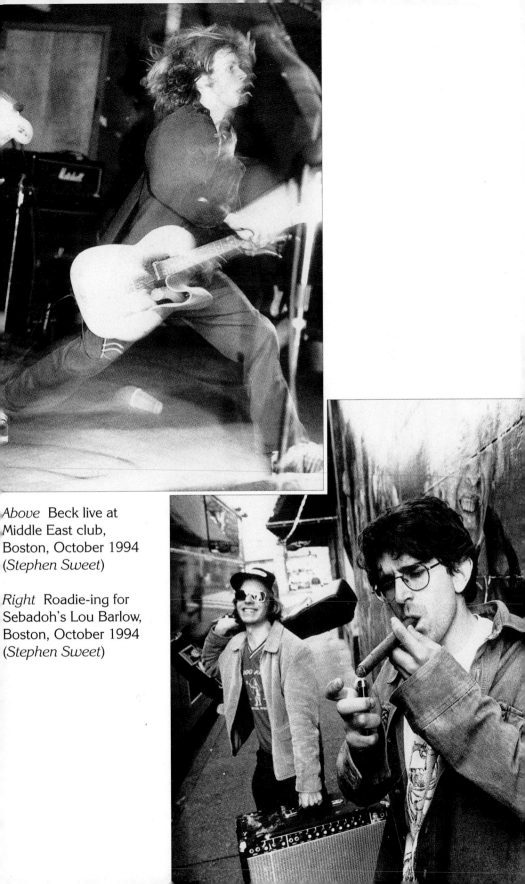

*Above*  Beck live at
Middle East club,
Boston, October 1994
(*Stephen Sweet*)

*Right*  Roadie-ing for
Sebadoh's Lou Barlow,
Boston, October 1994
(*Stephen Sweet*)

record in the food, so they get the owner (Mike D) to give Beck the push. The final scene sees the band dressed like Run DMC in an apartment with Beck next door in a re-creation of the 'Walk This Way' video before the camera goes outside to see a full moon showing the face of Flava Flav.

## Forcefield (1994)

This video has been spotted on a couple of late-night music shows. Not really something that you'd expect to see on prime-time viewing as it isn't promoting a single, it is very lo-fi in its production. Beck is seen in stark black and white playing acoustic guitar and some colour footage is also included of the band that appeared on the *One Foot In The Grave* album. This clip was directed by Pat Maley.

## Jack-ass (1997)

Steve Hanft's imagination was again allowed to run riot in this, the final video from *Odelay*. 'I listened to the song,' he remembers, 'and I came up with the idea of a young coal miner, even though there were no lyrics about coal mining.' The opening shot is of a miner smoking a pipe, the smoke from which contains an image of a man rowing a boat with a woman – this is bassist Justin Meldal-Johnsen with girlfriend Corrine in Victorian-era clothing. As the clips moves on a coal shaft is seen with miners (including guitarist Smokey Hormel) working along the wall. Beck walks by singing in full mining gear complete with sooty face. Later as he's working a cart rolls by with Willie Nelson sitting in it. He throws some sparkling powder over Beck as he passes by, surreal indeed.

At the end of the shift the whistle blows and the miners start to leave, and Hanft's Captain Beefheart preferences come into play once again: 'Towards the end, this kind of Middle Eastern bassline comes into the song, quite happy and psychedelic,' he told *Select* magazine. 'That reminded me of "Plastic Factory" by Captain Beefheart, and this line in it, "Be in flower/Growing boy and girl are glowing", so I had the miners go into this bright world with a beekeeper and a little boy and girl.' Meldal-Johnsen and girlfriend are seen again as the miners emerge into the Technicolor world outside.

## Loser (1994)

This video was never meant to be played on MTV, let alone in super-heavy rotation, it was just Steven Hanft, Beck and a few friends messing around. Hanft had agreed to do the video in return for Beck contributing some songs and music to the soundtrack of his *Kill The*

*Moonlight* film. 'At first I didn't want to do it,' says Hanft. 'But we had all these ideas. Like I'd say, "Let's have some people doing aerobics in the graveyard – that would be a 'Loser' thing." Or, "Yeah, the grim reaper should be squeegeeing blood off your window – that's a 'Loser' thing." Then I was like, "Everything will be on fire!" and Beck was like, "Yeah!" . . . It was total chaos.'

The video opens with someone walking along in a yellow sweatshirt but their face is fuzzed out; this is because it's a Star Wars Stormtrooper helmet that couldn't be shown. Eventually the walker removes it and . . . it's Beck. The footage includes lots of random and seemingly unconnected footage including: stock car racing (from *Kill The Moonlight*); Beck in the woods wearing an Indian head-dress; two aerobics dancers in a graveyard (one of whom is Lisa Demerol of Sexy Death Soda and Liquor Cabinet); Beck rapping outside a store (the mime that walks up to him is Steve Moramarco of *The Abe Lincoln Story* and *Bean*); Beck and Steven Hanft are seen squeegeeing the window of a car (Beck's squeegie is on fire, Hanft is dressed as the Grim Reaper wiping blood from the window); Eddie Lopez of Sukia is seen playing guitar on a roof; the list goes on.

### Love Spreads (1994)

When the Stone Roses returned from their lengthy between-albums exile with *Second Coming*, Steve Hanft was commissioned to direct the 'Love Spreads' video for their North American fans. Roses' guitarist John Squire is a long-time Beck fan and welcomed his cameo appearance as a gold panner.

### Mutations (1998)

As the 1990s progressed so did the use of the EPK (Electronic Press Kit). In order to avoid sitting through hundreds of interviews each time a new album is released, artists will pre-record a series of questions and answers along with audio clips from the album and circulate the video to journalists when review copies of the album are sent out. In October 1998, for the first time Beck took this route with *Mutations*. As his original intention had been to release the album on Bong Load with no promotion at all, it's not too surprising that he chose this approach for promoting the album.

The video itself runs for nine minutes and is shot mainly in black and white. For the most part Beck sits in a chair giving answers to a computer-like voice on the usual *Mutations* questions – why Nigel Godrich? how was it recorded? when were the songs written? etc. Slightly more off-the-cuff moments arise when Beck is asked which

fruit he would equate the album to – 'pomegranate' he replies and when he's asked what he would say if he could have seen himself in this situation ten years previously – 'Get a haircut,' he quips.

Short audio samples of 'Cold Brains' and 'Nobody's Fault But My Own' are played to black and white stills taken during the recording of the album. 'Bottle Of Blues' is also played with accompanying grainy live footage in colour, but not matching the song – probably taken during the *Odelay* tour for the 'Computer Chips And Salsa' project. Other verbal highlights include Beck being asked if he feels under pressure – 'No, I feel de-pressurized by the altitude' – and how he envisages people listening to the album: 'I hope people have a nice meal and later a bath, or if they don't bath they can just hose themselves down.'

Of course 'Tropicalia' is also played ('A good summertime record for the winter', according to Beck) and this covers the credits which end with a still photograph of Beck holding up a sign reading 'The End'.

## Pay No Mind (1995)

Not exactly your average MTV staple but this clip got Beck on to *Beavis and Butthead* none the less. Steve Hanft directed this video which showcases late-night skateboarding, middle-aged people with fancy drinks and Beck sitting on some bales of hay strumming away at a battered acoustic guitar, oh and some volcanic eruptions and lava flows. Ross Harris of Sukia can briefly be seen holding a drink with his mother.

Beavis and Butthead watched the clip with the usual indifference that they show to anything that didn't have the word 'fire' in the title:

(Beck sings 'Tonight, the city is full of morgues')
Butthead:    Tonight the city is full of whores?
Beavis:      I wish our city was full of whores, that'd be cool!
Butthead:    His shirt says 'Kick me' (note: it actually said 'Rock Me')
Beavis:      Someone should kick him in the nads! Who is this
             fartknocker anyway?
Butthead:    He's like one of the dudes from the gifted class or
             something.

## The New Pollution (1997)

To date this has been the only video totally directed by Hansen himself and, it has to be said, it's one of the best. Described by the director himself as 'a cross between *McCabe and Mrs Miller* and *The Lawrence Welk Show*'. It was filmed predominantly on a soundstage in Los Angeles and has a very 1960s *American Bandstand* type feel to it. It tips

its hat to several 1960s influences. The opening shot of Beck and band cavorting around a field in livestock masks recalls The Beatles and they arrive on the stage by jumping through an American flag à la The Who. The original backdrop, vertical stripes, was changed at the last minute because 'it was too Dick Cavett'. The band sing and play among a weird collection of characters dancing in the studio.

Old-school computer animation cuts in between Beck singing and dancing in various guises, including 'Livewire' era Motley Crue and Kraftwerk (a homage to their 'Pocket Calculator' video). However some of these not-too-subtle points still managed to pass some people by. 'When I'm doing the dancing with the girls, that was sort of a Serge Gainsbourg reference with all the landscaping lawnmower machines behind us,' Beck told Mark Lamarr on British TV. 'Somebody came up to me and said "Hey, that was a funny Robert Palmer thing you did there." So you think you're nailing the target but it's just going over people's heads.'

Beck found Serge Gainsbourg to be a big influence on his film-making:

> I discovered him in about 1995. In France, in the sixties, they had these machines where you put a couple of francs in and you could watch these little movie vignettes of your favourite singer. So all these French artists made these really primitive videos – he's got an extraordinary amount of them. Some are mundane, some are genius. They're really refreshing to watch 'cos they'll contain a couple of brilliant shots – maybe something as simple as him standing in front of a black background, gesturing. Or him sitting in a chair in a reading room, looking really paranoid. Or him behind some weird lamps, arms folded. He doesn't move much, the smallest gesture is huge. And every video has him smoking.

Beck hired a Rolls-Royce for a day for the scene of his driving and the woman statue coming to life on the front of the car. Again this can be linked back to Gainsbourg. He told *Melody Maker*:

> My favourite Gainsbourg is 'Melody Nelson', because that fits into that whole dangerous area where rock meets orchestra. The dynamic of that record is insane. His band have totally got that early seventies electric guitar, heavy bass, solos filled, dead sounding drums, cliched rock sound. They're wailing and he's whispering, but he's about five times louder. And then there's this creepy orchestra . . . and it's a concept record! One of the videos features Jane Birkin as Melody, this little schoolgirl, who he hits while driving a Rolls-Royce.

Tony Maxwell of That Dog is seen dancing on the slide with two girls near the end.

## Tropicalia (1999)

During the NME 1998 Review show on British TV (see later), a non-official promo clip for 'Tropicalia' was shown. Although the track had been released as a single there was no 'official' video for it. This TV show's version shows footage of Beck superimposed on a tropical fish tank to give the impression that he's tiny and inside the tank. He sits down while fish swim by, he drinks from a mug then puts on a pair of goggles and a snorkel before walking around the tank while larger than life goldfish and the like swim about him. Finally he pulls out a cine-camera from under his coat and points it at his head before wandering past a 'No Fishing' sign and walking off screen as the song ends.

## Where It's At (1996)

For the opening video from *Odelay* Steve Hanft got the call once again. Along with Beck he combined a whole host of ideas into one video. The opening scene shows some workers toiling by the side of a hot road while the boss watches on. 'It was pretty much a stream of consciousness thing,' explains Hanft. 'Listening to the record and pooling ideas. Beck wanted to have some community service guys working, so we re-created the *Cool Hand Luke* scene with the boss-man oppressing the workers.'

The next idea was a parking lot fair with Beck singing on the back of a truck with a 'Value Days' banner in the background. Watching on is Beck's partner Leigh Limon (seen holding a balloon) while Grace Marks of the band Sukia and her brother are two of the breakdancers. A disco robot calls out 'Two turntables and a microphone'. Hanft let the cat out of the bag by saying 'The disco robot just came about because I thought that bit sounded like a disco robot.' Insight indeed!

Beck's input was wanting to re-create the image from the label of a vitamin bottle that he'd seen (that's where the family jump into the air holding hands and are frozen in mid-air with the coloured circles behind them) and recording a scene in the style of a 1960s family planning booklet that he'd spied (the field where it was recorded was actually next to a toxic waste dump!).

Next up on the ideas turntable was a re-creation of William Shatner's 1978 reading of Elton John's 'Rocket Man'. Here Beck is seen in dinner jacket being joined confusingly by two more versions of himself. Then Beck is wandering through some trees with a hook on his hand. Steve Hanft wanted to pay homage to one of his idols: 'The bit where Beck's walking with a hook, I just wanted him to look like a kind of Captain Beefheart guy.'

The final scene shows that Beck doesn't take his own advice (he'd said 'There is a danger in organised dancing, caution is the word') as he plays to a line-dancing club. 'The stuff with the line-dancing came from The Nashville Network, which is like a really suburban country MTV,' Hanft explains. 'We wanted to do that mini-mall thing.' The line dance in the video was actually made up specially for the song by the Glendale, CA, residents that appeared on film. At the video's conclusion Eddie Lopez again makes an appearance, this time with oranges over his eyes. So far this is the only Beck video to make it on to VH-1's *Pop Up Video*.

## Wiltern Theater (1999)

Beck's show at this Los Angeles art-deco theatre on 8 May 1999 was filmed for future use. The show was centred around nine songs from *Mutations* in an acoustic setting with two string players and the usual Brass Menagerie. As it was the first show he'd played in Los Angeles since the El Rey Theater in December 1997 he was greeted like a long-lost son with screams reminiscent of the Beatles fans in the early 1960s. The performance was shown in part on the HBO show *Reverb* in October 1999, when half a dozen tracks were screened.

## Television shows (in alphabetical order)

### 120 Minutes Promo (1994) DGC, MTV, USA

Filmed on 16 February 1994 this footage became central in the ongoing myth of Beck-as-a-goof-ball. Taped for MTV's *120 Minutes* show, it was later sent out as a promo by DGC to promote their latest signing. Thurston Moore of Sonic Youth was the show's guest host and was involved in a bizarre series of mini-scenes with Beck.

To begin with, Moore produces a copy of *A Western Harvest Field By Moonlight* and pulls out the enclosed finger-painting, Beck whips it out of his hand, rips it into several pieces and says 'There you go' as he hands it back. 'Now you've got a couple of extra ones.' The interview goes downhill from there on. When asked about 'Loser' he pulls out a mini tape-recorder and answers by playing back some garbled noise from the tape, to which Moore deadpans 'That explains a lot, man.' Moore finally gets some comic value of his own when he asks Beck's age. 'Twenty-three,' he answers, to which Moore quips 'Oh, 'cos you look a lot older.'

Beck plays two acoustic tracks, both while seated on a stool – 'Crystal Clear (Beer)' and 'Pay No Mind'. Before each song he reads Moore's auto-cue in a slow drawl, but with his own variations on the

script. 'Hi, I'm Thurston Moore of Chronic Youth,' he reads before his first song and later he changes it to 'Hi, I'm Kim Deal of Sonic Youth.' The promo ends with the pair being joined by Beastie Boy Mike D for some impromptu noise-making.

### 120 Minutes (1996) MTV, USA

Early in the year Beck, with Abe Lincoln beard attached, dropped by for an interview with Matt Pinfield. Discussion centred around Beck's recent Grammy nominations and his *Rolling Stone* and *Spin* awards. 'It's nice to be acknowledged,' beamed Beck. 'But it's only by the critics. I know that in the real world Kenny G is number 1.'

When asked about the Dust Brothers he claimed that 'We showered together everyday, lots of massages and deep seated conversations.' He also introduced clips of 'Devils Haircut' and 'Pay No Mind', commenting on the latter as 'one of the first songs I ever wrote, it originally had ten verses'. Later he requested Kraftwerk's 'Pocket Calculator' – 'I remember hearing this when I was about 12, it sounded like something my watch did. You could tell that there was something not quite right with them.'

### Brit Awards (1997) ITV, UK

As Beck was unable to collect his award in person, a short clip was filmed and shown on the night. Beck is seen getting into a trailer where Snoop Doggy Dogg is waiting to present the 'Best International Male' award. Beck removes his sunglasses to reveal another pair of glasses underneath, collects the award and says 'All right'.

### Howard Stern Birthday Party (1997) USA

Beck performed two live songs on this show that was live on the radio and also filmed for TV. 'Novacane' and 'Where It's At' were played to a motley crew of an audience that included a mixture of large-breasted women and extras from a Marilyn Manson video. A lively interview took place during the show, some of the highlights of which are as follows:

| | |
|---|---|
| Stern: | See, I was reading about you – you're not like a rock star type, 'cause you don't have like even groupies, like you don't even have women backstage or anything like that. Is that true? |
| Beck: | We have a, uh, 400-person boys choir . . . |
| Stern: | Yeah . . . |
| Beck: | Uh, they just kinda hang out and sing. |
| Stern: | Really? |
| Beck: | Lots of harmonies . . . |

157

Stern:    That's what goes on backstage? Typically rock stars will have like lots of broads . . .

Beck:    Lots of milk and cookies . . .

Stern:    Yeah, but you have just young choir boys hanging around.

Beck:    Exactly.

Stern:    Seriously. Was it hard in high school?

Beck:    Um . . . I didn't really go to high school, so . . .

Stern:    How'd you get outta that?

Beck:    I just, you know, stopped going after awhile.

Stern:    Are you serious? You just went home and told your parents, 'Hey man, I'm not going to high school anymore?'

Beck:    Well, I kinda didn't have the best high school . . .

Stern:    Tell me! No one did! [laughs]

Beck:    It was kinda a matter of health, ya know . . .

Stern:    Oh, seriously? Like, mental health?

Beck:    No, no. Uh . . . you know, physical . . .

Stern:    Oh, you mean like you were getting beat up and stuff?

Beck:    Well, you know . . .

Stern:    . . . kicked your ass and stuff?

Beck:    Well, you know. Not at . . . no, of course, not everyone.

Stern:    [laughing]: Oh, there were some people who were nice! No, I got beat up. I grew up in an all-black neighbourhood and there were three white families and I know I got my ass kicked a lot.

Beck:    Right.

Stern:    Because, quite frankly, look at me . . . I'm pretty sure everyone could kick my ass!

Beck:    Right, right.

## Later with Jools Holland (1997) BBC TV, UK

This show has become *the* live music showcase on British TV after a decade on the air. The winning formula sees a series of diverse acts arranged around presenter Jools Holland in the same studio taking turns to play with the odd interview snippet thrown in for good measure. Most bands play one or two songs, but Beck was allowed to play three tunes *and* was interviewed by the ex-Squeeze man as well. Taking a break from the *Odelay* tour on 6 May 1997 he joined Dru Hill, Spanish pianist Ruben Gonzales, The Brand New Heavies, the Rollins Band, David Byrne and Morcheeba at the BBC studios in London.

After being introduced as 'He's not a loser and we don't want to kill him', Beck and band pelted headlong into a heavy version of 'Devils Haircut'. 'Lovely, superb,' commented Holland at the song's conclusion. 'I will be enquiring just exactly what is a "Devil's haircut" later in the show.'

The interview segment saw Beck and Holland sat by a piano surrounded by fans. The questions were pretty standard Beck-fare ('What music did you first listen to?', 'What does "Odelay" mean?') and then he was asked about the Devils Haircut – 'Is a Devils Haircut frightening?'

'It's a blues thing,' Beck replied.

'Oh,' said a slightly bemused presenter. 'Well, it didn't frighten me until I heard you sing it!'

To end the show Beck was invited back to perform again, but not before Holland had got the whole audience to call out 'Odelay' a few times. The very smartly dressed band then ran through 'Jack-ass' and 'Sissyneck' to end the proceedings.

## Monsieur Beck (1997) Canada

This show was a collage of Beck footage old and new. Older footage included interviews on Canadian TV from 1994 and 1996, with a 1994 street performance in Toronto and a 1996 solo studio rendition of 'Lord Only Knows'. The new footage included an interview and film from the April 1997 show in Montreal.

## MTV Video Music Awards (1996) MTV, USA

The 1996 version of these awards saw Beck win his first 'Spaceman'. He received it for the 'Best Male Video' ('Where It's At') and it was presented to him by Van Halen. 'Best Male Award – I'm not sure what that means,' said Beck by way of an acceptance speech. He'd earlier presented the award for Best R'n'B Video with Chris Rock to the Fugees. Before the awards he'd put in one of his more bizarre TV appearances when he'd appeared outside the Radio City Music Hall on top of a bus. While Mike Simpson provided some scratching and turntable action inside the bus, Beck and Rozelle stood on the roof and rapped through a version of 'Where It's At', while Greg Hormel, Justin Meldal-Johnsen, Joey Waronker and Theo Mondle provided shouts and hand-claps from beside the bus. It was a sight to behold indeed.

## MTV Video Music Awards (1997) MTV, USA

The VMAs of 1997 were Beck's finest hour as far as videos are concerned. He walked away with five in total – Best Male Video and Best Editing, for 'Devils Haircut', and Best Direction in a Video, Best Choreography in a Video and Best Art Direction, all for 'The New Pollution'. He also took part in a handful of interviews and played live too. Comedian Mike Myers introduced him as 'one of my all-time favourite artists' as Beck and band burst into 'The New Pollution',

complete with a six-member choir. Greg Hormel and Justin Meldal-Johnsen arrived by sliding down two ramps while Beck put on some snazzy dance moves and did the splits as well as managing to use a feather fan, a whip and even to stop and comb his hair in a mirror at one point.

### MTV Video Music Awards (1998) MTV, USA

September 1998 saw Beck's third consecutive appearance at these awards. This time he presented the award for Best Rap Video to Will Smith for 'Gettin' Jiggy With It.' His co-presenter was Tori Amos who played along with Beck's fascination with unnatural acts with drum machines.

### Odebeck (1996) Much Music, Canada

This cunningly titled show was filmed in Toronto for Canadian TV in August 1996. Filmed in front of a 'live studio audience', it was hard to tell how much of the performance was actually live as at one point Beck dropped his microphone but the singing was unaffected. Strange.

### Planet Showbiz (1997), Channel Four, UK

British TV 'personality' Mark Lamarr was sent by Channel Four to Normal, Il., to interview Beck and shoot some live footage. He also ventured to Silverlake and visited the Dust Brothers. While talking to the Dust Brothers, Lamarr described Beck as 'quite serious and mellow' off-stage but very different on it. Mike Simpson agreed: 'It was amazing for us seeing him play these songs we wrote with him – the transformation was amazing.' Of his own live performance, Beck described it as 'a dinner party and I'm the host, making the toast'.

### Playing With Matches (1997) VH-1, USA

Filmed at the opening of the Playing With Matches exhibition in Santa Monica, the footage shows some of the exhibits and interviews with Beck, Bibbe Hansen and Vaginal Creme Davis. 'When I was four,' says Beck, 'my grandfather thought my head looked like a grapefruit. He was going to turn me into a Fluxus art-piece. He was going to put a big "Sunkist" stamp on my forehead.'

### Playing With Matches: In Concert (1997) ABC TV, USA

Another show from the Santa Monica exhibition. Not really in concert at all, but it does show some songs ('The New Pollution' and 'Devils Haircut') from Glastonbury in 1997.

## Playing With Matches (1998) MTV News, USA

MTV sent a film crew along to the Thread Waxing Space in New York for the opening of the Playing With Matches exhibition there on 5 September 1998. After showing clips of Marianne Faithfull and Thurston Moore at the show there was a short interview with Beck. Dressed in a green and grey camouflage T-shirt he discussed his grandfather and his leading role in experimental art: 'He really made beautiful things from things that you wouldn't think of as artistically valid. He enthused them with something beyond their limited possibilities. He validated any sort of leaning towards experimenting with your environment, experimenting with sounds, with an idea. There was some elder there in the background making that acceptable.'

## Reading Festival (1995) MTV Europe

Beck's set at this festival in 1995 was filmed and several songs have since been shown on MTV Europe. Dressed in a bright red shirt and matching trousers, Beck was filmed playing 'Novacane' (introduced as 'Novacane Express') and 'Thunderpeel'. The camera tends to spend a lot of time focused on bassist Abby Travis as the only woman on stage and there are a few close-ups of drummer Joey Waronker, complete with semi-afro haircut.

## Rockpalast (1997) WDR TV, Germany

This long-running German live music showcase captured Beck's August 1997 show at the Bizarre Festival in Cologne. Starting with 'Devils Haircut' and 'Novacane', the band were in playful mood, blasting through a 'greatest hits' set. For the encore the band wore horse masks while Beck returned in his black rhinestone suit for 'High Five'.

## Rolling Stone State Of The Union (1998) USA

In May 1998, Beck made an appearance on this TV special with the likes of Jewel and Bruce Springsteen. He sat on a step in a studio and played a solo version of 'Hollow Log' after introducing it with a short speech: 'The old-time music, the country blues and the delta blues, it was something that I gravitated towards. There's something fairly timeless about it and it's not adorned with the commercial trickery of the time that it came out of. It's like sitting in plastic furniture all your life then finding a good old rocking chair.'

## Saturday Night Live (1997) NBC, USA

Beck continued his early 1997 TV rounds with a stop by on *Saturday Night Live*. Before singing he took part in a short sketch about drugs

with Kevin Spacey and Michael Palin. 'I've come for the prescription drugs for the Black Crowes,' he told Spacey, who replied, 'There's a truck full waiting outside.'

Two songs were played on the show, 'Where It's At' and 'Devils Haircut'. Joey Waronker wore a cowboy hat and western tie, while Justin Meldal-Johnsen sported a mini-afro. The end credits rolled over as Beck and band passed a dead parrot in a cage around with Michael Palin and John Cleese.

### Saturday Night Live (1999) NBC, USA

Filmed on the day before his show at the Town Hall in New York City, Beck showcased some *Mutations* material for a national audience. First off he took part in a spoof sketch, sending up VH-1's *Behind The Music* series before performing 'Nobody's Fault But My Own' and 'Tropicalia'.

### Sessions at West 54th (1997) USA

This show is similar to the BBC's *Later with Jools Holland* in that a series of bands play live while surrounded by a few lucky fans in an intimate setting. Beck arrived in the studio in what was billed as the final show of the *Odelay* tour. Introduced by ex-KCRW man Chris Douridas, Beck played part of the show in a white suit and part in a black one. Only a fraction of the show was actually broadcast so viewers had to be content with just 'Devils Haircut', 'Debra' (after which Beck was helped from the stage by the band while crying mock tears), 'Jack-ass' and a lengthy version of 'Where It's At'.

### Space Ghost (1997) USA

This children's cartoon features a 'Roger Rabbit' approach to getting interviews with various 'pop' stars. A filmed interview with the guest is interwoven into the cartoon featuring the hero, Space Ghost, and his cohorts. When asked what he likes to do, Beck replied: 'I like to plug things in, and then I like to unplug them, and then I go to sleep.' Later Beck goes to sleep with a lampshade on his head while another cartoon character, Moltar, sings a song in German. Kids today don't know how lucky they really are!

### The 39th Annual Grammy Awards (1997) USA

Filmed and broadcast in varying degrees around the world, Beck was the star of the show. He played a spectacularly grand version of 'Where It's At' and walked away with two awards. During rehearsal he had been interviewed by MTV. He spoke about the dressing-room arrangements which included all 'older' performers (Bruce Spring-

steen, Bonnie Raitt etc.) at one end of the backstage area and all the younger ones at the other. 'There's a segregation and I'd like to speak out on that right now,' he joked.

An interview with the Dust Brothers was also broadcast. After a bit of their general history they spoke in detail about the recording of 'Where It's At'. John King explained that it had begun with Beck playing the intro on a Wurlitzer while they recorded everything on to a MAC computer using 'Studiovision' software. It was revealed that the 'Where It's At' chant in the chorus is not a gang of people all shouting but Beck taking on the voices of several different characters (the big guy, the small guy, the real energetic guy and the old guy) that were all then superimposed on top of each other. Asked about possible future collaborations with King and Simpson, Beck replied: 'We have some unfinished business.'

**The Best Of Beck** (1998) Sky 1, Europe
This late-night programme on Europe's largest cable and satellite station showcases one-hour collections of videos by a chosen artist. The summer of 1998 was deemed to be the time that Beck was worthy of this honour and seven of his videos were collected together. 'Where It's At', 'Jack-ass', 'Devils Haircut', 'The New Pollution', 'Pay No Mind', 'Deadweight' and 'Loser' made the final cut.

**The Late Show with David Letterman** (1996) CBS TV, USA
Beck's network TV debut was here for him to sing 'Where It's At'. After introducing him as a 'most interesting new talent', Letterman then proceeded to ask some most uninteresting questions (how old are you? where were you born? what's touring like?) before concluding with '*Odelay* – it's a monster!' at which point Beck corrected him: 'A gentle monster.'

**The Late Show with David Letterman** (1997) CBS TV, USA
Just before the MTV Awards, Beck returned to this show to perform 'Jack-ass'. In the interview that followed Letterman remarked to Beck that it was a year since his last appearance on the show and that he should drop by more often. 'I like the anniversary thing,' replied Beck. Letterman then enquired if Beck was in any way related to the Hanson's of 'Mmmbop' fame. 'It's interesting that you should ask me that,' smirked Beck, ''cos they're a bunch of holograms that I projected from the top of Mount Fuji. I meditated for about 18 years . . .' at which point Letterman butted in to quip, 'I think you're right about that one year thing.'

**The NME Review of 1998** (1999) Channel Four, UK
This one-hour show broadcast in January 1999 looked back over the previous year from a British perspective with interviews, live snippets and promo clips. Large portions of the review were dedicated to Robbie Williams, Fat Boy Slim, Asian Dub Foundation and the death of Britpop. Beck showed up in the American section (along with Elliott Smith); a non-official promo video for 'Tropicalia' (see promo videos section, above, for details) was shown with voice-over interview answers from the *Mutations* EPK.

**The Tonight Show with Jay Leno** (1996) USA
Beck's debut on this show was his most amusing. After he played 'Devils Haircut', the usual interview section turned to focus on Al Hansen. He had appeared on the show in the mid-to-late 60s with Johnny Carson, but had been kicked off. When asked why his grandfather had been asked to leave the show, Beck leaned forward with a pair of scissors and snipped off Leno's tie. 'That'll be $175,' snapped the host. Leno soon gained revenge, however, by snipping off Beck's tie. 'Jay, that wasn't very fair,' complained Beck. 'You have a lot more ties than I do.'

**The Tonight Show with Jay Leno** (1997) USA
When Beck made his second appearance on this show, to promote the 'Jack-ass' single, he also offered an olive branch. He brought along a selection of ties to replace the one that he cut from around the host's neck on his previous visit. After the original incident was reshown he offered them to Leno to make a choice (he eventually took the whole lot) while Leno also had a couple for Beck to choose from. He offered the singer a choice between a dandy-looking 'Roswell-Alien' design and one featuring 'Mr Potato-Head'. 'Ah, that's real classy,' said Beck as he chose the latter.

**The Tonight Show with Jay Leno** (1997) USA
Beck's hat-trick appearance was a duet with Willie Nelson just before the 1997 Farm Aid benefit at which the two also appeared. They strolled through a version of Jimmie Rodgers' 'Peach Pickin' Time In Georgia', taking it in turns to sing a verse each.

**Top Of The Pops** (1994) BBC TV, UK
To promote the Geffen release of 'Loser', Beck was shipped over to England to perform on the long-running *Top Of The Pops* in February 1994. 'At that time the song was so old, I tried to make it more

interesting,' Beck said of his appearance. To liven it up he hired a group of old men to stand in as his backing band as the music was on tape and only Beck would sing live. 'I'd never had a band,' he commented. 'That cliché of the folk singer turning electric – I tried to subvert it by using elderly people.' The result was pretty hilarious.

## Soundtracks *(in alphabetical order)*

### Kill The Moonlight (1997)

Steve Hanft began making this film as far back as 1991 and finished it in 1995 before it was finally released in 1997. It tells the story of the character Chance, a toxic waste worker, and his quest to find enough money to enter his speedway car in the big race. This parallels the story of Hanft trying to collect enough money together to fund the finishing of the film, the final cost of which was $14,000. 'It's the opposite of the Spielberg "feel good" type movie that was everywhere when I started filming,' says Hanft.

Soon after Beck and Hanft met they agreed to help each other out. Hanft directed Beck's first video – 'Loser' – and Beck contributed three tracks to the soundtrack of this movie. The country tinge of 'Leave Me On The Moon', the instrumental 'Last Night I Traded My Soul's Innermost For Some Pickled Fish' and the noise-fest of 'Underwater Music' were finally added to the album, along with Martha Atwell (previously with Beck in 'Ten Ton Lid'), Go To Blazes and The Pussywillows.

There are various cross-overs between this film and the 'Loser' video – the line 'I'm a driver, I'm a winner, things are gonna change I can feel it' in 'Loser' was taken from the film, and the CD booklet of the soundtrack shows two people in toxic spill protection suits cleaning up. They are the same two guys who seem to be wearing space suits as they are driven away on the back of a pick-up truck in the 'Loser' clip.

The film premiered on 12 June 1997 with a special showing at the Sunset 5 Theater in Los Angeles. Beck was on hand to play a special mini-acoustic set including 'Leave Me On The Moon' from the film as well as 'No Money, No Honey', 'Waitin' For A Train', 'Rowboat' and a cover of the Doors' 'Light My Fire'.

### A Life Less Ordinary (1997)

As mentioned earlier in this appendix, Beck's 'Deadweight' was released as a single from the soundtrack to this Ewan McGregor–Cameron Diaz movie. The soundtrack was heavily promoted and

BECK! ON A BACKWARDS RIVER

featured R.E.M., Ash and The Cardigans among others. 'Deadweight' itself was also heavily promoted with at least three different promo sleeves available before the single itself arrived in October 1997. The song had its own video produced (see video promos section above) and appears during the final credits.

### She's The One (1996)
Beck indirectly contributed to this film when Tom Petty decided to cover 'Asshole' for the project. Originally Petty was going to provide a couple of songs for the soundtrack but soon had an album's worth on tape. After the album was released Beck was heard to substitute the words 'Tom Petty' in place of 'Asshole' when playing the song live. The album sleeve attributes 'Asshole' to 'Beck Campbell'. Petty and 'Campbell' interviewed each other shortly after in a syndicated piece that appeared in several magazines around the world.

### subUrbia (1997)
With Mark Kates as one of the executive producers of this film, it wasn't surprising that a Beck track should be included on the soundtrack. The chosen song was a 1994 version of 'Feather In Your Cap' featuring Beck and Joey Waronker. The inclusion of a Beck song on a Richard Linklater soundtrack may be seen by some as ironic after Beck took such pains to play down the whole 'slacker' image after 'Loser'. After all, it was Linklater who had previously made the movie *Slacker*. As it is, Beck sits proudly alongside pals Stephen Malkmus (who performs with Elastica) and Thurston Moore (both with Sonic Youth and solo).

### The Hi-Lo Country (1999)
This Woody Harrelson tale of postwar cowboys featured another Willie Nelson–Beck collaboration. After the live performances of 'Peach Pickin' Time In Georgia' and Nelson's cameo in the 'Jack-ass' video they reunited to perform the Jack Irby song 'Drivin' Nails In My Coffin'.

### The Rugrats Movie (1998)
This children's TV cartoon show made it to the big screen in 1998, and perhaps somewhat surprisingly Beck made an appearance on the soundtrack. Along with tracks by Lisa Loeb and Busta Rhymes the main ensemble piece, 'This World Is Something New To Me', featured a right motley crew – Beck, The B52s, Patti Smith, Lenny Kravitz, Jakob Dylan, Iggy Pop and half a dozen more.

*Above left* Live at MTV
Awards, 1997
(*Dave Hogan/Rex*) …

*Above right*
… supporting The Verve,
Wigan, 1998
(*M Flowers/All
Action*) …

*Left* … and a Las
Vegas showman, 1999
(*Marie Cox*)

Introducing the band:

Stagecoach (Joey Waronker)...

...Showboat
(Justin Meldal-Johnson)...

...Smokestack (Smokey Hormel)...

... and DJ Swamp
(all pics: *Deborah Gilmore*)

*Above*  Beck's longtime love, Leigh Limon
(*Deborah Gilmore*)

*Right*  Not everyone was Kung Foo fighting; with Dave Grohl, Tokyo, 1997
(*Steve Double/S.I.N*)

*Above* Beck turns his back on flower power, 1995 (*Chris Floyd/All Action*)

*Right* "Don't call me Elvis;" *that* infamous cowboy suit, *Odelay* tour, 1997 (*Justin Thomas/All Action*)

*Left* "Hey, isn't he that slacker guy?" Post-'Loser' breakthrough, 1994 (*Jake Chessum*)

# II Art Always Wins – Artwork

'Art Always Wins.' Al Hansen's quote was not a statement open to debate, he was merely pointing out a fact. It was something that he passed on to his daughter Bibbe and grandsons Channing and Beck. It wasn't until after his death, however, that his victories were properly documented and presented to the general public at large. Bibbe's husband, Sean Carrillo, had been collecting together ideas and ephemera which led to the Playing With Matches exhibitions. 'My grandfather was an originator of so many ideas,' says Beck, 'but he never had it together enough to present them. He never documented himself like other artists did. He was pushing all these ideas, but he struggled with being recognised.'

On 21 June 1995, Al Hansen died aged 67. At the memorial service, Beck played a few songs including 'Lord Only Knows' and 'Ramshackle' and watched performances by Al's friends and contemporaries. He recalls:

> It involved a gay wedding. A projection of 16mm film, the throwing of toilet paper around – it created a sort of toilet paper tent, a mini-amphitheatre of toilet paper – and people walking around with toy guns. It was all choreographed, but there was a certain element of chance, and the two who were getting married were tied up and they had to saw a chair in half. I remember being so overwhelmed with this spirit of I don't know what. Some other force overtaking me.

The city of Cologne presented a retrospective of Al's work at the Kolnisches Stadt Museum in the autumn of 1996. Beck clearly misses his grandfather both as a person and as an artist:

> I wish he'd been alive to see what's happened. He was around when 'Loser' came out, and he was incredibly proud. He kept all the articles. He connected with the things I was doing with hip-hop because he came out of the hipster, Beat thing – using language as freestyle

Programme of events for New York launch of Playing With Matches

expression, coming up with the most outlandish combinations of slang and rhyming things. But he didn't get to see what I'm doing now.

After having an initial run at a gallery in Winnipeg, the collection of Beck and Al's work finally got a high-profile position at the Santa Monica Museum of Art in May 1998 under the name Playing With Matches. The exhibit contained work by Beck and his grandfather in a series of different media. 'It's a bunch of biker–body builder collages I did when I was like 19, when I was living with my grandfather in Germany,' Beck said of his contribution to the exhibition and accompanying book. To kick things off a special gala benefit evening was held at the museum with a series of performance art pieces conducted to entertain the hundreds of attendees. The new gallery complex at the museum, the Bergamot Station, was officially opened on 7 May to coincide with the show.

Beck provided the most reported on aspect of the show with a piece called 'New Age Evisceration 1'. Prior to the performance, Beck called the piece 'a combination of Yanni and Tony Robbins . . . it will be the longest twenty minutes of your life'. When questioned further he gave away a little more: 'The death of the age of Aquarius – think about naked dolphins fucking computers.' Well, this second description came a little closer to the mark of what actually happened.

Performed in a garage, with a basketball hoop over the door, Beck and his band played about 20 minutes of synthesiser music with some semi-mystical words over the top. Beck was dressed as a sort of 1960s or 70s hippie, with a long wig and fake moustache. The musicians, dubbed as 'Dreamcatcher' for the night, were dressed in white boiler-suits and horse-head masks. Beck, in a deep voice, mumbled out such quotes as 'this is the eruption of your inner teenager' and 'imagine naked dolphins' before a band member in dolphin suit ran on and rammed a dildo into a mock computer. Beck then chainsawed it in half – the keyboard that is – to some hysterical laughter and an equal amount of puzzled looks. At the end of the year Beck looked back on this performance:

> One of this year's personal highpoints was the debut of my band Dreamcatcher at the opening of 'Playing With Matches'. I've been working on it for years. It's a sort of motivational New Age musical and visual experience. I prepared by meditating 29 hours a day at least three days beforehand, and I shed my skin about five times to prepare myself to give the gift of wisdom. We had a sort of dolphin healing ceremony . . . you kinda had to be there, I think.

Others included in the night's festivities were Channing Hansen and spoken-word terrorist Karen Finley who gave an X-rated monologue. As an avant-garde performance artist, Channing has followed more directly in his grandfather's footsteps than Beck and on this night he re-enacted the 'Yoko Ono Piano Drop' and performed his own 'Elegy For The Fluxus Dead'. This is where he wraps himself up in tape while calling out the names of Fluxus members who have passed away – 'Rudolf Shwartzkogler, Richard Maxfield, Ken Dewey, James Waring, Addi Koepcke, Marcel Duchamp, Albert Fine, George Maciunas, Brian Buczak, Robert Filliou, Bob Watts, Charlotte Moorman, John Cage, Piero Helickzer, Joe Jones, Al Hansen, Wolf Vostell, Dieter Rot, Dick Higgins'. Beck spoke of his watching the piano drop:

> I was really taken aback at how moving it was. First, there was this huge sound of the piano hitting the ground. There were 400 people there, and as soon as the piano hit the ground they were swarming around it, ripping it apart, giving pieces to Channing to sign. And there

were all these sounds of the hammers and the strings and the keys being ripped out of the piano. I wasn't expecting that at all.

After a stay on the West Coast the exhibition moved cross-country to New York and the Thread Waxing Space gallery in mid-September. Again there was an event to kick things off, this time at New York's Roxy where a gang of celebrities wanted to be seen at this Happening. Lou Reed, Laurie Anderson, Kate Moss, Liv Tyler, Yoko Ono, Evan Dando and Gwyneth Paltrow were among the many spotted by a sizeable media crowd that turned up to report on the show.

Having 'Twister' mats for tablecloths and featuring performance art and Lower East Side Noise – Cat Power, J Mascis and Foot (a Thurston Moore Experience) – the assembled throngs saw Fluxus veteran Larry Miller screaming his way through 'Danger Music, No. 17' and Channing Hansen again performing his 'Elegy For The Fluxus Dead'. Beck thought about putting on another of his performances but explained why he changed his mind: 'I don't really have time, there's too much stuff going on. That last piece took two weeks to put together. It was almost as much work as doing a video. There were a lot of, for lack of a better word, production values involved. We had to build different set pieces.' He did however find the time to appear at the Rizzoli bookstore to sign copies of the *Playing With Matches* book.

Many TV crews showed up to film footage of this event and interviews with Yoko Ono and Beck were broadcast. Ono remembered Al Hansen by saying, 'He was a unique and interesting artist, and a friend. I have one of his Hershey's-chocolate collages. It somehow wandered my way – it was the sixties, you know.'

The exhibition had a powerful effect on Beck: 'There's a lot of memories here for me – like the Hershey-bar kite with the bottom knocked off. It was hanging in our house when I was five, and my brother Channing ran into it and it fell on his foot and broke.'

After leaving New York, the exhibition showed up in Vancouver and at the LaForet Gallery in Tokyo to coincide with Beck's April 1999 shows there. Sean Carrillo taped the opening in Tokyo for a documentary that he's been preparing for a couple of years and Channing again performed.

I'll let Beck have the final word on Al:

He puts things together, finds a bizarre name and sells his creations for lots of money. He makes fun of the world. He enjoys himself more than the people who buy his works. My music is also ridiculous, I'm just an impostor. Thanks to his teaching I could never take myself seriously.

## Single artwork *(in alphabetical order)*

### Beercan (1994)

This is a bit of a curate's egg. The front cover is hard to make out but it looks like a close-up photo of an empty tin and a pile of cigarette butts on some grass. The US maxi-single came in a standard CD box and the insert had a Polaroid photo with the words 'Formula Zero Bjeck' in cut-out letters plastered on top of it. The back cover shows another Polaroid, this time of two dogs and the words 'Dis-Go!' spelt out in more cut-out letters underneath. The French-produced European version has the same front and back covers as the US maxi-single.

### Cold Brains (1999)

When this five-track CD EP came out in 1999, it was originally as a US-only radio promo in a card sleeve. The cover had a picture of Beck from the Town Hall show in January 1999 along with some quotes from various magazines about *Mutations* and a small picture of that album's cover. The reverse had a line drawing by Jason Mason of two people shaking hands and sharing the same thought bubble of 'I think what you think.' This design was used on Beck T-shirts sold at gigs that spring.

The Australian release came in a standard jewel case with the same artwork, but minus the quotes and *Mutations* picture on the front cover.

### Deadweight (1997)

This Beck release has more cover variations than any other, with at least four different ones in circulation. The most common, on the UK CD, shows 'Kleine Sonne' (1969) (meaning 'Little Sun') by Hannah Hoch on the front and an airplane on the insert. The UK promo is a plain yellow card sleeve with just 'Beck Deadweight' written in white. Two other European promo CDs are a Dutch version with a big red heart on the cover which has a hole in the centre of it, and a French one with McGregor and Diaz on the cover and all the songs from the *A Life Less Ordinary* soundtrack album listed on the reverse.

### Devils Haircut (1996)

Not surprisingly, all versions of this single feature the Manuel Ocampo painting of the demon sitting on a pot, from the *Odelay* collage, on their cover. The reverse of each cover shows other detail from the same painting, while the second UK CD shows a zoomed in picture of just the demon's top half – a handy fact to know if you're after the Noel Gallagher remix of the title track.

### It's All In Your Mind (1994)

This low-key K Records release on 7" vinyl only comes in a wrap-around paper sleeve. Most of the front cover is taken up with the title with a thin photo of Beck standing in a garden with his back to the camera. The back is taken up with the song titles in large blue and orange letters. The whole package was designed by Tae Won Yu.

### Jack-ass (1996)

The cover of this single features a braying donkey. Both the CD and double 7" singles were gatefold sleeves with the centre showing a portrait of Beck with Willie Nelson, by Autumn deWilde, from the 'Jack-ass' video shoot. The back cover shows a smoking pipe with an image of a man and woman in a boat rising in the smoke – an image that was recreated in the accompanying video. Promotional versions of this single came with plain non-picture sleeves.

### Loser (1993)

The original Bong Load version of this single in 1993 featured a cover of Beck stepping over the photographer while wearing a strange goggle-eyed mask and carrying a pitchfork. The whole thing was shaded red and had an oval logo in the centre simply saying 'Beck'. The reissue in 1994 had the same front cover but had 'Beck' in the centre in white letters. The US version has 'Loser' written in white in the bottom left of the cover while the UK version has 'Loser' written directly below 'Beck' for some unknown reason. The CD insert showed Beck passed out on a floor that looked like a bright blue sky.

In 1994 there was also a 7" jukebox single which came in a plain blue paper sleeve and a 12" promo in a white sleeve with a red sticker on it proclaiming 'Beck Loser'.

### MTV Makes Me Wanna Smoke Crack (1992)

Beck's debut, most collectible, release came as a split 7" single with Bean on Flipside Records. Beck's 'MTV Makes Me Wanna Smoke Crack' and 'To See That Woman Of Mine' came on blue vinyl. The foldout picture sleeve showed a black and white photo of Beck with a flaming acoustic guitar and came with a foldout lyric sheet insert.

### Nobody's Fault But My Own (1999)

This Japanese-only jewel-case CD was one of the least imaginative of Beck's covers to date. It's a Charlie Gross photo of Beck sitting in an empty theatre wearing a bright red shirt among empty bright red seats. This was possibly taken at the Town Hall in New York.

## Pay No Mind (1995)

All formats of this single show what looks like a close-up of a ball of twine on the cover. The back shows a photo of Beck wearing glasses, similar to the ones he wore on his '120 Minutes' appearance with Thurston Moore in 1994, and with 'Got No Mind' plastered across his forehead. The actual CDs copy the front cover with a yellow design; the Japanese version is blue. The small print claims that the three backing tracks were 'Evacuated onto 4 track in 1998'. This single was issued in 1995 and the three tracks in question ('Special People', 'Trouble All My Days' and 'Supergolden (Sunchild)') are all actually from the *Golden Feelings* tape in 1993.

## Sissyneck (1997)

As this song was Beck's updated take on country, it was apt that the cover should be of him wearing a cowboy hat. The reverse showed a colourful drawing of a cowboy riding a horse while there was a funky swirly design on the disc. The 'Australian Tour Edition' said exactly that on the cover but was otherwise identical to the other versions. A single-track promo CD was available in a brown cardboard sleeve with the braying donkey from the 'Jack-ass' sleeve on the back.

## Steve Threw Up (1994)

The cover of this Bong Load 7" single shows the German folk singer Heino. His super-deep voice featured on many a 1960s release. The front cover also carries the logo 'Stereo-Pathetic High Fidelity' which Beck used on his Flipside album. The back shows a picture of Beck on his bike wearing a flying helmet taken by Ross Harris. The sides of the record are numbered as '2' and '3'. The unlisted song on side 3, 'Cupcake', is represented by a childlike drawing of a cupcake on the centre of the record which is accredited to 'Clare no.1 dream girl USA'.

## The New Pollution (1997)

The sixties theme from the video to this single translated on to the designs for the CDs and vinyl that were released. The best way to differentiate between the many versions of this release is to look at the swirls, which hold the secret. The US CD version featured red and blue swirls on a black background, the UK versions had red swirls on a green background (this was copied, confusingly, for the US promo CD as well) and an alternate cover of yellow and orange bubbles on a black background. This bubble effect was copied on the Japanese release which came with a total of eight tracks and was titled *The New Pollution And Other Favourites*. If you want to be sure what you're buying, read the label, carefully.

## Tropicalia (1998)

This had been planned as the only single from *Mutations* and featured a very distinctive cover. The keyboard design is taken from Beck's own mixed-media piece 'Emergency Flag' (1998), as is the inner design with all the numbers listed down the left-hand side. The actual CD, and the centre of the 7", also shows a drawing by Beck that is a detail of the same art-piece. The UK version was mispressed and so the design is only really visible when held up to the light, while the European version shows a bold blue on yellow design. There was also a card-sleeved UK promo CD with a different sleeve showing 'Beck Tropicalia' written seven times in bold orange and green lettering.

## Twig (1995)

Chris Ballew and Beck put out this 7" under the names Caspar and Mollusk on Cosmic Records in 1995. The yellow vinyl was housed in a black and yellow sleeve which shows a trio of alien like creatures on a kind of lunar landscape.

## Where It's At (1996)

All versions of this single have exactly the same artwork, just to confuse you. And confusing it can be as there are at least 11 versions of this single spread over 12", cassette and CD. All of them show the famous blue and white 'Two turntables and a microphone' logo that was seen on so many T-shirts during 1996 and 1997. The predominantly blue and green reverse has a small bird with the 'Compact Disc' logo in its mouth watching over a speckled brown egg. While the front cover connection is obvious, the back cover connection is far from it. Any suggestions?

## Album artwork *(in alphabetical order)*

### A Western Harvest Field By Moonlight (1994)

The cover of this 10" vinyl album shows exactly what it says in the title, while for some reason, the spine states 'A Western Harvest Moon By Moonlight'. If you turn the back cover 90 degrees you see another harvest field by moonlight in strips which alternate with a floral pattern. The initial 2,000 copies of this record came with a free finger-painting and an orange sticker on the cover saying 'original finger painting enclosed'. These mini-artworks came in various shapes and sizes, some were merely blurs of colour while others depicted mini-portraits. All of them were painted at parties hosted by Beck and Fingerpaint Records. The middle of each record has a series of doodles among the song titles. The two sides of the record are listed as the 'Bic' side and the 'Beek' side. If you hold the latter in front of a mirror you can read the message 'Happiness grows in your own backyard'.

## Banjo Story (1993)

Not an official release but this tape did have a cover designed by a mysterious individual going by the name of Marcel. It shows a bald-headed person (possibly a baby) riding on the back of a centipede.

## Mellow Gold (1994)

For Beck's debut album on Geffen he chose a dramatic cover shot. The anarchic-looking robot backed by the Armageddon-like sky is titled 'The Last Man After Nuclear War' by Eddie Lopez. Lopez can be seen in the 'Loser' and 'Where It's At' videos and also in the band Sukia. Beck explains:

> A friend of mine, Eddie, made that. He's from Guatemala and he does autobody work, I went down to the garage one day and he showed it to me and I was just blown away, it was so beautiful. That thing shoots fire and it moves as well – he brought it down to a show and it started following me. When I asked the record company to put it on the cover it was hilarious, they wanted a good shot so they took it to a fashion studio – they even had a make-up man there for him! He didn't have much to do, that robot looks beautiful anyway.

The back cover shows Beck in his flying goggles (as on the 'Steve Threw Up' sleeve), over a collage of lots of oranges. For some reason, when this album was reissued on vinyl by Geffen in 1998 (rather than Bong Load) it showed an orange-coloured sky with Beck on the back cover instead of the oranges. The CD insert has Beck photographed with an acoustic guitar and a close-up picture of some children's toys. The Japanese release came with an extra CD booklet with the lyrics to all of the songs in both Japanese and English. The whole package was designed by Robert Fisher.

## Midnite Vultures (1999)

Unfortunately, for such a great album, this is an awful cover. While Beck was careful to give *Odelay* a cover that had no connection to the music, and he gave the simply recorded *Mutations* a simple cover shot of himself, this one is an attempt to capture his mood, circa 1999.

The dayglo-green background is a bad start and the waist-down shot of someone wearing some oh-too-tight pink plastic trousers is just too much to take. The blue graffiti-like lettering of 'Beck' and 'Midnite

175

Vultures' is OK, and maybe the whole thing does somehow fit in with the mood of the album, but it won't be everyone's cup of tea. The back cover shows some surreal colour swirls similar to the 'New Pollution' sleeves from 1997, while the figure in black has been airbrushed in a similar way to the 'Sexx Laws' sleeve. Overall it's a mess and an eye-straining one at that. Maybe that was the whole point.

## Mutations (1998)

Beck decided to make an appearance on this cover. He is seen in Charlie Gross's photo wearing a hotel laundry bag. The CD booklet is filled with the bizarre artwork of Tim Harkinson. His model, 'Finger' (1997), has two shots of it on the CD insert and his strange-looking 'balloon sculptures', 'Pneuman' (1994), 'Latex Balloon Installation: Balloon Self Portrait' (1993) and 'Reservoir' (1995), are also featured. His 'Wall Chart of World History From Earliest Times to the Present' (Detail, 1997) is used to accompany the lyric pages as Beck prints them all for the first time.

The vinyl version of the album came with a 7" single with it to fit the last two songs into the whole package and also housed a 7" × 7" colour booklet of similar artwork with a couple of extra pages than the CD. The German issue of the CD came in a gatefold digipack while the Japanese version also had an extra booklet with an article about Beck and all the lyrics – both in Japanese. The image of Beck on the actual CD is from a photograph by Autumn deWilde which can be seen when held up to the light.

## Odelay (1996)

The cover of *Odelay* features one of the most memorable cover images of recent years. It was chosen almost by accident: 'I was looking at this dog book, and I came to a picture of the most extreme dog,' said Beck. 'He looked like a bundle of flying udon noodles attempting to leap over a hurdle. I couldn't stop laughing for about 20 minutes. Plus the deadline for the cover was about a day away.'

The dog is actually a Hungarian sheep dog or Komondor. Beck found it in *The Complete Dog Book* published by the American Kennel Club. The front cover is out of kilter with the rest of the book though. Much of the artwork comes from the hand of Filipino artist and friend of Beck, Manuel Ocampo. The back cover with the egg-man is from Ocampo's *Junior Masturbator* (1996) and if you look at the bottom right-hand corner you can see the word 'Hansen'.

'I wanted to be Beck Hansen for this album,' says Beck. 'If you look on the back cover, in the lower right corner – they didn't want to put it on the front cover – it says in really tiny print, "Hansen". It's kind of too late to change though.'

The CD booklet has a collage of images from Al Hansen, Zarim Osborn and more paintings by Ocampo. Some of the images in the collage were taken out and used for the covers of singles from the album. Beck had lived near to Ocampo, whose work is full of religious imagery and strange views of animals and insects, and had known him for a while. His work has been well known in Southern California for over a decade and has been the subject of a film, *God Is My Co-Pilot*.

The vinyl album's booklet features a large fold-out poster with extra line-drawings on the reverse that aren't in the CD booklet and the back of the vinyl sleeve has a little more artwork at the top of the collage with the words 'Tabula IV' visible at the top left and a painting of a skinned turkey in the top right corner.

### One Foot In The Grave (1994)

This simply recorded album has an equally simply constructed cover to go with it. The cover shows a black and white picture of Beck and bassist James Bertram standing outside a front door. The back has a picture of Beck sitting on a swing playing an acoustic guitar. While the vinyl version has a plain white inner sleeve, the CD insert has five black and white photos of the various guest musicians.

### Stereopathetic Soul Manure (1994)

The cover for this album is taken from the cover of a record called *Brahms, Gigi, And All That* by the Clayton Valley Singers. It shows a corner of the original album's cover. The CD booklet contains some of the stranger photos from Beck releases. One shows Beck in his beloved Star Wars Stormtrooper mask playing a banjo outside an ice-cream store; another is of two chimpanzees in human clothing playing a guitar and tambourine respectively (possibly from the TV series *Lancelot Link the Secret Chimp*) while the opposite side of the page shows Beck, and friend, with a banjo – a subtle self-put-down? The CD itself has a line drawing by Bob Gundermen showing a crude map.

# III Sing It Again – An A–Z Directory of Songs

**000.000**

| | |
|---|---|
| BECK HANSEN | vocals and all instruments |
| WRITTEN BY | Beck Hansen |
| RECORDED | G-Son Studios, Los Angeles, CA, USA, May 1995 |
| PRODUCED BY | Beck Hansen and Mario Caldato Jr |
| RELEASE DATES | Japan: February 1997 (CD 'The New Pollution And Other Favourites' single) |
| | UK: November 1997 (CD 'Devils Haircut' single, part 1) |

I don't know if you can make your CD player play backwards, but if you can this is what it might sound like. Five and a half minutes of mid-paced backwards guitar and bass with some shakers over the top. The vocal is so distorted that it's hard to work out if it's going forwards or backwards.

**11.6.45**

| | |
|---|---|
| BECK HANSEN | spoken word vocals |
| WRITTEN BY | Beck Hansen |
| RELEASE DATE | US: February 1994 (CD *Stereopathetic Soul Manure*) |

After giving the date as 6 November 1945, Beck (if it is indeed he) tells what he's been doing that day. Presumably this is a tape recording of an eleven or twelve year old Beck playing around with an old cassette recorder giving us his audio diary of that summer. If not, and it was recorded later and made to sound like he's only twelve, then he must have had way too much spare time on his hands. This day consisted of watching MTV and playing Pac-Man.

**8.4.82**

| | |
|---|---|
| BECK HANSEN | spoken word vocals |
| WRITTEN BY | Beck Hansen |
| RELEASE DATE | US: February 1994 (CD *Stereopathetic Soul Manure*) |

'I'm really bored,' states Beck to begin this segment; you'd never have guessed. 'My friend Scott slipped on a Twinkie,' he says. Riveting stuff.

## 8.6.82

| | |
|---|---|
| BECK HANSEN | spoken word vocals |
| WRITTEN BY | Beck Hansen |
| RELEASE DATE | US: February 1994 (CD *Stereopathetic Soul Manure*) |

Another bizarre snippet from the Flipside collection. This one gives the date and claims that Beck's pants were on fire. Then there's a really interesting monologue about when he had some food.

## Alcohol

| | |
|---|---|
| BECK HANSEN | vocals, guitars |
| WRITTEN BY | Beck Hansen |
| PRODUCED BY | Tom Rothrock and Rob Schnapf |
| RELEASE DATES | US: February 1994 (CD, MC, 7″ 'Loser' single) |
| | UK: February 1994 (MC, 7″ 'Loser' single) |

A gentle acoustic ballad that would have fitted nicely on *One Foot In The Grave*. Occasionally played live but has never been a regular part of the set. 'Alcohol leaving me dry/Alcohol please give me some,' sings Beck as he strums away.

## American Wasteland

| | |
|---|---|
| BECK HANSEN | vocals and all instruments |
| MARIO P | guitar |
| SEAN ROSS | bass |
| WRITTEN BY | Beck Hansen |
| PRODUCED BY | Beck Hansen, Mike Simpson and John King |
| RELEASE DATES | Japan: June 1996 (CD, 'Where It's At' single) |
| | Australia: 1996 (CD, 'Devils Haircut' single) |
| | UK: November 1996 (CD, 'Devils Haircut' single) |
| | US: November 1996 (12″ 'Devils Haircut' single) |

One of many 'Devils Haircut' remixes, this hardcore rock version was perhaps the most radical. Mixed to sound like it was recorded live in concert, it begins with the end of a hardcore thrash song; a bit of crowd noise is heard before someone announces, 'This next song is called "American Wasteland".' The high-speed version follows with extra guitar and bass added for good measure. The song abruptly ends and the next song, 'Go To Hell', starts up as the track fades out. Beck has actually played this version of 'Devils Haircut' live.

## Aphid Manure Heist

| | |
|---|---|
| BECK HANSEN | vocals, guitar |
| WRITTEN BY | Beck Hansen |
| RECORDED | Poop Alley Studios, Los Angeles, CA, USA |
| PRODUCED BY | Tom Grimley |
| RELEASE DATE | US: February 1994 (CD *Stereopathetic Soul Manure*) |

After a short burst of unidentified classical music this track abruptly turns into a kind of sea-shanty. The vocalist is uncredited but sounds like it could a 1940s country artist or Beck singing through a clever distortion device. The real Beck takes over the vocal for less than three seconds at the end.

## Asshole

| | |
|---|---|
| BECK HANSEN | vocals, guitars |
| WRITTEN BY | Beck Hansen |

*Studio version:*

| | |
|---|---|
| RECORDED | Dub Narcotic Studios, Olympia, WA, USA, October 1993 |
| PRODUCED BY | Calvin Johnson |

*Live version:*

| | |
|---|---|
| RECORDED | Golden Gate park, San Francisco, CA, USA, 16 June 1996 |
| PRODUCED BY | Pat McCarthy |

*Release dates:*

| | |
|---|---|
| STUDIO VERSION | US: November 1994 (CD, LP, MC *One Foot In The Grave*) |
| LIVE VERSION | UK: 1997 (CD *Tibetan Freedom Concert*, 3CD set – live version) |
| | US: 1997 (CD *Tibetan Freedom Concert*, 3CD set – live version) |

Possibly the best song from his Olympia sessions with Calvin Johnson, this song has been a live favourite from the start and is still regularly played today. It was recorded at the first Tibetan Freedom concert and released the following year. Tom Petty covered this track as part of his soundtrack to the movie *She's The One* in 1996. Beck has sometimes changed the lyric to 'Make's me feel like Tom Petty'.

## Asskizz Powergrudge (Payback '94)

| | |
|---|---|
| BECK HANSEN | vocals, guitar, drums, noise |
| WRITTEN BY | Beck Hansen |
| RECORDED | Poop Alley Studios, Los Angeles, CA, USA |
| PRODUCED BY | Beck Hansen and Tom Grimley |
| RELEASE DATE | US: 1994 (CD, 'Beercan' single) |

Stunted strumming and biscuit-tin-lid percussion accompany Beck's low spoken vocal on the 'Beercan' B-side. The song deteriorates into some serious noise for the finale.

## Atmospheric Conditions

| | |
|---|---|
| BECK HANSEN | vocals, guitar |
| SCOTT PLOUF | drums |
| CALVIN JOHNSON | vocals |
| CHRIS BALLEW | guitar |
| WRITTEN BY | Beck Hansen |
| RECORDED | Dub Narcotic Studios, Olympia, WA, USA, January 1994 |

| | |
|---|---|
| PRODUCED BY | Calvin Johnson |
| RELEASE DATE | US: November 1994 (CD, LP, MC *One Foot In The Grave*) |

Beck sings backing vocals to Johnson's deep lead vocals on this, the last track on his K Records debut. Not to be confused with 'Atmospheric Recordings', this sprightly little number is one of the better moments on the album and one of the few that includes an electric guitar.

### Atmospheric Recordings

| | |
|---|---|
| BECK HANSEN | laughter |
| RECORDED | live to cassette |
| RELEASE DATE | not officially released, available on *Banjo Story* tape |

Not a musical track but a short recording of Beck (and friend?) watching a cartoon on TV. Between the exaggerated laughter an episode of what sounds like *Daffy Duck* can be heard.

### Baby

This is not really a new Beck track at all but one which was mistitled. The *Quodlibet* bootleg (later reissued simply as *Beck*) contained this track from a BBC radio session, but it's actually the original version of 'Static'.

### Bad Energy

| | |
|---|---|
| BECK HANSEN | vocals, guitar |
| WRITTEN BY | Beck Hansen |
| PRODUCED BY | Beck Hansen |
| RELEASE DATE | US: January 1993 (MC *Golden Feelings*) |

Beck begins this oddity by wailing 'I know who you are, but you don't know me' in his best Mick Jagger impression. He then talks in an overly deep voice about some 'bad' things.

### Beautiful Way

| | |
|---|---|
| BECK HANSEN | vocals, guitar, bass, harmonica |
| ROGER MANNING JR | keyboards, tambourine |
| GREG LEISZ | pedal steel |
| JAY DEE MANESS | pedal steel |
| SMOKEY HORMEL | guitar |
| BETH ORTON | background vocals |
| WRITTEN BY | Beck Hansen |
| RECORDED | Beck's house, Silverlake, CA, USA, February 1999 |
| PRODUCED BY | Beck Hansen and Mickey Petralia |
| RELEASE DATES | US: November 1999 (CD, MC, LP *Midnite Vultures*) |
| | UK: November 1999 (CD, MC, LP *Midnite Vultures*) |

One of the best tracks on *Midnite Vultures* and the one that stands out like a sore thumb, both musically and lyrically. An understated country tune with gentle percussion and pedal steel nicely complementing Beth Orton's sparse backing vocals to 'beautiful' effect.

## Beercan

| | |
|---|---|
| BECK HANSEN | vocals and all instruments |
| MIKE BIOTO | organ |
| WRITTEN BY | Beck Hansen and Carl Stephenson |
| RECORDED | Carl Stephenson's house, Los Angeles, CA, USA |
| PRODUCED BY | Beck Hansen and Carl Stephenson |
| RELEASE DATES | UK: March 1994 (CD, LP, MC *Mellow Gold*) |
| | US: March 1994 (CD, LP, MC *Mellow Gold*) |
| | UK: 1994 (CD, 7" 'Beercan' single) |
| | US: 1994 (CD, 'Beercan' single) |

The second single from *Mellow Gold*, this upbeat track features Carl Stephenson's trademark hip-hop loops and a typically whacky Beck lyric. In this catchy tune he sings and raps of 'Wino's throwing frisbees at the sun', 'Now I'm running like a flaming pig.' Stephenson also throws in several uncredited samples during the break then asks 'How'd you like me now?' 'Pretty good.' By the way, the uncredited guitar sample is apparently from the Melvins' song 'Hog Leg'.

## Big Stompin' Mama

| | |
|---|---|
| BECK HANSEN | vocals, percussion |
| WRITTEN BY | Beck Hansen |
| RECORDED | Los Angeles, CA, USA, 1992–93 |
| PRODUCED BY | Beck Hansen |
| RELEASE DATE | not officially released, available on *Fresh Meat And Old Slabs* tape |

Starting with a strange crackly sample, Beck screams about the Mama in question while playing some bizarre percussion in this quasi-marching tune. Not essential.

## Blackfire Choked Our Death

| | |
|---|---|
| BECK HANSEN | vocals |
| WRITTEN BY | Beck Hansen |
| PRODUCED BY | Beck Hansen |
| RELEASE DATE | US: January 1994 (10" *A Western Harvest Field By Moonlight*) |

Beck went overboard on his distorted vocals for this one. An a cappella blues wail about a big fire.

## Blackhole

| | |
|---|---|
| BECK HANSEN | vocals, guitars |
| DAVID HARTE | drums |
| ROB ZABRECKY | bass |
| PETRA HADEN | violin |
| WRITTEN BY | Beck Hansen |

| | |
|---|---|
| PRODUCED BY | Beck Hansen, Rob Schnapf and Tom Rothrock |
| RELEASE DATES | UK: March 1994 (CD, LP, MC *Mellow Gold*) |
| | US: March 1994 (CD, LP, MC *Mellow Gold*) |

After the weird and crazy characters running about through Beck's major label debut, this is perhaps a surprisingly downbeat and sober ending to the album. It was a trick that he'd repeat with 'Ramshackle' at the end of *Odelay*. Petra Haden guests from That Dog.

## Bogus Flow

| | |
|---|---|
| BECK HANSEN | vocals, guitars, harmonica |
| WRITTEN BY | Beck Hansen |
| RELEASE DATE | US: 1994 (CD *Geffen Rarities Vol. 1* promo) |

Described by Beck as 'Pulling up roots ... again. Stranded in the decaying harbour. Surfing in the oil spillage.' Well, you can't really argue with that; especially if you don't know what it means. One of Beck's rambling, bizarre lyrics similar to 'Pay No Mind', he could change the words to this from performance to performance. It contains some of his most astute observations ('People with cordless personalities') and at one point he almost has to stop as he struggles to contain his laughter.

## Bogus Soul

| | |
|---|---|
| BECK HANSEN | vocals, guitars |
| WRITTEN BY | Beck Hansen |
| PRODUCED BY | Beck Hansen |
| RELEASE DATE | US: January 1993 (MC *Golden Feelings*) |

Sounding like a live performance, Beck wails away over some acoustic guitar while being heckled. A song that had never been anywhere, and wasn't likely ever to go anywhere either.

## Bonus Beats

| | |
|---|---|
| BECK HANSEN | vocals and all instruments |
| WRITTEN BY | Beck Hansen, Mike Simpson and John King |
| RECORDED | PCP Labs, Silverlake, CA, USA , 1995 |
| PRODUCED BY | John King |
| RELEASE DATES | US: June 1996 (CD, 12" 'Where It's At' single) |
| | UK: June 1996 (CD, 12" 'Where It's At' single) |

This remix of 'Where It's At' is quite a departure from the original. John King adds some heavy beats to the mix while stripping almost everything else away, vocals included. What vocals he does leave are basically the some robotic sounding calls of 'Make-out city' and 'California, where it's at', and the clips of 'What about those who swing both ways?' and 'That's beautiful'.

## Bonus Noise

| | |
|---|---|
| BECK HANSEN | noise making |
| WRITTEN BY | Beck Hansen |

| RELEASE DATES | US: March 1994 (CD *Mellow Gold*) |
| | UK: March 1994 (CD *Mellow Gold*) |
| | US: March 1994 (CD 'Beercan' single) |
| | UK: June 1996 (CD *Odelay*) |

Two different versions of 'Bonus Noise' have been inflicted upon Beck's fans. The first was found unlisted at the end of *Mellow Gold* and another version was found at the end of some copies of *Odelay*. Of the second version, Beck said 'That was a freeze-up on the recording machine. The recording machine froze. It was playing the same part of a song over and over. We just taped it. That was the machine's two cents, its attempt to contribute to the album in some way.'

## Bottle Of Blues

| BECK HANSEN | vocals, guitar, harmonica, synthesiser |
| ROGER MANNING | synthesiser, backing vocals |
| JUSTIN MELDAL-JOHNSEN | bass |
| JOEY WARONKER | drums |
| WRITTEN BY | Beck Hansen |
| RECORDED | Ocean Way Studios, Los Angeles, CA, USA |
| PRODUCED BY | Nigel Godrich and Beck Hansen |
| RELEASE DATES | UK: 2 November 1998 (CD, LP, MC *Mutations*) |
| | US: 3 November 1998 (CD, LP, MC *Mutations*) |

One of the more rockin' tracks on *Mutations*, this song had been in Beck's live catalogue for a while. A straight ahead track that was recorded and mixed in one afternoon.

## Bottle Of Wine

| BECK HANSEN | vocals, banjo, drums |
| RECORDED | live to cassette |
| RELEASE DATE | not officially released, available on *Banjo Story* tape |

One of Beck's first ever recordings – it's listed on the original early sleeve for *Banjo Story*. Typical of the rest of the tape, just Beck, banjo and crude, biscuit-tin-lid percussion. He 'Smoked the wallpaper, sniffed the glue' then moved on to the subject of this song.

## Broken Train

| BECK HANSEN | vocals, guitar, mariambas, keyboards, background vocals |
| ROGER MANNING JR | synthesiser, clavinet, percussion, guitar |
| JOEY WARONKER | drums |
| JUSTIN MELDAL-JOHNSEN | bass, percussion |
| WRITTEN BY | Beck Hansen |
| RECORDED | Beck's house, Silverlake, CA, USA |
| PRODUCED BY | Beck Hansen and Mickey Petralia |
| RELEASE DATES | US: November 1999 (CD, MC, LP *Midnite Vultures*) |
| | UK: November 1999 (CD, MC, LP *Midnite Vultures*) |

Almost released as 'Out Of Kontrol', but changed to its present title at the last moment. Beck sings of a strange place where 'The snipers are passed out/In the bushes again/I'm glad I got my suit dry-cleaned/ Before the riots started' to the accompaniment of a jazzy little instrumental track with some even jazzier percussion. 'Did you ever let a cowboy sit on your lap?' asks Beck in one of the most straightforward tracks on a very unstraightforward album.

## Brother

| | |
|---|---|
| BECK HANSEN | vocals, guitar, bass, piano |
| WRITTEN BY | Beck Hansen |
| RECORDED | Sunset Sound Studio, Los Angeles, CA, USA, January 1995 |
| PRODUCED BY | Tom Rothrock and Rob Schnapf |
| RELEASE DATES | UK: September 1997 (CD 'Jack-ass' single) |
| | US: September 1997 (12" 'Jack-ass' single) |
| | Australia: 1997 (CD 'Sissyneck' Tour EP) |

One of the songs originally composed for *Odelay* and one of the few that actually survived. Not typical of Beck by a long way, it features very prominent piano and a longing vocal performance. Maybe an indication of what *Odelay* might have turned out like or maybe of some material he still has hidden away somewhere.

## Burnt Orange Peel

| | |
|---|---|
| BECK HANSEN | vocals, guitar |
| SCOTT PLOUF | drums |
| CHRIS BALLEW | guitar |
| JAMES BERTRAM | bass |
| WRITTEN BY | Beck Hansen |
| RECORDED | Dub Narcotic Studios, Olympia, WA, USA, January 1994 |
| PRODUCED BY | Calvin Johnson |
| RELEASE DATE | US: November 1994 (CD, LP, MC *One Foot In The Grave*) |

A rowdy track full of 'Whoo-hoo's', maybe an early influence for Blur's 'Song 2'? Maybe not. From Beck's second trip to Olympia, this track rocks along at quite a pace, full of distorted guitar. This is what anti-folk probably sounded like in 1989.

## Burro

| | |
|---|---|
| BECK HANSEN | vocals |
| PERFORMED BY | Mariachi Los Camperos de Nati Cana |
| ARRANGED BY | David Campbell and Juan Morales |
| WRITTEN BY | Beck Hansen |
| RECORDED | Sunset Studios, Los Angeles, CA, USA, 1997 |
| PRODUCED BY | Beck Hansen |
| RELEASE DATES | UK: September 1997 (CD 'Jack-ass' single) |

US: September 1997 (12″ 'Jack-ass' single)
US: 1999 (CD *The Best Latin Party Album In The World
... Ever!* compilation)
Australia: 1997 (CD 'Sissyneck' Tour EP)

Sometimes referred to as the 'Mariachi Version' or 'Mariachi Mix', this is the Spanish version of 'Jack-ass'. After hearing Mariachi Los Camperos de Nati Cana perform at a local restuarant, La Fonda, Beck asked them into the studio to record this song. Stepfather Sean Carrillo translated the lyric and father David Campbell helped to arrange it; the outcome was this amazing version.

## Canceled Check

| | |
|---|---|
| BECK HANSEN | vocals, slide guitar |
| ROGER MANNING | piano, synthesiser, percussion |
| JUSTIN MELDAL-JOHNSEN | bass |
| JOEY WARONKER | drums |
| SMOKEY HORMEL | acoustic guitar |
| GREG LEISZ | pedal steel |
| DAVID RALICKE | trombone |
| ELLIOTT CAINE | trumpet |
| WRITTEN BY | Beck Hansen |
| RECORDED | Ocean Way Studios, Los Angeles, CA, USA, March 1998 |
| PRODUCED BY | Beck Hansen and Nigel Godrich |
| RELEASE DATES | UK: November 1998 (CD, LP, MC *Mutations*) |
| | US: November 1998 (CD, LP, MC *Mutations*) |

This track is somewhat of a rarity in that Beck played it live for several years before finally recording it for *Mutations*. Therefore you can see the lyrical progression from the early live versions of the song to the final one which appeared on the album. Written in Japan during August and September 1994 it was inspired by motivational speaker Tony Robins in a story well told by Beck during numerous gigs. Late one night he was trying to get to sleep in a hotel and channel surfing Japanese TV when he stumbled on an English language channel which was showing an 'infomercial' by Mr Robins. Robins, as usual, was expatiating on the various 'easy' ways of making money and expanding real estate and his catchphrase was 'The past is a cancelled check, your maximum point of power is now!' Beck reminisced that 'The song just fit in with my life at the time and how certain things were at the time.'

On returning to the US that autumn Beck put this song straight into his set-list for the rest of the tour. Early versions were musically identical to the final one but lyrically some tweaking took place along the way. Initially the first verse had the line 'I heard you moaning' which was replaced by 'You're so helpless' but otherwise it remained intact. The chorus was not changed at all but the second verse has gone through at least three different versions. Version 1 in 1994 started 'You're building momentum/Something you want to avoid doing'; by his 1995 radio appearance on KCRW it had become 'Stumbling religion/starting to get annoyed' before he finally settled on 'Count your blessings/And do the things that you should'. There may have been even more in-studio changes as Beck attempted to record it for *Odelay* in 1995. 'I tried to record this for *Odelay*,' he told *Rolling Stone*, 'but it just didn't fit.'

By the time the *Mutations* sessions were underway, producer Nigel Godrich was becoming more confident about putting his own ideas forward. He thought that 'Canceled Check' was too smooth and wanted a few imperfections to come to the surface, even if they were manufactured. 'We made everyone play with bags over their heads,' he recalled. 'The idea was to increase the chances of playing wrong notes because the musicians were too proficient. We wanted to loosen up the feel, and it worked quite well, actually.'

Beck had trouble in finalising the song, so it was decided to get their money's worth from all the hired percussion instruments that were sitting unused in the back room of the studio. The lights were switched off and everyone just let rip, throwing things around and generally making a heck of a racket. 'We decided on a jam where they throw stuff around the studio, so it sounds pretty anarchic,' laughed Godrich. 'I think blood was drawn on at least one occasion,' deadpanned Beck when asked to comment on the noisefest – and after five years the song was done.

### Captain Brain

| | |
|---|---|
| BECK HANSEN | vocals, guitar |
| WRITTEN BY | Beck Hansen |
| RECORDED | Los Angeles, CA, USA, 1992–93 |
| PRODUCED BY | Beck Hansen |
| RELEASE DATE | not officially released, available on *Fresh Meat And Old Slabs* tape |

Another song from the *Fresh Meat And Old Slabs* tape recorded for his mother's birthday. A very stark song, sung very slowly in a deep voice similar to the one he used for 'Trouble All My Days'. 'Captain Brain is coming down/Thinking about nothing at all/Who could it be?' he sings, and it's all over in under a minute.

### Casio (Good Stuff)

| | |
|---|---|
| WRITTEN BY | Beck Hansen |
| RELEASE DATE | unreleased |

Part of the live collection in 1993–94, this funky little number was so named because Beck would pull out his Casio keyboard and play it guitar style. A studio version has never been released, either officially or otherwise, so it is uncertain whether it has actually ever been recorded.

## Chewin' Like Gilligan

| | |
|---|---|
| BECK HANSEN | vocals, banjo |
| WRITTEN BY | Beck Hansen |
| RECORDED | New York, NY, USA, 1988 |
| PRODUCED BY | Beck Hansen |
| RELEASE DATE | not officially released, available on *Banjo Story* tape |

Recorded in New York some time around 1988, this track was included on the *Banjo Story* tape, featuring just Beck and his banjo. Starting with Beck stomping and hitting what sounds like a bisucit tin lid, he then basically talks his way through a jumbled story about joining a travelling show and leaving town before aburptly halting with the words 'Chewin' like Gilligan'.

## Clock

| | |
|---|---|
| BECK HANSEN | vocals, all instruments |
| WRITTEN BY | Beck Hansen/Mike Simpson/John King |
| RECORDED | PCP Labs, Silverlake, CA, USA, 1995 |
| PRODUCED BY | Beck Hansen/Mike Simpson/John King |
| RELEASE DATES | Japan: June 1996 (CD, LP, MC *Odelay*) |
| | Japan: June 1996 (CD 'Where It's At' single) |
| | UK: November 1997 (CD free with *Select* magazine) |
| | UK: June 1996 (CD *Odelay* limited edition version) |
| | US: November 1996 (12" 'Devils Haircut' single) |
| | US: 1996 (CD, *Swagalicious* compilation) |

This track from the *Odelay* sessions was used as a bonus track on the Japanese version of said album and also the 'Where It's At' single. In the UK it was chosen by Beck for a freebie CD given away by *Select* magazine. The song is a steady march with a distorted Beck vocal asking numerous rhetorical questions ('Is it long before the spirit shaves its legs') with all kinds of noise effects and string samples along the way.

## Close To God

| | |
|---|---|
| BECK HANSEN | drums, vocals |
| CALVIN JOHNSON | guitar, vocals |
| WRITTEN BY | Beck Hansen |
| RECORDED | Dub Narcotic Studios, Olympia, WA, USA, 28 October 1993 |
| PRODUCED BY | Beck Hansen and Calvin Johnson |
| RELEASE DATE | US: 1998 (CD *Selector Dub Narcotic* compilation) |

It's often been quoted that Beck has 'at least' a whole album's worth of unreleased material recorded with K Records guru Calvin Johnson from late 1993 and early 1994. Five years after the first of these sessions another track saw the light of day when this song was included on the *Selector Dub Narcotic* compilation CD. Beck's track sat snuggly alongside the John Spencer Blues Explosion and Johnson's own Dub Narcotic Sound System. Scott Plouf, who played drums on some *One Foot In The Grave* songs, plays on this album with the band Telepathic Youth and also with Calvin Johnson on the track 'Ambulance Driver Blues'.

'Close To God' features joint vocals pitting Johnson's incredibly deep singing voice against Beck's, which is being put through a vocoder. The result of this is that the words are almost impossible to understand. Beck's disjointed drum-beat and 'space invader' sound effects and Johnson's occasional wah-wah guitar licks add into the mix of this track which stands alone from the material previously released from these sessions.

## Cold Brains

| | |
|---|---|
| BECK HANSEN | vocals, guitars, piano, harmonica, glockenspiel |
| JUSTIN MELDAL-JOHNSEN | bass |
| ROGER MANNING | synthesiser |
| JOEY WARONKER | drums and percussion |
| WRITTEN BY | Beck Hansen |
| RECORDED | Ocean Way Studios, Los Angeles, CA, USA, 21 February 1998 |
| PRODUCED BY | Nigel Godrich and Beck Hansen |
| RELEASE DATES | US: October 1998 (CD, *CMJ New Music Volume 63* compilation) |
| | UK: November 1998 (CD, LP, MC *Mutations*) |
| | US: November 1998 (CD, LP, MC *Mutations*) |
| | US: March 1999 (CD promo EP 'Cold Brains') |

This understated folk-rock opener to *Mutations* had been in the Beck live canon since as far back as 1994. It was the first song attempted with Nigel Godrich as producer in order to find out if the working relationship between him and Beck was going to be appropriate for the recording of *Mutations*. It was and they went on to record the album the next month.

Full of references to death and decay that would litter the album, this track soon found its way to the head of Beck's set-list for the few gigs that he played in support of the album during early 1999.

## Color Coordinated

| | |
|---|---|
| WRITTEN BY | Beck Hansen |

Another live staple from the 1993–94 period that has presumably never been recorded. This instrumental starts off as a fast guitar track before becoming a Faith No More-style drum, guitar and bass work-out and finishes at a slow plodding pace.

## Convalescent

| | |
|---|---|
| WRITTEN BY | Beck Hansen |

A loud indie-guitar styled song that would have had student unions up and down the country jumping drunkenly about had it been released as a single. Unfortunately it seems that it was never even recorded, although it can be found on numerous live tapes from 1993 and 1994. Although it's quite a departure from other Beck songs of the time, it is actually pretty good.

### Corvette Bummer

| | |
|---|---|
| BECK HANSEN | vocals, guitars, drums, bass |
| WRITTEN BY | Beck Hansen |
| RECORDED | Poop Alley Studios 1993 |
| PRODUCED BY | Tom Grimley |
| RELEASE DATES | UK: March 1994 (CD single 'Loser') |
| | US: March 1994 (CD single 'Loser') |

In typically playful Beck fashion, the sleeve to the 'Loser' single claims this track to have been recorded in either 1996 (on the US sleeve) or in 1997 (on the UK sleeve). It was actually part of the Poop Alley sessions from 1993 that also spawned several tracks on *Stereopathetic Soul Manure*. Sometimes used as the show opener on the *Mellow Gold* tour in 1994, it starts up with an infectious hip-hop beat leading into one of Beck's stream-of-consciousness lyrics. The lyric actually includes mini-references to other Beck songs of around this period – 'Ziplock Bag', 'Whiskey Can' and 'Cupcake' – while it twists and turns its way through a whole host of unlikely images, including dancing like a worm and taking off his shoes to smell his socks! Uncredited DJ scratching is a prelude to Beck's ending the song in a crazy high-pitched voice before cracking up with laughter to bring a halt to proceedings.

### Crystal Clear (Beer)

| | |
|---|---|
| BECK HANSEN | vocals, acoustic guitar |
| WRITTEN BY | Beck Hansen |
| RECORDED | Wire Works Studios |
| PRODUCED BY | Rusty Cusak |
| RELEASE DATE | US: February 1994 (CD *Stereopathetic Soul Manure*) |

Only Beck could write a song that begins with the line 'Plastic donut, can of spam/There's no kindness in this land' and sound sincere about it. Another finger-picking song, basically about not being caught getting drunk by his girlfriend. This was recorded for Beck's MTV *120 Minutes* appearance in February 1994, but had been around for quite a while before that.

### Cupcake

| | |
|---|---|
| BECK HANSEN | shouting |
| WRITTEN BY | Beck Hansen |
| RECORDED | Poop Alley Studios 1993 |
| PRODUCED BY | Tom Grimley |
| RELEASE DATE | US: 1994 (7" 'Steve Threw Up' single) |

The untitled noise after 'Motherfucker' is actually known as 'Cupcake'. Basically some distorted shouting and expletives, the song presumably got its name from just about the only discernible word on the track that wasn't x-rated. The centre of the record also shows a drawing of a cupcake by 'clare no.1 dream girl USA'.

## Curses

| | |
|---|---|
| BECK HANSEN | vocals, guitar |
| WRITTEN BY | Beck Hansen |
| RECORDED | KCRW, Santa Monica, CA, USA, 6 January 1995 |

Performed live on KCRW in 1995, this song was another in the long line of finger-picking songs. Beck sings of a list of curses that he'd like to put on different people.

## Cut 1/2 Blues

| | |
|---|---|
| BECK HANSEN | vocals, guitar |
| DON BURNETTE | drums |
| BOBBY | guitar |
| WRITTEN BY | Beck Hansen |
| RECORDED | Wire Works Studios |
| PRODUCED BY | Rusty Cusak |
| RELEASE DATE | US: February 1994 (CD *Stereopathetic Soul Manure*) |

Pronounced as 'The Cut In Half Blues', this song originally turned up on the *Fresh Meat And Old Slabs* tape but dates back as far as the late 1980s when Beck was in New York. The officially released *Stereopathetic Soul Manure* version cuts out the original first verse and chorus from the *Fresh Meat And Old Slabs* version as Beck sings about the love of his life cutting him in half with a chainsaw during the night. The missing first verse goes 'Some folks get their kicks steppin' on ants/Some folks fall for love and romance/Some like to roll in the mud and laugh/My baby just like to cut people in half.' This is supposedly the song that inspired Bong Load to approach Beck to record with them.

## Cyanide Breath Mint

| | |
|---|---|
| BECK HANSEN | vocals, guitar |
| WRITTEN BY | Beck Hansen |
| RECORDED | Dub Narcotic Studios, Olympia, WA, USA, October 1993 |
| PRODUCED BY | Calvin Johnson |
| RELEASE DATE | US: November 1994 (CD, LP, MC *One Foot In The Grave*) |

Recorded during the first sessions for the *One Foot In The Grave* album with Calvin Johnson in his basement. Comprising just vocal and guitar to put forth another of Beck's early 1990s trademark lyrics about being in a bad place at a bad time – 'Definitely this is the wrong place to be/There's blood on the futon/There's a kid drinking fire'. The song gives a very cynical vibe about all you encounter. 'I got a funny feeling they got plastic in the afterlife,' he intones as everything seems to be a fake. Beck used the title of this song for the company that deals with the publishing of his songs – Cyanide Breathmint Music.

## Dark And Lovely

| | |
|---|---|
| BECK HANSEN | vocals and all instruments |
| SAMPLES FROM | 'Out Of Sight' (James Brown) performed by Them |
| WRITTEN BY | Beck Hansen, Mike Simpson and John King |
| RECORDED | PCP Labs, Silverlake, CA, USA , 1995 |
| PRODUCED BY | Beck Hansen, Mike Simpson and John King |
| RELEASE DATES | UK: November 1996 (CD 'Devils Haircut' single) |
| | Japan: June 1996 (CD 'Where It's At' single) |
| | Australia: 1996 (CD 'Devils Haircut' single) |
| | US: November 1996 (12″ 'Devils Haircut' single) |
| | Australia: 1997 (CD 'Sissyneck' Tour EP) |

Another 'Devils Haircut' remix, this time by the Dust Brothers. This one is pretty straightforward but does add some male opera singer vocals in parts! A funkier than usual bassline and added Mike Simpson scratching also make it stand out.

## Dead Man With No Heart

| | |
|---|---|
| BECK HANSEN | vocals, banjo |
| CHRIS BALLEW | banjo |
| WRITTEN BY | Beck Hansen |
| RECORDED | KCRW, Santa Monica, CA, USA, 1 March 1994 |

Performed live as a pair of 'duelling banjos', Beck and pal Chris Ballew zipped through this track in no time at all. It hasn't been heard since.

## Dead Melodies

| | |
|---|---|
| BECK HANSEN | vocals, guitar |
| ROGER MANNING JR | keyboards |
| JUSTIN MELDAL-JOHNSEN | upright bass, background vocals |
| JOEY WARONKER | percussion |
| SMOKEY HORMEL | guitar, background vocals |
| WRITTEN BY | Beck Hansen |
| RECORDED | Ocean Way Studios, Los Angeles, CA, USA, March 1998 |
| PRODUCED BY | Nigel Godrich and Beck Hansen |
| RELEASE DATES | UK: November 1998 (CD, LP, MC *Mutations*) |
| | US: November 1998 (CD, LP, MC *Mutations*) |

Another song to make it on to *Mutations* after being around for a while. Beck played this when supporting Bob Dylan in late 1997. The baroque feel to this song is heightened by the upright bass playing of Justin Meldal-Johnsen and the whole mood of the album is summed up in Beck's simple but atmospheric lyric.

## Deadweight

| | |
|---|---|
| BECK HANSEN | vocals, guitars, bass, drum machine, keyboards |
| WRITTEN BY | Beck Hansen, Mike Simpson and John King |
| RECORDED | PCP Labs, Silverlake, Los Angeles, CA, USA, 1995 |
| PRODUCED BY | Beck Hansen, Mike Simpson and John King |
| RELEASE DATES | UK: October 1997 (CD, 7" 'Deadweight' single) |
| | UK: November 1997 (CD, MC *A Life Less Ordinary* soundtrack) |
| | UK: January 1998 (MC *Bratpack 98* compilation free with *NME*) |

Part one of Beck's supposed 'Latin Trilogy', this classy tune formed the cornerstone of the excellent soundtrack to the 1997 film *A Life Less Ordinary*. Beck is in fine form playing everything in sight and single-handedly starting off a Brazilian revival that he'd continue with 'Tropicalia'. He comments:

I get asked to do soundtracks all the time, but I met with the film-makers of *A Life Less Ordinary* early in the spring, and they talked about the movie and the scene that it was going to be for. I knew they were capable, and I also knew what they were into aesthetically, so I would do something in their vein, which is also my vein. When I was home I had two days, so I created it, and there are no samples on that song, which I'm really glad about. On a lot of soundtracks, bands give their throwaway songs. But you know, if I'm going to commit to something, it's got to be quality.

## Dead Wild Cat

| | |
|---|---|
| PRODUCED BY | Beck Hansen |
| RELEASE DATE | US: February 1994 (CD *Stereopathetic Soul Manure*) |

This is the taped conversation of someone telling Beck about finding a dead wildcat and a bottle of beer in rural Georgia. The bottle hadn't been opened so they drank it.

## Death Is Coming To Get Me

| | |
|---|---|
| BECK HANSEN | vocals, guitar |
| WRITTEN BY | Beck Hansen |
| RELEASE DATE | not released, available on the *Fresh Meat And Old Slabs* tape |

Inspired by Nimrod Workman, an old bluesman/coalminer as he told KCRW in 1993 before playing a banjo version of it.

## Debra

| | |
|---|---|
| BECK HANSEN | vocals |
| JUSTIN MELDAL-JOHNSEN | upright bass |
| ROGER MANNING JR | organ |
| JOEY WARONKER | drums |

| SMOKEY HORMEL | guitar |
| FERNANDO PULLUM | horns |
| STEVE BAXTER | horns, background vocals |
| JOE TURANO | horns, background vocals |
| CONTAINS ELEMENTS OF | 'My Love For You' (written by Ed Greene) performed by Ramsey Lewis |
| WRITTEN BY | Beck Hansen, Mike Simpson and John King |
| RECORDED | PCP Labs, Silverlake, CA, USA |
| PRODUCED BY | Beck Hansen, Mike Simpson and John King |
| RELEASE DATES | US: November 1999 (CD, MC, LP *Midnite Vultures*) |
| | UK: November 1999 (CD, MC, LP *Midnite Vultures*) |

A standard in the Beck live canon since 1996 when it almost made it on to *Odelay* and originally known as 'I Wanna Get With You (And Your Sister Debra)', this slo-jam has been a fan favourite ever since. On the eve of releasing *Midnite Vultures*, Beck had this to say about the track:

I realize that it doesn't represent what we would like to think ideal soul music is all about. No matter how slick an R&B track is, you can always rely on the lyrics to be unique. Even when they're generic, you get lines like 'I want to lick you up and down/make you real hot.' And that's what turns me on. 'Debra' embraces the absurdity and trashiness of that.

### Derelict

| BECK HANSEN | vocals and all instruments |
| WRITTEN BY | Beck Hansen, John King and Mike Simpson |
| RECORDED | PCP Labs, Silverlake, CA, USA, 1995 |
| PRODUCED BY | Beck Hansen, Mike Simpson and John King |
| RELEASE DATES | UK: June 1996 (CD, LP, MC *Odelay*) |
| | US: June 1996 (CD, LP, MC *Odelay*) |

One of the earlier songs completed for *Odelay*, this track was described by Beck as 'Coming into town on a ghost ship. The stowaways are finding themselves naked in the back of a police car, smelling like herring and birdshit.' Beck explained the line 'Gave my clothes to the policeman' as 'Sometimes the authorities need to see everybody naked; the police would be better able to govern the citizens of their town if they could see them naked.'

### Devil Got My Woman

| BECK HANSEN | vocals, guitar |
| WRITTEN BY | Skip James |
| RECORDED | Sun Studios, Memphis, TN, USA, March 1994 |
| PRODUCED BY | Beck Hansen |
| RELEASE DATES | UK: September 1997 (CD, 7" 'Jack-ass' single) |
| | Australia: 1997 (CD 'Sissyneck' Tour EP) |

A Skip James cover that is pretty much true to the original. Slide blues guitar and lots of complaints about the devil getting his woman and making her run off with his best friend.

## Devils Haircut

| | |
|---|---|
| BECK HANSEN | vocals, all instruments |
| SAMPLES FROM | 'Out Of Sight' (James Brown) performed by Them |
| | 'Soul Drums' (Bernard Purdie) performed by Pretty Purdie |
| ELEMENTS OF | 'I Can Only Give You Everthing' (Coulter/Scott) by Terry and The Pirates |
| WRITTEN BY | Beck Hansen, Mike Simpson and John King |
| RECORDED | PCP Labs, Silverlake, CA, USA, 1995 |
| PRODUCED BY | Beck Hansen, Mike Simpson and John King |
| RELEASE DATES | UK: June 1996 (CD, LP, MC *Odelay*) |
| | US: June 1996 (CD, LP, MC *Odelay*) |
| | UK: November 1996 (CD, 7″ 'Devils Haircut' single) |
| | US: November 1996 (CD 'Devils Haircut' single) |

Written during the ill-fated Lollapalooza tour in the summer of 1995, this blazing *Odelay* opener started life as 'Electric Music And The Summer People'. Described by Beck as a blues song, this single included the recurring guitar riff of 'I Can Only Give You Everything' and was remixed several times. The Noel Gallagher remix featured extra heavy guitars.

Beck went to great lengths to explain that this song could be about anything you wanted it to be about. 'I've got five stories about "Devils Haircut",' he claimed. 'It's a bogus poetic allusion to the evils of vanity. Or it could be just something that sounds good to sing to. Or it might be that I was putting my own lyrics to a Can song where I can't work out the real lyrics. And there's also a tradition of blues people talking about haircuts – gimme that wig back that I boughtcha.'

OK, only four but who cares. He also described it thus: 'The summer of '99, electric music and the summer people. Stag-o-Lee has just got out of a penitentary in Florida. He joins a schoolbus of camouflage artists tracking across the southern part of the United States. It's like an inverse freedom ride. Stag-o-Lee has lost his hat, he's hatless in this new environment.'

## Diamond Bollocks

| | |
|---|---|
| BECK HANSEN | vocals, guitars |
| ROGER MANNING JR | background vocals, harpsichord, synthesiser |
| JUSTIN MELDAL-JOHNSEN | electric bass, background vocals |
| JOEY WARONKER | drums, percussion |
| WRITTEN BY | Beck Hansen |
| RECORDED | Ocean Way Studios, Los Angeles, CA, USA, March 1998 |
| PRODUCED BY | Nigel Godrich and Beck Hansen |

| RELEASE DATES | UK: November 1998 (CD, LP, MC *Mutations*) |
| | US: November 1998 (CD, LP, MC *Mutations*) |

The black sheep of *Mutations*, this song was at complete odds with the rest of the album. 'It just didn't fit. It seemed to disrupt the whole mood. It was like a pleasant party with the obnoxious, surly guest, so we put it at the end,' said Beck. It was the only song of the *Mutations* sessions to be written in the studio and includes parts of four songs that were edited together over three days. It was named after a compliment that Beck received after a UK show when someone came up to him and said, 'That was top bollocks you diamond geezer', or words to that effect. 'It's kind of a nice indicator of things to come,' said Beck as a tease about *Midnite Vultures*.

### Diamond In The Sleaze

| BECK HANSEN | vocals, guitars, bass |
| ROGER MANNING JR | keyboards, drums, percussion |
| DAVID RALICKE | flute |
| WRITTEN BY | Beck Hansen |
| RECORDED | Los Angeles, CA, USA, 1999 |
| ENGINEERED BY | Tony Hoffer |
| MIXED BY | Mickey P |
| RELEASE DATES | Japan: April 1999 (CD 'Nobody's Fault But My Own' single) |
| | Australia: May 1999 (CD 'Cold Brains' single) |

A tribute to how far Beck's songwriting had progressed was that this B-side was better than some things that made it on to his previous albums. A catchy pop song with a difference that benefits greatly from Roger Manning's flirty keyboards.

### Diskobox

| BECK HANSEN | vocals, all instruments |
| JON SPENCER | keychain |
| WRITTEN BY | Beck Hansen, Mike Simpson and John King |
| RECORDED | PCP Labs, Silverlake, CA, USA, 1995 |
| PRODUCED BY | Beck Hansen, Jon Spencer, Mike Simpson and John King |
| RELEASE DATE | UK: June 1996 (CD *Odelay*) |

To pay back for Beck's appearance on 'Flavor', Jon Spencer made a brief appearance on this *Odelay* bonus track. Another distorted Beck vocal screams over a funky backbeat in a sort of cross between 'High Five' and Spencer's own 'Flavor'.

### Don't You Mind People Grinnin' In Your Face

| BECK HANSEN | vocals, piano |
| WRITTEN BY | Son House |
| RECORDED | KCRW Radio, Santa Monica, CA, USA, 23 July 1993 |
| | Radio Free LA, CA, USA, 20 January 1997 |

Beck treated listeners of KCRW's *Morning Becomes Eclectic* to a rare piano performance of this song in 1995. It was performed as a lonesome blues song, but unfortunately had to be faded out as the show came to an end. Two years later, on another radio session, he played a more traditional guitar version of the song.

### Drivin' Nails In My Coffin

| | |
|---|---|
| BECK HANSEN | vocals |
| WILLIE NELSON | vocals |
| WRITTEN BY | Jerry Irby |
| RECORDED | ASC studios, Dallas, TX, USA, 1998 |
| PRODUCED BY | Marty Stuart and Gary Hogue |
| RELEASE DATE | US: January 1999 (CD *Hi-Lo Country* soundtrack) |

After playing together at Farm Aid and on the Jay Leno show in 1997, Beck and Willie Nelson finally recorded together for this soundtrack. Again it was a lively old country tune with pedal steel and fiddle.

### Electric Music And The Summer People

| | |
|---|---|
| WRITTEN BY | Beck Hansen |

*Original version:*

| | |
|---|---|
| BECK HANSEN | vocals, guitar, percussion, robot |
| JUSTIN MELDAL-JOHNSEN | keyboards |
| RECORDED | PCP Labs, Silverlake, CA, USA |
| ENGINEERED BY | Beck Hansen, Justin Meldal-Johnsen and John King |
| RELEASE DATES | US: 1997 (CD 'The New Pollution' single) |
| | UK: February 1997 (CD 'The New Pollution' single) |

*Re-recorded version:*

| | |
|---|---|
| BECK HANSEN | vocals, sitar, guitar, synthesiser, organ |
| ROGER MANNING JR | piano, organ, synthesiser, background vocals |
| JUSTIN MELDAL-JOHNSEN | bass |
| JOEY WARONKER | percussion, timpani |
| RECORDED | Ocean Way Studios, Los Angeles, CA, USA, March 1998 |
| PRODUCED BY | Nigel Godrich and Beck Hansen |
| RELEASE DATES | Japan: 1998 (CD *Mutations*) |
| | US: March 1999 (CD 'Cold Brains' promo EP) |
| | Australia: May 1999 (CD 'Cold Brains' single) |

The original straight ahead version of this song had been an *Odelay* outtake. Beck decided to reuse it as a surf-style song for a practice session with Nigel Godrich before the *Mutations* sessions proper. The new version made it on to the Japanese *Mutations* and various EPs.

### Erase The Sun

| | |
|---|---|
| BECK HANSEN | vocals, guitar, bass, piano, harmonica, synthesiser |
| JOEY WARONKER | drums |
| WRITTEN BY | Beck Hansen |
| RECORDED | G-Son Studios, Los Angeles, CA, USA, May 1995 |
| PRODUCED BY | Beck Hansen and Mario Caldato Jr |
| RELEASE DATE | UK: October 1997 (CD 'Deadweight' single) |

A noisy little acoustic number that Beck had had in reserve for a while. Anti-folk still lived in 1998! Some of the lyric was later reworked and used in 'Diamond Bollocks'; 'Offices and fountains they named for you' and 'Hari-Kari's spinning the golden looms' were used on the *Mutations* track.

### Feather In Your Cap

| | |
|---|---|
| BECK HANSEN | vocals, bass, acoustic guitar, piano |
| JOEY WARONKER | drums |
| WRITTEN BY | Beck Hansen |
| RECORDED | The Shop, Los Angeles, CA, USA, October 1994 |
| PRODUCED BY | Tom Rothrock and Rob Schnapf |
| RELEASE DATES | Japan: 1997 (CD 'The New Pollution' single) |
| | Germany: 1997 (CD 'Jack-ass' single) |
| | UK: September 1997(CD, 7″ 'Sissyneck' single) |
| | US: 1994 (7″ 'It's All In Your Mind' single) |
| | US: 1997 (CD *subUrbia* soundtrack) |

Another song that Beck has reworked several times and has released different versions of. As well as the basic Hansen-Waronker version, an alternate take with 'That Dog' is available.

### Feelings

| | |
|---|---|
| BECK HANSEN | vocals, guitar |
| WRITTEN BY | Beck Hansen |
| PRODUCED BY | Beck Hansen |
| RELEASE DATE | US: January 1993 (MC *Golden Feelings*) |

A fairly tuneless, dirge-like strum which has Beck singing that he has 'feelings' and lots of 'em too.

### Feel Like A Piece Of Shit (Cheetoes Time!)

| | |
|---|---|
| BECK HANSEN | vocals, keyboards |
| WRITTEN BY | Beck Hansen |
| PRODUCED BY | Beck Hansen |
| RELEASE DATE | US: January 1994 (10″ *A Western Harvest Field By Moonlight*) |

This is the third of the 'Feel Like A Piece Of Shit' songs on this album and it's just a slower version than the other two.

### Feel Like A Piece Of Shit (Crossover Potential)

| | |
|---|---|
| BECK HANSEN | vocals, keyboards |
| WRITTEN BY | Beck Hansen |
| PRODUCED BY | Beck Hansen |
| RELEASE DATE | US: January 1994 (10″ *A Western Harvest Field By Moonlight*) |

This is just a speeded-up version of the first 'Feel Like A Piece Of Shit', detailed below.

## Feel Like A Piece Of Shit (Mind Control)

| | |
|---|---|
| BECK HANSEN | vocals, keyboards |
| WRITTEN BY | Beck Hansen |
| PRODUCED BY | Beck Hansen |
| RELEASE DATE | US: January 1994 (10″ *A Western Harvest Field By Moonlight*) |

The first of the three 'Feel Like A Piece Of Shit' songs on this album. A minute of keyboard programmed drum beats and yet another distorted Beck vocal saying 'Feel Like A Piece Of Shit' over and over.

## Feel The Strain Of Sorrow Never Ceasing

| | |
|---|---|
| BECK HANSEN | vocals, guitar |
| WRITTEN BY | Beck Hansen |
| RECORDED | KCRW, Santa Monica, CA, USA, 6 January 1995 |

On his third KCRW session Beck played a collection of songs that were neither on his last album, *Mellow Gold*, nor being prepared for his next one, *Odelay*. Instead he played a few rarities that he was warming up for a show with Johnny Cash the following night. 'This is just a scrap, I have a surplus of stuff that isn't going anywhere,' said Beck by way of introduction.

## Forcefield

| | |
|---|---|
| BECK HANSEN | vocals, guitar |
| SAM JAYNE | vocals |
| WRITTEN BY | Beck Hansen |
| RECORDED | Dub Narcotic Studios, Olympia, WA, USA, |
| PRODUCED BY | Calvin Johnson |
| RELEASE DATE | US: November 1994 (CD, LP, MC *One Foot In The Grave*) |

Despite not being released as a single, this track has a promo video that has been played on MTV (allbeit in the early hours) showing some black and white footage of Beck in Olympia, WA. Sam Jayne adds some great alternative vocals, as both he and Beck sing different choruses at the same time to great effect.

## Fourteen Rivers Fourteen Floods

| | |
|---|---|
| BECK HANSEN | vocals, guitar |
| WRITTEN BY | Mississippi John Hurt |
| RECORDED | Dub Narcotic Studios, Olympia, WA, USA, October 1993 |
| PRODUCED BY | Calvin Johnson |
| RELEASE DATE | US: November 1994 (CD, LP, MC *One Foot In The Grave*) |

The second cover version from Beck's Olympia sessions, and another Mississippi John Hurt song. A slide guitar song that is just oozing with the Delta blues that Beck was so captured by in his teenage years.

## F**kin' With My Head (Mountain Dew Rock)

| | |
|---|---|
| BECK HANSEN | vocals, all instruments |
| WRITTEN BY | Beck Hansen |
| RECORDED | Rob Schnapf's house, Los Angeles, CA, USA, 1993 |
| PRODUCED BY | Beck Hansen, Rob Schnapf and Tom Rothrock |
| RELEASE DATES | UK: March 1994 (CD, LP, MC *Mellow Gold*) |
| | US: March 1994 (CD, LP, MC *Mellow Gold*) |

This mid-paced rocker often opened Beck shows of 1994. The vinyl version prints the title in full while CD versions carry the abbreviated spelling, as above. This song is very indicative of the material that Beck was writing about this time.

## Fume

| | |
|---|---|
| WRITTEN BY | Beck Hansen |

*Original version:*

| | |
|---|---|
| BECK HANSEN | vocals, guitar, harmonica |
| RECORDED | Los Angeles, CA, USA, 1992–93 |
| PRODUCED BY | Beck Hansen |

*Officially released version:*

| | |
|---|---|
| BECK HANSEN | vocals, guitar |
| RECORDED | Poop Alley Studios, Los Angeles, CA, USA |
| PRODUCED BY | Tom Grimley |
| RELEASE DATES | original version available on *Fresh Meat And Old Slabs* tape |
| | US: March 1994 (CD 'Loser' single) |

Based on a true story that Beck heard on the radio about the tragic deaths of two teens who had parked their pickup truck at the side of a mountain road and inhaled a can of nitrous with the windows up. They died of asphyxiation in their attempt to get high.

## Get Real Paid

| | |
|---|---|
| BECK HANSEN | vocals, synthesiser |
| ROGER MANNING JR | synthesiser |
| JUSTIN MELDAL-JOHNSEN | bass |
| ARNOLD MCCULLER | background vocals |
| VALERIE PINKTON | background vocals |
| CHOIR | Arroyo Tabernacle Mens Chorale |
| WRITTEN BY | Beck Hansen |
| RECORDED | Beck's house, Silverlake, CA, USA |
| PRODUCED BY | Beck Hansen, Tony Hoffer and Mickey Petralia |
| RELEASE DATES | US: November 1999 (CD, MC, LP *Midnite Vultures*) |
| | UK: November 1999 (CD, MC, LP *Midnite Vultures*) |

Co-producer Tony Hoffer managed to conjure up some really weird intro sounds for this track – a kind of sound-bite from a computer-driven assembly line. The vocals are really distorted so that they sound like a trio of women singing through a futuristic vocoder while a Star Wars laser battle takes place somewhere in the background. 'We like the boys/With the bullet proof vests/We like the girls/With the cellophane chests.' Ah, so that's what it's all about!

## Gettin' Home

| | |
|---|---|
| BECK HANSEN | vocals, guitar |
| WRITTEN BY | Beck Hansen |
| PRODUCED BY | Beck Hansen |
| RELEASE DATES | US: January 1993 (MC *Golden Feelings*) |
| | US: January 1994 (10" *A Western Harvest Field By Moonlight*) |

The hidden gem of the *Golden Feelings* tape. This finger-picking song could have been written by any of the blues giants in the pre-war period. Beck obviously liked it too as he re-recorded it for his 10" mini-album on Fingerpaint Records.

## Girl Dreams

| | |
|---|---|
| BECK HANSEN | vocals, guitar |
| WRITTEN BY | Beck Hansen |
| RECORDED | Dub Narcotic Studios, Olympia, WA, USA, October 1993 |
| PRODUCED BY | Calvin Johnson |
| RELEASE DATES | US: November 1994 (CD, LP, MC *One Foot In The Grave*) |
| | US: 1996 (CD *The Poop Alley Tapes* compilation titled as 'Girl Of My Dreams') |

Possibly Beck's first direct love song. A different version of this straightforward acoustic song was included on the *Poop Alley* compilation under a slightly different name. This song features a basic, almost childlike lyric, 'I first met you down on Lover's Lane/The birds they were insane/flapping all about/You're just a girl of my dreams/but it seems my dreams never come true.'

## Goin' Nowhere Fast

| | |
|---|---|
| WRITTEN BY | Beck Hansen |
| *Banjo Story version:* | |
| BECK HANSEN | vocals, banjo |
| RECORDED | New York City, NY, 1988–89 |
| PRODUCED BY | Beck Hansen |
| *Fresh Meat And Old Slabs version:* | |
| BECK HANSEN | harmonica, guitar, vocals |
| RECORDED | Los Angeles, CA, USA, 1992–93 |
| CONTAINS SAMPLE OF | 'Talking Hard Work' written and performed by Woody Guthrie |
| PRODUCED BY | Beck Hansen |
| RELEASE DATES | originally available on unofficial *Banjo Story* tape |
| | different version available on unofficial *Fresh Meat And Old Slabs* tape |

The original *Banjo Story* version could easily be a mid-period Woody Guthrie song as Beck laments his impoverished position in a very lo-fi take. The second version starts with a snippet of Woody Guthrie followed by a more polished sounding Beck (though still pretty raw) on acoustic guitar telling the same story as his *Banjo* version.

### Got No Mind

| | |
|---|---|
| BECK HANSEN | vocals, guitar |
| WRITTEN BY | Beck Hansen |
| RECORDED | Poop Alley Studios, 1993 |
| PRODUCED BY | Beck Hansen and Tom Grimley |
| RELEASE DATES | France: March 1994 (CD single 'Beercan') |
| | US: March 1994 (CD single 'Beercan') |

An alternate lyric version of 'Pay No Mind' which supposedly had over ten verses originally. This song may just be a collection of the ones that were cut.

### Go Where U Want

| | |
|---|---|
| BECK HANSEN | vocals, guitar |
| WRITTEN BY | Beck Hansen |
| RECORDED | Los Angeles, CA, USA, 1993 |
| PRODUCED BY | Beck Hansen |
| RELEASE DATE | not officially released, available on *Fresh Meat And Old Slabs* tape |

This was the original version of 'Hollow Log' which Beck included on his mother's birthday tape. He re-recorded it later that year for *One Foot In The Grave* after slightly changing the lyric.

### Grease

| | |
|---|---|
| BECK HANSEN | vocals, guitar, harmonica |
| WRITTEN BY | Beck Hansen |
| RECORDED | Los Angeles, CA, USA, 1992–93 |
| PRODUCED BY | Beck Hansen |
| RELEASE DATE | not officially released, available on *Fresh Meat And Old Slabs* tape |

A storming acoustic song which has its tongue firmly planted in its cheek. After an introduction of Beck on the telephone calling for pizzas, the song bursts into life and contains some of Beck's best lines, 'Life is short, can I have it go/If it's not in the "TV Guide" then I don't know' among them.

### Groovy Sunday

| | |
|---|---|
| BECK HANSEN | vocals, all instruments |
| WRITTEN BY | Beck Hansen, Mike Simpson, John King |
| RECORDED | PCP Labs, Silverlake, CA, USA, 1995 |
| PRODUCED BY | Mike Simpson |
| RELEASE DATE | UK: November 1996 (CD single 'Devils Haircut') |

Remix of 'Devils Haircut' with a subtle organ riff added to the mix. The vocal is unchanged and apart from a few shakers, that's about it.

## Halo Of Gold

| | |
|---|---|
| BECK HANSEN | vocals, keyboards, guitars, programming |
| MICKEY P | programming |
| JUSTIN MELDAL-JOHNSEN | bass |
| ROGER MANNING | keyboards |
| WRITTEN BY | Alexander Lee Spence |
| PRODUCED BY | Beck Hansen |
| RELEASE DATES | UK: 6 December 1998 (CD, 7" single 'Tropicalia') |
| | US: March 1999 (CD promo EP 'Cold Brains') |
| | UK: 1999 (CD *More Oar: A Tribute To Alexander 'Skip' Spence* compilation) |

Of all the cover versions ever attempted this must be one of the most radical reworkings ever released; that's a compliment by the way. Beck took the sparse, disjointed original and turned it into something truly memorable.

## Hard To Compete

| | |
|---|---|
| BECK HANSEN | vocals, guitar |
| CHRIS BALLEW | bassitar |
| WRITTEN BY | Beck Hansen |
| RECORDED | KCRW, Santa Monica, CA, USA, 1 March 1994 |

Probably best known for being played on a couple of radio sessions in 1994 – KCRW in Los Angeles and on JJJ Radio in Australia. On the former Beck played with help from Chris Ballew on his patented two-stringed bass guitar or 'Bassitar'. The song is a gentle complaint about not being able to do the right thing in a relationship.

## Heartland Feeling

| | |
|---|---|
| WRITTEN BY | Beck Hansen |

*Fresh Meat and Old Slabs version:*

| | |
|---|---|
| BECK HANSEN | vocals, guitar |
| SAMPLE FROM | 'Thunder Road' written and performed by Bruce Springsteen |
| RECORDED | Los Angeles, CA, USA, 1992–93 |

*Golden Feelings version:*

| | |
|---|---|
| BECK HANSEN | vocals, guitar |
| PRODUCED BY | Beck Hansen |
| RELEASE DATES | available on *Fresh Meat And Old Slabs* tape – original version |
| | US: January 1993 (MC *Golden Feelings*) |

This is a song of many introductions. The *Fresh Meat* version has Beck talking while dealing out a pack of cards – 'What we're talking about here is a "heartland feeling" ... John Cougar Mellencamp, Bruce Springsteen, Bob Seger, a melon feeling, powerful approving music';

this is followed by a brief, distorted sample of Springsteen's 'Thunder Road'. On the *Golden Feelings* version, video collaborator Steven Hanft provides the spoken intro which sounds like a snippet of an answerphone message before Beck gives the same spoken intro, while dealing a pack of cards as in the *Fresh Meat* version. The actual song is a catchy, melodic tale of a series of characters going through their boring everyday lives.

### Hell

| | |
|---|---|
| UNKNOWN GIRL | vocals |
| RELEASE DATE | not officially released, available on *Banjo Story* tape |

Not a song at all but a short spoken piece by an uncredited girl who sounds about nine years old. 'You could stay in hell for about 15 years and they wouldn't even let you [. . .]' she explains. This is the final offering on the *Banjo Story* tape from 1988.

### He's A Mighty Good Leader

| | |
|---|---|
| BECK HANSEN | vocals, guitar |
| WRITTEN BY | Mississippi John Hurt |
| RECORDED | Dub Narcotic Studios, Olympia, WA, USA, October 1993 |
| PRODUCED BY | Calvin Johnson |
| RELEASE DATE | US: November 1994 (CD, LP, MC *One Foot In The Grave*) |

Perhaps a strange choice to use this track to open the 1994 album on Calvin Johnson's K Records. A traditional finger-picking guitar arrangement, complete with mis-picks, showing that Beck did indeed know his blues history. Recorded on Beck's initial trip to Olympia before signing with Geffen a month later.

### High Five (Rock The Catskills)

| | |
|---|---|
| BECK HANSEN | vocals, guitar, bass |
| JOEY WARONKER | percussion |
| MIKE BIOTO | organ |
| ELEMENTS OF | 'Mr. Cool' (Vincent Willis) performed by Rasputin's Sash |
| WRITTEN BY | Beck Hansen, Mike Simpson, John King |
| RECORDED | PCP Labs, Silverlake, CA, USA, 1995 |
| PRODUCED BY | Beck Hansen, Mike Simpson, John King |
| RELEASE DATES | UK: June 1996 (CD, LP, MC *Odelay*) |
| | US: June 1996 (CD, LP, MC *Odelay*) |

Beck gave this straight-to-the-point explanation: 'Waiting for a train. San Francisco Bay Blues, Jesse Fuller as an android in his own private sex militia.' What he didn't say is that this song was a vital part of his live show, often the last song of the night where he'd come out in his rhinestone suit with the band in horse head masks. 'How do you rock the Catskills? You play Lollapalooza there!' Beck screamed. Among the beats and scratching you can even hear a sample of Schubert's 'Unfinished Symphony'.

## Hollow Log

| | |
|---|---|
| BECK HANSEN | vocals, guitar |
| WRITTEN BY | Beck Hansen |
| RECORDED | Dub Narcotic Studios, Olympia, WA, USA, October 1993 |
| PRODUCED BY | Calvin Johnson |
| RELEASE DATE | US: November 1994 (CD, LP, MC *One Foot In The Grave*) |

Originally known as 'Go Where You Want', this classic finger-picker has been around for a while. Beck changed one of the lines from 'Sleeping in a log' to 'Sleeping in a hollow log' and renamed the song accordingly. He chose to play this track as his contribution to *Rolling Stone* magazine's *State Of The Union* TV special in 1998. He introduced it by saying 'The old time music, country blues and delta blues – I gravitated towards it. It's like sitting on plastic furniture all your life then finding a good old rocking chair' before giving an enthralling solo perfomance.

## Hollywood Freaks

| | |
|---|---|
| BECK HANSEN | vocals, bass synthesiser |
| JUSTIN MELDAL-JOHNSEN | bass |
| ROGER MANNING JR | synthesiser |
| ARNOLD MCCULLER | background vocals |
| VALERIE PINKTON | background vocals |
| MIKE SIMPSON | scratching |
| JOHN KING | scratching |
| WRITTEN BY | Beck Hansen, Mike Simpson and John King |
| RECORDED | PCP Labs, Silverlake, CA, USA |
| PRODUCED BY | Beck Hansen, Mike Simpson and John King |
| RELEASE DATES | US: November 1999 (CD, MC, LP *Midnite Vultures*) |
| | UK: November 1999 (CD, MC, LP *Midnite Vultures*) |

Beck sang a few lines of this as far back as November 1998 on KCRW before giving it a full debut at the post-Oscars show in March 1999. This was originally known as 'Jockin' My Mercedes' – one of the lines in the song – and was almost released as 'Hlwd. Freaks' but the pronunciation was expected to cause problems and so it was changed late in the day. Some bizarre lyrics are included – heck, even Norman Schwarzkopf gets a mention!

## Hotwax

| | |
|---|---|
| BECK HANSEN | Vocals, all instruments |
| SAMPLES FROM | 'Song For Aretha' (Purdie/Ott/Thiele) perfomed by Pretty Purdie |

'Up On The Hill' (Higgins/Brown) performed by Monk Higgins & The Specialities

| | |
|---|---|
| WRITTEN BY | Beck Hansen, Mike Simpson and John King |
| RECORDED | PCP Labs, Silverlake, CA, USA, 1995 |
| PRODUCED BY | Beck Hansen, Mike Simpson and John King |
| RELEASE DATES | UK: June 1996 (CD, MC, LP *Odelay*) |
| | US: June 1996 (CD, MC, LP *Odelay*) |

'It's sort of a travelling song. Just down in the town lookin' for a dream that sticks,' says Beck about this song which was the first recorded for *Odelay*. It took quite a while to finish as layer upon layer was added. Another Spanish chorus was added – this one meant 'I am a broken record/I have bubblegum in my brain.' Ross Harris of Sukia makes an appearance as 'The Wizard'.

### Howling Wolves (Demo)

| | |
|---|---|
| BECK HANSEN | vocals, noise |
| CHRIS BALLEW | vocals, noise |
| WRITTEN BY | Beck Hansen and Chris Ballew |
| RECORDED | Los Angeles, CA, USA, March 1994 |
| PRODUCED BY | Beck Hansen and Chris Ballew |
| RELEASE DATE | not officially released |

During Beck's KCRW *Morning Becomes Eclectic* performance on 1 March 1994 with Chris Ballew, they pulled out a tape containing a demo that they'd just recorded and played it on air. This was the track they played. Ballew claimed it was from a new side-band they were forming called the Howling Wolves. The track comprises noise and guitar feedback with some spoken vocals about 'Drawing pictures with God' and 'Covering yourselves with masking tape' shouted over the top. 'Sort of like Bon Jovi in a vacuum cleaner,' claimed Beck. How they got away with playing this on the radio I'll never know.

### I Feel Low Down

| | |
|---|---|
| BECK HANSEN | vocals, guitar, bottle-top blowing |
| WRITTEN BY | Beck Hansen |
| RECORDED | Los Angeles, CA, USA, 1992–93 |
| PRODUCED BY | Beck Hansen |
| RELEASE DATE | not released, available on *Fresh Meat And Old Slabs* tape |

A strange introduction of what sounds like Beck blowing across a range of bottle-tops is followed by an energetic vocal from Beck saying that he feels low down. Then he explains that he went to the store and bought some coffee.

### I Get Lonesome

| | |
|---|---|
| BECK HANSEN | vocals, guitar |
| CALVIN JOHNSON | vocals |

| | |
|---|---|
| SCOTT PLOUF | drums |
| WRITTEN BY | Beck Hansen |
| RECORDED | Dub Narcotic Studios, Olympia, WA, USA, January 1994 |
| PRODUCED BY | Calvin Johnson |
| RELEASE DATE | US: November 1994 (CD, LP, MC *One Foot In The Grave*) |

A stark acoustic number with Scott Plouf's spare drumming, Calvin Johnson's amazingly deep voice and Beck's finger-picking. It's quite easy to close your eyes and imagine the three of them sitting in Johnson's cold basement studio playing this.

## In A Cold Ass Fashion

| | |
|---|---|
| BECK HANSEN | vocals, sitar, banjo |
| WRITTEN BY | Beck Hansen and Carl Stephenson |
| RECORDED | Carl Stephenson's house, Los Angeles, CA, USA, 1992 |
| PRODUCED BY | Beck Hansen |
| RELEASE DATES | US: 1994 (CD *Jabberjaw: Good To The Last Drop* compilation) |
| | US: 1994 (7″ *Jabberjaw No.2* four-track compilation) |

A left-over track from Beck's earliest LA sessions with his 'Loser' companion. Again Beck does a semi-'Loser' rap over a sampled drum loop with a catchy chorus and some added sitar and banjo thrown in for good measure.

## Instrumental Rag

| | |
|---|---|
| BECK HANSEN | banjo, percussion, hollering |
| WRITTEN BY | Beck Hansen |
| PRODUCED BY | Beck Hansen |
| RELEASE DATE | not officially released, available on *Banjo Story* tape |

This jolly little tune is mostly instrumental although it's occasionally punctuated by a bit of yokel-like hollering. A typical banjo and 'biscuit-tin-lid' type of song from this early tape.

## Interlude #1

| | |
|---|---|
| BECK HANSEN | noise |
| CONTAINS SAMPLE OF | 'I Hear Trumpets Blow' performed by the Tokens |
| WRITTEN BY | Beck Hansen |
| RELEASE DATE | US: January 1993 (MC *Golden Feelings*) |

Not really a Beck track but a sample with Beck adding some screeching noise over the top. The sample is a 16-second clip of the Tokens' 1966 song 'I Hear Trumpets Blow' – 'I am not of royalty/I'm an ordinary guy', it says.

## Interlude #2

| | |
|---|---|
| BECK HANSEN | vocals, noise |
| WRITTEN BY | Beck Hansen |
| PRODUCED BY | Beck Hansen |
| RELEASE DATE | US: January 1993 (MC *Golden Feelings*) |

'Interlude' is a good description of this effort. It's 16 seconds of heavy breathing and hard to hear vocals, no more, no less.

## It's All In Your Mind

| | |
|---|---|
| BECK HANSEN | vocals, guitar |
| WRITTEN BY | Beck Hansen |
| RECORDED | Dub Narcotic Studios, Olympia, WA, USA |
| PRODUCED BY | Calvin Johnson |
| RELEASE DATES | US: 1994 (7″ 'It's All In Your Mind' single) |
| | US: 1997 (CD *The Bridge School Concerts* compilation – live version) |
| | UK: 1997 (CD *The Bridge School Concerts* compilation – live version) |

A simple acoustic track from the Dub Narcotic sessions with another of Beck's multi-repeating lyrics. In the tradition of 'No Money, No Honey' and 'My Head Is Gonna Break In Two', Beck sings this song's title over and over.

## I've Seen The Land Beyond

| | |
|---|---|
| BECK HANSEN | vocals, guitar |
| SAM JAYNE | background vocals |
| WRITTEN BY | Mississippi John Hurt |
| RECORDED | Dub Narcotic Studios, Olympia, WA, USA, January 1994 |
| PRODUCED BY | Calvin Johnson |
| RELEASE DATE | US: November 1994 (CD, LP, MC *One Foot In The Grave*) |

A faithful run through of this Mississippi John Hurt song, with some energetic guitar playing and vocalising. Unfortunately it's all over in under 1:40, which is a shame.

## Jack-ass

| | |
|---|---|
| BECK HANSEN | vocals, bass, drums, guitars |
| SAMPLE FROM | 'It's All Over Now, Baby Blue' (Bob Dylan) performed by Them |
| WRITTEN BY | Beck Hansen, Mike Simpson, John King and Bob Dylan |
| RECORDED | PCP Labs, Silverlake, CA, USA, 1995 |
| PRODUCED BY | Beck Hansen, Mike Simpson and John King |
| RELEASE DATES | UK: June 1996 (CD, LP, MC *Odelay*) |
| | US: June 1996 (CD, LP, MC *Odelay*) |
| | The 'Butch Vig Mix' appears on: |

UK: September 1997 (CD, 7" 'Jack-ass' single)
Germany: 1997 (CD 'Jack-ass' single)
The 'Lowrider Mix' appears on:
UK: September 1997 (CD, 7" 'Jack-ass' single)

'The midst of summer, when the only goal is movement,' says Beck about this country song that he has presented in his own unique way. When released as a single, several remixes of this song were available and also a Spanish version, 'Burro'. To tie in with the title Beck does his damn fine impression of a donkey at the end. When asked about the line 'Tyin' a noose in the back of my mind', Beck replied: 'That's part of an interest in ropes in general. Could have been a lasso, too. Could have been a ship docking rope, but I don't know what the term for that is. I'm not too good with terminology. The attraction? With rope, you can hang something if you need to.' Speaking of remixes, the Insane Clown Posse blatantly stole from this track for their song 'Another Love Song' in 1999.

## Jagermeister Pie

| | |
|---|---|
| BECK HANSEN | accordion |
| WRITTEN BY | Beck Hansen |
| RECORDED | Poop Alley Studios, Los Angeles, CA, USA |
| PRODUCED BY | Tom Grimley |
| RELEASE DATES | US: February 1994 (CD *Stereopathetic Soul Manure*) |
| | Australia: 1995 (CD *Mellow Gold* bonus tour disc) |

This is an accordion solo lasting 1:08 minutes.

## Lampshade

| | |
|---|---|
| BECK HANSEN | vocals, guitar, harmonica |
| WRITTEN BY | Beck Hansen |
| RELEASE DATES | US: January 1994 (10" *A Western Harvest Field By Moonlight*) |
| | Australia: 1995 (CD *Mellow Gold* bonus tour disc) |
| | US (CD *Modern Day Paintings* compilation CD) |

One of the few real songs on this album. A nice acoustic song that manages to last past the one-minute mark. Beck pulled this one from nowhere at a concert in Los Angeles in May 1999 and explained how it came from a New Year's Eve memory from the early 1990s which saw him break his collarbone at a party.

## Last Night I Traded My Soul's Innermost For Some Pickled Fish

| | |
|---|---|
| BECK HANSEN | guitar, harmonica |
| WRITTEN BY | Beck Hansen |
| RECORDED | Los Angeles, CA, USA |
| PRODUCED BY | Beck Hansen |
| RELEASE DATE | US: 1997 (CD *Kill The Moonlight* soundtrack) |

One of Beck's more amusing titles failed to hide the fact that it wasn't really one of his better efforts. This Ry Cooder-like instrumental with Beck also jamming away on his harmonica could have been a B-side. The whole thing is less than two minutes long.

### Lazy Flies

| | |
|---|---|
| BECK HANSEN | vocals, guitars |
| ROGER MANNING JR | keyboards |
| JUSTIN MELDAL-JOHNSEN | electric bass, percussion |
| JOEY WARONKER | drums, percussion |
| WRITTEN BY | Beck Hansen |
| RECORDED | Ocean Way Studios, Los Angeles, CA, USA, April 1998 |
| PRODUCED BY | Nigel Godrich and Beck Hansen |
| RELEASE DATES | UK: November 1998 (CD, LP, MC *Mutations*) |
| | US: November 1998 (CD, LP, MC *Mutations*) |

A very dramatic drum sound carries this song along in a kind of baroque style, with a lyric that asks 'Who wants to be there/To sweep the debris/To harness dead horses/To ride in the sun?' Beck comments:

> I tend to try to say a lot of different things in one song. I want a song lyric to be a funky brew. My words have to feel good, sound good, look good and make sense to me. Where other songwriters tend to describe one feeling or one situation per song, I rarely write songs that are about one thing. 'Lazy Flies', for example, is this imaginary movie about some colonial, futuristic backwater. But it also contains elements of the barrio I grew up in. I grew up in that seedy part of LA where all the Salvadorian mechanics and maids who work in the big mansions of the super-rich elite in the Hollywood hills live.

### Leave Me On The Moon

| | |
|---|---|
| BECK HANSEN | vocals, guitar, piano, sound effects |
| RUSSELL SIMINS | drums (updated version) |
| WRITTEN BY | Beck Hansen |
| *Original version:* | |
| RECORDED | Los Angeles, CA, USA, 1992–93 |
| PRODUCED BY | Beck Hansen |
| RELEASE DATE | not officially released, available on *Fresh Meat And Old Slabs* tape |
| *Updated version:* | |
| RECORDED | Los Angeles, CA, USA |
| PRODUCED BY | Beck Hansen |
| RELEASE DATE | US: 1997 (CD *Kill The Moonlight* soundtrack) |

Beck had promised some tracks for Steve Hanft's first feature film after Hanft had agreed to do the 'Loser' video. This was the only actual song he offered, the other two were merely throw-away instrumentals. The original *Fresh Meat* version had been part of his mother's 1993 birthday present tape. It was slower and Beck's vocal was really slow and drawn out. The lyric was the same as the released version, but featured some sound effects in the background. The updated version featured luscious pedal steel and honky-tonk piano. 'Everything's good, so long as it sits still,' sings Beck, before claiming, 'Seems like everyone is just floating away', so he must 'Tie myself down'.

## Lemonade

| | |
|---|---|
| BECK HANSEN | vocals, guitars, piano |
| JOEY WARONKER | drums |
| REBECCA GATES | background vocals |
| WRITTEN BY | Beck Hansen |
| RECORDED | March 1994 |
| PRODUCED BY | Beck Hansen and Brian Paulson |
| RELEASE DATES | Japan: 1997 (CD *The New Pollution And Other Favorites*) |
| | UK: February 1997 (CD 'The New Pollution' single) |
| | US: 1997 (12" 'The New Pollution' single) |
| | Germany: 1997 (CD 'Jack-ass' single) |

A furious drum-and-acoustic-interlude blast that almost defies explanation. A distorted vocal screams over the raucous drumming only to be halted every 40 seconds or so for a gentle acoustic guitar and piano interlude. The Spinanes' Rebecca Gates makes a guest appearance.

## Let's Go Moon Some Cars

| | |
|---|---|
| WRITTEN BY | Beck Hansen |
| *Banjo Story version:* | |
| BECK HANSEN | vocals, guitar, banjo |
| PRODUCED BY | Beck Hansen |
| *Fresh Meat version:* | |
| BECK HANSEN | vocals, guitar |
| RECORDED | Los Angeles, CA, USA, 1992–93 |
| PRODUCED BY | Beck Hansen |
| RELEASE DATE | not officially released, available on *Banjo Story* tape; also available on *Fresh Meat And Old Slabs* tape |

This is interesting if only because it's the first recorded Beck song of which we have a record. It opened up his 1988 *Banjo Story* tape. This original version is the epitome of hillbilly country with just Beck and his banjo. It's also the opening track on the *Fresh Meat* tape and sees Beck throwing out an oddball call to arms. After 'Let's go moon some cars', it's 'Let's go steal some beer', then 'Let's go set something on fire' and 'Let's go shoot some pigs'. For the latter, whether it's the LAPD variety or not is unclear.

## Lloyd Price Express

| | |
|---|---|
| BECK HANSEN | vocals, all instruments |
| WRITTEN BY | Beck Hansen, Mike Simpson and John King |

| SAMPLE FROM | 'Needle To The Groove' (Embden Toure/Khaleel Kirk) performed by Mantronix |
|---|---|
| ELEMENTS FROM | 'Personality' written by Lloyd Price and Harold Logan |
| RECORDED | PCP Labs, Silverlake, CA, USA, 1995 |
| PRODUCED BY | Beck Hansen, Mike Simpson and John King |
| REMIXED BY | John King |
| RELEASE DATES | Japan: 1996 (CD 'Where It's At' single) |
| | US: November 1996 (12″ 'Devils Haircut' single) |
| | UK: November 1996 (7″ 'Devils Haircut' single) |

Yet another 'Where It's At' remix, this time by John King. Here he pretty much leaves the vocals intact but severely changes the music, beats and all, giving a very seventies TV theme to the song.

## Lord Only Knows

| BECK HANSEN | vocals, guitars, bass |
|---|---|
| JOEY WARONKER | drums |
| MIKE MILLIUS | screams |
| ELEMENTS OF | 'Lookout For Lucy' (Millius/Thomas) performed by Mike Millius |
| WRITTEN BY | Beck Hansen |
| RECORDED | PCP Labs, Silverlake, CA, 1995 |
| PRODUCED BY | Beck Hansen, Mike Simpson and John King |
| RELEASE DATES | UK: June 1996 (CD, MC, LP *Odelay*) |
| | US: June 1996 (CD, MC, LP *Odelay*) |

Acoustic versions of this great song were heard as early as 1994, when Beck played it on a Radio 1 session. It also made regular appearances during Beck's stint supporting Sonic Youth in April 1996. The Mike Millius scream gets things going in this pseudo-country song. 'It's a fare-thee-well tune, my closing-time song, a last salute, the last hurrah. Another mis-spent evening,' said Beck about this song which he played at his grandfather Al's memorial sevice. It was originally called 'Orale'.

## Loser

| BECK HANSEN | vocals, guitar, sitar |
|---|---|
| CARL STEPHENSON | programming, sampling |
| SAMPLES FROM | 'I Walk on Guilded Splinters' (Dr John) |
| | *Kill The Moonlight* (a Steven Hanft film) |
| WRITTEN BY | Beck Hansen and Carl Stephenson |
| RECORDED | Carl Stephenson's house, Los Angeles, CA, USA, 1992 |
| PRODUCED BY | Beck Hansen and Carl Stephenson |
| RELEASE DATES | US: March 1993 (12″ 'Loser' single) |
| | UK: March 1994 (CD, LP, MC *Mellow Gold*) |
| | US: March 1994 (CD, LP, MC *Mellow Gold*) |

The song that changed Beck's life. Recorded at hiphop producer Carl Stephenson's house then forgotten about until Bong Load put it out as a 12″ in 1993. Sparked massive record company interest for the rest of the year. Geffen re-released it as a single a year later. The opening slide guitar riff made it one of the most instantly recognisable songs of the 1990s and made Beck a star. The chorus of 'Soy un perdidor/I'm a loser baby, so why don't you kill me' unwittingly cast Beck into the spotlight as a reluctant spokesperson for the slacker generation. He'd actually meant his rap to be an imitation of Chuck D. What all of the hype and column inches seemed to forget is that this is actually a pretty good song that includes classic lines like 'Drive by body pierce'. The line 'I'm a driver, I'm a winner/Things are gonna change I can feel it' is from Steven Hanft's *Kill The Moonlight* film.

### Magic Stationwagon

| | |
|---|---|
| BECK HANSEN | vocals, guitar, drums, percussion |
| WRITTEN BY | Beck Hansen |
| PRODUCED BY | Beck Hansen |
| RELEASE DATE | US: January 1993 (MC *Golden Feelings*) |

A noisy, distorted guitar bash that features some doubly and maybe even triply recorded vocals. Beck would record himself, then play along to the tape to double-up his vocals and repeat.

### Mango Vader Rocks

| | |
|---|---|
| BECK HANSEN | vocals, all instruments |
| WRITTEN BY | Beck Hansen |
| RECORDED | Carl Stephenson's house, Los Angeles, CA, 1991 |
| PRODUCED BY | Carl Stephenson |
| RELEASE DATES | US: January 1994 (10″ *A Western Harvest Field By Moonlight*) |

Random noise, strange percussion, dog barks and occasional spoken vocals (in a kind of Darth Vader voice). After one listen it's easy to see, or rather hear, how this became a *Mellow Gold* outtake.

### Mayonnaise Salad

| | |
|---|---|
| BECK HANSEN | vocals, guitars, drums |
| WRITTEN BY | Beck Hansen |
| PRODUCED BY | Beck Hansen |
| RELEASE DATE | US: January 1994 (10″ *A Western Harvest Field By Moonlight*) |

Feedback, wailing guitars, drums for just over a minute. Like a bad Nirvana B-side without a lyric.

### Mexico

| | |
|---|---|
| BECK HANSEN | vocals, guitar |
| WRITTEN BY | Beck Hansen |
| RECORDED | Los Angeles, CA, USA, 1992–93 |
| PRODUCED BY | Beck Hansen |
| RELEASE DATES | available on unofficial *Fresh Meat And Old Slabs* tape |

US: 1994 (CD *Rare On Air Vol. 1* compilation)
Australia: 1995 (CD *Mellow Gold* bonus tour disc)

Loosely based on Woody Guthrie's 'Buffalo Skinners', this song originally made it on to *Fresh Meat And Old Slabs* under the title 'Ballad Of Mexico'. It tells the story of Beck working at McDonald's, getting sacked, going back and robbing the McDonald's that sacked him and running over the border to live in Mexico. What did Beck do when he got to Mexico? He got a job at McDonald's of course. The *Rare On Air* version was recorded on Beck's first KCRW appearance on 23 July 1993.

## Milk And Honey

| | |
|---|---|
| BECK HANSEN | vocals, guitar, synthesiser, vocoder |
| ROGER MANNING JR | synthesiser, piano, guitar, electronic drums, clavinet, vocoder |
| JOEY WARONKER | drums |
| JUSTIN MELDAL-JOHNSEN | bass, hammer-ons |
| DJ SWAMP | scratching |
| JOHNNY MARR | guitar |
| TONY HOFFER | guitar |
| WRITTEN BY | Beck Hansen and Buzz Clifford |
| | 'embodies a portion of' 'I Am I See', written by Buzz Clifford |
| RECORDED | Beck's house, Silverlake, CA, USA, 1999 |
| PRODUCED BY | Beck Hansen and Tony Hoffer |
| RELEASE DATES | US: November 1999 (CD, MC, LP *Midnite Vultures*) |
| | UK: November 1999 (CD, MC, LP *Midnite Vultures*) |

Taking inspiration from one-hit wonder Buzz Clifford, Beck presents this rocker with a twist and a new guest guitarist – Johnny Marr. 'I had him do a Lynyrd Skynyrd guitar lead on,' recalls Beck. 'It was fairly surreal watching Johnny Marr play Skynyrd riffs. I don't think he was too enthused, but he said he would do it, but only for me.' Mid-way through the song it goes all messed up again as Beck chants over a disco strut before the arena-rock returns: 'Bangkok athletes in the biosphere/Arkansas wet dreams/We all disappear/Kremlin mistress/ Rings the buddah chimes'. To end with Beck gives us a gently strummed coda with just the words 'Milk and honey' repeated over and over as the track drifts away.

## Minus

| | |
|---|---|
| BECK HANSEN | vocals, all instruments |
| WRITTEN BY | Beck Hansen |
| PRODUCED BY | Beck Hansen, Brian Paulson and Mario Caldato Jr |
| RELEASE DATES | UK: June 1996 (CD, LP, MC *Odelay*) |
| | US: June 1996 (CD, LP, MC *Odelay*) |

One of the few *Odelay* tracks that Beck had written before going into the studio with the Dust Brothers in 1995, this song is simply described by Beck as 'a rebuttal'. Originally debuted in 1994, it is probably the hardest song on the album and gave Beck a real chance to 'rock out' when played live. It was previously titled 'Minus (Karaoke Bloodperm)'. 'It's sort of a mixture between a Korean business meeting, and the movie *Carrie*,' says Beck.

## Mixed Bizness

| | |
|---|---|
| BECK HANSEN | vocals, vocoder |
| ROGER MANNING JR | synthesiser, background vocals, vocoder |
| JOEY WARONKER | drums |
| SMOKEY HORMEL | guitar |
| JUSTIN MELDAL-JOHNSEN | bass, shaker, background vocals |
| TONY HOFFER | guitar |
| DAVID RALICKE | trombone |
| JON BIRDSONG | trumpet |
| DAVID BROWN | tenor saxophone |
| WRITTEN BY | Beck Hansen |
| RECORDED | Beck's house, Silverlake, CA, USA |
| PRODUCED BY | Beck Hansen and Tony Hoffer |
| RELEASE DATE | US: November 1999 (CD, MC, LP *Midnite Vultures*) |
| | UK: November 1999 (CD, MC, LP *Midnite Vultures*) |

In what must surely be a sure-fire single choice for the future Beck cooks up a funk-fest for the millennium. 'I'm mixing business with leather/Christmas with Heather,' sings Beck to a can't-sit-down beat. The funky guitars and horns give the album an encore feel on only its third track. Excellent.

## Modesto

| | |
|---|---|
| BECK HANSEN | vocals |
| LISA | drums |
| LEO LE BLANC | pedal steel |
| WRITTEN BY | Beck Hansen |
| RECORDED | Wire Works Studio |
| PRODUCED BY | Rusty Cusak |
| RELEASE DATE | US: February 1994 (CD *Stereopathetic Soul Manure*) |

Named after a northern Californian town, this country-tinged song showcases some nice pedal steel from Leo Le Blanc who died in 1995. Beck sings of looking through a bag of Frit-O-Lays.

## MTV Makes Me Want To Smoke Crack

| | |
|---|---|
| BECK HANSEN | vocals, guitar, harmonica |
| MIKE BIOTO | piano (on 'Lounge Act Version') |
| WRITTEN BY | Beck Hansen |

| RELEASE DATES | US: 1992 (7″ 'MTV Makes Me Want To Smoke Crack' single) |
| | UK: 1994 (CD 'Loser' single – 'Lounge Act Version') |

Beck's first official release sees him in hilarious form as he sends up MTV. On acoustic guitar and harmonica he claims 'Everything's perfect and everything's bright/Everyone is perky and everyone's uptight/The colours are nice and the pictures are nice/The girls are nice and everything's so nice'. Beck also sings about working in the video store. Quite a debut indeed. Welsh band Catatonia later responded with 'S4C Makes Me Want To Smoke Crack'.

The 'Lounge Act Version' was debuted on KCRW. It's where Beck stops the tape and continues the song in a Tony Bennett-like crooner vocal with only a piano as accompaniment. 'It's my friend Mike [Bioto],' replies Beck when asked the identity of the pianist. 'He's sort of the reincarnated Jerry Lewis of the West Coast jazz scene. He plays keyboards on the albums usually.'

## Motherfucker

| BECK HANSEN | vocals, drums, guitar |
| WRITTEN BY | Beck Hansen |
| PRODUCED BY | Beck Hansen |
| RELEASE DATE | US: January 1993 (MC *Golden Feelings*) |

Different spelling, but the same song as the one that appeared on *Mellow Gold*, just a little more rough around the edges.

## Motherfucker

| BECK HANSEN | vocals |
| DAVID HARTE | drums |
| WRITTEN BY | Beck Hansen |
| RECORDED | Rob Schnapf's house, Los Angeles, CA, USA |
| PRODUCED BY | Beck Hansen, Rob Schnapf and Tom Rothrock |
| RELEASE DATES | UK: March 1994 (CD, LP, MC *Mellow Gold*) |
| | US: March 1994 (CD, LP, MC *Mellow Gold*) |

Another X-rated title from *Mellow Gold*. Described by Beck as 'Paying homage to that great tradition of the hate song inaugurated by Johnny Rotten. I love that violence, to be able to play without giving the slightest fuck.' The main point of the song is that 'Everyone's out to get you motherfucker'.

## My Head Is Gonna Break In Two

| BECK HANSEN | vocals, banjo |
| UNKNOWN CHILD | vocals |
| WRITTEN BY | Beck Hansen |
| RELEASE DATE | not officially released, available on *Banjo Story* tape |

Beck is aided on this track by an uncredited young girl, who sounds about four years old, as they sing 'My Head Is Gonna Break In Two' over and over and over and over.

## Nicotine And Gravy

| | |
|---|---|
| BECK HANSEN | vocals, guitar, synthesiser, piano |
| ROGER MANNING JR | synthesiser, clavinet, piano |
| JUSTIN MELDAL-JOHNSEN | bass, synthesiser |
| HERB PETERSON | banjo |
| EVE BUTLER | violin |
| JOEL DEROUIN | violin |
| DAVID CAMPBELL | viola |
| LARRY CORBETT | cello |
| DJ SWAMP | scratching |
| VALERIE PINKTON | background vocals |
| ARNOLD MCCULLER | background vocals |
| DAVID RALICKE | trombone |
| JON BIRDSONG | trumpet |
| DAVID BROWN | tenor saxophone |
| WRITTEN BY | Beck Hansen |
| RECORDED | Beck's house, Silverlake, CA, USA |
| PRODUCED BY | Beck Hansen and Mickey Petralia |
| RELEASE DATES | US: November 1999 (CD, MC, LP *Midnite Vultures*) |
| | UK: November 1999 (CD, MC, LP *Midnite Vultures*) |

After the full-out bluster of album opener 'Sexx Laws', Beck tones it down and gets all sultry on this, the next track. His lyrics have never been this explicit, but they also become oblique too – the typical Beck contradiction. One moment he's singing 'I'll feed you fruit that don't exist/I'll leave graffiti/Where you've never been kissed' and the next he tells us that 'It takes a miracle just to survive/Buried animals call your name/You keep on sleeping/Through the poignant rain' just to keep us on our toes. The overall feel is classic Prince – there's even a telephone ring part-way through reminiscent of the sound effects employed by the purple on albums like *Sign O' The Times*.

## Nitemare Hippy Girl

| | |
|---|---|
| BECK HANSEN | vocals, guitars |
| DAVID HARTE | drums |
| WRITTEN BY | Beck Hansen |
| RECORDED | Rob Schnapf's house, Los Angeles, CA, USA |
| PRODUCED BY | Beck Hansen, Rob Schnapf and Tom Rothrock |
| RELEASE DATES | UK: March 1994 (CD, LP, MC *Mellow Gold*) |
| | US: March 1994 (CD, LP, MC *Mellow Gold*) |

Another of Beck's goofy songs, this one is about an imaginary friend (we assume) who has 'Dried-up flowers, flakey skin/A beaded necklace and a bottle of gin'. This 'whimsical, tragical beauty' has many gifts including 'tofu the size of Texas' and 'a thousand lonely husbands'. A charming little song that Beck will sometimes pull out of the bag for a live treat.

## Nobody's Fault But My Own

| | |
|---|---|
| BECK HANSEN | vocals, guitar |
| JUSTIN MELDAL-JOHNSEN | bass |
| JOEY WARONKER | percussion |
| DAVID CAMPBELL | viola, strings, composer and arranger |
| LARRY CORBETT | cello |
| WARREN KLEIN | sitar, tambura |
| FRED SESLIANO | esraj |
| WRITTEN BY | Beck Hansen |
| RECORDED | Ocean Way Studios, Los Angeles, CA, USA, March 1998 |
| PRODUCED BY | Nigel Godrich and Beck Hansen |
| RELEASE DATES | UK: November 1998 (CD, LP, MC *Mutations*) |
| | US: November 1998 (CD, LP, MC *Mutations*) |
| | Japan: April 1999 (CD 'Nobody's Fault But My Own' single) |

One of the more ambitious songs on *Mutations*. Warren Klein and Fred Sesliano's Indian influences on this song make it stand out from the rest of the album. After being debuted on the short 1998 tour as a fairly sparse ballad, the album version goes to completely new places. This was better re-created during live dates in the spring of 1999 (and on *Saturday Night Live*) as the Indian instruments were brought along to add a new dimension to the live presentation of this song.

## No Money, No Honey

| | |
|---|---|
| WRITTEN BY | Beck Hansen |
| *Original version:* | |
| BECK HANSEN | vocals |
| *Second version:* | |
| KEN | vocals |
| BECK HANSEN | backing vocals, guitar |
| RECORDED | Los Angeles, CA, USA |
| RELEASE DATES | US: January 1993 (MC *Golden Feelings* – original version) |
| | US: February 1994 (CD *Stereopathetic Soul Manure* – second version) |

One of Beck's earliest compositions, possibly inspired by his hard time in New York in the late 1980s, this song first showed up on his Sonic Enemy tape in 1993. He later added a second version of it to *Stereopathetic Soul Manure* with his homeless friend, Ken, on vocals. This version was preceded by a snippet of 'Hall of Mirrors' by the B12s.

## Novacane

| | |
|---|---|
| BECK HANSEN | vocals, all instruments |
| WRITTEN BY | Beck Hansen, John King and Mike Simpson |
| RECORDED | PCP Labs, Silverlake, CA, USA, 1995 |

| | |
|---|---|
| PRODUCED BY | Beck Hansen, Mike Simpson and John King |
| RELEASE DATES | UK: June 1996 (CD, LP, MC *Odelay*) |
| | US: June 1996 (CD, LP, MC *Odelay*) |
| | US (CD *Big Shiny Tunes* compilation) |
| | US (CD *Buy Product 2* compilation) |

One of the first batch of *Odelay* tracks to be completed, Beck played this during his stint on the Lollapalooza tour in the summer of 1995. Under the title of 'Novacane Express' he also played it at Reading 1995 where it was filmed and shown on MTV Europe. A real blast to play live, it also features a full tour de force of Dust Brothers studio wizardry. Beck described the song as 'The last convoy, a convoy with no destination, fully powered, unlimited supply of diesel. The convoy is continually growing. A concatenation of brakeless trucks are speeding towards an invisible doom.'

## O Maria

| | |
|---|---|
| BECK HANSEN | vocals |
| ROGER MANNING JR | piano, organ |
| JUSTIN MELDAL-JOHNSEN | upright bass |
| JOEY WARONKER | drums |
| SMOKEY HORMEL | guitar |
| DAVID RALICKE | trombone |
| WRITTEN BY | Beck Hansen |
| RECORDED | Ocean Way Studios, Los Angeles, CA, USA, March 1998 |
| PRODUCED BY | Nigel Godrich and Beck Hansen |
| RELEASE DATES | UK: 2 November 1998 (CD, LP, MC *Mutations*) |
| | US: 3 November 1998 (CD, LP, MC *Mutations*) |

This is one of the more poignant songs on Beck's most poignant album. The downbeat lyric ('Cos everybody knows, death creeps in slow/Till you feel safe in his arms') is somewhat offset by the slightly jaunty melody.

## One Foot In The Grave

| | |
|---|---|
| BECK HANSEN | vocals |
| WRITTEN BY | Beck Hansen |
| RELEASED DATE | US: February 1994 (CD *Stereopathetic Soul Manure*) |

Despite not making it on to the album of the same name, this song has been a staple of the Beck live canon for about six years and is a big fan favourite. This version was recorded live somewhere in the early 1990s. Beck has described this song as being his tribute to the harmonica-playing blues maestro, Sonny Terry. In concert it constantly throws up interesting variations as the crowd will inevitably clap along, but as almost every crowd claps at a different speed, the song is rarely the same. In London in 1997, Beck had to stop mid-song, out of breath, and ask the crowd to clap a little slower. 'I don't want no jungle beats!' he hollered.

## One Of These Days
| | |
|---|---|
| BECK HANSEN | vocals, guitar, synthesiser |
| JUSTIN MELDAL-JOHNSEN | bass |
| ROGER MANNING JR | keyboards, percussion |
| WRITTEN BY | Beck Hansen |
| RECORDED | Los Angeles, CA, USA, 1999 |
| ENGINEERED BY | Tony Hoffer and Justin Meldal-Johnsen |
| MIXED BY | Mickey P |
| RELEASE DATES | Japan: April 1999 (CD 'Nobody's Fault But My Own' single) |
| | Australia: May 1999 (CD 'Cold Brains' single) |

It may only be a B-side, but this is one of Beck's better songs, a fairly straightforward one in the same mould as many of those on *Mutations*. The dreamy vocals give a new dimension to it that builds all the way through to a lively finish. Beck played it extensively on his mini-tour in April and May 1999.

## Outcome
| | |
|---|---|
| BECK HANSEN | vocals, guitars |
| SCOTT PLOUF | drums |
| SAM JAYNE | backing vocals |
| JAMES BERTRAM | bass |
| WRITTEN BY | Beck Hansen |
| RECORDED | Dub Narcotic Studios, Olympia, WA, USA, January 1994 |
| PRODUCED BY | Beck Hansen and Calvin Johnson |
| RELEASE DATE | US: November 1994 (CD, LP, MC *One Foot In The Grave*) |

A mid-paced rocker that could have been a Pearl Jam B-side. Recorded with the full band on Beck's second trip to Olympia in early 1994, the shared vocal duties with Sam Jayne work very well and provide one of the highlights on this album.

## Ozzy
| | |
|---|---|
| BECK HANSEN | vocals |
| DON BURNETTE | drums |
| WRITTEN BY | Beck Hansen |
| RELEASE DATE | US: February 1994 (CD *Stereopathetic Soul Manure*) |

A live favourite that sees Beck cut loose and have some fun. He sings the verse in an artificially high voice and sings 'Ozzy' over and over in an echo effect for the chorus. 'Ozzy, you're the man,' cries Beck.

## Painted Eyelids
| | |
|---|---|
| BECK HANSEN | vocals |
| SCOT PLOUF | drums |
| JAMES BERTRAM | bass |
| SCOTT JAYNE | backing vocals |

| | |
|---|---|
| WRITTEN BY | Beck Hansen |
| RECORDED | Dub Narcotic Studios, Olympia, WA, USA, January 1994 |
| PRODUCED BY | Beck Hansen and Calvin Johnson |
| RELEASE DATE | US: November 1994 (CD, LP, MC *One Foot In The Grave*) |

A real traditional country tune and one of the more melodic songs on the album. Rarely played live, but it's a treat when it is.

## Pay No Mind (Snoozer)

| | |
|---|---|
| BECK HANSEN | vocals |
| DAVID HARTE | drums |
| WRITTEN BY | Beck Hansen |
| RECORDED | Rob Schnapf's house, Los Angeles, CA, USA |
| PRODUCED BY | Beck Hansen, Rob Schnapf and Tom Rothrock |
| RELEASE DATES | UK: March 1994 (CD, LP, MC *Mellow Gold*) |
| | US: March 1994 (CD, LP, MC *Mellow Gold*) |
| | US: 1995 (CD, 12" 'Pay No Mind' single) |
| | UK: 1995 (CD, 12" 'Pay No Mind' single) |
| | Japan: 1995 (CD 'Pay No Mind' single) |

One of Beck's oldest songs, this was originally said to have about ten verses. When played live Beck often changes the words and he also released a different vocal arrangement as 'Got No Mind'. The vinyl version of *Mellow Gold* includes a different version of this song. In the UK, the single was initially withdrawn but later released. A pretty straightforward, gentle song it addresses many of Beck's concerns of the early 1990s. 'Give the finger to the rock and roll singer/As he's dancing upon your pay cheque,' he sings on the album, but he often changed 'rock and roll singer' to 'folk singer' when he played it live.

## Peaches & Cream

| | |
|---|---|
| BECK HANSEN | vocals, guitar, keyboards, background vocals, handclaps |
| ROGER MANNING JR | synthesiser, organ, percussion, handclaps |
| JUSTIN MELDAL-JOHNSEN | bass, percussion, handclaps |
| DAVID RALICKE | trombone |
| JON BIRDSONG | trumpet |
| DAVID BROWN | tenor saxophone |
| CHOIR | Arroyo Tabernacle Men's Choir |
| WRITTEN BY | Beck Hansen |
| RECORDED | Beck's house, Silverlake, CA, USA |
| PRODUCED BY | Beck Hansen and Mickey Petralia |
| RELEASE DATES | US: November 1999 (CD, MC, LP *Midnite Vultures*) |
| | UK: November 1999 (CD, MC, LP *Midnite Vultures*) |

Another *Midnite Vultures* track that recalls Prince not only because of the title, but because of the lyrics that include such couplets as 'Give those pious soldiers/Another lollipop/Cause we're on the good ship/Ménage à trois'. After a few minutes of serious bumping and grinding a choir strikes up in full effect to sing 'Keep your lamplight trimmed and burning' in a very surreal moment.

### People Gettin' Busy

| | |
|---|---|
| BECK HANSEN | vocals, harmonica, guitars |
| WRITTEN BY | Beck Hansen |
| PRODUCED BY | Beck Hansen |
| RELEASE DATE | US: January 1993 (MC *Golden Feelings*) |

Starting out as a jolly little acoustic strum for the first 30 seconds, it then abruptly turns into an electric monster. Beck supplies at least three different voices for the chorus that he layers on top of each other.

### Piece Of Shit

| | |
|---|---|
| BECK HANSEN | vocals |
| WRITTEN BY | Beck Hansen |
| RECORDED | Los Angeles, CA, USA, 1992–93 |
| PRODUCED BY | Beck Hansen |
| RELEASE DATE | not officially released, available on *Fresh Meat And Old Slabs* tape |

Delightfully titled song from his mother's birthday present tape consisting of 12 seconds of sampled disco music and a few Beck words distorted over the top.

### Pinefresh

| | |
|---|---|
| BECK HANSEN | guitars |
| WRITTEN BY | Beck Hansen |
| PRODUCED BY | Beck Hansen |
| RELEASE DATE | US: January 1994 (10″ *A Western Harvest Field By Moonlight*) |

Gentle acoustic guitar, like small waves lapping on the side ofa lake. Just when it seems like the introduction has ended . . . that's it, the song's over.

### Pink Noise (Rock Me Amadeus)

| | |
|---|---|
| BECK HANSEN | vocals |
| ANNA WARONKER | bass |
| RACHEL HADEN | drums |
| WRITTEN BY | Beck Hansen |
| RECORDED | Poop Alley Studios, Los Angeles, CA, 1992–93 |
| PRODUCED BY | Tom Grimley |
| RELEASE DATE | US: February 1994 (CD *Stereopathetic Soul Manure*) |

After starting with some electric blues guitar this track quickly becomes a typical shambling Beck noise fest. Amid the screamin' and hollerin', the only discernible lyrics seem to be 'Pink noise/Delicious potato/The victims/Demeanin' religion', followed by a second verse of 'Two rights/Two wrongs/Horrific/Control'. People's poet indeed. Joey Waronker's sister, Anna, provides some fuzzed-up bass before some suitably Casio breakdown effects to round it off.

## Puttin' It Down

| | |
|---|---|
| BECK HANSEN | vocals, guitar |
| WRITTEN BY | Beck Hansen |
| RELEASE DATE | US: February 1994 (CD *Stereopathetic Soul Manure*) |

A great little acoustic song that Beck still occasionally plays. 'Well, you treat me like a clown, but I don't wanna be funny,' sings Beck in what could be a comment on his early LA acoustic shows that were greeted with total apathy. 'I'm puttin' it down, but you're not picking it up.'

## Ramshackle

| | |
|---|---|
| BECK HANSEN | vocals, guitars |
| CHARLIE HADEN | bass |
| JOEY WARONKER | percussion |
| WRITTEN BY | Beck Hansen |
| PRODUCED BY | Tom Rothrock and Rob Schnapf |
| RELEASE DATES | UK: June 1996 (CD, LP, MC *Odelay*) |
| | US: June 1996 (CD, LP, MC *Odelay*) |

As on *Mellow Gold* before it, and *Mutations* after it, Beck ended *Odelay* with an acoustic calm-down from the madness that had preceeded it. 'Ramshackle' pre-dated the Dust Brothers' involvement with the album and featured jazz legend Charlie Haden on upright bass. Beck described this song as 'Just south-western, San Fernando Valley, San Gabriel ... the ranchhouses, like cardboard cut-outs. Brown atmosphere.'

## Readymade

| | |
|---|---|
| BECK HANSEN | vocals, all instruments |
| EXCERPTS FROM | 'Desafinado' (Antonio Carlos Jobim/Newton Mendonca) performed by Laurindo Almeida and the Bossa Nova All Stars |
| WRITTEN BY | Beck Hansen, John King and Mike Simpson |
| RECORDED | PCP Labs, Silverlake, CA, USA, 1994–95 |
| PRODUCED BY | Beck Hansen, Mike Simpson and John King |
| RELEASE DATES | UK: June 1996 (CD, LP, MC *Odelay*) |
| | US: June 1996 (CD, LP, MC *Odelay*) |

Here Beck could have been singing about his grandfather's art studio: 'Rubbish piles, fresh and plain/Empty boxes and a pawn shop brain.' This fairly slow, plodding song was described by its singer as simply 'Standing in the bread line'.

### Richard's Hairpiece

| | |
|---|---|
| BECK HANSEN | vocals |
| WRITTEN BY | Beck Hansen, John King and Mike Simpson |
| PRODUCED BY | Aphex Twin |
| RELEASE DATES | Japan: 1997 (CD 'The New Pollution And Other Favourites' single) |
| | US: February 1997 (CD, 12″ 'The New Pollution' single) |
| | UK: February 1997 (CD 'The New Pollution' single) |

Possibly the most radical remix of a Beck song ever. Aphex Twin, Richard James, sped the song up to 'jungle' proportions and added some classic strings into the mix too. Quite an achievement.

### Rollins Power Sauce

| | |
|---|---|
| BECK HANSEN | vocals, all instruments |
| WRITTEN BY | Beck Hansen |
| RECORDED | Poop Alley Studios, Los Angeles, CA, USA, 1993 |
| PRODUCED BY | Tom Grimley |
| RELEASE DATE | US: February 1994 (CD *Stereopathetic Soul Manure*) |

A slow beat accompanies this, Beck's take on a Henry Rollins song. 'My throat muscles are completely shredded,' drawls Beck at the start of the song. It's not surprising if he's going to keep singing like this.

### Rowboat

| | |
|---|---|
| BECK HANSEN | vocals |
| LISA | drums |
| LEO LE BLANC | pedal steel |
| WRITTEN BY | Beck Hansen |
| RECORDED | Wire Works Studio, Los Angeles, CA, USA |
| PRODUCED BY | Rusty Cusak |
| RELEASE DATE | US: February 1994 (CD *Stereopathetic Soul Manure*) |

This traditional country tune was given to Johnny Cash to cover after Beck decided that the first song he wrote for the country legend, 'Sing It Again', was not up to the required standard. Cash was impressed with this song and declared that Beck has 'got that mountain music in his blood'. Beck himself worked this song more into his live set during his 1998 shows and played it regularly during his spring 1999 mini-tour. The version on *Stereopathetic Soul Manure* features some exquisite pedal-steel playing from Leo Le Blanc who sadly died in 1995.

### Runners Dial Zero

| | |
|---|---|
| BECK HANSEN | vocals |
| ROGER MANNING JR | synthesiser, piano |
| JUSTIN MELDAL-JOHNSEN | bass |
| JOEY WARONKER | percussion |
| WRITTEN BY | Beck Hansen |
| RECORDED | Ocean Way Studios, Los Angeles, CA, USA, April 1998 |

PRODUCED BY      Nigel Godrich and Beck Hansen
RELEASE DATE      UK: November 1998 (CD, LP, MC *Mutations*)

This song stands out from Beck's back catalogue in a big way. A hauntingly lonely song that features little more than drums and vocals, it has been compared to Big Star's 'Kangaroo' and Dennis Wilson's 'Carry Me Home'. This was the last song of the *Mutations* sessions because producer Nigel Godrich had to leave before it was completed.

## SA-5

| | |
|---|---|
| BECK HANSEN | vocals, drum machine, guitar |
| WRITTEN BY | Beck Hansen |
| PRODUCED BY | Beck Hansen |
| RELEASE DATE | UK: October 1997 (CD 'Deadweight' single) |

A half-brother to 'Cyanide Breath Mint' is this song. Aggressive acoustic guitar, fucked vocals and a drum machine make this the perfect Beck B-side.

## Satan Gave Me A Taco

| | |
|---|---|
| WRITTEN BY | Beck Hansen |
| *Original version:* | |
| BECK HANSEN | vocals, guitar |
| *Second version:* | |
| BECK HANSEN | vocals, banjo |
| DON BURNETTE | drums |
| JOHNNY CASH | machine backing vocals |
| RECORDED | Los Angeles, CA, USA, 1992–93 |
| PRODUCED BY | Rusty Cusak |
| RELEASE DATES | original version available on *Fresh Meat And Old Slabs* tape |
| | US: February 1994 (CD *Stereopathetic Soul Manure*) |

Some sampled laughing begins the original version of this track – an all-time favourite of Beck's fans. The original one is slightly faster and Beck's vocal a little rawer than the version that was officially released the next year. It's impossible to do this song justice in my words so I'll just quote the opening of the lyrics: 'Satan gave me a taco and it made me really sick/The chicken was all raw and the grease was mighty thick/The rice was all rancid and the beans were so hard/I was gettin' kinda dizzy eatin' all the lard/There was aphids on the lettuce and I ate every one/And after I was done the salsa melted off my tongue/Pieces of tortilla got stuck in my throat/And the stains on my clothes burned a hole through my coat.'

## Say Can You See

| | |
|---|---|
| BECK HANSEN | vocals |
| WRITTEN BY | Beck Hansen |
| RECORDED | Los Angeles, CA, USA, 1992–93 |

| PRODUCED BY | Beck Hansen |
| RELEASE DATE | not officially released, available on *Fresh Meat And Old Slabs* tape |

An awful trawl through 45 seconds of deep voiced, semi-spoken vocals over some tortured untuned acoustic guitar. Horrible.

### Scavenger

| BECK HANSEN | vocals |
| WRITTEN BY | Beck Hansen |

Played live on JJJ Radio in Sydney, Australia in 1994, Beck introduced this unreleased song by the title 'Scavenger'.

### Schmoozer

| BECK HANSEN | vocals, guitars, drums, harmonica |
| WRITTEN BY | Beck Hansen |
| PRODUCED BY | Beck Hansen |
| RELEASE DATE | US: January 1993 (MC *Golden Feelings*) |

A slowed-down Buddy Holly drum beat carries this song along. Again it's (like 'Special People') a kind of 'list song' with lyrics like 'You been atalkin' now/You been arockin' now/You been aguessin' now/You been undressin' now' and so it goes for about twelve more 'You beens'.

### See Water

| BECK HANSEN | vocals |
| SCOTT PLOUF | drums |
| JAMES BERTRAM | bass |
| CHRIS BALLEW | guitar |
| WRITTEN BY | Beck Hansen |
| RECORDED | Dub Narcotic Studios, Olympia, WA, USA, January 1994 |
| PRODUCED BY | Calvin Johnson |
| RELEASE DATE | US: November 1994 (CD, LP, MC *One Foot In The Grave*) |

Another of the 'band' songs from Olympia, this one is an achingly slow stroll with plenty of percussion and overdubbed guitar. The title is the whole point of the song: 'Close your eyes and see water/sliding up the back of your head/folding into your clothing/covering everything you said.'

### Sexx Laws

| BECK HANSEN | vocals |
| ROGER MANNING JR | synthesiser, piano, tambourine, shaker |
| SMOKEY HORMEL | guitar |
| JUSTIN MELDAL-JOHNSEN | bass |
| DAVID RALICKE | trombone |
| JON BIRDSONG | trumpet |

| | |
|---|---|
| DAVID BROWN | tenor saxophone |
| HERB PETERSON | banjo |
| JAY DEE MANESS | pedal steel |
| ARNOLD MCCULLER | background vocals |
| VALERIE PINKTON | background vocals |
| WRITTEN BY | Beck Hansen |
| RECORDED | Beck's house, Silverlake, CA, USA |
| PRODUCED BY | Beck Hansen and Mickey Petralia |
| RELEASE DATES | US: November 1999 (CD, MC, LP *Midnite Vultures*) |
| | UK: November 1999 (CD, MC, LP *Midnite Vultures*) |
| | UK: November 1999 (CD 'Sexx Laws' single) |

'I want to defy the logic of all sex laws,' screamed Beck at some late 1998 shows. Eventually this between-song banter evolved into a complete song. Setting the scene for the raunchy album that followed, Beck sings that if you 'Let the handcuffs slip off your wrists/I'll let you be my chaperone/At the halfway home.' Musically this is more energetic than many of the other album tracks and has the only truly rousing chorus of the whole album, that is driven by some enthusiastic horn playing. As the song comes to an end the banjo interlude is just pure 'Wacky Races'.

### Sexy Boy (Sex Kino Mix) by Air

| | |
|---|---|
| WRITTEN BY | J. B. Dunckel and N. Godin |
| REMIXED BY | Beck Hansen |
| RELEASE DATES | US: 1998 (CD 'Sexy Boy' single) |
| | UK: 1998 (CD 'Kelly Watch The Stars' single) |
| | US (CD *MTV Amp 2* compilation) |

With a little help from Mickey P, Beck remixed this breakthrough track by the French phenomenon Air. The track was changed to make it sound like someone was walking into a cinema and tucking into some popcorn. Roger Manning and Justin Meldal-Johnsen also toured with them to solidify the Beck connections.

### She Is All (Gimme Something To Eat)

| | |
|---|---|
| BECK HANSEN | vocals |
| ANNA WARONKER | bass |
| RACHEL HADEN | drums |
| WRITTEN BY | Beck Hansen |
| RECORDED | Poop Alley Studios, Los Angeles, CA, USA |
| PRODUCED BY | Tom Grimley |
| RELEASE DATE | US: January 1994 (10″ *A Western Harvest Field By Moonlight*) |

Like most songs on this mini-album, this track clocks in at just over a minute. The lyric basically consists of the title in repetition. The girls from That Dog make a guest appearance again.

## Sin City

| | |
|---|---|
| BECK HANSEN | vocals, guitar |
| EMMYLOU HARRIS | vocals |
| JOEY WARONKER | drums |
| JUSTIN MELDAL-JOHNSEN | bass |
| SMOKEY HORMEL | guitar |
| JAYDEE MANESS | pedal steel |
| GABE WUTCHER | fiddle |
| BILLY PANE | piano |
| WRITTEN BY | Gram Parsons and Chris Hillman |
| RECORDED | Ocean Way Studios, Los Angeles, CA, USA, 1998 |
| PRODUCED BY | Beck Hansen |
| RELEASE DATES | UK: July 1999 (CD *Return Of The Grievous Angel* compilation) |
| | US: July 1999 (CD *Return Of The Grievous Angel* compilation) |
| | UK: July 1999 (CD *Unconditionally Guaranteed – Volume 7* compilation – free with *Uncut* magazine) |

An unradical interpretation of this song that Gram Parsons co-wrote with fellow Byrd Chris Hillman. Beck's vocal is somewhat over-shadowed by Emmylou's but it doesn't really detract from the overall song.

## Sing It Again

| | |
|---|---|
| BECK HANSEN | vocals |
| ROGER MANNING JR | piano |
| JUSTIN MELDAL-JOHNSEN | upright bass |
| JOEY WARONKER | drums |
| SMOKEY HORMEL | guitar |
| WRITTEN BY | Beck Hansen |
| RECORDED | Ocean Way Studios, Los Angeles, CA, USA, March 1998 |
| PRODUCED BY | Nigel Godrich and Beck Hansen |
| RELEASE DATES | UK: November 1998 (CD, LP, MC *Mutations*) |
| | US: November 1998 (CD, LP, MC *Mutations*) |

'Shall we do another one then?' asks Beck to start this one off. A semi-waltz which features a great bit of guitar work by Smokey Hormel, it had originally been written by Beck for Johnny Cash but Beck had put it to one side until recording *Mutations* because he called it 'a piece of shit'. He couldn't have been more wrong.

## Sissyneck

| | |
|---|---|
| BECK HANSEN | vocals |
| MIKE BIOTO | organ |
| GREGORY LEISZ | pedal steel |
| ELEMENTS OF | 'The Moog And Me' (Dick Hyman) performed by Dick Hyman |
| | 'A Part Of Me' (Paris/Taylor) |
| WRITTEN BY | Beck Hansen, John King and Mike Simpson |

| | |
|---|---|
| RECORDED | PCP Labs, Silverlake, CA, USA, 1995 |
| PRODUCED BY | Beck Hansen, Mike Simpson and John King |
| RELEASE DATES | UK: June 1996 (CD, LP, MC *Odelay*) |
| | US: June 1996 (CD, LP, MC *Odelay*) |
| | UK: May 1997 (CD, MC, 7" 'Sissyneck' single) |
| | Australia: 1997 (CD *Odelay* tour edition) |

Hiphop meets country on this track. Beck gets down with some beats among lines like 'I got a stolen wife/And a rhinestone life/And some good old boys' and 'Now let me tell you about my baby/She was born in Arizona/Sitting in the jailhouse/Trying to learn some good manners.' Maybe he could have given this one to Johnny Cash. Beck bizarrely described this track as 'David Allen Coe got a perm and decided to get a job at the Casio store at the mall.' When asked about the line 'My pants ain't gettin' no bigger', he answered, 'Y'know, sometimes they just can't. You try to hold your breath and bloat yourself, but those clothes are just not gonna make room for any of your follies.'

## Sleeping Bag

| | |
|---|---|
| BECK HANSEN | vocals, guitar |
| SCOTT PLOUF | drums |
| JAMES BERTRAM | bass |
| WRITTEN BY | Beck Hansen |
| RECORDED | Dub Narcotic Studios, Olympia, WA, USA, January 1994 |
| PRODUCED BY | Calvin Johnson |
| RELEASE DATES | US: November 1994 (CD, LP, MC *One Foot In The Grave*) |
| | US (CD *Yo Yo A Go Go* compilation) |

A jazzy little acoustic number and a live favourite too. Seems to get played more often with age. Perhaps it's one of those songs that Beck likes to 'marinate'.

## Soul Sucked Dry

| | |
|---|---|
| BECK HANSEN | vocals, guitar, harmonica |
| WRITTEN BY | Beck Hansen |
| PRODUCED BY | Beck Hansen |
| RELEASE DATE | US: January 1993 (MC *Golden Feelings*) |

A slightly bluesy number with stabs of blues guitar and a wailing harmonica in the far background. Could have been written by Beck during his lowest moments of LA semi-poverty. 'My soul's suckin' dry/My soul's been sucked dry/Emptiness surrounds me/Bitterness crowns me.'

## Soul Suckin Jerk

| | |
|---|---|
| BECK HANSEN | vocals, all instruments |
| WRITTEN BY | Beck Hansen and Carl Stephenson |

| RECORDED | Carl Stephenson's house, Los Angeles, CA, USA |
|---|---|
| PRODUCED BY | Beck Hansen and Carl Stephenson |
| RELEASE DATES | UK: March 1994 (CD, LP, MC *Mellow Gold*) |
| | US: March 1994 (CD, LP, MC *Mellow Gold*) |

Typical of Beck's songs about working for the 'man' – 'Throwing chicken in the bucket with the soda pop can, puke green uniform on my back, I had to set it on fire in a vat of chicken fat.' A progression form his earlier song 'Mexico' where he gets fed up with his low-paid job and goes on the rampage. The difference is, in 'Mexico' he doesn't have a choice but here he just does a runner. After burning his uniform he's left cold that night, but is resolute that 'I ain't washing dishes in the ditch no more/I ain't going to work for no soul-sucking jerk.'

## Soul Suckin Jerk (Reject)

| BECK HANSEN | vocals, all instruments |
|---|---|
| WRITTEN BY | Beck Hansen |
| RECORDED | Poop Alley Studios, Los Angeles, CA, USA |
| PRODUCED BY | Tom Grimley |
| RELEASE DATE | UK: March 1994 (CD 'Loser' single) |

This version of 'Soul Suckin Jerk' is a more groove-filled version than that on *Mellow Gold* with a more prominent bassline. Beck first sings the second half of the album version's lyric, then goes on to a mid-song break of 'you know it/that's right/rockin' the town like a moldy crouton/flyin' through the air with breeze' before singing the initial half of the album version's lyric to end with. This version is a good two minutes longer than the album version and goes into an organ solo towards the end.

## Spanking Room

| BECK HANSEN | vocals |
|---|---|
| WRITTEN BY | Beck Hansen |
| RECORDED | Poop Alley Studios, Los Angeles, CA, USA, 1993 |
| PRODUCED BY | Beck Hansen and Tom Grimley |
| RELEASE DATES | France: March 1994 (CD 'Beercan' single) |
| | US: March 1994 (CD 'Beercan' single) |

A real grunge out ensues on this track. Maybe it was a reflection of US music in 1994, but it's just a lot of screams and heavy guitar riffs over an unimaginative drum beat.

## Special People

| BECK HANSEN | vocals |
|---|---|
| WRITTEN BY | Beck Hansen |
| PRODUCED BY | Beck Hansen |
| RELEASE DATES | US: January 1993 (MC *Golden Feelings*) |
| | UK: 1995 (CD, 12″ 'Pay No Mind' single) |
| | US: 1995 (CD 'Pay No Mind' single) |
| | Japan: 1995 (CD 'Pay No Mind' single) |

This is an a cappella vocal by Beck telling us what the 'Special People' do in his deepest voice.

### Static

| | |
|---|---|
| BECK HANSEN | vocals, guitars |
| ROGER MANNING JR | electric piano, organ |
| JUSTIN MELDAL-JOHNSEN | bass |
| JOEY WARONKER | drums, percussion |
| WRITTEN BY | Beck Hansen |
| RECORDED | Ocean Way Studios, Los Angeles, CA, USA, March 1998 |
| PRODUCED BY | Nigel Godrich and Beck Hansen |
| RELEASE DATES | UK: 2 November 1998 (CD, LP, MC *Mutations*) |
| | US: 3 November 1998 (CD, LP, MC *Mutations*) |

Beck has had two songs called 'Static'. The original was to have been released as a single on Domino Records in the UK, but Beck changed his mind. It was a finger-picking song that threatened to become 'Hollow Log' at any moment. The version on *Mutations* is one of that album's more electric moments.

### Steal My Body Home

| | |
|---|---|
| BECK HANSEN | vocals, all instruments |
| WRITTEN BY | Beck Hansen |
| RECORDED | Carl Stephenson's House, Los Angeles, CA, USA, 1992 |
| PRODUCED BY | Beck Hansen, Rob Schnapf and Tom Rothrock |
| RELEASE DATES | UK: March 1994 (CD, LP, MC *Mellow Gold*) |
| | US: March 1994 (CD, LP, MC *Mellow Gold*) |

A slow, laborious song that could have been a forerunner for 'Nobody's Fault But My Own'. The Indian feel and depressing lyric would have fitted nicely onto *Mutations*. 'Watch my troubles all unwind/Drinkin' gasoline and wine/Catchin' chill up the storm/The trees are fake, the air is dead/The birds are stuffed with poison lead/And the ground is much too clean.' Towards the end the whole atmosphere changes from one of an eastern culture to a bizarre Beck world of kazoos and strange percussion.

### Steve Threw Up

| | |
|---|---|
| BECK HANSEN | vocals |
| WRITTEN BY | Beck Hansen |
| RECORDED | Los Angeles, CA, USA, 1992–93 |
| PRODUCED BY | Beck Hansen |
| RELEASE DATE | available on *Fresh Meat And Old Slabs* tape |
| | US: 1994 (7" 'Steve Threw Up' single) |

This song is based on the story of Beck's friend, Steve Moramarco, who threw up on a Ferris wheel at a fairground. After taking some 'bad acid' he looked down on the fairground and threw up on a girl. Beck then goes into a long list, which is way too detailed, of everything that Steve had eaten – and he'd eaten a lot!

### Strange Invitation

| | |
|---|---|
| BECK HANSEN | vocals, guitars |
| SMOKEY HORMEL | guitars |
| JUSTIN MELDAL-JOHNSEN | bass |
| JON CLARKE | English horn, bass clarinet |
| DAVID CAMPBELL | celesta |
| WRITTEN BY | Beck Hansen |
| RECORDED | Sunset Sound Studio, Los Angeles, CA, USA |
| PRODUCED BY | Beck Hansen |
| RELEASE DATE | UK: September 1997 (CD, 7" 'Jack-ass' single) |

This lush, orchestral version of 'Jack-ass' was arranged and conducted by David Campbell who also played celesta on the track

### Styrofoam Chicken (Quality Time)

| | |
|---|---|
| BECK HANSEN | keyboards |
| WRITTEN BY | Beck Hansen |
| PRODUCED BY | Beck Hansen |
| RELEASE DATE | US: January 1994 (10" *A Western Harvest Field By Moonlight*) |

This song, the last on *A Western Harvest Field By Moonlight*, never ends. It is just a short burst of garbled keyboard noise that is cut into the run-out groove of the record to keep playing for ever as the groove is cyclical.

### Sucker Without A Brain (Fresh Meat)

| | |
|---|---|
| WRITTEN BY | Beck Hansen |
| *Banjo Story version:* | |
| BECK HANSEN | vocals, banjo |
| *Fresh Meat And Old Slabs version:* | |
| BECK HANSEN | vocals, guitar |
| RECORDED | Los Angeles, CA, USA, 1992–93 |
| PRODUCED BY | Beck Hansen |
| RELEASE DATE | not officially released, available on *Fresh Meat And Old Slabs* and *Banjo Story* tapes |

An almost waltz-like song that tells of a horrific bus-crash. 'Here comes that bus/Right into your face/Now you're flying home,' sings Beck. 'The driver tried to swerve/But he just didn't see ya/Now you're buried b'neath the wheel/Just like a tortilla.' Humorous stuff.

### Supergolden Black Sunchild/Supergolden (Sunchild)

| | |
|---|---|
| BECK HANSEN | vocals, guitar |
| WRITTEN BY | Beck Hansen |
| PRODUCED BY | Beck Hansen |
| RELEASE DATES | US: January 1993 (MC *Golden Feelings*) |

US: 1995 (CD 'Pay No Mind' single)
UK: 1995 (CD, 12″ 'Pay No Mind' single)
Japan: 1995 (CD 'Pay No Mind' single)

When this song was originally included on the *Golden Feelings* tape it was referred to as its original title of 'Supergolden Black Sunchild', but by the time of its inclusion on the 'Pay No Mind' single two years later it had taken the abbreviated name of 'Supergolden (Sunchild)'. The start of the song sounds like Jimmy Saville yodelling but it then abruptly becomes a gentle acoustic song. This could be the kind of folk music that Beck and the anti-folk gang were rebelling against in the late 1980s. Beck sings lines like 'Bless this sceptre' and 'Slice the mango' in a kind of warble. Of course this song is a sarcastic take, isn't it?

## Sweet Sunshine

| | |
|---|---|
| BECK HANSEN | vocals, all instruments |
| WRITTEN BY | Beck Hansen and Carl Stephenson |
| RECORDED | Carl Stephenson's house, Los Angeles, CA, USA |
| PRODUCED BY | Beck Hansen and Carl Stephenson |
| RELEASE DATES | UK: March 1994 (CD, LP, MC *Mellow Gold*) |
| | US: March 1994 (CD, LP, MC *Mellow Gold*) |

It sounds like a car race has been sampled on this track, or maybe a swarm of bees. Beck sings with a heavily distorted vocal in what could almost be a love song, in Beck's world of course: 'Touch me on the inside with a finger full of gravy/Wanna get you on the sofa, lady, wanna Shake and Bake me.'

## Talkin Demolition Expert

| | |
|---|---|
| BECK HANSEN | vocals, banjo, drums |
| WRITTEN BY | Beck Hansen |
| RELEASE DATE | not officially released, available on *Banjo Story* tape |

A real 'down-home' feel to this song – it could be any one of a number of 1950s country singers, if you ignore the lyric, that is! Beck sings that 'I got all kinds of devices that I'm gonna detonate/I got bazookas, hand-grenades', as he tells the story of quitting his office job and killing his boss before going on the rampage, Rambo-style.

## Tasergun

| | |
|---|---|
| WRITTEN BY | Beck Hansen |
| *Original version:* | |
| BECK HANSEN | vocals, guitar |
| RECORDED | Los Angeles, CA, USA, 1992–93 |
| PRODUCED BY | Beck Hansen |
| *Stereopathetic Soul Manure version:* | |
| BECK HANSEN | vocals |
| DON BURNETTE | drums |

| | |
|---|---|
| BOBBY CO | bass |
| RECORDED | Wire Works Studio, Los Angeles, CA, USA |
| PRODUCED BY | Rusty Cusak |
| RELEASE DATES | original version available on *Fresh Meat And Old Slabs* tape |
| | US: February 1994 (CD *Stereopathetic Soul Manure*) |

Whether or not this is based on a true story is up for debate. It is, however, a humorous little tale of Beck's experiences in a Hollywood boarding house. An old man in the next room took offence at Beck playing his guitar and exclaimed 'Watch out son, I got a tasergun.' After an incident involving stolen toilet paper Beck moved out. The officially released version is painfully slow compared to the speedy original and, in my opinion, not half as good.

### The Fucked Up Blues

| | |
|---|---|
| BECK HANSEN | vocals, drums, guitar, harmonica |
| WRITTEN BY | Beck Hansen |
| RECORDED | Los Angeles, CA, USA, 1992 |
| PRODUCED BY | Beck Hansen |
| RELEASE DATE | US: January 1993 (MC *Golden Feelings*) |

The opening song on Beck's first release on an actual label, Sonic Enemy. After a primitive drum opening, Beck sings in a deep Calvin Johnson-like voice. As with many of his songs written about this time, it contains a fairly high number of profanities; for example, the chorus goes – 'I got the fucked up blues, I got the fucked up blues, oh what can you do about the fucking, fucked up blues.' After a short harmonica solo the verbal garbage continues to the end.

### The Little Drum Machine Boy

| | |
|---|---|
| BECK HANSEN | vocals |
| WRITTEN BY | Beck Hansen |
| RELEASE DATES | US: December 1996 (CD *Just Say Noel* compilation) |
| | UK: November 1997 (CD *Clock* promo, free with *Select* magazine) |

This Christmas compilation song – 'The holiday robot funk,' says Beck on this lengthy 7 minute track – is loosely based on the melody for 'The Little Drummer Boy'. Beck usually plays this in shows during December, but will sometimes play it in July too just for a change. Other highlights in the song include Beck's 'I get down, I get down, I get down all the way' to the tune of 'Jingle Bells'.

### The New Pollution

| | |
|---|---|
| BECK HANSEN | vocals, guitars, drums, bass |
| SAMPLE FROM | 'Venus' (Brad Baker) performed by Joe Thomas |
| WRITTEN BY | Beck Hansen, Mike Simpson and John King |
| RECORDED | PCP Labs, Silverlake, CA, USA, 1994–95 |
| PRODUCED BY | Beck Hansen, Mike Simpson and John King |

| | |
|---|---|
| RELEASE DATES | UK: 24 June 1996 (CD, LP, MC *Odelay*) |
| | US: June 1996 (CD, LP, MC *Odelay*) |
| | UK: 24 February 1997 (CD, 7" 'The New Pollution' single) |
| | US: February 1997 (CD 'The New Pollution' single) |
| | US: (CD, *MTV Alternative Nation V.1//V.2* compilation) |
| REMIXES | Remix by Mario C & Mickey P on the following: |
| | Japan: 1997 (CD 'The New Pollution' single) |
| | UK: February 1997 (CD 'The New Pollution' single) |
| | US: February 1997 (12" 'The New Pollution' single) |
| | Remix by Mickey P on the following: |
| | Japan: 1997 (CD 'The New Pollution' single) |
| | US: February 1997 (12" 'The New Pollution' single) |
| | UK: May 1997 (CD 'Sissyneck' single) |

At first Beck thought this to be just a throw-away song and wasn't going to include it on the album at all after writing it in just half a day. The bassline is a rip-off from the Beatles' 'Taxman' and the whole thing trots along at quite a pace. The ambiguous lyric in the chorus ('She's alone in the new pollution') was something that Beck intended to get people thinking about what he was saying. As he explained to *Rolling Stone*:

I'm not trying to confuse people. I want to communicate. A song like 'The New Pollution', I mean, pollution, it's a presence in our lives. And isn't it interesting to use a word like that, something with such horrible connotations, in the context of almost a love song? That's where you create friction. That's where you can start to get to someplace where you aren't dealing in the banalities of everyday, pedestrian rock lyrics. Not that I mean to be snobby about it, I can appreciate the good ol' song, and I still like to write that way sometimes.

In a separate interview, Beck said that this song 'Is about industrial waste as a stimulant and actually a delicacy that's marketed in new ways. And every few months [there's] a new angle, a new level of exposure.'

## The Spirit Moves Me

| | |
|---|---|
| BECK HANSEN | vocals |
| DON BURNETTE | drums |
| LEO LE BLANC | pedal steel |
| WRITTEN BY | Beck Hansen |
| RECORDED | Wire Works Studio, Los Angeles, CA, USA |
| PRODUCED BY | Rusty Cusak |
| RELEASE DATE | US: February 1994 (CD *Stereopathetic Soul Manure*) |

There's a real country feel to this song, due both to the luscious pedal steel and also the lyric. The slow pace tells of a disgruntled husband: 'Lately I've been spitting out the things that I didn't mean to say/But that's alright now because you don't listen to me anyway.' A shame that it only just lasts two minutes.

### This Is My Crew

| | |
|---|---|
| BECK HANSEN | vocals |
| ROGER MANNING JR | synthesiser |
| JUSTIN MELDAL-JOHNSEN | bass |
| DJ SWAMP | scratching |
| WRITTEN BY | Beck Hansen |
| RECORDED | Beck's house, Silverlake, CA, USA |
| PRODUCED BY | Beck Hansen and Tony Hoffer |
| RELEASE DATE | UK: November 1999 (CD 'Sexx Laws' single) |

*Midnite Vultures* outtake that found its way on to the first single release from said album.

### This World Is Something New To Me

| | |
|---|---|
| BECK HANSEN | vocals |
| DAWN ROBINSON | vocals |
| LISA LOEB | vocals |
| PATTI SMITH | vocals |
| LAURIE ANDERSON | vocals |
| FRED SCHNEIDER | vocals |
| KATE PEIRSON | vocals |
| CINDY WILSON | vocals |
| LENNY KRAVITZ | vocals |
| JAKOB DYLAN | vocals |
| IGGY POP | vocals |
| WRITTEN BY | Mark Mothersbaugh |
| PRODUCED BY | Mark Mothersbaugh and Robert Casale |
| RELEASE DATE | UK: 1999 (CD *The Rugrats Movie* soundtrack compilation) |

This massive ensemble track has different people singing every line, and it's pretty difficult to work out exactly who sings what. For a song with so many singers, it's a little surprising that it lasts less than two minutes.

### Thunderpeel

| | |
|---|---|
| WRITTEN BY | Beck Hansen |
| *Original version:* | |
| BECK HANSEN | vocals |
| DON BURNETTE | drums |
| RECORDED | Wire Works Studio, Los Angeles, CA, USA |
| PRODUCED BY | Rusty Cusak |
| *Second version:* | |
| BECK HANSEN | vocals |
| JOEY WARONKER | drums |
| PRODUCED BY | Beck Hansen and Mario Caldato |

| | |
|---|---|
| RELEASE DATES | US: February 1994 (CD *Stereopathetic Soul Manure* – original version) |
| | Japan: 1997 (CD 'The New Pollution And Other Favourites' single – second version) |

A straight-ahead rock song but with a Beck slant. The original version is a little more loopy and off kilter while the second version is closer to the live version of this song, which Beck plays fairly often.

## Today Has Been A Fucked Up Day

| | |
|---|---|
| BECK HANSEN | vocals, banjo |
| WRITTEN BY | Beck Hansen |
| RECORDED | Poop Alley Studios, Los Angeles, CA, USA |
| PRODUCED BY | Tom Grimley |
| RELEASE DATE | US: February 1994 (CD *Stereopathetic Soul Manure*) |

This is Beck's version of the Woody Guthrie classic 'Today Has Been A Lonesome Day'. Part way through he puts down the banjo and stomps along with the next chorus from what sounds like the other side of a kitchen. Beck can then be heard to run back to the tape player, pick up his banjo and finish off the song.

## Together We Found Misery

| | |
|---|---|
| BECK HANSEN | vocals, banjo, harmonica |
| WRITTEN BY | Beck Hansen |
| RECORDED | live to cassette, New York City, 1988 |
| PRODUCED BY | Beck Hansen |
| RELEASE DATE | not officially released, available on *Banjo Story* tape |

As you'd guess from the title, this is a sad tale of woe. A gentle strum with some passionate vocals that stand out from the rest of the tape.

## To See That Woman Of Mine

| | |
|---|---|
| BECK HANSEN | vocals, guitar, harmonica |
| WRITTEN BY | Beck Hansen |
| RELEASE DATE | US: 1992 (7″ 'MTV Makes Me Want To Smoke Crack' single) |

Singing in a gravelly voice, Beck sings of having to 'make it to Texas' to see his woman. A pretty straightforward acoustic/country song but a pretty good start nonetheless.

## Totally Confused

| | |
|---|---|
| WRITTEN BY | Beck Hansen |
| *Golden Feelings version:* | |
| BECK HANSEN | vocals, guitar |
| RECORDED | Los Angeles, CA, USA, 1992 |
| PRODUCED BY | Beck Hansen |
| *A Western Harvest Field By Moonlight version:* | |
| BECK HANSEN | vocals, guitar, drums |
| ANNA WARONKER | guitar, background vocals |

| PETRA HADEN | violin |
|---|---|
| RACHEL HADEN | bass, background vocals |
| WRITTEN BY | Beck Hansen |
| RECORDED | Poop Alley Studios, Los Angeles, CA, USA, 1993 |
| PRODUCED BY | Tom Grimley |
| RELEASE DATES | US: January 1993 (MC *Golden Feelings*) |
| | US: January 1994 (10" *A Western Harvest Field By Moonlight*) |
| | Australia: 1995 (CD *Mellow Gold* bonus tour CD) |
| | UK: March 1994 (CD 'Loser' single) |
| | US: 1994 (CD 'Beercan' single, listed as 'Totally Kunfused') |
| | UK: November 1997 (CD *Clock* promo CD given away with *Select* magazine) |

One of Beck's older songs, it was finally released as a solo take (lasting 1:50) on the *Golden Feelings* tape. The following year Beck re-recorded it with the girls from That Dog. This beefed up version is the one that subsequently found its way on to five different releases.

### Total Soul Future (Eat It)

| BECK HANSEN | vocals |
|---|---|
| DON BURNETTE | drums, backing vocals |
| BOBBY HECKSHER | guitar |
| WRITTEN BY | Beck Hansen |
| RECORDED | Wire Works Studio, Los Angeles, CA, USA |
| PRODUCED BY | Rusty Cusak |
| RELEASE DATES | US: February 1994 (CD *Stereopathetic Soul Manure*) |
| | US: 1998 (CD *Wired: Music Futurists* compilation) |

This bluesy, shuffling number features some weird Beck backing vocals and a funky guitar solo. The typically obscure lyric includes such turns of phrase as 'She got finger snap/She got the lips like a rat.'

### Tropicalia

| BECK HANSEN | vocals |
|---|---|
| ROGER MANNING JR | synthesiser, organ, percussion |
| JUSTIN MELDAL-JOHNSEN | acoustic bass, percussion |
| JOEY WARONKER | drums, percussion, synth drums |
| SMOKEY HORMEL | percussion, quica, acoustic guitars |
| DAVID RALICKE | flute, trombone |
| WRITTEN BY | Beck Hansen |
| RECORDED | Ocean Way Studios, Los Angeles, CA, USA, March 1998 |
| PRODUCED BY | Nigel Godrich and Beck Hansen |
| RELEASE DATES | UK: 2 November 1998 (CD, LP, MC *Mutations*) |
| | UK: 6 December 1998 (CD, 7" 'Tropicalia' single) |
| | US: 3 November1998 (CD, LP, MC *Mutations*) |

The one and only single taken from *Mutations* – and Beck didn't even want that many. The second part of his supposed 'Brazilian Trilogy' ('Deadweight' was the first instalment). Beck sings of misery waiting 'in big hotels' and living 'under an air conditioned sun'. 'The song "Tropicalia",' says Beck, 'covers the dichotomy and contrast between the fact that when these [immigrant] workers, who come from a culture which is very exotic and lively and exuberant, emigrate from Mexico or El Salvador to California, their life ends up being anything but exotic.' The breakdown was just ad-libbed live in the studio while recording.

## Trouble All My Days

| | |
|---|---|
| BECK HANSEN | vocals |
| WRITTEN BY | Beck Hansen |
| PRODUCED BY | Beck Hansen |
| RELEASE DATES | US: January 1993 (MC *Golden Feelings*) |
| | US: 1995 (CD, 12" 'Pay No Mind' single) |
| | UK: 1995 (CD, 12" 'Pay No Mind' single) |
| | UK: November1996 (CD 'Devils Haircut' single) |
| | US (CD *Fast Forward 2* compilation) |

This track originally surfaced back in 1993 and was, for some reason, still being released three years later, which comes as a bit of a surprise as it's only an average blues romp.

## Truckdrivin' Neighbors Downstairs (Yellow Sweat)

| | |
|---|---|
| BECK HANSEN | vocals, guitars |
| WRITTEN BY | Beck Hansen |
| RECORDED | Beck's 4-track machine, Los Angeles, CA, USA |
| PRODUCED BY | Beck Hansen, Rob Schnapf and Tom Rothrock |
| RELEASE DATES | UK: March 1994 (CD, LP, MC *Mellow Gold*) |
| | US: March 1994 (CD, LP, MC *Mellow Gold*) |

The introduction to this song is allegedly a real fight that Beck inadvertently recorded on his tape machine. You can hear a father and son arguing; this drove Beck out from his apartment but he accidentally left the tape recording. When he returned, he found that the fight had been recorded and the story goes that one of the two downstairs neighbours lost an arm in an axe-battle that followed. The song itself deals with the less than perfect neighbours that live downstairs. 'Acid casualty with a repossessed car/Vietnam vet playing air guitar/It's just the shit-kickin', speed-takin', truck-drivin' neighbors downstairs/Whiskey stained buck-toothed backwoods creep/Grizzly bear motherfucker never goes to sleep/It's just the shit-kickin', speed-takin', truck-drivin' neighbors downstairs.'

## Underwater Music

| | |
|---|---|
| BECK HANSEN | guitars, noise |
| WRITTEN BY | Beck Hansen |
| RECORDED | Los Angeles, CA, USA |
| PRODUCED BY | Beck Hansen |
| RELEASE DATE | US: 1997 (CD *Kill The Moonlight* soundtrack) |

Hardly a 'track' at all, this is just 54 seconds of tortured guitar and noise which gives way to a sample of a car or motorcycle speeding by.

### Waiting For A Train

| | |
|---|---|
| BECK HANSEN | backing vocals |
| KEN | vocals |
| ROSS HARRIS | spoken word introduction |
| WRITTEN BY | J. Rodgers and E. McWilliams |
| RELEASE DATE | US: February 1994 (CD *Stereopathetic Soul Manure*) |

The version to appear on *Stereopathetic Soul Manure* features a spoken-word intro from Ross Harris (of the band Sukia) taken from *Normal* a Steve Hanft film. The singer on the album is actually Ken, a guy who used to live rough and occasionally appeared outside Beck's Los Angeles home in the early 1990s. He disappeared into the night one time but before he vanished Beck managed to get this a cappella version of the Jimmie Rodgers song on to tape. The song itself is a classic hobo song from the late 1920s which helped secure fame for the 'Singing Brakeman' before his early death in 1933 at the age of 35.

### We Live Again

| | |
|---|---|
| BECK HANSEN | vocals, guitars |
| ROGER MANNING JR | harpsichord |
| JUSTIN MELDAL-JOHNSEN | upright bass |
| JOEY WARONKER | drums |
| DAVID CAMPBELL | strings (arranger and composer) |
| WRITTEN BY | Beck Hansen |
| RECORDED | Ocean Way Studios, Los Angeles, CA, USA, March 1998 |
| PRODUCED BY | Nigel Godrich and Beck Hansen |
| RELEASE DATES | UK: 2 November 1998 (CD, LP, MC *Mutations*) |
| | US: 3 November 1998 (CD, LP, MC *Mutations*) |

With a lush string arrangement by Beck's father, David Campbell, this is one of the most beautiful songs on an album that is full of beautiful songs. Roger Manning's harpsichord and Justin Meldal-Johnsen's upright bass are just perfect for this song. Beck even manages to get a favourite line of his, 'Turns shit to gold', into the song.

### Where It's At

| | |
|---|---|
| BECK HANSEN | vocals, guitars, drums, bass, organ, synthesiser |
| MIKE BIOTO | trumpet, organ |
| DAVID BROWN | saxophone |
| SAMPLE FROM | 'Needle To The Groove' (Embden Toure/Khaleel Kirk) performed by Mantronix |
| WRITTEN BY | Beck Hansen, John King and Mike Simpson |
| RECORDED | PCP Labs, Silverlake, CA, USA, 1995 |
| PRODUCED BY | Beck Hansen, Mike Simpson and John King |
| RELEASE DATES | UK: June 1996 (CD, LP, MC *Odelay*) |
| | US: June 1996 (CD, LP, MC *Odelay*) |

UK: June 1996 (CD, 12″, MC 'Where It's At' single)
US: June 1996 (CD, 12″, MC 'Where It's At' single)

The pivotal track from *Odelay* and also the first single to be taken from it. Based around a looped organ riff played by Beck and the refrain 'Turntables and a microphone', Beck played homage to the old-school rappers. Many remixes were available including ones by John King, Mario C. & Mickey P and U.N.K.L.E. as well as ones that were given different names like 'American Wasteland' and 'Make Out City'. Uncredited samples on this song include the line 'That Was A Good Drum Break' which was originally on the Frogs' 'I Don't Care If You Disrespect Me (Just So You Love Me)' and the 'What about people who swing both ways, you know AC/DCs?' sample is taken from an educational album from the sixties called *Sex For Teens (Where It's At)*.

Beck described the song as 'The anti-thunderdome party in the "2 Pac"/"Dr. Dre" video. It's directly through the core of the Earth on the other side of the Earth. It's a party and it's happening, but it's a phantom party. It never happened but it's still there. It's a celebration, without a specific location.'

### Whimsical Actress

| | |
|---|---|
| BECK HANSEN | vocals |
| DON BURNETTE | drums |
| WRITTEN BY | Beck Hansen |
| RECORDED | KCRW, Santa Monica, CA, USA, 23 July 1993 |

'A flight of fancy, a flight of whimsy,' says Beck about this song, one of his strangest yet. Sung in the voice of a high-pitched Englishwoman on his first-ever radio appearance, this helped Beck's live shows to start selling out in no time.

### Whiskey Can Can

| | |
|---|---|
| BECK HANSEN | vocals, guitar |
| WRITTEN BY | Beck Hansen |
| RECORDED | Dub Narcotic Studios, Olympia, WA, USA |
| PRODUCED BY | Calvin Johnson |
| RELEASE DATE | US: 1994 (7″ 'It's All In Your Mind' single) |

B-side to his only K Records single in 1994. A lively track with some fairly odd lyrics – 'She's the old boat in the sewer/She's the old man with manure' – but it's charming nonetheless.

### Whiskeyclone, Hotel City 1997

| | |
|---|---|
| BECK HANSEN | vocals, guitars |
| WRITTEN BY | Beck Hansen |
| RECORDED | Rob Schnapf's house, Los Angeles, CA, USA |
| PRODUCED BY | Beck Hansen, Rob Schnapf and Tom Rothrock |
| RELEASE DATES | UK: March 1994 (CD, LP, MC *Mellow Gold*) |
| | US: March 1994 (CD, LP, MC *Mellow Gold*) |

A stark acoustic song with haunting vocals. It sums up Beck's songs about unlucky characters in dead-end situations: 'I was born in this hotel/Washing dishes in the sink/Magazines and free soda/Trying hard not to think.' Occasionally played live during the acoustic sections of Beck shows.

### Will I Be Ignored By The Lord?

| | |
|---|---|
| BECK HANSEN | vocals |
| WRITTEN BY | Beck Hansen |
| RECORDED | Los Angeles, CA, USA, 1992 |
| PRODUCED BY | Beck Hansen |
| RELEASE DATE | US: January 1993 (MC *Golden Feelings*) |

An a cappella, religiously influenced song sung by Beck in a deep voice with the title being the chorus. 'When I was born/Lots of people sayin'/I looked like a dead man,' he sings in another jolly early lyric.

### You Can Be So Careless

| | |
|---|---|
| BECK HANSEN | vocals, harmonica, banjo |
| RELEASE DATE | not officially released, available on *Banjo Story* tape |

One of the better efforts on Beck's debut tape. A longer song with a lengthy harmonica solo too. A sign of the better things to come on the *Golden Feelings* and *Fresh Meat* . . . tapes.

### Ziplock Bag

| | |
|---|---|
| BECK HANSEN | vocals, guitar, harmonica |
| SCOTT PLOUF | drums |
| JAMES BERTRAM | bass |
| CHRIS BALLEW | guitar |
| WRITTEN BY | Beck Hansen |
| RECORDED | Dub Narcotic Studios, Olympia, WA, USA, January 1994 |
| PRODUCED BY | Calvin Johnson |
| RELEASE DATE | US: November 1994 (CD, LP, MC *One Foot In The Grave*) |

An odd song out on this album as Beck reverts back to the general type of song that he'd been recording elsewhere at about this time. A slightly distorted vocal fights to be heard over an even more distorted guitar. One minute forty later and the noise is over, thankfully.

## Addenda

Some other songs that don't appear in the main list are included here for one of the following reasons:

- they were never released;
- they have not yet been released;
- they were played live and their name and/or origin is uncertain;
- they slipped through the net.

Almost A Ghost
Cock
Grizzly
Inferno
It's All Gonna Come To Be
Jimi Carter
Let The Doctor Rock You
Make Out City
Maximum Potential
Megaboob
Plague
Protein Summer
Sandman
Scavenger
Sports Convention
Sweet and Low
The World May Lose Its Motion
Touch Of Class
Twig
Whiskey-Faced Radioactive Blowdryin' Lady

# IV Puttin' It Down – Discography

Please note: quoted prices are for mint condition copies

## Singles

### MTV Makes Me Want To Smoke Crack

| Label | Cat. No. | Country | Format | Title | Year | Price |
|---|---|---|---|---|---|---|
| Flipside | FLIP46 | US | 7" | MTV Makes Me Want To Smoke Crack/To See That Woman Of Mine/Privates On Parade – by Bean/Rock Scissors Paper – by Bean – clear blue vinyl, 500 only | 1992 | £60 |

### Loser

| Label | Cat. No. | Country | Format | Title | Year | Price |
|---|---|---|---|---|---|---|
| Bong Load | BL5 | US | 12" | Loser/Steal My Body Home | 1993 | £10 |
| Geffen | DGCS 7-19270 | US | 7" | Loser/Alcohol | 3/94 | £5 |
| Geffen | DGCCS-12270 | US | Cassette | Loser/Alcohol | 3/94 | £3 |
| Geffen | DGCDM-21930 | US | CD | Loser/Corvette Bummer/Alcohol/Soul Suckin Jerk (Reject)/Fume | 3/94 | £7 |
| Geffen | PRO-CD-4613 | US | CD promo | Loser | 1994 | £8 |
| Geffen | PRO-A-4629 | US | 12" promo | Loser/Loser | 1994 | £10 |
| Geffen | GFS 67 | UK | 7" | Loser/Alcohol/Fume | 2/94 | £8 |
| Geffen | GFSJB 67 | UK | 7" | Loser/Loser – jukebox version | 2/94 | £5 |
| Geffen | GFSC 67 | UK | Cassette | Loser/Alcohol/Fume | 2/94 | £4 |
| Geffen | GFSTD 67 | UK | CD | Loser/Totally Confused/Corvette Bummer/MTV Makes Me Want To Smoke Crack (Lounge Act Version) | 2/94 | £6 |
| Geffen | GED 21891 | Sweden | CD | Loser/Totally Confused/Corvette Bummer/MTV Makes Me Want To Smoke Crack (Lounge Act Version) | 1994 | £6 |

**Steve Threw Up**

| Label | Cat. No. | Country | Format | Details | Year | Price |
|---|---|---|---|---|---|---|
| Bong Load | BL 11 | US | 7" | Steve Threw Up/Motherfuker/Cupcake – not listed | 1994 | £6 |

**Beercan**

| Label | Cat. No. | Country | Format | Details | Year | Price |
|---|---|---|---|---|---|---|
| Geffen | DGC DM-22000 | US | CD | Beercan/Got No Mind/Asskizz Powergrudge (Payback 94)/Totally Confused/Spanking Room/Bonus Noise | 1994 | £8 |
| Geffen | PRO-CD-4648 | US | CD | Beercan | 1994 | £10 |
| Geffen | GED 21939 | France | CD | Beercan/Got No Mind/Spanking Room/Bonus Noise – not listed on sleeve | 1994 | £10 |

**It's All In Your Mind**

| Label | Cat. No. | Country | Format | Details | Year | Price |
|---|---|---|---|---|---|---|
| K | IPU 45 | US | 7" | It's All In Your Mind/Feather In Your Cap/Whiskey Can – fold over sleeve, brown vinyl | 1994 | £50 |
| K | IPU 45 | US | 7" | It's All In Your Mind/Feather In Your Cap/Whiskey Can – fold over sleeve, black vinyl | 1994 | £5 |
| K | IPU 45 | US | 7" | It's All In Your Mind/Moedown – mis-press | 1994 | £30 |

**Pay No Mind**

| Label | Cat. No. | Country | Format | Details | Year | Price |
|---|---|---|---|---|---|---|
| Geffen | GED 21911 | US | CD | Pay No Mind/Special People/Trouble All My Days/Supergolden (Sunchild) – jewel case or card sleeve | 1995 | £6 |
| Geffen | PRO-CD 4939 | US | CD promo | Pay No Mind (Snoozer)/Special People/Trouble All My Days/Supergolden (Sunchild) | 1995 | £8 |
| Geffen | PRO-CD-4639 | US | CD promo | Pay No Mind (Snoozer) | 1995 | £10 |
| Geffen | GFS 73 | UK | 7" | Pay No Mind (Snoozer)/Special People – unreleased | 4/94 | £20 |
| Geffen | GFSC 73 | UK | Cassette | Pay No Mind (Snoozer)/Special People – unreleased | 4/94 | £10 |
| Geffen | GFST 73 | UK | 12" | Pay No Mind (Snoozer)/Special People/Trouble All My Days/Supergolden (Sunchild) – withdrawn | 4/94 | £20 |
| Geffen | GFSTD 73 | UK | CD | Pay No Mind (Snoozer)/Special People/Trouble All My Days/Supergolden (Sunchild) – withdrawn | 4/94 | £15 |
| Geffen | GES 19223 | Holland | 7" | Pay No Mind (Snoozer)/Special People | 1995 | £10 |
| Geffen | MVCG-13017 | Japan | CD | Pay No Mind (Snoozer)/Special People/Trouble All My Days/Supergolden (Sunchild) | 1995 | £25 |

**Where It's At**

| Label | Cat. no. | Country | Format | Tracklisting | Year | Price |
|---|---|---|---|---|---|---|
| Geffen | – | US | CD | Where It's At (Edit)/Where It's At (Remix by Mario C and Mickey P)/Bonus Beats | 1996 | £5 |
| Geffen | DGC 12-22214 | US | 12" | Where It's At (Edit)/Make Out City/Where It's At (Remix by Mario C and Mickey P)/Bonus Beats/Where It's At (Remix by U.N.K.L.E.) | 1996 | £6 |
| Geffen | DGC 9180 | US | 12" | Where It's At (LP Version)/Make Out City (Remix by Mike Simpson)/Where It's At (Remix by Mario C and Mickey P)/Where It's At (Remix by John King)/Bonus Beats | 1996 | £6 |
| Geffen | PRO-A-4875 | US | 12" promo | Where It's At (Promo Edit)/Where It's At (Remix by John King)/Where It's At (Remix by Mario C and Mickey P)/Bonus Beats – White label, stamped sleeve | 1996 | £8 |
| Geffen | PRO-CD-4887 | US | CD promo | Where It's At (Edit)/Where It's At (LP Version) | 1996 | £7 |
| Geffen | PRO-CD-1014 | US | CD promo | Where It's At/Make Out City (Remix by Mike Simpson) | 1996 | £8 |
| Geffen | GFST 22156 | UK | 12" | Where It's At (Edit)/Where It's At (Remix by Mario C and Mickey P)/Bonus Beats/Where It's At (Remix by U.N.K.L.E.) | 6/96 | £5 |
| Geffen | GFSC 22156 | UK | Cassette | Where It's At (Edit)/Where It's At (Remix by Mario C and Mickey P) | 6/96 | £3 |
| Geffen | GFSTD 22156 | UK | CD | Where It's At (Edit)/Where It's At (Remix by Mario C and Mickey P)/Bonus Beats | 6/96 | £5 |
| Geffen | WGFSTD 22156 | UK | CD promo | Where It's At + 2 – Card sleeve | 1997 | £6 |
| Geffen | MVCZ-15001 | Japan | CD | Where It's At (Edit)/Where It's At (Remix by John King)/Lloyd Price Express/Dark And Lovely/American Wasteland/Clock | 1996 | £15 |
| Geffen | – | Australia | CD | Where It's At (Edit)/Where It's At (Remix by Mario C and Mickey P)/Bonus Beats | 1996 | £6 |
| Geffen | – | Spain | CD promo | Where It's At – Odelay cover | 1997 | £15 |
| Geffen | GED 22157 | France | CD | Where It's At (Edit)/Where It's At (Remix by Mario C and Mickey P) – Card sleeve | 1996 | £10 |
| Telecine | – | UK | Video | Where It's At (3:30) | 1996 | £10 |

## Devils Haircut

| Label | Catalogue | Country | Format | Title | Year | Price |
|---|---|---|---|---|---|---|
| Geffen | GED 22175 | US | CD | Devils Haircut/Dark And Lovely (Remix by The Dust Brothers)/American Wasteland (Remix by Mickey P) | 1996 | £5 |
| Geffen | DGC 12-22222 | US | 12" | Devils Haircut (LP Version)/Dark And Lovely (Remix by The Dust Brothers)/American Wasteland (Remix by Mickey P) Lloyd Price Express (Remix by John King)/Clock | 1996 | £6 |
| Geffen | PRO-CD-1016 | US | CD promo | Devils Haircut | 1996 | £6 |
| Geffen | PRO-CD-1066 | US | CD promo | Devils Haircut (Mike Simpson Remix) | 1996 | £6 |
| Geffen | GFS 22183 | UK | 7" | Devils Haircut/Lloyd Price Express (Remix by John King) | 11/96 | £3 |
| Geffen | GFSTD 22183 | UK | CD | Devils Haircut/Dark And Lovely (Remix by The Dust Brothers)/American Wasteland (Remix by Mickey P)/000.000 | 11/96 | £5 |
| Geffen | GFSXD 22183 | UK | CD | Devils Haircut/Devils Haircut (Remix by Noel Gallagher)/Groovy Sunday (Remix by Mike Simpson)/Trouble All My Days | 11/96 | £8 |
| Geffen | BECK1 | UK | CD | Devils Haircut | 1996 | £5 |
| – | – | UK | Video | Devils Haircut (3:12) | 1996 | £10 |
| Geffen | – | Australia | CD | Devils Haircut/Dark And Lovely/American Wasteland | 1996 | £6 |

## The New Pollution

| Label | Catalogue | Country | Format | Title | Year | Price |
|---|---|---|---|---|---|---|
| Geffen | GED 22204 | US | CD | The New Pollution/Electric Music And The Summer People/Richard's Hairpiece | 1997 | £5 |
| Geffen | DGC 12-22300 | US | 12" | The New Pollution/The New Pollution (Remix by Mario C and Mickey P)/The New Pollution (Remix by Mickey P)/Lemonade/Richard's Hairpiece | 1997 | £6 |
| Geffen | – | US | 12" promo | The New Pollution/The New Pollution (Remix by Mario C) | 1996 | £7 |
| Geffen | PRO-CD-1082 | US | CD promo | The New Pollution | 1996 | £6 |
| Geffen | PRO-CD-1090 | US | CD promo | The New Pollution (Remix by Mickey P) | 1996 | £7 |

| Label | Catalogue | Country | Format | Description | Year | Price |
|---|---|---|---|---|---|---|
| Geffen | GFS 22205 | UK | 7" | The New Pollution/Electric Music And The Summer People | 2/97 | £3 |
| Geffen | GFSTD 22205 | UK | CD | The New Pollution/Richards Hairpiece (Remix by Aphex Twin)/Electric Music And The Summer People | 2/97 | £4 |
| Geffen | GFSXD 22205 | UK | CD | The New Pollution/The New Pollution (Remix by Mario C and Mickey P)/Lemonade | 2/97 | £4 |
| Geffen | MVCZ-10005 | Japan | CD | The New Pollution/The New Pollution (Remix by Mickey P)/The New Pollution (Remix by Mickey P and Mario C)/Richards Hairpiece/Thunderpeel/Lemonade/000.000/Feather In Your Cap | 1997 | £25 |
| Geffen | — | Australia | CD | The New Pollution/Electric Music And The Summer People/Richard's Hairpiece – card sleeve | 1997 | £6 |
| Geffen | — | Holland | CD | The New Pollution/ + 2/ + video track | 1997 | £10 |
| Telecine | — | UK | Video | The New Pollution (3:41) | 1997 | £10 |

**Sissyneck**

| Label | Catalogue | Country | Format | Description | Year | Price |
|---|---|---|---|---|---|---|
| Geffen | GFS 22253 | UK | 7" | Sissyneck/Feather In Your Cap | 5/97 | £3 |
| Geffen | GFSC 22253 | UK | Cassette | Sissyneck/The New Pollution (Remix By Mickey P) | 5/97 | £2 |
| Geffen | GFSTD 22253 | UK | CD | Sissyneck/The New Pollution (Remix by Mickey P)/Feather In Your Cap | 5/97 | £4 |
| Geffen | WGFSTD 22253 | UK | CD promo | Sissyneck – brown card picture sleeve | 1997 | £5 |
| Geffen | GEFDM 22310 | Australia | CD | Sissyneck/Burro/Dark And Lovely/Devil Got My Woman/Brother | 1997 | £8 |

**Jack-ass**

| Label | Catalogue | Country | Format | Description | Year | Price |
|---|---|---|---|---|---|---|
| Geffen | DGC 12-22303 | US | 12" | Jack-ass/Strange Invitation/Burro/Brother | 1997 | £6 |
| Geffen | PRO-CD-1077 | US | CD promo | Jack-ass (Butch Vig Remix)/Jack-ass (LP Version) – no p/s | 1997 | £7 |
| Geffen | GFS 22276 | UK | 2 × 7" | Jack-ass (Butch Vig Remix)/Strange Invitation/Devil Got My Woman/Jack-ass (Lowrider Mix)/Burro/Brother | 1997 | £5 |
| Geffen | GFSTD 22276 | UK | CD | Jack-ass (Butch Vig Remix)/Jack-ass (Lowrider Mix)/Burro/Strange Invitation/Devil Got My Woman/Brother | 1997 | £4 |

| Label | Cat. No. | Country | Format | Tracklisting | Date | Price |
|---|---|---|---|---|---|---|
| Telecine | | UK | Video | Jack-ass (3:12) | 1997 | £10 |
| **Deadweight** | | | | | | |
| Geffen | PRCD 7637-2 | US | CD promo | Deadweight – blue stickered case | 1997 | £6 |
| Geffen | GFS 22293 | UK | 7" | Deadweight (Edit)/Erase The Sun | 10/97 | £3 |
| Geffen | GFSC 22293/ | UK | Cassette | Deadweight/Erase the Sun | 10/97 | £2 |
| Geffen | GFSTD 22293 | UK | CD | Deadweight (Edit)/Erase The Sun/SA-5 | 10/97 | £4 |
| Geffen | WGFTSD 22293 | UK | CD promo | Deadweight – yellow card sleeve | 10/97 | £6 |
| A&M | 3703 | France | CD promo | Deadweight (Edit) – unique 'Cameron Diaz-Ewan McGregor' sleeve | 1997 | £10 |
| Geffen | BECKCDJ1 | Holland | CD promo | Deadweight (Radio edit) – unique 'Heart' sleeve | 1997 | £10 |
| **Clock** | | | | | | |
| — | — | UK | CD promo | Clock/The Little Drum Machine Boy/Totally Confused – given away free with December 1997 issue of *Select* magazine | 11/97 | £6 |
| **Tropicalia** | | | | | | |
| Geffen | GFS 22365 | UK | 7" | Tropicalia/Halo Of Gold | 12/98 | £2 |
| Geffen | GFSTD 22365 | UK | CD | Tropicalia/Halo Of Gold/Black Balloon | 12/98 | £4 |
| Geffen | WGFSTD22365 | UK | CD promo | Tropicalia – unique sleeve | 1998 | £6 |
| **Cold Brains** | | | | | | |
| Geffen | INT5P-6561 | US | CD promo | Cold Brains/Electric Music And The Summer People/Halo Of Gold/Runners Dial Zero/Diamond Bollocks – card sleeve | 1/99 | £8 |
| Geffen | INTDM-97093 | Australia | CD | Cold Brains/One Of These Days/Diamond In The Sleaze/Halo Of Gold/Electric Music And The Summer People | 4/99 | £10 |
| **Nobody's Fault But My Own** | | | | | | |
| Geffen | MVCF-12015 | Japan | CD | Nobody's Fault But My Own/One Of These Days/Diamond In The Sleaze | 4/99 | £10 |

## Sexx Laws

| Label | Cat. no. | Country | Format | Tracks | Date | Price |
|---|---|---|---|---|---|---|
| Geffen | | US | 12" | Sexx Laws/Salt In The Wound | 11/99 | £5 |
| Geffen | 497180-4 | UK | Cassette | Sexx Laws/Salt In The Wound | 11/99 | £2 |
| Geffen | | US | 12" promo | Sexx Laws/remix (limited edition, 1,000 only) | 11/99 | £10 |
| Geffen | 4971812 | UK | CD | Sexx Laws/Salt In The Wound/Sexx Laws (The Wiseguys remix) | 11/99 | £3 |
| Geffen | 4971822 | UK | CD | Sexx Laws/This Is My Krew/Sexx Laws (Malibu Mix) | 11/99 | £3 |
| Geffen | 4971827 | UK | 7" | Sexx Laws/Salt In The Wound (Wiseguyz Remix) | 11/99 | £2 |
| Geffen | MVCF-12016 | Japan | CD | Sexx Laws/Salt In The Wound/Sexx Laws (Wiseguyz Remix) | 11/99 | £10 |

## Albums

### Golden Feelings

| Label | Country | Format | Tracks | Date | Price |
|---|---|---|---|---|---|
| Sonic Enemy | US | Cassette | The Fucked Up Blues/Special People/Magic Station Wagon/No Money, No Honey/Trouble All My Days/Bad Energy/Schmoozer/Heartland Feeling/Interlude 1/Supergolden Black Sunchild/Soul Sucked Dry/Interlude 2/Feelings/Gettin' Home/Will I Be Ignored By The Lord?/Bogus Soul/Totally Confused/Motherfucka/People Gettin' Busy | 1/93 | £35 |
| Sonic Enemy | US | Cassette | some titles spelt differently – duplicated by 52nd street | 1993 | £15 |
| Sonic Enemy | US | CD | as original cassette | 9/99 | £12 |

### A Western Harvest Field By Moonlight

| Label | Cat. no. | Country | Format | Tracks | Date | Price |
|---|---|---|---|---|---|---|
| Fingerpaint | 02 | US | 10" | Totally Confused/Mayonnaise Salad/Gettin' Home/Blackfire Choked Our Death/Feel Like A Piece Of Shit (Mind Control)/She Is All (Gimme Something To Eat)/Pinefresh/Lampshade/Feel Like A Piece Of Shit (Crossover Potential)/Mango Vader Rocks/Feel Like A Piece Of Shit (Cheetoes Time)/Styrofoam Chicken | 1994 | £20 |

| Label | Cat. No. | Country | Format | Tracklisting / Notes | Date | Price |
|---|---|---|---|---|---|---|
| Fingerpaint | 02 | US | 10" | (Quality Time) – 2,000 copies with fingerpainting by Beck | 9/95 | £15 |
| Fingerpaint | 02 | US | 10" | as above – 3,000 copies, no fingerpainting | 1997? | £10 |
|  |  |  |  | as above |  |  |
| **Mellow Gold** |  |  |  |  |  |  |
| Geffen | DGCD-24634 | US | CD | Loser/Pay No Mind (Snoozer)/Fuckin' With My Head (Mountain Dew Rock)/Whiskeyclone, Hotel City 1997/Soul Suckin Jerk/Truckdrivin' Neighbors Downstairs (Yellow Sweat)/Sweet Sunshine/Beercan/Steal My Body Home/Nitemare Hippy Girl/Motherfucker/Blackhole | 3/94 | £10 |
| Geffen | DGCC-24634 | US | Cassette | as above | 3/94 | £7 |
| Geffen | #DGCC-24634 | US | Cass promo | as above, blue and white insert | 3/94 | £15 |
| Bong Load | BL 12 | US | LP | as above – with 12" insert | 3/94 | £10 |
| Geffen | – | US | 10" promo | some of above tracks missing + Corvette Bummer | 1994 | £20 |
| Geffen | PRO-CD-4633 | US | CD promo | as above, omits Fuckin' With My Head (Mountain Dew Rock) and Truckdrivin' Neighbors Downstairs (Yellow Sweat) | 1994 | £15 |
| Geffen | GED 24634 | UK | CD | as above + Analogue Odyssey – unlisted | 3/94 | £10 |
| Geffen | GEC 24634 | UK | Cassette | as above + Analogue Odyssey – unlisted | 3/94 | £7 |
| Geffen | MVCF-153 | Japan | CD | as above + Analogue Odyssey – unlisted – includes lyric booklet | 1994 | £20 |
| Geffen | GEFD-24634 | Australia | CD | as above + 2nd bonus CD: Mexico/Totally Confused/Jagermeister Pie/Lampshade/Rowboat | 1995 | £18 |
| Geffen | SVLP 0044 | UK | LP | 180g vinyl re-pressing | 1999 | £20 |
| **Stereopathetic Soul Manure** |  |  |  |  |  |  |
| Flipside | FLIP 60 | US | CD | Pink Noise (Rock Me Amadeus)/Rowboat/Thunderpeel/Waitin' For A Train/The Spirit Moves Me/Crystal Clear (Beer)/No Money, No Honey/8.6.82/Total Soul Future (Eat It)/One Foot In The Grave/Aphid Manure Heist/Today Has been A Fucked Up Day/Rollins Power Sauce/Puttin' It Down/11.6.45/ | 4/94 | £12 |

Cut 1/2 Blues/Jagermeister Pie/Ozzy/Dead Wild Cat/Satan Gave Me A Taco/8.4.82/Tasergun/Modesto

## One Foot In The Grave

| Label | Cat. no. | Country | Format | Tracklisting | Date | Price |
|---|---|---|---|---|---|---|
| K | KLP 28 | US | CD | He's A Mighty Good Leader/Sleeping Bag/I Get Lonesome/Burnt Orange Peel/Cyanide Breath Mint/See Water/Ziplock Bag/Hollow Log/Forcefield/Fourteen Rivers Fourteen Floods/Asshole/I've Seen The Land Beyond/Outcome/Girl Dreams/Painted Eyelids/Atmospheric Conditions | 11/94 | £12 |
| K | KLP 28 | US | Cassette | as above | 11/94 | £7 |
| K | KLP 28 | US | LP | as above | 11/94 | £8 |
| K | KLP 28 | UK | CD | as above | 8/96 | £10 |
| K | KLP 28 | UK | LP | as above | 8/96 | £8 |

## Odelay

| Label | Cat. no. | Country | Format | Tracklisting | Date | Price |
|---|---|---|---|---|---|---|
| Geffen | DGCD-24823 | US | CD | Devils Haircut/Hotwax/Lord Only Knows/The New Pollution/Derelict/Novacane/Jack-ass/Where It's At/Minus/Sissyneck/Readymade/High Five (Rock The Catskills)/Ramshackle | 6/96 | £10 |
| Geffen | DGCD-24823 | US | Cassette | as above | 6/96 | £7 |
| Bongload | BL 30 | US | LP | as above – 180g vinyl + tri-foldout poster | 6/96 | £10 |
| Geffen | DGCDA 24823 | US | CD promo | as above | 1996 | £12 |
| Bongload | BL 30 | UK | LP | as above – 180g vinyl + tri-foldout poster | 6/96 | £10 |
| Geffen | GED 24908 | UK | CD | as above + Diskobox | 6/96 | £10 |
| Geffen | GED 24926 | UK | CD | as above + Diskobox + Clock – unlisted | 6/96 | £15 |
| Geffen | GEC 24908 | UK | Cassette | as above | 6/96 | £7 |
| Geffen | GEFD-24948 | Australia | CD | as above + 2nd bonus CD | 1997 | £16 |

## Mutations

| Label | Cat. no. | Country | Format | Tracklisting | Date | Price |
|---|---|---|---|---|---|---|
| Geffen | — | US | CD | Cold Brains/Nobody's Fault But My Own/Lazy Flies/Canceled Check/We Live Again/Tropicalia/Dead Melodies/Bottle Of Blues/O Maria/Sing It Again/Static/Diamond Bollocks | 11/98 | £10 |

| Label | Cat. No. | Country | Format | Description | Date | Price |
|---|---|---|---|---|---|---|
| Geffen | – | US | Cassette | as above | 11/98 | £7 |
| Bong Load | BL 39 | US | LP | as above, 180g vinyl + bonus 7" containing Diamond Bollocks + Runners Dial Zero | 11/98 | £12 |
| Geffen | GED 25184 | UK | CD | as above + Runners Dial Zero | 11/98 | £10 |
| Geffen | GEC-25184 | UK | Cassette | as above + Runners Dial Zero | 11/98 | £7 |
| Geffen | – | UK | CD promo | as above + Runners Dial Zero | 1998 | £15 |
| Geffen | GED 25188 | Germany | CD | as above + Runners Dial Zero + Halo Of Gold + Black Balloon | 11/98 | £15 |
| Geffen | MVCF-24047 | Japan | CD | as above + Runners Dial Zero + Electric Music And The Summer People | 11/98 | £25 |
| Geffen | – | Australia | CD | as above + 2nd bonus CD | 11/98 | £20 |

**Midnite Vultures**

| Label | Cat. No. | Country | Format | Description | Date | Price |
|---|---|---|---|---|---|---|
| Geffen | – | US | CD | Sexx Laws/Nicotine & Gravy/Mixed Bizness/Get Real Paid/Hollywood Freaks/Peaches & Cream/Broken Train/Milk & Honey/Beautiful Way/Pressure Zone/Debra | 11/99 | £11 |
| Geffen | – | US | Cassette | as above | 11/99 | £8 |
| Bong Load | – | US | LP | as above | 11/99 | £10 |
| Geffen | – | UK | CD | as above | 11/99 | £11 |
| Geffen | – | UK | Cassette | as above | 11/99 | £8 |
| Geffen | – | Japan | CD | as above + Arabian Nights | 11/99 | £20 |

**Miscellaneous**

| Label | Cat. No. | Country | Format | Description | Date | Price |
|---|---|---|---|---|---|---|
| Geffen | PRO-CD-4653 | US | CD | BECK SAMPLER (5 tracks) | 1994 | £8 |
| Geffen | – | US | Cass promo | A HISTORY OF BECK Loser/Mexico/Death Is Coming To Get Me/Whimsical Actress/Pay No Mind/MTV Makes Me Want To Smoke Crack/Totally Confused/Lampshade/Steve Threw Up/Pink Noise/Rowboat/The Spirit Moves Me/Plain Wrap [actually 'Crystal Clear (Beer)']/One Foot In the Grave | 1994 | £25 |

| Label | Catalogue | Country | Format | Title | Year | Price |
|---|---|---|---|---|---|---|
| Chatback | CHATCD6 | UK | CD | The Interview Sessions (30 minutes of radio interviews 1993–1996) | 1997 | £5 |
| Geffen | PRO-CD-1235A | US | CD | The Mutations Conversations (interview with Neil Strauss about Mutations) | 9/98 | £8 |
| Geffen | — | UK | CD | Interview with Neil Strauss (as above, different sleeve) | 9/98 | £12 |

### Compilations featuring Beck tracks

| Label | Catalogue | Country | Format | Title | Year | Price |
|---|---|---|---|---|---|---|
| Mammoth | MR0074-2 | US | CD | RARE ON AIR: LIVE PERFORMANCES VOLUME 1 (contains Mexico) | 1994 | £12 |
| No Life | KLXU | US | CD | KXLU LIVE VOLUME ONE (contains Whiskey-Faced, Radioactive Blowdryin' Lady) | 1994 | £15 |
| Geffen | PRO-CD-4643 | US | CD promo | SWAG (contains Corvette Bummer) | 1994 | £10 |
| Mammoth | MR0081-2 | US | CD | JABBERJAW: GOOD TO THE LAST DROP (contains In A Cold Ass Fashion) | 1994 | £10 |
| Mammoth | MR0078 | US | 7" | JABBERJAW (contains In A Cold Ass Fashion) Limited Edition of 1500 | 1994 | £15 |
| CMJn | — | US | CD | CMJ NEW MUSIC MONTHLY (contains It's All In Your Mind) | 9/94 | £12 |
| Geffen | GFLD-19247 | US | CD, LP, Cass | GEFFEN RARITIES VOL.1 (contains Bogusflow) | 1994 | £10/£12/£7 |
| Yo Yo | YOYO-3 | US | CD | PERISCOPE: ANOTHER YO YO COMPILATION (contains The World May Lose Its Motion) | 1994 | £12 |
| Nardwuar the Human Serviette | CLEO 8 | US | CD, LP | SKOOKUM CHIEF POWERED TEENAGE ZIT ROCK ANGST PRESENTED (contains Naardwar vs Beck) | 1995 | £10 |
| Brinkman | — | Holland | CDx2 | FAST FORWARD #2 (contains Trouble All My Days) | 1995 | £10 |
| Geffen/ Carrere Music | — | France | CD | UN HIVER 95 (contains Beercan) CD came with issues of the French magazine *Les Inrockuptibles* | 1995 | £12 |
| WIN | WIN010 | US | CDx2 | THE POOP ALLEY TAPES (contains Girl Dreams re-recorded with That Dog) | 1996 | £10 |

| Label | Catalogue | Country | Format | Title | Date | Price |
|---|---|---|---|---|---|---|
| — | VOL 16 | US | CDx2 | VOLUME 16: COPULATION EXPLOSION (contains Thunderpeel) | 1996 | £15 |
| Yo Yo | YOYO-4 | US | CDx2 | YO YO A GO GO (contains Untitled (actually Satellite Of Love) and Sleeping Bag) | 1996 | £15 |
| Geffen/Almo | DGCD-24963 | US | CD promo | BUY PRODUCT 2: BRIEF ENCOUNTERS (contains Novacane) | 1996 | £12 |
| Vans | VAND-900 | US | CD promo | VANS WARPED MUSIC SAMPLER (contains Make Out City) | 1996 | £10 |
| Geffen | PRO-CD-7035 | US | CD promo | SWAGALICIOUS (contains Clock) | 1996 | £10 |
| — | — | Canada | CD | MUCH MUSIC PRESENTS: BIG SHINY TUNES (contains Novacane) | 1996 | £12 |
| Geffen | GEFD-25107 | US | CD | JUST SAY NOEL (contains The Little Drum Machine Boy) | 1996 | £10 |
| — | — | UK | CD | JUST SAY NOEL (contains The Little Drum Machine Boy) | 1996 | £10 |
| Maxim | MAXIM 003 | UK | CD | CLASS OF '96 (contains Where It's At) | 12/96 | £5 |
| SFTR | SFTR1482 | US | CD | KILL THE MOONLIGHT soundtrack (contains Leave Me On The Moon, Last Night I Traded My Soul's Innermost For Some Pickled Fish and Underwater Music) | 1997 | £11 |
| Geffen | GED25121 | UK | CD, Cass | SUBURBIA soundtrack (contains Feather In Your Cap) | 1997 | £10/£5 |
| Geffen | 9362-46824-2 | US | CD, Cass | SUBURBIA soundtrack (contains Feather In Your Cap) | 1997 | £10/£5 |
| Arista | — | UK | CD | THE BRIDGE SCHOOL BENEFITS VOL.1 (contains It's All In Your Mind (live)) | 1997 | £10 |
| — | — | US | CD | THE BRIDGE SCHOOL BENEFITS VOL.1 (contains It's All In Your Mind (live)) | 1997 | £10 |
| Fingerpaint | NR40003 | US | CD | MODERN DAY PAINTINGS BY ORIGINAL MUSIC ARTISTS (contains Lampshade) | 1997 | £10 |
| Hollywood Records | PRCD-10762-2 | US | CD promo | THE H.O.R.E. FESTIVAL 1997 (contains Jack-ass) | 1997 | £10 |
| Wicked Disc | WIC 1008-2 | US | CD | WBCN NAKED DISC (contains One Foot In The Grave live at Fort Apache Studios, 9 August 1997) | 1997 | £12 |

| Label | Catalogue | Country | Format | Title | Date | Price |
|---|---|---|---|---|---|---|
| No Life | KLXU | US | CD | DEMOLISTEN VOL.2 (contains Untitled) | 1997 | £10 |
| Capitol | 859 911-0 | UK | CDx3 | TIBETAN FREEDOM CONCERT (contains Asshole live version) | 1997 | £20 |
| NME | BRAT 98 | UK | Cassette | BRATPACK 98 (contains Deadweight (Edit)) | 1/98 | £2 |
| CMJ | DIDX018179 | US | CD | CMJ NEW MUSIC (contains Cold Brains) free with magazine, in paper sleeve | 10/98 | £6 |
| TVT Soundtracks | TVT 8290-2 | US | CD | THE HI-LO COUNTRY soundtrack (contains Drivin' Nails In My Coffin) | 1/99 | £11 |
| Rhino | — | US | CD | WIRED MAGAZINE PRESENTS: MUSIC FUTURISTS (contains Total Soul Future (Eat It)) | 2/99 | £12 |
| Virgin | — | US | CD | THE BEST LATIN PARTY ALBUM IN THE WORLD .... EVER! (contains Burro (Mariachi version)) | 4/99 | £10 |
| Birdman Records | — | US | CD | MORE OAR: A TRIBUTE TO ALEXANDER 'SKIP' SPENCE (contains Halo Of Gold) | 7/99 | £11 |
| — | — | UK | CD | MORE OAR: A TRIBUTE TO ALEXANDER 'SKIP' SPENCE (contains Halo Of Gold) | 1999 | £11 |
| UNCUT | UG-8-14 | UK | CD | UNCONDITIONALLY GUARANTEED 7 (contains Sin City) free with Uncut magazine, August 1999 | 7/99 | £2 |
| — | — | US | CD | RETURN OF THE GRIEVOUS ANGEL: TRIBUTE TO GRAM PARSONS (contains Sin City) | 7/99 | £11 |
| ALMO | ALMCD66 | UK | CD | RETURN OF THE GRIEVOUS ANGEL: TRIBUTE TO GRAM PARSONS (contains Sin City) | 1999 | £11 |
| — | — | US | CD | MOM III: MUSIC FOR OUR MOTHER OCEAN (contains Electric Music And The Summer People) | 8/99 | £11 |
| CMJ | — | US | CD | CMJ NEW MUSIC (contains Halo Of Gold, listed as One Of These Days) free with magazine, in paper sleeve | 9/99 | £6 |

**Guest appearances**

| Label | Catalogue | Country | Format | Title | Date | Price |
|---|---|---|---|---|---|---|
| SFTRI | SFTRI 314 | US | 10" | THE GERALDINE FIBBERS: GET THEE GONE Beck co-wrote and appears on Blue Cross | 1994 | £8 |
| Matador | OLE 105-2 | US | CD, LP | JON SPENCER BLUES EXPLOSION: ORANGE Beck provides a rap on Flavor | 1994 | £11/£8 |

| Label | Catalogue | Country | Format | Title / Description | Year | Price |
|---|---|---|---|---|---|---|
| Cosmic Records | COS 002 | US | 7" | TWIG (yellow vinyl) | 1994 | £8 |
| Matador | OLE 111-2 | US | CD | JON SPENCER BLUES EXPLOSION: EXPERIMENTAL REMIXES Beck appears on remix of Flavor with Mike D and Mario Caldato Jnr | 1995 | £10 |
| SFTRI | SFTRI 481 | US | CD | THE GERALDINE FIBBERS: WHAT PART OF GET THEE GONE DON'T YOU UNDERSTAND? Beck co-wrote and appears on Blue Cross | 1996 | £8 |
| Dreamworks | DMRD-50002 | US | CD | FOREST FOR THE TREES Beck plays harmonica on Fall | 1997 | £10 |
| Vast Records | — | US | CD | HEAR YOU ME! Beck plays banjo on the That Dog track Silently | 1/98 | £10 |
| Caroline | CAR 6645-2 | UK | CD | AIR: SEXY BOY Beck remixes the track Sexy Boy (Sex Kino Mix) | 1998 | £6 |
| Virgin | 7243 8 95072 2 5 | UK | CD | AIR: KELLY WATCH THE STARS Beck remixes the track Sexy Boy (Sex Kino Mix) | 1998 | £5 |
| Supreme | 314-524 527-2 | US | CD | AMNESIA: LINGUS Beck plays harmonica on Drop Down | 1998 | £10 |
| Polygram | 232TP7CD | UK | CD | BJÖRK: ALARM CALL Beck remixes the track Alarm Call (Bjeck Mix) | 1998 | £4 |
| Polygram | 232tp21p1 | UK | 12" | BJÖRK: ALARM CALL Beck remixes the track Alarm Call (Bjeck Mix) | 1998 | £8 |
| Polygram | 567 201-2 | France | CD | BJÖRK: HUNTER Beck remixes the track Alarm Call (Bjeck Mix) | 1998 | £5 |
| — | — | US | CD | KAHIMI KARIE Beck plays harmonica on Lolitapop Dollhouse | 9/98 | £10 |
| Dreamworks | — | US | CD | FOREST FOR THE TREES: THE SOUND OF WET PAINT Beck appears on Jet Engine | 3/99 | £6 |
| Interscope | IND 90181 | UK | CD | THE RUGRATS MOVIE soundtrack Beck appears on the track This World Is Something New To Me | 1999 | £11 |

## Miscellaneous

The following is a cut and paste sampling CD of actual Beck tracks to make new ones, put out by a group of internet pranksters:

Seeland 507CD/
Records

| Illegal Art | 001 | US | CD | 1997 | £10 |
|---|---|---|---|---|---|

Mr Meridies (Paving The Road To Hell)/Jane Dowe (Puzzels & Pagans)/Huk Don Phun (Killer Control Enters Blackhole)/Steev Hise (Stuck Together, Falling Apart)/The International Bankers (Void Transaction)/Corporal Blossom (Burnig Today's Memory)/The Evolution Control Committee (One Beck In The Grave)/Spacklequeen (Eggs, Eggs, Arms, Legs)/Hromlegn Kainn (Doublefolded)/Mr Meridies (Carpet Tunnel Syndrome)/Jane Drowe (Bust A Move)/J. Teller (Fat Zone)

The following is a Beck tribute by fans and unsigned bands, and very good it is too:

| Alt.Music.Beck Recordings | US | CD | 8/99 | £10 |
|---|---|---|---|---|

C (Death Is Coming To Get You)/Justin Bennett (Motherfucker)/Chonk (Satan Gave Me A Taco)/Crut (Crystal Clear (Beer))/Thrillo (Sleeping Bag)/Molokoplus (Truck Drivin' Neighbours Downstairs)/Madame Q (U-Boat (Rowboat)/Adam Flaherty (One Of These Days/Flavor)/Bandsaw (Baby)/Equatorial (Bogusflow)/Mortimer Nasty (Special People)/The Dropkicks (Pay No Mind)/Jergens Mcflurry Quartet (Special People/Let's Go Moon Some Cars)/Copter (Thunderpeel)/Greg M (Trouble All My Days)/Electroluxica (Puttin' It Down)/Simon Wilkinson (Sing It Again)/Je$U$ Po$$E Inc (Steve Threw Up)/Dead White Babies (Will I Be Ignored By The Lord?)/Michael Roddy Potvin (Strange Invitation)/Sacha Sojic (Whiskeyclone, Hotel City 1997)/Dj Spooky Mulder (One Foot In The Grave (Mini-Mix))

# V Canceled Check – Gig List

**1993**

| 23 July | KCRW Radio, Santa Monica, CA, USA | Loser/Mexico/Death Is Coming To Get Me/Whimsical Actress |
| 23 July | Troy Café, Los Angeles, CA, USA | Pay No Mind/MTV Makes Me Want to Smoke Crack |

**1994**

| 3 Jan. | unknown venue, Los Angeles, CA, USA | |
| Feb. | *Top Of The Pops*, BBC TV, London, England | Loser |
| 1 Mar. | KCRW Radio, Santa Monica, CA, USA | Bogusflow/Dead Man With No Heart/Hard To Compete/Howling Wolves/It's All In Your Mind/It's All Gonna Come To Be |
| 2 Mar. | Aaron's Records, Los Angeles, CA, USA | |
| March | SXSW, Austin, TX, USA | |
| 20 Mar. | Goat's Head, Houston, TX, USA | |
| 22 Mar. | The Boot, New Orleans, LA, USA | |
| 24 Mar. | Dark Horse Tavern, Atlanta, GA,USA | |
| 25 Mar. | The Shoebox, Athens, GA, USA | |
| 26 Mar. | Duke University, Durham, NC, USA | The Fucked Up Blues/I Get Lonesome/Bogusflow/One Foot In The Grave/The Spirit Moves Me/Fuckin' With My Head – incomplete set list |
| 27 Mar. | American University, Washington, DC, USA | |
| 29 Mar. | Knitting Factory, New York, NY, USA | |
| 30 Mar. | Axis, Boston, MA, USA | Mexico/Special People/One Foot In The Grave/Color Coordinated/Pay No Mind/Fuckin' With My |

Head/Fume/Soul Suckin Jerk/
Blackhole/Loser/Burnt OrangePeel/
Sleeping Bag/Truckdrivin' Neighbors
Downstairs

| | | |
|---|---|---|
| 31 Mar. | Middle East Café, Cambridge, MA, USA | |
| 1 Apr. | The Grand, New York, NY, USA | |
| 2 Apr. | JC Dobbs, Philadelphia, PA, USA | |
| 4 Apr. | The Rivoli, Toronto, ONT, Canada | |
| 6 Apr. | Detroit Science, Detroit, MI, USA | |
| 7 Apr. | The Distillery, Columbus, OH, USA | |
| 12 Apr. | Cicero's, St Louis, MO, USA | |
| 13 Apr. | Rhumba Box, Kansas City, MO, USA | |
| 15 Apr. | Ground Zero, Boulder, CO, USA | |
| 16 Apr. | DV-8, Salt Lake City, UT, USA | |
| 18 Apr. | Slim's, San Francisco, CA, USA | |
| 19 Apr. | The Troubadour, Los Angeles, CA, USA | |
| 20 Apr. | World Beat Center, San Diego, CA, USA | |
| 22 Apr. | McCabes, Santa Monica, CA, USA | |
| 8 May | Beale Street Music, Memphis, TN, USA | |
| 3 June | Price Center, La Jolla, CA, USA | Fuckin' With My Head/Got No Mind/One Foot In The Grave/ Loser/Fume/Beercan – incomplete set list, radio broadcast |
| 4 June | The Roxy Club, Phoenix, AZ, USA | |
| 5 June | Huntridge Theater, Las Vegas, NV, USA | |
| 10 June | unknown venue, Mountain View, CA, USA | Fuckin' With My Head/Pay No Mind/One Foot In The Grave/ Loser/Fume/Beercan |
| 11 June | unknown venue, Los Angeles, CA, USA | |
| 13 June | DV-8, Salt Lake City, UT, USA | |

| 15 June | Ogden Theater, Denver, CO, USA | |
| 17 June | Deep Ellum Live, Dallas, TX, USA | |
| 18 June | Toad's, Houston, TX, USA | |
| 19 June | Liberty Lunch, Austin, TX, USA | |
| 21 June | Mississippi, St Louis, MO, USA | |
| 22 June | Bogarts, Cincinnati, OH, USA | |
| 24 June | Eastwood Theater, Indianapolis, IN, USA | |
| 25 June | Phoenix Plaza, Pontiac, MI, USA | |
| 27 June | The Metro, Chicago, IL, USA | Corvette Bummer/Instrumental/ Motherfucker/Fume/Whiskeyclone Hotel City 1997/Minus/Soul Suckin Jerk/Pink Noise (Rock Me Amadeus)/Got No Mind/Bogusflow/ Cyanide Breath Mint/Nitemare Hippy Girl/One Foot In The Grave/Alcohol/John Hardy/Loser/ Colour Coordinated/Blackhole/ Spanking Room/Beercan/Fuckin' With My Head/The Soul Of Gina Arnold |
| 28 June | The Rave, Milwaukee, WI, USA | |
| 29 June | 1st Avenue Club, Minneapolis, MN, USA | *Total Paranoia* CD Bootleg: Corvette Bummer/Color Coordinated/Fuckin' With My Head/Motherfucker/ Fume/Pay No Mind/Asskizz Powergrudge (Payback '94)/Burnt Orange Peel/Scavenger/Bogusflow/ unknown/One Foot In The Grave/John Hardy/Alcohol/Loser/ Minus/Blackhole/Spanking Room/ Beercan |
| 2 July | Howden Ballroom, Vancouver, BC, Canada | |
| 3 July | Oz, Seattle, WA, USA | |
| 4 July | La Luna, Portland, OR, USA | |
| 6 July | The Fillmore, San Francisco, CA, USA | |
| 7 July | The Whisky, Los Angeles, CA, USA | |
| 5 Aug. | The Playroom, Goldcoast, Australia | |

| | | |
|---|---|---|
| 6 Aug. | The Roxy, Brisbane, Australia | |
| 9 Aug. | The Herdsman, Perth, Australia | |
| 11 Aug. | The Old Lion, Adelaide, Australia | |
| 12 Aug. | Prince of Wales, Melbourne, Australia | |
| 13 Aug. | Prince of Wales, Melbourne, Australia | |
| 14 Aug. | Wall Street, Melbourne, Australia | |
| 17 Aug. | Anu Bar, Canberra, Australia | |
| 18 Aug. | Newcastle University, Newcastle, Australia | |
| 19 Aug. | Sydney University, Sydney, Australia | |
| 22 Aug. | JJJ Radio Session, Sydney, Australia | Beercan/Color Coordinated/Minus/Scavenger/Thunderpeel/Hard To Compete/It's All In Your Mind/Grizzly |
| 23 Aug. | Powerstation, Auckland, New Zealand | |
| 25 Aug. | Neptune II, Wanchai, CHI | |
| 27 Aug. | Faces, Makati, CHI | |
| 29 Aug. | Club Citta, Kawasaki, Japan | |
| 31 Aug. | Diamond Hall, Nagoya, Japan | |
| 1 Sept. | IMP Hall, Osaka, Japan | |
| 2 Sept. | Skala Espacio, Fukuoka, Japan | |
| 4 Sept. | Club Citta, Kawasaki, Japan | |
| 5 Sept. | Club Citta, Kawasaki, Japan | |
| 6 Sept. | Liquid Room, Tokyo, Japan | *Strawberry Communion* CD Bootleg: Soul Suckin Jerk/Color Coordinated/Fuckin' With My Head/Maximum Potential/Corvette Bummer/Thunderpeel/Whiskeyclone, Hotel City 1997/Asshole/Puttin' It Down/StaggerLee/It's All Gonna Come To Be/Loser/Minus/Pay No Mind/Nitemare Hippy Girl/Blackhole/Beercan/Motherfucker |
| 7 Sept. | Liquid Room, Tokyo, Japan | |

| | | |
|---|---|---|
| 9 Sept. | After Dark, Honolulu, HI, USA | Soul Suckin Jerk/Fuckin' With My Head/Grizzly/Corvette Bummer/ Thunderpeel/Whiskeyclone, Hotel City 1997/Mexico/Asshole/One Foot In The Grave/Canceled Check/ Loser/Minus/Maximum Potential/ Static/Blackhole/Beercan/ Motherfucker/Truckdrivin' Neighbors Downstairs |
| 19 Oct. | Metropol, Pittsburgh, PA, USA | |
| 20 Oct. | Marquee, Buffalo, NY, USA | |
| 21 Oct. | The Opera House, Toronto, ONT, Canada | Soul Suckin Jerk/Cock/Fume/ Fuckin' With My Head/Asskizz Powergrudge (Payback)/ Thunderpeel/Corvette Bummer/ Scavenger/Beginner's Luck/ Brother/(title unknown)/One Foot In The Grave/He's A Mighty Good Leader/Trouble All My Days/Loser/ Convalescent/Ziplock Bag/ Maximum Potential/Blackhole/ Beercan/Motherfucker/Jimi Carter |
| 22 Oct. | Le Spectrum, Montreal, QUE, Canada | |
| 24 Oct. | Middle East Café, Cambridge, MA, USA | *I'm A Schmoozer Baby* CD Bootleg: Fume/Fuckin' With My Head/Casio (Good Stuff)/Thunderpeel/ Truckdrivin' Neighbors Downstairs/ Brother/Asshole/One Foot In The Grave/Canceled Check/Static/ Spirits/It's All In Your Mind/Flavor/ Loser/Convalescent/Sandman/ Blackhole/Beercan |
| 25 Oct. | Lupos Heartbreak, Providence, RI, USA | |
| 26 Oct. | Irving Plaza, New York, NY, USA | Soul Suckin Jerk/Cock/Fume/ Fuckin' With My Head/Casio (Good Stuff)/Thunderpeel/Ziplock Bag/ Sleeping Bag/Brother/Asshole/One Foot In The Grave/Static/Loser/ Glut/Outcome/Blackhole/Beercan/ Motherfucker/Jimi Carter |
| 28 Oct. | Toads Place, New Haven, CT, USA | *Suicidal Jerk* CD Bootleg: Soul Suckin Jerk/Fume/Fuckin' With My Head/Casio/Thunderpeel/Corvette Bummer/Whiskeyclone, Hotel City 1997/Asshole/I Get Lonesome/One Foot In The Grave/unknown/ |

|  |  | Maximum Potential/Blackhole/ Beercan/Motherfucker/Jimi Carter |
|---|---|---|
| 29 Oct. | Metropolis, Harrisburg, PA, USA | |
| 30 Oct. | Trocadero, Philadelphia, PA, USA | |
| 31 Oct. | 9:30 Club, Washington, DC, USA | Soul Suckin Jerk/Color Coordinated/Fume/Fuckin' With My Head/Casio (Good Stuff)/ Thunderpeel/Ziplock Bag/Asshole/ Puttin' It Down/Cyanide Breath Mint/Alcohol/I Get Lonesome/ Nitemare Hippy Girl/No Money, No Honey/Feather In Your Cap/Mighty Good Leader/Loser/Touch Of Class/ Glut/Blackhole/Beercan/ Motherfucker/Jimi Carter |
| 3 Nov. | Salle Des Fêtes, Vernier/ Le Ligne, France | |
| 5 Nov. | The Revolver, Madrid, Spain | Soul Suckin Jerk/Colour Coordinated/Outcome/ Motherfucker/Casio (Good Stuff)/ Maximum Potential/Thunderpeel/ Whiskeyclone, Hotel City 1997/ Medley: Puttin' it Down-Cyanide Breath Mint-Nitemare Hippy Girl-I Get Lonesome-Alcohol/Touch Of Class/Totally Confused/Blackhole/ Sleeping Bag/Beercan/Jimi Carter |
| 6 Nov. | Estandard, Barcelona, Spain | |
| 8 Nov. | Crossover, Torino, Italy | |
| 9 Nov. | Circolo Degli, Rome, Italy | |
| 10 Nov. | Factory, Milan, Italy | |
| 12 Nov. | Belmondo, Prague, Czech Republic | |
| 13 Nov. | Charterhalle, Munich, Germany | |
| 15 Nov. | Luxor, Cologne, Germany | |
| 16 Nov. | Grosse Freiheit, Hamburg, Germany | |
| 17 Nov. | Loft, Berlin, Germany | |
| 18 Nov. | Vision Boarde, Les Deux Alpes, France | |
| 20 Nov. | Vera, Groningen, Holland | |
| 21 Nov. | Loppen, Copenhagen, Denmark | |
| 22 Nov. | Gino, Stockholm, Sweden | |
| 23 Nov. | Rockefeller, Oslo, Norway | |

| 26 Nov. | Manchester University, Manchester, England | |
|---|---|---|
| 27 Nov. | King Tuts Wah, Glasgow, Scotland | |
| 28 Nov. | Astoria Theatre, London, England | Fuckin' With My Head/ Thunderpeel/Soul Suckin Jerk/ Color Coordinated/Casio (Good Stuff)/Maximum Potential/Ziplock Bag/Sports Convention/ Whiskeyclone, Hotel City 1997/ Puttin' It Down/Protein Summer/ One Foot In The Grave/It's All In Your Mind/Flavor/Feather In Your Cap/Interlude/Loser/Touch Of Class/Got No Mind/Blackhole/ Beercan/Motherfucker/Casio (Rappel) |
| 29 Nov. | Splash Club, London, England | |
| 1 Dec. | Transmusicales, Rennes, France | Fuckin' With My Head/ Thunderpeel/Soul Suckin Jerk/Got No Mind/Whiskeyclone, Hotel City 1997/Alcohol/It's All In Your Mind/One Foot In The Grave/ Loser/Touch Of Class/Sleeping Bag/Beercan/Motherfucker/Casio (Good Stuff) |
| 2 Dec. | Arapaho, Paris, France | |
| 4 Dec. | De Melkweg, Amsterdam, Holland | Corvette Bummer/Fume/Fuckin' With My Head/Thunderpeel/Soul Suckin Jerk/Minus/Casio (Good Stuff)/Asshole/It's All In Your Mind/Loser/Motherfucker/ Nitemare Hippy Girl/Blackhole/ Beercan |
| 5 Dec. | Vooruit, Gent, Belgium | Fuckin' With My Head/ Thunderpeel/Soul Suckin Jerk/ Casino (Ripoff)/Color Coordinated/ Truckdrivin' Neighbors Downstairs/ Ziplock Bag/Whiskeyclone, Hotel City 1997/Mexico/One Foot In The Grave/Feather In Your Cap/Devil Got My Woman/Loser/Got No Mind/Blackhole |
| 12 Dec. | unknown venue, Los Angeles, CA, USA | |
| 17 Dec. | Slim's, San Francisco, CA, USA | |

| | | |
|---|---|---|
| 18 Dec. | The Troubadour, Los Angeles, CA, USA | Fuckin' With My Head/ Thunderpeel/Soul Suckin Jerk/ Minus/Casio (Good Stuff)/Country Jam/Maximum Potential (Sandman)/Convalescent/ Instrumental Interlude/Asshole/ Puttin' It Down/Sleeping Bag/One Foot In The Grave/Beginner's Luck/Spirits/It's All In Your Mind/Trouble All My Days/Loser/ Touch Of Class/Pay No Mind/ Blackhole/Beercan |

## 1995

| | | |
|---|---|---|
| 6 Jan. | KCRW, Los Angeles, CA, USA | Devil Got My Woman/Feel The Strain Of Sorrow Never Ceasing/ Canceled Check/Curses/John The Revelator/Don't You Mind People Grinnin' In Your Face |
| 7 Jan. | Pantages Theater, Los Angeles, CA, USA | |
| 21 Apr. | Doornroosje, Nijmegen, Holland | |
| 20 June | Catalyst, Santa Cruz, CA, USA | |
| 21 June | Cactus Club, San Jose, CA, USA | |
| 22 June | Cattle Club, Sacramento, CA, USA | |
| 24 June | World Beat Center, San Diego, CA, USA | |
| 25 June | Music City, Fountain Valley, CA, USA | |

*Start of the Lollapalooza tour*

| | | |
|---|---|---|
| 4 July | The Gorge, George, WA, USA | Fuckin' With My Head/unknown/ Motherfucker/Pay No Mind/ unknown/Asshole/Loser/ unknown/Beercan |
| 5 July | UBC Stadium, Vancouver, BC, USA | |
| 8 July | Fiddlers, Denver, CO, USA | |
| 10 July | Sandstone Amphitheater, Kansas City, MO, USA | |
| 11 July | Riverport Amphitheater, St Louis, MO, USA | |
| 12 July | Deer Creek Amphitheater, Indianapolis, IN, USA | |
| 14 July | Polaris Amphitheater, Columbus, OH, USA | |

| | | |
|---|---|---|
| 15 July | New World Amphitheater, Chicago, IL, USA | *Main Stage*: Fuckin' With My Head/Novocane/Thunderpeel/Pay No Mind/Where It's At/Truckdrivin' Neighbors Downstairs/Cyanide Breath Mint/Diskobox/Static/Loser *Second Stage*: John Hardy/Fume/ Mexico/Asshole/Hollow Log/ Rowboat/Ozzy/Nitemare Hippy Girl |
| 18 July | Riverbend Amphitheater, Cincinatti, OH, USA | |
| 19 July | Pine Knob Amphitheater, Detroit, MI, USA | |
| 20 July | Pine Knob Amphitheater, Detroit, MI, USA | |
| 22 July | Blossom Music Center, Cleveland, OH, USA | |
| 23 July | Molson Park, Toronto, ONT, Canada | *Main Stage*: Fuckin' With My Head/Novacane/Thunderpeel/Pay No Mind/Fume/Plague/Loser/ Motherfucker/Blackhole/Beercan *Second Stage*: Cyanide Breath Mint/John Hardy/Asshole/ Heartland Feeling/Hollow Log/One Foot In The Grave/Puttin' It Down/Alcohol/It's All In Your Mind/improv/Nightmare Hippy Euro/Encore Medley: Ozzy-Asshole-I Get Lonesome-Satan Gave Me Some Vitamins-Mexico-Totally Confused-Rowboat |
| 25 July | Great Woods, Boston, MA, USA | |
| 26 July | The Meadows, Hartford, CT, USA | Fuckin' With My Head/ Thunderpeel/Fume/Pay No Mind/ Minus/Where It's At/unknown/ Loser/Heartland Feeling/Blackhole |
| 28 July | Randall's Island, New York, NY, USA | |
| 29 July | Randall's Island, New York, NY, USA | Intro/Fume/Novacane/Fuckin' With My Head/Pay No Mind/Diskobox/ Loser/Motherfucker/Blackhole/ Beercan/Jimi Carter |
| 30 July | Blockbuster/Sony Pavillion, Philadelphia, PA, USA | |
| 31 July | Starlake Amphitheater, Pittsburg, PA, USA | |
| 3 Aug. | Racetrack, Charleston, NC, USA | Thunderpeel/Novacane/Fuckin' With My Head/Pay No Mind/Where |

It's At/Fume/Loser/Motherfucker/
Blackhole/Beercan

| | | |
|---|---|---|
| 5 Aug. | Lakewood Amphitheater, Atlanta, GA, USA | |
| 6 Aug. | Walnut Creek Amphitheater, Raleigh, NC, USA | |
| 9 Aug. | Southpark Meadows, Austin, TX, USA | |
| 10 Aug. | Starplex Amphitheater, Dallas, TX, USA | Fuckin' With My Head/Fume/Pay No Mind/Cyanide Breath Mint/ Truck Drivin' Neighbors Downstairs/Puttin' It Down/One Foot In The Grave/Asshole/Sleeping Bag/Loser/Jimi Carter |
| 12 Aug. | Desert Sky Pavillion, Phoenix, AZ, USA | |
| 14 Aug. | Irvine Meadows, Los Angeles, CA, USA | |
| 15 Aug. | Irvine Meadows, Los Angeles, CA, USA | |
| 18 Aug. | Shoreline Amphitheater, San Francisco, CA, USA | Fuckin' With My Head/ Thunderpeel/Novacane/Pay No Mind/Where It's At/Motherfucker/ Loser (Beatbox)/Loser (Electric)/ Blackhole/Beercan/Jimi Carter |

*End of Lollapalooza tour*

| | | |
|---|---|---|
| 25 Aug. | Reading Festival, Reading, England | Pay No Mind/Loser/Asshole/ Beercan/Novacane/Thunderpeel – not in order |
| 26 Aug. | Pukkelpop, Open, Hasselt, Belgium | |
| 27 Aug. | Lowlands Festival, Dronton, Holland | Fume/Motherfucker/Pay No Mind/ Novacane/Truckdrivin' Neighbors Downstairs/Alcohol/Puttin' It Down/Loser/Minus/Asshole/ Beercan/Jimi Carter |
| 29 Aug. | Bataclan, Paris, France | |
| 31 Aug. | Fri-Son, Fribourg, Switzerland | |
| 1 Sept. | Winterthurer, Switzerland | |
| 2 Sept. | Holzstock '95, Ebensee, Austria | |
| 9 Sept. | El Pop Festival, Badalona, Spain | |
| 12 Sept. | Elysée Montmartre, Paris, France | |
| 18 Oct. | Shoreline Amphitheater, Mountain View, CA, USA | Pay No Mind/Sleeping Bag/John Hardy/Hollow Log/One Foot In The |

|  |  | Grave/Rowboat/Asshole/It's All In Your Mind |
|---|---|---|
| 28 Oct. | Bridge School Benefit, Mountain View, CA, USA | |
| 11 Nov. | Club Spaceland, Los Angeles, CA, USA | *Hi-Fi Pollution* CD Bootleg: Puttin' It Down/unknown/Painted Eyelids/ Pay No Mind/Alcohol/I Wanna Get With You (And Your Sister Debra)/Dead Melodies/One Foot In The Grave |
| 29 Dec. | unknown venue, Australia | |

## 1996

| | | |
|---|---|---|
| 7 Jan. | Summersault Festival, Perth, Australia | The Diamond Sea (intro)/Pay No Mind/Alcohol/Plague/One Foot In The Grave/Truckdrivin' Neighbors Downstairs/Hollow Log |
| 1 Mar. | unknown venue, Tilburg, Holland | |
| 18 Mar. | Noorderlicht, Tilburg, Holland | Pay No Mind/Cyanide Breath Mint/ Mexico part 1/I Get Lonesome/One Foot In The Grave/Truckdrivin' Neighbors Downstairs/Hollow Log/'Call Me Beck'/Plague/Mexico part 2/Asshole/Sleeping Bag/Mexico part 3/Lord Only Knows |
| 27 Mar. | unknown venue, Paris, France | |
| 31 Mar. | King's College, London, England | Puttin' It Down/Pay No Mind/ Cyanide Breath Mint/No Money, No Honey/Fume/Heartland Feeling (part 1)/Leave Me On The Moon/Truckdrivin' Neighbors Downstairs/Heartland Feeling (part 2)/Hollow Log/One Foot In The Grave |
| 3 Apr. | unknown venue, Germany | |
| 5 June | Regency Room, Toronto, ONT, Canada | |
| 16 June | Tibetan Freedom Concert, San Francisco, CA, USA | Pay No Mind/Alcohol/Truckdrivin' Neighbors Downstairs/Asshole/One Foot In The Grave/Burnt Orange Peel/High Five/Hollow Log |
| 16 June | Modern Rock Live – Tibet Special | Pay No Mind/Hollow Log |
| 16 June | Tower Records, Los Angeles, CA, USA | *Odelay* release |
| 17 June | KOME, San Jose, CA, USA | Jackass/Curses |

| | | |
|---|---|---|
| 19 June | KCRW, Santa Monica, CA, USA | Regular Song/Two Bit Cares/Jackass/Waitin' For A Train/It Ain't Your Time |
| 27 June | Galaxy, Santa Ana, CA, USA | |
| 28 June | The Glass House, Pomona, CA, USA | |
| 3 July | Quart Festival, Kristiansand, Norway | |
| 4 July | unknown venue, France | |
| 5 July | unknown venue, France | |
| 6 July | Les Eurockeene, Belfort, France | |
| 8 July | unknown venue, Austria | |
| 9 July | Backstage, Munich, Germany | |
| 10 July | unknown venue, Germany | |
| 12 July | Feile Festival, Thurles, Ireland | |
| 13 July | T-In-The-Park, Scotland | |
| 14 July | Dour Music Festival, Dour, Belgium | |
| 16 July | unknown venue, Italy | |
| 17 July | Vidia Club, Cesena, Italy | *Neogenetic Disco* CD Bootleg: Devils Haircut/Novacane/Hotwax/Where It's At/Minus/Freakout Eurobeat/ Loser/I Wanna Get With You (And Your Sister Debra) |
| 19 July | Phoenix Festival, Stratford, England | Filmed for UK TV, *Neogenetic Disco* CD Bootleg: Devils Haircut/Loser/ Where It's At/Lord Only Knows/ Beercan/Pay No Mind (incomplete set list) |
| 21 July | Paradiso, Amsterdam, Holland | *Electric Music For The Kool People* CD Bootleg: Fuckin' With My Head/ Devils Haircut/Novacane/Pay No Mind/Loser/Minus/Truckdrivin' Neighbors Downstairs/No Money, No Honey/Puttin' It Down/ Rowboat/Where It's At/East 17 Tribute/The New Pollution/Jackass/Beercan/I Wanna Get With You (And Your Sister Debra)/High Five/Motherfucker |
| 23 July | Rote-Fabrik, Zurich, Switzerland | |
| 24 July | unknown venue, Switzerland | |

| | | |
|---|---|---|
| 26 July | Lollipop Festival, Stockholm, Sweden | *Lollipop* CD Bootleg: Lord Only Knows/Devils Haircut/Novacane/Sissyneck/Minus/Pay No Mind/Loser/Truck Drivin' Neighbors Downstairs/Where It's At/The New Pollution/Jack-ass/Beercan/High Five |
| 27 July | unknown venue, France | |
| 2 Aug. | Live 105, San Francisco, CA, USA | Pay No Mind/Asshole/Leave Me On The Moon |
| 3 Aug. | Kitsap Bowl, Bremerton, WA, USA | |
| 4 Aug. | Timberbowl, Estacada, OR, USA | |
| 14 Aug. | First Avenue, Minneapolis, MN, USA | |
| 15 Aug. | Cabaret Metro, Chicago, IL, USA | |
| 17 Aug. | Sanctum, Pontiac, MI, USA | |
| 18 Aug. | Odeon, Cleveland, OH, USA | |
| 20 Aug. | Ogden Music Hall, Buffalo, NY, USA | Devils Haircut/Fuckin' With My Head/Hotwax/Readymade/Loser/Lord Only Knows/Jack-ass/Soul Suckin Jerk/Motherfucker/Minus/Beercan/Sissyneck/Where It's At/High Five |
| 21 Aug. | Concert Hall, Toronto, ONT, Canada | |
| 22 Aug. | Chumcity Building, Toronto, ONT, Canada | Filming for ODEBECK, MuchMusic TV: Devils Haircut/Novacane/Hotwax/Sissyneck/Derelict/I Wanna Get With You (And Your Sister Debra)/High Five/Thunderpeel/Where It's At/Ramshackle |
| 23 Aug. | La Spectrum, Montreal, QUE, Canada | |
| 24 Aug. | Avalon, Boston, MA, USA | |
| 25 Aug. | Lupos Heartbreak, Providence, RI, USA | |
| 27 Aug. | Supper Club, New York, NY, USA | *1st show*: Devils Haircut/Novacane/Thunderpeel/Loser/Lord Only Knows/Hotwax/I Wanna Get With You (And Your Sister Debra)/Pay No Mind/Truckdrivin' Neighbors Downstairs/No Money, No Honey/Manchild (Asshole)/One Foot In The Grave/Ramshackle/Where It's |

At/Sissyneck/Derelict/Beercan –
incomplete set list
*2nd show*: unknown set list

| | | |
|---|---|---|
| 28 Aug. | WXRK Radio, New York, NY, USA | |
| 30 Aug. | Trocadero, Philadelphia, PA, USA | |
| 31 Aug. | 9:30 Club, Washington, DC, USA | |
| 1 Sept. | Maxwell's, Hoboken, NJ, USA | Puttin' It Down/Dust In The Wind/ Cold Brains/Waiting For A Train/Girl Dreams/Cyanide Breath Mint/Asshole/instrumental/Hollow Log/One Foot In The Grave/Painted Eyelids/Ramshackle/Rowboat/ Totally Confused/Pay No Mind Medley: I Get Lonesome-Truckdrivin' Neighbors Downstairs-Alcohol-Modesto-Cyanide Breath Mint-Painted Eyelids-Fuckin' With My Head/Heartland Feeling |
| 2 Sept. | Columbia University, New York, NY, USA | |
| 6 Sept. | David Letterman, CBS TV, New York, NY, USA | Where It's At |
| 20 Sept. | unknown venue, Charlotte, NC, USA | Fuckin' With My Head/Loser/ Novacane/Hot Wax/The New Pollution/Asshole/Jack-ass/Where It's At/Devils Haircut/ Motherfucker/Beercan/High Five |
| 21 Sept. | 99-X Big Day Out Festival, Atlanta, GA, USA | Novacane/Devils Haircut/Loser/ Motherfucker/Beercan/Where It's At/The New Pollution/Sissyneck/ Hotwax/Pay No Mind |
| 23 Sept. | 328 Performance Hall, Nashville, TN, USA | Fuckin' With My Head/Hotwax/The New Pollution/Pay No Mind/ Asshole/No Money, No Honey/ Puttin' It Down/Sleeping Bag/ Truckdrivin' Neighbors Downstairs/ Beatbox (with guest)/Where It's At/Minus/Sissyneck/Beercan/I Wanna Get With You (And Your Sister Debra)/High Five |
| 28 Sept. | unknown venue, Tulsa, OK, USA | Devils Haircut/Novacane/Lord Only Knows/Hotwax-Bob Wills/ Motherfucker/Sissyneck/Pay No Mind/Truckdrivin' Neighbors Downstairs/One Foot In The Grave/Rowboat/Where It's At/ Thunderpeel/The New Pollution/ |

| | | |
|---|---|---|
| | | Fume/Jack-ass/Derelict/Beercan/I Wanna Get With You (And Your Sister Debra)/High Five |
| 11 Oct. | Civic Auditorium, Santa Monica, CA, USA | Devils Haircut/Novacane/Lord Only Knows/Pay No Mind/The New Pollution/Truckdrivin' Neighbors Downstairs/Asshole/One Foot In The Grave/Ramshackle/Fume/Derelict/Sissyneck/Where It's At/Minus/Beercan/I Wanna Get With You (And Your Sister Debra)/High Five |
| 12 Oct. | unknown venue, Los Angeles, CA, USA | |
| 23 Oct. | IMP Hall, Osaka, Japan | |
| 24 Oct. | Diamond Hall, Nagoya, Japan | |
| 25 Oct. | Skala Espacio, Fukuoka, Japan | |
| 27 Oct. | Blitz, Tokyo, Japan | |
| 28 Oct. | Blitz, Tokyo, Japan | |
| 30 Oct. | Blitz, Tokyo, Japan | |
| 31 Oct. | Blitz, Tokyo, Japan | |
| 1 Nov. | Liquid Room, Tokyo, Japan | |
| 3 Nov. | Bayside Jenny, Osaka, Japan | |
| 4 Nov. | CK Caf, Kyoto, Japan | |
| November | Forest National, Brussels, Belgium | |
| 15 Nov. | unknown venue, Madrid, Spain | Soul Suckin Jerk/Color Coordinated/Outcome/Motherfucker/Casio (Good Stuff)/Sandman/Thunderpeel/Whiskeyclone, Hotel City 1997/Puttin' It Down/Cyanide Breath Mint/Nitemare Hippy Girl/I Get Lonesome/Alcohol/Feather In Your Cap/Loser/Touch Of Class/Totally Confused/Blackhole/Beercan/Jimi Carter |
| 20 Nov. | unknown venue, Stuttgart, Germany | Loser/Thunderpeel/Novacane/Devils Haircut/Hotwax/Lord Only Knows/Readymade/Jack-ass/Sissyneck/Beercan – incomplete set list |
| 24 Nov. | The Cirkus, Stockholm, Sweden | *Cirkus* CD Bootleg: Loser/Novacane/Hotwax/One Foot In The Grave/Where It's At/Devils Haircut/ |

| | | |
|---|---|---|
| | | Beercan/I Wanna Get With You (And Your Sister Debra)/High Five |
| 29 Nov. | Le Bataclan, Paris, France | *Loser* CD Bootleg: Loser/Novacane/ Lord Only Knows/High Five/The New Pollution/Derelict/Pay No Mind/Ramshackle/No Money, No Honey/It's All In Your Mind/One Foot In The Grave/Mexico/Where It's At/Devils Haircut/Sissyneck |
| 9 Dec. | Academy, Manchester, England | Lord Only Knows/Minus/ Novacane/Thunderpeel/The New Pollution/Hotwax/Derelict/Loser/ Ramshackle/Where It's At/Devils Haircut/American Wasteland/ Beercan/Fuckin' With My Head/ High Five |
| 10 Dec. | Brixton Academy, London, England | *Swinging London* CD Bootleg: Thunderpeel/Lord Only Knows/ Minus/The New Pollution/Derelict/ Loser/Asshole/One Foot In The Grave/Pay No Mind/Where It's At/Devils Haircut/Sissyneck/I Wanna Get With You (And Your Sister Debra)/Beercan |
| 11 Dec. | SSX, Dublin, Ireland | |
| 14 Dec. | KROQ, Los Angeles, CA, USA | Loser/Novacane/Devils Haircut/ One Foot In The Grave/The New Pollution/Where It's At/Little Drum Machine Boy/High Five |
| December | Cow Palace, San Francisco, CA, USA | Live 105 Xmas show: Beatbox w/ Beastie Boys/Beck solo Beatbox/ Thunderpeel/Novacane/Loser/The New Pollution/Pay No Mind/One Foot In The Grave/Devils Haircut/ Where It's At/High Five |

## 1997

| | | |
|---|---|---|
| 11 Jan. | *Saturday Night Live*, New York, NY, USA | Where It's At/Devils Haircut |
| 12 Jan. | Roseland, New York, NY, USA | |
| 13 Jan. | Ventura Theater, Los Angeles, CA, USA | Devils Haircut/Novacane/Loser/ Lord Only Knows/Hotwax/The New Pollution/Sleeping Bag/One Foot In The Grave/Derelict/Where It's At – incomplete set list |
| 20 Jan. | Radio Free LA, Los Angeles, CA, USA | *Hi-Fi Pollution* CD Bootleg: I Ain't Got No Home In This World Anymore/ Don't You Mind People Grinnin' In Your Face |

| | | |
|---|---|---|
| 6 Feb. | UBC Student Recreation, Vancouver, BC, Canada | Devils Haircut/Novacane/Lord Only Knows/Hotwax/Diskobox/Minus/Loser/Derelict/Alcohol/Asshole/I Get Lonesome/Canceled Check/One Foot In The Grave/Jack-ass/Where It's At/Sissyneck/Beercan/High Five |
| 7 Feb. | Paramount Theater, Seattle, WA, USA | |
| 8 Feb. | Salem Armory, Salem, OR, USA | |
| 10 Feb. | EMU Ballroom, Eugene, OR, USA | DJ Swamp intro/Unit Is In Effect/Devils Haircut/Novacane/Lord Only Knows/Minus/Loser/Sissyneck/The New Pollution/Hotwax/Pay No Mind/Ozzy (new version)/Asshole/It's All In Your Mind/Regular Song/Interlude/Don't You Mind People Grinnin' In Your Face/Derelict/Where It's At/Thunderpeel/Motherfucker/Jack-ass/DJ Swamp solo/High Five |
| 12 Feb. | Pioneer Theater, Reno, NV, USA | |
| 13 Feb. | Freeborn Hall, Davis, CA, USA | Intro/Devils Haircut/Thunderpeel/Loser/The New Pollution/Hotwax/Sleeping Bag/Asshole/Hollow Log/beatbox/Truckdrivin' Neighbors Downstairs/Derelict/Where It's At/Minus/Lord Only Knows/Fuckin' With My Head/DJ Swamp solo/High Five |
| 14 Feb. | SC Civic Auditorium, Santa Cruz, CA, USA | Intro/Devils Haircut/Novacane/Lord Only Knows/The New Pollution/Fume/Hotwax/Jack-ass/Asshole/Hollow Log/Don't You Mind People Grinnin' In Your Face/Acoustic jam/Motherfucker/Derelict/Where It's At |
| 15 Feb. | Stanford Auditorium, Palo Alto, CA, USA | |
| 16 Feb. | Rainbow Ballroom, Fresno, CA, USA | |
| 19 Feb. | Rimac Arena, San Diego, CA, USA | |
| 20 Feb. | Celebrity Theater, Phoenix, AZ, USA | Devils Haircut/Novacane/Lord Only Knows/Hotwax/The New Pollution/Sissyneck/Loser/Puttin' It Down/Asshole/One Foot In The Grave/Hollow Log/Jack-ass/Where It's At/Thunderpeel/Beercan/High Five |

| | | |
|---|---|---|
| 21 Feb. | Huntridge Theater, Las Vegas, NV, USA | |
| 26 Feb. | Grammy Awards, New York, NY, USA | Where It's At |
| 28 Feb. | *TFI Friday*, Channel 4 TV, London, England | The New Pollution |
| 2 Mar. | Kilburn National, London, England | Unit Is In Effect/Devils Haircut/Novacane/Lord Only Knows/Thunderpeel/Sissyneck/Hotwax/Little Drum Machine Boy/Jack-ass/Asshole/I Get Lonesome/One Foot In The Grave/Rowboat/Derelict/Where It's At/The New Pollution/Beercan/Swamp Solo/High Five |
| 3 Mar. | Cardiff University, Cardiff, Wales | |
| 19 Mar. | The Edge, Fort Lauderdale, FL, USA | Devils Haircut/Novacane/Thunderpeel/Hotwax/The New Pollution/Derelict/Loser/Pay No Mind/Asshole/One Foot In The Grave/Cyanide Breath Mint/Jack-ass/Where It's At/Minus/Beercan/High Five |
| 20 Mar. | USF Special Events Center, Tampa, FL, USA | |
| 21 Mar. | Florida Theater, Gainesville, FL, USA | |
| 22 Mar. | Classic Center, Athens, GA, USA | |
| 24 Mar. | Ryman Auditorium, Nashville, TN, USA | |
| 25 Mar. | Reynolds Coliseum, Raleigh, NC, USA | Novacane/Thunderpeel/Lord Only Knows/The New Pollution/Minus/Loser/Sissyneck/Pay No Mind/Asshole/Truckdrivin' Neighbors Downstairs/One Foot In The Grave/Jack-ass/Where It's At/Fuckin' With My Head/Swamp Solo/American Wasteland/Motherfucker |
| 26 Mar. | Patriot Center, Fairfax, VA, USA | Unit Is In Effect/Devils Haircut/Novacane/Thunderpeel/Lord Only Knows/The New Pollution/Hotwax/Sissyneck/Derelict/Pay No Mind + (in no particular order) Where It's At/Jack-ass/Loser/Beercan/Truckdrivin' Nieghbors Downstairs/Hollow Log/One Foot In The Grave/Asshole/DJ Swamp solo/High Five |
| 28 Mar. | Lefrak Hall, Amherst, MA, USA | |

| | | |
|---|---|---|
| 29 Mar. | University of Rochester, Rochester, NY, USA | |
| 30 Mar. | The Spectrum, Philadelphia, PA, USA | Devils Haircut/Novacane/ Thunderpeel/Burnt Orange Peel/ Loser/Derelict/Truckdrivin' Neighbors Downstairs/Hollow Log/One Foot In The Grave/ Asshole/The New Pollution/I Wanna Get With You (And Your Sister Debra)/Jack-ass/Where It's At/Beercan/Swamp Solo/High Five |
| 2 Apr. | Metropolis, Montreal, QUE, Canada | |
| 3 Apr. | Varsity Arena, Toronto, ONT, Canada | |
| 5 Apr. | Rhodes Arena, Akron, OH, USA | Devils Haircut/Novacane/Burnt Orange Peel/Lord Only Knows/ Hotwax – The Little Drum Machine Boy/Diskobox/Derelict/The New Pollution/Pay No Mind/Fume/ Asshole/One Foot In The Grave/ Jack-ass/Where It's At/Loser/ Beercan/High Five |
| 7 Apr. | Music Hall, Cincinatti, OH, USA | Fuckin' With My Head/Novacane/ Devils Haircut/Burnt Orange Peel/Hotwax – The Little Drum Machine Boy/The New Pollution/ Diskobox/Loser/Asshole/ Truckdrivin' Neighbors Downstairs/ One Foot In The Grave/Feather In Your Cap/Where It's At/Beercan/ High Five |
| 8 Apr. | Stephan Center, South Bend, IN, USA | |
| 9 Apr. | Expo Hall, Indianapolis, IN, USA | |
| 11 Apr. | Branden Auditorium, Normal, IL, USA | Devils Haircut/Novacane/Lord Only Knows/Hotwax – The Little Drum Machine Boy/The New Pollution/I Wanna Get With You (And Your Sister Debra)/Sissyneck/Burnt Orange Peel/Derelict/Asshole/ Painted Eyelids/One Foot In The Grave/Jack-ass/Where It's At/ Beercan/High Five |
| 12 Apr. | Brit Awards, London, England | |
| 12 Apr. | University of Chicago, Chicago, IL, USA | |

| | | |
|---|---|---|
| 14 Apr. | Mancuso Theater, Omaha, NE, USA | |
| 15 Apr. | Shrine Mosque, Springfield, MO, USA | |
| 16 Apr. | TNT Building, Oklahoma City, OK, USA | |
| 18 Apr. | Performing Arts Center, Topeka, KS, USA | |
| 19 Apr. | River Park, Tulsa, OK, USA | Devils Haircut/Novacane/Thunderpeel/Loser/The New Pollution/Hotwax/Sissyneck/Asshole/One Foot In The Grave/Jack-ass/Where It's At/High Five |
| 20 Apr. | Starplex Amphitheater, Dallas, TX, USA | Devils Haircut/Novacane/Lord Only Knows/Loser/The New Pollution/Hotwax/One Foot In The Grave/Jack-ass/Where It's At/Beercan/High Five |
| 25 Apr. | Universal Amphitheater, Los Angeles, CA, USA | |
| 2 May | Festimad, Madrid, Spain | |
| 3 May | Heineken Festival, Dublin, Ireland | Unit Is In Effect/Devils Haircut/Novacane/Thunderpeel/The New Pollution/Hotwax/The Little Drum Machine Boy/Burnt Orange Peel/Sissyneck/Derelict/Asshole/Hollow Log/One Foot In The Grave/Jack-ass/Where It's At/DJ Swamp solo/High 5 |
| 6 May | *Later with Jools Holland*, BBC TV, London, UK | Devils Haircut/Jack-ass/Sissyneck |
| 7 May | Apollo, Manchester, England | Unit Is In Effect/Devils Haircut/Novacane/Thunderpeel/Hotwax/The New Pollution/Loser/Happy Birthday/I Wanna Get With You (And Your Sister Debra)/Sissyneck/Asshole/Truckdrivin' Neighbors Downstairs/Where It's At/DJ Swamp solo/High Five |
| 9 May | Aston Villa Leisure Centre, Birmingham, England | |
| 10 May | Brixton Academy, London, England | Thunderpeel/Novacane/The New Pollution/Loser/Minus/Sissyneck/I Wanna Get With You (And Your Sister Debra)/Derelict/Asshole/Truckdrivin' Neighbors Downstairs/One Foot In The Grave/Jack-ass/Where It's At/Devils Haircut/High Five |

| | | |
|---|---|---|
| 11 May | Rock City, Nottingham, England | Thunderpeel/Novacane/The New Pollution/Hotwax/Derelict/Minus/ Sissyneck/Feather In Your Cap/ Rowboat/I Get Lonesome/Jack-ass/ Where It's At/Devils Haircut/Swamp Solo/High Five |
| 13 May | Barrowlands, Glasgow, Scotland | |
| 14 May | Mayfair, Newcastle, England | |
| 17 May | Rock Am Ring, Nurburing, Germany | |
| 18 May | Rock Am Park, Nurnburg, Germany | |
| 19 May | Pinkpop Festival, Landgraaf, Holland | |
| 22 May | Red Rocks, Denver, CO, USA | |
| 24 May | Apple River Amphitheater, Minneapolis, MN, USA | |
| 25 May | New World Music Theater, Chicago, IL, USA | |
| 26 May | Marcus Amphitheater, Milwaukee, WI, USA | |
| 26 May | Riverport Amphitheater, St Louis, MO, USA | Devils Haircut/Novacane/The New Pollution/Minus/Loser/Sissyneck/ Derelict/Asshole/One Foot In The Grave/Jack-ass/Where It's At/High Five |
| 28 May | Phoenix Center, Detroit, MI, USA | |
| 30 May | Brandeis University, Boston, MA, USA | |
| 31 May | RFK Stadium, Washington, DC, USA | |
| 1 June | Blockbuster Amphitheater, Philadelphia, PA, USA | |
| 8 June | HFStival, 120 mins interview | |
| 12 June | Los Angeles, CA, USA | *Kill The Moonlight* premiere: country intro/Leave Me On The Moon/No Money, No Honey/Waitin' For A Train/Rowboat/Sunset 5 jam/Light My Fire |
| 27 June | Glastonbury Festival, Glastonbury, England | Where It's At/The New Pollution/ One Foot In The Grave/Devils Haircut/Loser (incomplete set list) |

| | | |
|---|---|---|
| 28 June | St Gallen Festival, St Gallen, Switzerland | |
| 29 June | Rosklide Festival, Roskilde, Denmark | |
| 2 July | Imperial Festival, Oporto, Portugal | |
| 5 July | Torhout Festival, Torhout, Belgium | |
| 6 July | Werchter Festival, Werchter, Belgium | Thunderpeel/Novacane/The New Pollution/Devils Haircut/Loser/ Jack-ass/Derelict/Where It's At/ Swamp Solo/High Five |
| 17 July | *Jay Leno Show*, USA | Jack-ass |
| 27 July | Mount Fuji Festival, Mount Fuji, Japan | |

*H.O.R.D.E. Festival*

| | | |
|---|---|---|
| 1 Aug. | 1st River's Edge, Sommerset, WI, USA | |
| 2 Aug. | Alpine Valley, East Troy, WI, USA | |
| 3 Aug. | New World Music Theater, Chicago, IL, USA | |
| 5 Aug. | Vernon Downs, Syracuse, NY, USA | |
| 6 Aug. | The Meadows, Hartford, CT, USA | |
| 8 Aug. | Great Woods, Boston, MA, USA | |
| 9 Aug. | Great Woods, Boston, MA, USA | |
| 10 Aug. | Space, Albany, NY, USA | Devils Haircut/Novacane/Minus/ Loser/The New Pollution/Hotwax/ Derelict/Beercan/Pay No Mind/One Foot In The Grave/Jack-ass/Where It's At/High Five |
| 12 Aug. | Jones Beach, Wantaugh, NY, USA | Devils Haircut/Novacane/The New Pollution/Sissyneck/Loser/Derelict/ I Wanna Get With You (And Your Sister Debra)/One Foot In The Grave/Jack-ass/Where It's At/ Swamp Intro (Block Rockin' Beats)/High Five |

*End of H.O.R.D.E. Festival*

| | | |
|---|---|---|
| 15 Aug. | Bizarre Festival, Cologne, Germany | Filmed for *Rockpalast*, German TV; *Pulling Up Roots* + more CD Bootlegs: Unit Is In Effect/Devils Haircut/ Novacane/The New Pollution/ Minus/Loser/Derelict/One Foot In The Grave/Jack-ass/Where It's At/ Swamp Solo/High Five |

| | | |
|---|---|---|
| 16 Aug. | V97 Festival, Leeds, England | |
| 17 Aug. | V97 Festival, Chelmsford, England | |
| 27 Aug. | Henry J. Kaiser, San Francisco, CA, USA | |
| 29 Aug. | Champoeg Amphitheater, Portland, OR, USA | Devils Haircut/Novacane/Burnt Orange Peel/Minus/The New Pollution/Beercan/Derelict/Jack-ass/I Wanna Get With You (And Your Sister Debra)/Asshole/One Foot In The Grave/Hot Wax/Where It's At/High Five |
| 30 Aug. | Bumbershoot Festival, Seattle, WA, USA | |
| 31 Aug. | P & E Fairgrounds, Vancouver, BC, Canada | |
| 2 Sept. | *Late Show with David Letterman*, NY, USA | Jack-ass |
| 4 Sept. | MTV Video Music Awards, New York, NY, USA | The New Pollution |
| 6 Sept. | Sessions at West 54th, New York, NY, USA | *Make Out City* CD Bootleg: D-Day intro/Devils Haircut/Novacane/Hotwax/I Wanna Get With You (And Your Sister Debra)/The New Pollution/Sissyneck/Derelict/Rowboat/Ramshackle/One Foot In The Grave/Asshole/Jack-ass/Where It's At/Swamp Solo/High Five |
| 29 Sept. | *Jay Leno Show*, USA | Peach Pickin' Time In Georgia |
| 4 Oct. | Farm Aid Benefit, Chicago, IL, USA | Peach Pickin' Time In Georgia (duet with Willie Nelson)/Leave Me On the Moon/Sissyneck/Rowboat/Ramshackle/One Foot In The Grave/Jack-ass |
| 28 Oct. | VH-1 Fashion Awards, USA | |
| 18 Nov. | The El Rey Theater, Los Angeles, CA, USA | Intro (Redball country instrumental)/Light My Fire/Peach Pickin' Time In Georgia/I Get Lonesome/Redball (country instrumental)/Leave/Cold Brains/Ella Speed/Totally Confused/Static/Dead Melodies/No Money, No Honey/Asshole/One Foot In The Grave/He's A Mighty Good Leader/Heartland Feeling/Rowboat/Ramshackle/Redball Finale/Sissyneck/Jack-ass/Redball (country acoustic) |

| | | |
|---|---|---|
| 5 Dec. | KROQ Almost Acoustic X-Mas, Los Angeles, USA | Loser/Novacane/Devils Haircut/ One Foot In The Grave/The New Pollution/Where It's At/High Five |
| 16 Dec. | The El Rey Theater, Los Angeles, CA, USA | Waitin' For A Train/Lampshade/ Cold Brains/Girl Of My Dreams/Sing It Again/Leave Me On The Moon/One Foot In The Grave/Dead Melodies/Rowboat/Little Sparrow/ Nobody's Fault But My Own/He's A Mighty Good Leader/I Get Lonesome |
| 31 Dec. | Bondi Pavillion, Sydney, Australia | |

## 1998

| | | |
|---|---|---|
| 3 Jan. | Mudslingers Festival, Perth, Australia | Devils Haircut/Novacane/The New Pollution/Loser/Sissyneck/ Deadweight/Jack-ass/Where It's At/DJ Swamp Solo/High Five |
| 4 Jan. | Mudslingers Festival, Perth, Australia | |
| 6 Jan. | Barton, Adelaide, Australia | |
| 8 Jan. | Forum, Melbourne, Australia | |
| 9 Jan. | Forum, Melbourne, Australia | |
| 12 Jan. | Enmore, Sydney, Australia | Devils Haircut/Novacane/ Thunderpeel/The New Pollution/ Lord Only Knows/Derelict/Loser/ Minus/Beercan/Where It's At/DJ Swamp solo/High Five/Sissyneck/I Wanna Get With You (And Your Sister Debra)/Deadweight/ Ramshackle/Lampshade/One Foot In The Grave/Jack-ass |
| 13 Jan. | Festival Hall, Brisbane, Australia | |
| 17 Jan. | Logan Campbell Centre, Auckland, New Zealand | |
| 18 Jan. | Town Hall, Wellington, New Zealand | |
| 18 May | Santa Monica Art Museum, Santa Monica, CA, USA | |
| 17 May | Galaxy Theater, Santa Ana, CA, USA | Unit Is In Effect/Devils Haircut/ Novacane/The New Pollution/I Wanna Get With You (and Your Sister Debra)/Tropicalia/Cold Brains/Hotwax/Thunderpeel/ |

Sissyneck/Diamond Bollocks/
Nobody's Fault But My Own/One
Foot In The Grave/Jack-ass/Electric
Music And The Summer People/
Deadweight/Swamp Solo/Where It's
At

| | | |
|---|---|---|
| 23 May | Rockshow, Copenhagen, Denmark | |
| 24 May | Haigh Hall, Wigan, England | Devils Haircut/Novacane/I Wanna Get With You (And Your Sister Debra)/Loser/Diamond Bollocks/ One Foot In The Grave/Nobody's Fault But My Own/Jack-ass/The New Pollution/DJ Swamp Solo/ Where It's At |
| 26 May | Zeleste, Barcelona, Spain | |
| 28 May | Lisbon Coliseum, Lisbon, Portugal | filmed by MTV |
| 1 June | Blossom Amphitheater, Cleveland, OH, USA | Unit Is In Effect/Devils Haircut/ Novacane/Thunderpeel/The New Pollution/I Wanna Get With You (And Your Sister Debra)/Diamond Bollocks/Nobody's Fault But My Own/Sissyneck/Deadweight/ Beercan/One Foot In The Grave/ Electric Music And The Summer People/Derelict/Jack-ass/Loser/ Swamp solo/Where It's At |
| 2 June | Pine Knob Amphitheater, Detroit, MI, USA | Devils Haircut/Novacane/I Wanna Get With You (And Your Sister Debra)/The New Pollution/Loser/ Tropicalia/Diamond Bollocks/ Nobody's Fault But My Own/One Foot In The Grave/Hotwax/ Sissyneck/Minus/Deadweight/Jack- ass/Beercan/Swamp Solo/Where It's At |
| 3 June | Molson Amphitheater, Toronto, ONT, Canada | Unit Is In Effect/Devils Haircut/ Novacane/I Wanna Get With You (And Your Sister Debra)/Burnt Orange Peel/Derelict/Loser/ Tropicalia/Cold Brains/Diamond Bollocks/Electric Music And The Summer People/Nobody's Fault But My Own/One Foot In The Grave/ Deadweight/Sissyneck/Jack-ass/ Beercan/Swamp Solo/Where It's At |
| 5 June | Foxboro Stadium, Foxboro, MA, USA | (opening for Dave Matthews) Unit Is In Effect/Devils Haircut/Novacane/ Deadweight/I Wanna Get With You |

|  |  |  |
|---|---|---|
|  |  | (And Your Sister Debra)/Loser/ Nobody's Fault But My Own/One Foot In The Grave/Jack-ass/The New Pollution/DJ Swamp Solo/ Where It's At |
| 6 June | Performing Arts Center, Saratoga, NY, USA | Unit Is In Effect/Loser/Novacane/ Beercan/I Wanna Get With You (and Your Sister Debra)/Electric Music And The Summer People/ Deadweight/Sissyneck/Diamond Bollocks/Nobody's Fault But My Own/One Foot In The Grave/Jack-ass/Derelict/Thunderpeel/DJ Swamp solo/The New Pollution/ Where It's At |
| 7 June | Giants Stadium, East Rutherford, NJ, USA |  |
| 8 June | unknown venue, Philadelphia, PA, USA | Unit Is In Effect/Loser/Novacane/ Beercan/Fuckin' With My Head/ Sissyneck/Lord Only Knows/I Wanna Get With You (and Your Sister Debra)/Deadweight/Nobody's Fault But My Own/One Foot In The Grave/Hollow Log/Girl Dreams/ Asshole/Truckdrivin' Neighbors Downstairs/Cold Brains/ Thunderpeel/Devils Haircut/The New Pollution/Jack-ass/DJ Swamp solo/Where It's At |
| 9 June | Darien Lakes, Buffalo, NY, USA |  |
| 10 June | Starlake Amphitheater, Pittsburgh, PA, USA | Loser/Novacane/Beercan/Fuckin' With My Head/Sissyneck/Lord Only Knows/I Wanna Get With You (And Your Sister Debra)/Deadweight/ Nobody's Fault But My Own/One Foot In The Grave/Hollow Log/Girl Dreams/Asshole/Truckdrivin' Neighbors Downstairs/Cold Brains/ Thunderpeel/Devils Haircut/The New Pollution/Jack Ass/Where It's At |
| 11 June | Jones Beach, New York, NY, USA | Unit Is In Effect/Loser/Novacane/ Beercan (Electric Avenue)/Fuckin' With My Head/Sissyneck/Lord Only Knows/I Wanna Get With You (And Your Sister Debra)/Deadweight/ Nobody's Fault But My Own/One Foot In The Grave/Hollow Log/Sing It Again/Dead Melodies/Jack-ass/ |

|            |                                          | Thunderpeel/The New Pollution/Devils Haircut/Tropicalia/DJ Swamp solo/Where It's At |
|------------|------------------------------------------|---|
| 1 Aug.     | Mt. Fuji Festival, Mt. Fuji, Japan       | |
| 21 Sept.   | The Cooler, New York, NY, USA            | |
| 10 Oct.    | Silicon Planet, San Jose, CA, USA        | |
| 3 Nov.     | KROQ, Los Angeles, CA, USA               | Cold Brains/Dead Melodies |
| 8 Nov.     | *Modern Rock Live*, USA                  | Dead Melodies/O Maria/Sing It Again/Nobody's Fault But My Own/Canceled Check/Jack-ass |
| 24 Nov.    | KCRW Radio, Santa Monica, CA, USA        | Cold Brains/Bottle Of Blues/Sing It Again/O Maria/Dead Melodies/Nobody's Fault But My Own/Tropicalia/Hollywood Freaks/I Wanna Get With You (And Your Sister Debra) |
| 30 Nov.    | National Public Radio, USA               | |
| 18 Dec.    | Rosemont Horizon, Rosemont, IL, USA      | Loser/Novacane/The New Pollution/Mixed Bizness/Tropicalia/The Little Drum Machine Boy/I Wanna Get With You (And Your Sister Debra)/Defying The Logic Of All Sex Laws/Devils Haircut/Jack-ass/Beercan/Where It's At/Electric Avenue |
| 19 Dec.    | Target Center, Minneapolis, MN, USA      | |
| 20 Dec.    | Joe Louis Arena, Detroit, MI, USA        | Loser/Novacane/The New Pollution/Mixed Bizness/Tropicalia/Deadweight/The Little Drum Machine Boy/I Wanna Get With You (And Your Sister Debra)/Jack-ass/Defying The Logic Of All Sex Laws/Devils Haircut/Jack-ass/Where It's At |

**1999**

|          |                                      |   |
|----------|--------------------------------------|---|
| 10 Jan.  | Town Hall, New York, NY, USA         | Cold Brains/Bottle Of Blues/Sing It Again/O Maria/We Live Again/Canceled Check/Asshole/Sissyneck/One Foot In The Grave/He's A Mighty Good Leader/Stagolee/Dead Melodies/Rowboat/Lazy Flies/Tropicalia/Nobody's Fault But My Own/Deadweight/I Wanna Get With |

|  |  | You (And Your Sister Debra)/Static/Jack-ass |
|---|---|---|
| 5 Feb. | Largo, Los Angeles, CA, USA |  |
| 21 Mar. | House Of Blues, Los Angeles, CA, USA | Loser/Novacane/The New Pollution/Hotwax/Deadweight/Lord Only Knows/Beercan/I Wanna Get With You (And Your Sister Debra)/Jockin' My Mercedes/Tropicalia/Jack-ass/Where It's At/DJ Swamp solo/Devils Haircut/Electric Avenue |
| 11 Apr. | Shibuya Kokaido, Tokyo, Japan | Lazy Flies/Cold Brains/Bottle Of Blues/We Live Again/Sing It Again/Jack-ass/Tropicalia/Dead Melodies/O Maria/Sissyneck/Asshole (with band + strings)/Nobody's Fault But My Own/Deadweight/Novacane/Diamond Bollocks/The New Pollution/I Wanna Get With You (And Your Sister Debra)/Where It's At/DJ Swamp solo/Devils Haircut |
| 12 Apr. | Shibuya Kokaido, Tokyo, Japan | Deadweight/Lord Only Knows/Cold Brains/Lazy Flies/Canceled Check/We Live Again/Jack-ass/Sing It Again/Sissyneck/Diamond Bollocks/One Of These Days/Dead Melodies/Nobody's Fault But My Own/Tropicalia/The New Pollution/I Wanna Get With You (And Your Sister Debra)/Where It's At/DJ Swamp solo/Devils Haircut |
| 14 Apr. | Shiminkaikan, Fukuoka, Japan | Cold Brains/Lazy Flies/We Live Again/Bottle Of Blues/Sing It Again/One Of These Days/O Maria/Tropicalia/Dead Melodies/Nobody's Fault But My Own/Deadweight/The New Pollution/Beercan/Diamond Bollocks/I Wanna Get With You (And Your Sister Debra)/Where It's At – incomplete set list |
| 16 Apr. | Shiminkaikan, Osaka, Japan | Cold Brains/Lazy Flies/We Live Again/Sleeping Bag/One Of These Days/Sing It Again/O Maria/Sissyneck/Dead Melodies/Nobody's Fault But My Own/Tropicalia/Novacane/Beercan/The New Pollution/Deadweight/Diamond |

|  |  |  |
|---|---|---|
|  |  | Bollocks/Where It's At/DJ Swamp/ Devils Haircut |
| 18 Apr. | Sun Plaza, Sendai, Japan | Cold Brains/Lazy Flies/We Live Again/Sing It Again/Bottle Of Blues/Sissyneck/O Maria/One Of These Days/Dead Melodies/ Nobody's Fault But My Own/ Tropicalia/Novacane/The New Pollution/Beercan/I Wanna Get With You (And Your Sister Debra)/Deadweight/Diamond Bollocks/Where It's At/DJ Swamp solo/Devils Haircut |
| 19 Apr. | Sun Plaza, Tokyo, Japan | Cold Brains/Lazy Flies/We Live Again/Sing It Again/Bottle Of Blues/Sissyneck/O Maria/One Of These Days/Dead Melodies/ Nobody's Fault But My Own/ Tropicalia/Novacane/The New Pollution/Beercan/I Wanna Get With You (And Your Sister Debra)/Deadweight/Diamond Bollocks/Where It's At/DJ Swamp solo/Devils Haircut |
| 21 Apr. | Kouseinekin, Tokyo, Japan | Cold Brains/Lazy Flies/We Live Again/Sing It Again/Bottle Of Blues/Girl Dreams/Lampshade/ Rowboat/One Foot In The Grave/O Maria/One Of These Days/Dead Melodies/Nobody's Fault But My Own/Tropicalia/The New Pollution/Deadweight/I Wanna Get With You (And Your Sister Debra)/Where It's At/DJ Swamp solo/Devils Haircut |
| 24 Apr. | Andrews Amphitheater, Honolulu, HI, USA | Novacane/Lord Only Knows/ Beercan/Sissyneck/I Wanna Get With You (And Your Sister Debra)/Pass The Dutchie/Electric Avenue/Tropicalia/The New Pollution/Nobody's Fault But My Own/Cold Brains/Sing It Again/One Foot In The Grave/DJ Swamp solo/ Loser/Jack-ass/Hotwax/Where It's At/High Five/Minus/Devils Haircut |
| 6 May | Tiffany Theater, Tropicana Hotel, Las Vegas, USA | Novacane/The New Pollution/ Beercan/Lord Only Knows/Loser/ Sissyneck/Tropicalia/I Wanna Get With You (And Your Sister Debra)/Pass The Dutchie/Minus/ |

|  |  |  |
|---|---|---|
|  |  | Hotwax/Cold Brains/Sing It Again/ Girl Dreams/One Foot In The Grave/Nobody's Fault But My Own/Jack-ass/Deadweight/Where It's At/DJ Swamp solo/Electric Avenue/Devils Haircut |
| 8 May | Wiltern Theater, Los Angeles, CA, USA | Cold Brains/Lazy Flies/We Live Again/Rowboat/Sing It Again/Bottle Of Blues/One Of These Days/ Tropicalia/Sissyneck/O Maria/Dead Melodies/Girl Dreams/Lampshade/ Nobody's Fault But My Own/Jack-ass/Deadweight/I Wanna Get With You (And Your Sister Debra)/Devils Haircut |
| 9 May | Wiltern Theater, Los Angeles, CA, USA | Cold Brains/Lazy Flies/We Live Again/Canceled Check/Sing It Again/Bottle Of Blues/One Of These Days/Tropicalia/Sissyneck/O Maria/Dead Melodies/Asshole/ Sleeping Bag/One Foot In The Grave/Lampshade/Nobody's Fault But My Own/Jack-ass/Diamond Bollocks/Deadweight/I Wanna Get With You (And Your Sister Debra)/Devils Haircut |
| 16 May | Playstation E3 show, Los Angeles, CA, USA | Beercan/Novacane/Loser/Lord Only Knows/Hotwax/Tropicalia/I Wanna Get With You (And Your Sister Debra)/Pass The Dutchie/ Jack-ass/Nobody's Fault But My Own/Where It's At/DJ Swamp solo/ Electric Avenue/Devils Haircut |
| 6 July | El Rey Theater, Los Angeles, CA, USA | Played under the name 'Silverlake Menza' as support to Beth Orton: Tropicalia/Nobody's Fault But My Own/Cold Brains/Lazy Flies |
| 6 Oct. | UCSB Student Center, Santa Barbara, CA, USA |  |
| 7 Oct. | Satellite Student Union, CSU, Fresno, CA, USA |  |
| 9 Oct. | Coachella Festival, Indio, CA, USA | Novacane/The New Pollution/Sexx Laws/Deadweight/Sissyneck/Mixed Bizness/Debra/Jackass/Nobody's Fault But My Own/Minus/Pressure Zone/Beercan/Electric Avenue/ Where It's At |

# Index